Political Communication Research:

Approaches, Studies, Assessments

edited by

David L. Paletz

Duke University

A Volume in the Series
COMMUNICATION AND INFORMATION SCIENCE
Melvin J. Voigt, series editor

ABLEX PUBLISHING CORPORATION
NORWOOD, NEW JERSEY 07648

Copyright © 1987 by Ablex Publishing Corporation.

All rights reserved. No part of this publication may be reproduced, stored in a retrieval system, or transmitted, in any form or by any means, electronic, mechanical, photocopying, microfilming. recording, or otherwise, without permission of the publisher.

Printed in the United States of America.

Library of Congress Cataloging-in-Publication Data

Political communication research.

(Communication and information science)
Bibliography: p.
Includes index.
1. Communication in politics. 2. Mass media—Political aspects.
I. Paletz, David L., 1934– II. Series.
JA74.P625   1986   306'.2   86-17475
ISBN 0-89391-329-4

Ablex Publishing Corporation
355 Chestnut Street
Norwood, New Jersey 07648

Contents

The Editor and Contributors vi
Introduction x
  David L. Paletz

PART I APPROACHES

1. Hegemony: The American News Media from Vietnam to El Salvador, 3
A Study of Ideological Change and Its Limits
Daniel C. Hallin
2. The Media-Policy Connection: Ecologies of News 26
Harvey Molotch, David L. Protess, and Margaret T. Gordon
3. The Publicity of State Subjects 49
Graham Knight and Bruce Curtis
4. The Influence of Camera Perspectives on the Perception 62
of a Politician by Supporters, Opponents, and Neutral Viewers
Hans Mathias Kepplinger and Wolfgang Donsbach

PART II STUDIES

5. The Role of Private Television Stations in Italian Elections 75
Gianpietro Mazzoleni
6. Journalism versus Public Relations in the Federal Republic of Germany 88
Barbara Baerns
7. Media and Conscientious Objection in the Federal Republic of Germany 108
Hans Mathias Kepplinger and Michael Hachenberg
8. Changes in American News in Two Chinese Newspapers 129
Kuan-Hsing Chen
9. The Press and Redemocratization in Brazil 148
Celina R. Duarte

PART III ASSESSMENTS

10. Election Communication and the Democratic Political System 167
Jay G. Blumler
11. Media Agenda-Setting and Elections: Assumptions and Implications 176
David Weaver

12. **Uses and Gratifications Research and the Study of Social Change**   194
    Carl R. Bybee
13. **Towards the Democratization of Mass Communication:**   213
    A Social Search for Equality
    Jerzy Oledzki
14. **Information Technology and National Development in Latin America**   230
    Joseph Rota and Tatiana Galvan
15. **International Information: Bullet or Boomerang?**   245
    René-Jean Ravault

Author Index   267
Subject Index   272

This book is for Gabriel: your remarkable courage and strength of character during a year of cruel adversity inspire, even more, my love and admiration. Susannah, equally brave, your turn will come. Darcy, we will always remember you.

The Editor and Contributors

David L. Paletz is Professor of Political Science at Duke University (Durham, North Carolina) where he teaches a year-long sequence of courses entitled Politics and the Media, as well as courses on the American Presidency, Political Participation, and the relationships between Politics and the Libido. In 1984 he received the University's Alumni Distinguished Undergraduate Teaching Award. He is co-author of *Media Power Politics* (Free Press/Macmillan, 1981) and *Politics in Public Service Advertising on Television* (Praeger, 1977). His numerous articles have appeared in scholarly journals in the United States and abroad.

Barbara Baerns is Professor of Publizistik- und Kommunkationswissenschaft at Ruhr University of Bochum, Federal Republic of Germany. Her research interests include problems of interactions within the field of mass communication, media history, and different media systems. She has been political editor and staff member of two German newspapers, as well as head of a public relations department. Her latest book is *Journalism or Public Relations? On Influence Within the Media System*.

Jay G. Blumler is Director of the Centre for Television Research at the University of Leeds in England as well as Associate Director of the Center for Research in Public Communication at the University of Maryland. He has written extensively on political communication topics, including the following books: *Television in Politics: Its Uses and Influence* (1968); *The Challenge of Election Broadcasting* (1978); *La Television: Fait-Elle L'Election?* (1978); and edited and contributed to *Communicating to Voters: Television in the First European Parliamentary Elections* (1983).

Carl R. Bybee is Director of the Communication Research Center at the University of Oregon. He is serving or has served on the editorial boards of a number of scholarly journals, and has written extensively on the impact of election campaign communications and on audience motivations for the use of political communication. His current research interests are centered on the relationship between power and language in mass mediated communications, particularly with respect to news and organized labor.

Kuan-Hsing Chen is a Ph.D. candidate in the School of Journalism and Mass Communication, University of Iowa. His dissertation is on postmodern culture and politics.

THE EDITOR AND CONTRIBUTORS

Bruce Curtis is completing post-doctoral research at the Ontario Institute for Studies in Education on the organization of public education in the mid-nineteenth century. His *Building the Educational State* should appear in late 1986. He has published a number of essays dealing with subjects such as the politics of literacy, comparative educational development, and state building.

Wolfgang Donsbach is Assistant Professor for Communications at the Johannes Gutenberg-University in Mainz, Germany. His M.A. and Ph.D. are from the University in Mainz. He has been a Lecturer at the School of Journalism, University of Dortmund. His main fields of research and teaching are comparative research in journalism as a profession, mass media effects, and public opinion research.

Celina R. Duarte is a graduate in Economics at the Pontifícia Universidade Católica de São Paulo where she is finishing her M.A. Political Science dissertation on "Redemocratization in Brazil and the Press." She has conducted research on CEBRAP (Centro Braseleiro de Análise e Planejamento) and at IDESP (Instituto de Estudos Econômicos, Sociais e Políticos de São Paulo). Since 1983 she has been working as Technical Advisor for the Secretary of Finance of São Paulo. She has published articles in a number of scholarly journals.

Tatiana Galvan is Professor of Communications Theory at the Facultad de Ciencias Politicas y Sociales of the Universidad Nacional Autonoma de Mexico (UNAM), where she has been chairperson of the Department of Communication Sciences. She has been an editorial writer for Mexican newspapers, and was Editorial Director at the Mexican New Agency NOTIMEX. She has written extensively on the Mexican press as legitimator of the Mexican political system, on Mexican political parties, and on communication and social theory.

Margaret T. Gordon is Director of the Center for Urban Affairs and Policy Research at Northwestern University. She is also Professor of Journalism in Northwestern's Medill School of Journalism, and is the School's Director of Research. Her media-related publications include work on media coverage of violent crime, and on journalism and public policy. During 1985 she was a Senior Fellow at the Gannett Center for Media Studies at Columbia University.

Michael Hachenberg has been a teaching assistant at the Institut für Publizistik, University of Mainz, and now is director of a marketing organization in Munich.

Daniel C. Hallin is Assistant Professor of Communication and Political Science at the University of California, San Diego. He is author of a book on news coverage of the Vietnam war, forthcoming from Oxford University Press. Other publications include "Speaking of the President: Political Structure and Representational Form in U.S. and Italian Television News," in *Theory and Society,* and "The American News Media: A Critical Theory Perspective," in John Forester, ed., *Critical Theory and Public Life.*

Hans Mathias Kepplinger received his doctoral degree from the University of Mainz, where he worked as a research assistant with Elisabeth Noelle-Neumann. In 1978 he received a 3-year grant from the German Science Foundation (Heisenberg Stipendium) which made possible a research fellowship at the University of California, Berkeley. He is now Professor and Director of the Institut für Publizistik at the University of Mainz, Federal Republic of Germany. He has written several books and published articles in international journals.

Graham Knight is Associate Professor in the Department of Sociology at McMaster University, Hamilton, Ontario, Canada. He is currently at work on a book about local news in television and the press. This is part of a wider interest in media, ideology, and popular discourse. His writings have appeared in scholarly journals in Canada and United States.

Gianpietro Mazzoleni is Senior Researcher in the Sociology Department of the University of Milan. He holds a B.A. from St. Anselm's College (Manchester, NH) and a doctorate from the University of Rome. His research interests are in the areas of mass media content, political information, and campaign communication. His most recent book is *Televisione Elettorale e Televisione Politica* (Milan, 1984), on the political effects of television newscasts and advertising.

Harvey Molotch is Professor and Chair of Sociology at the University of California, Santa Barbara. With Marilyn Lester, he is co-author of a series of articles on "News as Purposive Behavior." He has also carried out extensive research on urban growth and development; his most recent book (with John Logan) is *Urban Fortunes,* forthcoming from the University of California Press.

Jerzy Oledzki is Associate Professor in the Department of Journalism and Political Science, University of Warsaw, Poland. His Ph.D. is in political science, with an M.A. in Polish literature and postgraduate study in journalism. Since 1984 he has been a visiting professor of journalism and political science at Ohio University in Athens, Ohio. Widely published in Polish periodicals, Oledzki has also authored several articles on mass media and international understanding in foreign publications. In 1984 his "Developing Countries and the World Communication Systems" was published by Warsaw University.

THE EDITOR AND CONTRIBUTORS

David Protess is Associate Professor of Journalism and Urban Affairs at Northwestern University. He is the author of articles on the agenda-setting impact of the news media, and is writing a book on the subject for the University of Wisconsin Press. He holds M.A. and Ph.D. degrees in public policy from the University of Chicago, and a B.A. in political science from Roosevelt University.

René Jean Ravault holds a Ph.D. in Mass Communication from the University of Iowa and a M.A. in Sociology from the Sorbonne. He is a Professeur-Chercheur in the Department of Communications at l'Université du Québec à Montréal. His current research interest is in the elaboration of a communication paradigm accounting for and improving decision making processes when intercultural and transnational issues are involved. The results of his findings have been published in scholarly journals in Canada, U.S.A., France, and Great Britain.

Joseph Rota (Ph.D. and M.A., Michigan State University; B.A., Universidad Iberoamericana, Mexico) is Associate Professor, School of Telecommunications, and Associate Faculty, Latin American Studies Program at Ohio University. He has taught at the National University of Mexico, Universidad Ibroamericana, and Universidad Anahuac, Mexico City. He is the author of over 40 scholarly papers.

David Weaver is Professor of Journalism at Indiana University and Director of the Bureau of Media Research in the School of Journalism. He received his Ph.D. in mass communication research from the University of North Carolina in 1974. He is the author of *Videotex Journalism* (Erlbaum, 1983), senior author of *Media Agenda-Setting in a Presidential Election* (Praeger, 1981), co-author of *Newsroom Guide to Polls and Surveys* (American Newspaper Publishers Association, 1980), and author of numerous book chapters on media agenda-setting, newspaper readership, and foreign news coverage.

Introduction

DAVID L. PALETZ
Department of Political Science
Duke University
Durham, NC 27706

Political communication research has blossomed around the world during the past decade, as scholars study the often intricate relations between politics and the media in their individual contries. At the same time, institutional arrangements have developed for this research to be aired and shared. Among these forums are the meetings of the International Political Science Association, the International Sociological Association, and the International Communication Association (which, despite its name, is predominantly North American in orientation and composition). Most notable is the International Association for Mass Communication Research (IAMCR), with its ideologically and geographically diverse membership. Within the IAMCR, the Political Communication Research Group, which I founded and have the distinct pleasure of chairing, has the specific purpose of enabling political communication scholars to report their latest research.

These paper-presentation sessions are often quite fruitful. Papers are variously—and not always deservingly—excoriated, disdained, neglected, ignored, approved, lauded, or beatified. Authors, discussants, and audience members report that the animated discussions resonate into their subsequent research. They also share an abiding concern with me that this benefit is unnecessarily limited to the conference participants and to scholars fortunate enough to obtain copies of what often become fugitive papers.

Inevitably, then, the idea arose of capturing some of the most provocative of these conference papers for interested scholars and, without being presumptuous, for posterity. This I have done. My purpose is to convey a sense of the subjects and issues deemed salient by political communication scholars around the world, and to do so by selecting research that is innovative and provocative.

All 15 of the papers were written in English, but 9 of them are by scholars whose native language is not English. The resulting prose and composition were inevitably more serviceable than fluent. In editing these contributions I have tried, consonant with coherence, to retain the original eloquence and flavor of expression.

INTRODUCTION

The papers themselves fall into three general, although not entirely distinct, categories: approaches, studies, and assessments. By approaches, I mean ways of thinking about and conceptualizing media-politics relations. One such approach, popular in Western Europe, and increasingly prevalent in the United States, is Antonio Gramsci's concept of hegemony. This is the argument "that political power in liberal capitalist societies...rests...on the strength of a world view, a system of assumptions and social values accepted as 'common sense' which legitimates the existing distribution of power and, indeed, renders opposition to it *inconceivable* for most of the population" (emphasis in original). Professor Daniel Hallin, whose definition I have just quoted (from pp. 2-3 of his essay), analyzes the viability of this concept and its applicability to the United States through the prism of media coverage of Vietnam and El Salvador. Hegemony emerges from his scrupulous scrutiny, it seems to me, questioned, modified, and, within limits, essentially intact—at least for the time being.

The second approach is dubbed by its authors, Professors Harvey Molotch, David L. Protess and Margaret Gordon, "Ecologies of News." With graphic and muck-raking examples, they trace (in their words) the "mutually determinative" relations between the media and participants in the policy process, and concomitant effects on media, public policies, and society.

Two quite different approaches conclude this section. From Canada, Professors Graham Knight and Bruce Curtis offer a highly theoretical discussion of themes raised in the preceding papers concerning state-media relations. Their essay is likely to inspire some readers as it bemuses others. It is followed by an account of an experiment attempting to measure the influence of camera angles on perceptions of politician. While there is a tradition of such experimental research in the United States, its occurrence elsewhere is less common. Useful, therefore, to learn how Professors Hans Mathias Kepplinger and Wolfgang Donsbach conducted their work in West Germany.

The book's second section, its heart, is devoted to original, empirical research. Professor Gianpietro Mazzoleni identifies and explains the impact of private television stations on Italian elections. The creation of such stations is likely to change elections in his country, localizing and personalizing them, while weakening the power of the parties. Since this phenomenon has occurred to some extent in the United States, and could be repeated elsewhere, Mazzoleni's work is highly illuminating.

Next are two empirical studies from West Germany. Professor Barbara Baerns examines the extent to which public relations determines news media content. She finds a relatively strong influence, and explains why. Then Professor Kepplinger and Michael Hachenberg present the results of their investigation of the links between the rise of conscientious objection to participation in military service in West Germany and media coverage of the topic. They find and carefully identify connections between social change, media legitimization of particular behavior, and public opinion.

The final two case studies are about China and from Brazil. Given their size, importance, and plethora of internal and political changes now taking place, both countries deserve the kind of extended and detailed research on their political communication processes they have yet to receive. The papers included here are a worthy beginning. Kuan-Hsing Chen describes changes over time in Chinese newspapers' depictions of the United States. And Professor Celina Duarte fascinatingly charts the complex involvement of the Brazillian press, and the military men in power who manipulate it, in that country's path to redemocratization.

The third and final section of the book is devoted to assessments. It begins with three critical appraisals: Professor Jay Blumler on media and election campaigns, Professor David Weaver on agenda-setting research, and Professor Carl Bybee on uses and gratifications. Their temperate essays outline the general thrust of past research, identify what they perceive as its deficiencies, and suggest new directions.

From Poland comes Professor Jerzy Oledzki's unusual essay on the links between political power, the media, and the people in his country. Then two scholars from Mexico, Professors Joseph Rota and Tatiana Galvan, chronicle the effects of communications technology on national development in Latin America, with specific reference to Mexico. Finally, Professor René Jean Ravault, in a striking polemic, attacks the assumptions and inadequacies of the conventional literature on the new world information order.

This book displays a blend of leading and young scholars who are trying to think seriously about political communication in their countries. Their work represented here offers a wide range of topics and themes, assessments of past studies, and directions for future research. The authors are united by a concern for the larger issues of political communication research. It is this unity that makes the book less time bound than timely and perhaps, for some of its insights and analysis, even timeless.

Acknowledgments. The indomitable Melvin Voigt encouraged me to go ahead with the idea of collecting some of the best political communication research from around the world; without him, this book would not exist. A trio of Duke University Political Science graduate students were of inestimable help. Paul Feldman and Jarvis Hall read and revised manuscripts for the book, and Patty Farnan took first cut at proofing the copyedited manuscript. Thanks also to stalwart Mark Dorosin. My then secretary Mary Umstead was her unique self. A word of appreciation, too, to the authors who responded to my request for submissions but whose works are not included herein because, in the end, they did not fit the book's organization and focus; there will be another book, another day.

PART I
APPROACHES

Chapter 1
Hegemony: The American News Media From Vietnam to El Salvador, A Study of Ideological Change and Its Limits

DANIEL C. HALLIN

Department of Communication
University of California, San Diego
La Jolla, CA 92093

In February, 1981, the Reagan administration, as its first major foreign policy action, released the State Department "White Paper" entitled "Communist Interference in El Salvador." In the process of writing a book on coverage of the Vietnam war by the American news media (Hallin, forthcoming), I was struck by the similarity between the reporting of the 1981 White Paper and the reporting of the White Paper released by the Johnson administration in February of 1965, and decided to write an article on the remarkable persistence of the old practice of reporting official statements on foreign policy at face value, without consulting alternative sources or historical parallels, and without commenting on their accuracy, significance, or motivation. I was quickly "scooped" by numerous critiques of White Paper coverage (Maslow & Arana, 1981). But in the meantime a much more complicated and theoretically more significant story was developing.

The purpose of the El Salvador White Paper, like that of its 1965 predecessor, was to "frame" the situation in El Salvador as a Cold War confrontation between the United States and the Soviet Union, on the assumption that a "Cold War" interpretation would maximize public support for American intervention. But, within a few days, alternative "frames"—most notably the parallel with the "quagmire" of Vietnam—were becoming common enough in news coverage that the Reagan administration, which had made a major effort to put Central America in the spotlight, was beginning to complain of "excessive publicity." The publicity following the White Paper was in fact very extensive, much more so than at a comparable stage of American involvement in Vietnam. And, as the focus of coverage began to shift

---

An earlier version of this paper was presented under the auspices of the Political Communication Research Group at the International Association for Mass Communication Research Conference, Paris, Sept. 6–10, 1982. See also Hallin (1983).

somewhat from Washington to El Salvador itself, much of it was strikingly *different* from the foreign policy coverage of the early and mid-1960s. The crisis in Central America has thus become an excellent case for an exploration of the dynamics and the limits of change in the ideological orientation of the American news media and in their relation to the structure of political authority.

I will center my discussion around Antonio Gramsci's concept of "hegemony," which is just now beginning to cross the Atlantic and has established a small but promising beachhead in American media research (Anderson, 1976-1977; Gitlin, 1980; Gramsci, 1971; Hall, 1979; Miliband, 1969; Williams, 1977). Gramsci was concerned with the nature of power in a liberal-democratic political system. Briefly, he argued that political power in liberal capitalist societies depends relatively little, except in times of extreme crisis, on the coercive apparatus of the state. It rests instead on the strength of a world view, a system of assumptions and social values accepted as "common sense" which legitimates the existing distribution of power and, indeed, renders opposition to it *inconceivable* for most of the population. The state plays a role in the propagation of that world view, but the legitimating cultural system so crucial to political power is maintained largely by private, autonomous, and in many cases "nonpolitical" institutions: the family, the church, the political party, and, of course, the mass media.

The concept of hegemony plays a double role in the study of the media. It is used, first, to conceptualize the political "function" of the media. (I'll have a few things to say a little later about the problem of functionalism.) The media, according to this neo-Marxist perspective, play the role of maintaining the dominant political ideology: they propagate it, celebrate it, interpret the world in its terms, and, at times, alter it to adapt to the demands of legitimation in a changing world. At the same time, the concept of hegemony is employed to explain the "behavior" of the media, the process of cultural production itself. The media themselves are subject to the hegemonic process. The dominant ideology shapes the production of news and entertainment; this explains why the media can be expected to function as agents of legitimation, despite the fact that they are independent of direct political control.

Central America coverage is a significant case on which to test this perspective. Conservatives in the United States have been arguing ever since the later years of the Vietnam war that the media have shifted away from the legitimating role they played earlier, to become part of an "adversary culture" now established in opposition both to formal political authority and to established ideological assumptions (Huntington, 1981; Robinson, 1975, 1976). Recent coverage of Central America has provoked a new round of this sort of commentary. As we shall see, it is not entirely off the mark. Since Vietnam, a major ideological rift has developed over what is likely to prove the most sensitive political question of the coming decades: the United States' relation to revolution in the Third World. In the current crisis, the Reagan administration and the media have often stood on opposite sides of that rift. As a result, the Reagan administration has in fact had a great deal of trouble "managing" public opinion on Central America. More significant still for the long-term development of American political ideology, questions about the American stance toward revolution not publicly aired in the United States since the onset of the Cold War have broken into the arena of mass political communication.

Nevertheless, I shall argue that the hegemonic process can be seen very strongly at work in the Central American case. The Vietnam era shook the ground from beneath a number of the key assumptions of the view that has been taken as "common sense" on foreign affairs since the late 1940s. The shaking of those assumptions initiated a period of both ideological and institutional change that has profoundly affected the way the American news media report world politics. But at the same time, there are powerful "centrifugal forces" at work which limit the scope of those changes and the threat they could potentially pose either to the power of foreign policy elites within the United States or to the basic shape of the U.S. role in world politics. I will begin by examining the extent of the changes in foreign policy coverage since Vietnam, and the implications of those changes for the analysis of the hegemonic process, and then move to a discussion of the limits of change.

This article is based on a continuing study of Central America coverage, and its conclusions must therefore be taken as tentative. It is based on an analysis of network television coverage of Central America from the October 1979, coup in El Salvador through the present, a somewhat less systematic monitoring of coverage in major American newspapers, and on a series of interviews with reporters, producers, and editors involved in Central America coverage, both in Central America and in Washington, New York, and Miami bureaus. Eventually, many of the points made here about television coverage will be backed up by quantitative content analysis.

THE FRAGMENTATION OF THE COLD WAR CONSENSUS

Conflict between the government and the media is nothing new, even in the area of foreign policy. The early escalation of American involvement in Vietnam provoked a particularly intense conflict, the history of which is by now well known (Halberstam, 1965, 1979; Mecklin, 1965). Reports from the field in 1962-1963 contradicted official optimism, and tensions rose to the point that the administration carried out a public campaign to discredit the Saigon press corps. President John F. Kennedy asked the *New York Times* to remove its Saigon correspondent, David Halberstam; and *Time*'s correspondents Charles Mohr and Mert Perry resigned when their own organization failed to back them in the dispute over the accuracy—or the patriotism—of Vietnam reporting.

But as intense as these conflicts seemed to those involved in them, they took place within the narrow bounds of a powerful consensus on foreign policy. News coverage was held within those bounds by two factors. First, the dominant professional ideology of objective journalism held that it was the reporter's job simply to provide a record of what was said and done by those in positions of authority (Cohen, 1963). The news therefore tended most of the time—especially from Washington, where this principle was strongest, and especially on the front page—to reflect official views, whatever the reporter's personal beliefs. Second, reporters themselves almost all accepted the basic outlines of the "bipartisan" consensus on foreign policy that had been established with the onset of the Cold War. That consensus held that the central fact of world politics was the conflict between the "Free World," led by the United States, and an expansionist Communist bloc, led by the Soviet Union. Given the centrality and the irreconcilability of this conflict, any local conflict, whether in Europe or what would later come to be called the Third World, had to be interpreted in terms of its "global"— that is, its Cold War—significance.

A word is necessary here about the power of ideology.[1] All human communication requires a structure of rules for the production of meaningful statements or utterances. Language is such a structure; its rules at the same time make it *possible* for us to apprehend and represent the world in a social way, and also *limit* the range of representations open to us. An ideology is also such a structure, on a higher level. It provides the basic framework within which political thought and communication take place. A language, of course is very broad: it develops over a period of centuries, shaped by the speech acts of millions of very different individuals. Its limits are therefore wide enough that it generally does not make sense to see them as constraints, although, as recent controversies over the sexual assumptions embedded in ordinary language attest, this is not always the case. But an ideology is a much more specific historical structure, often developed, to some extent at least, by a limited number of individuals for conscious political purposes. Its limits are much narrower; and in a period when a single ideology dominates a particular area of discourse, the constraints it imposes can be powerful and of great political significance.

The early 1960s were precisely such a period—a period of consensus on foreign policy, when the Cold War ideology was accepted as defining the limits of "responsible" political discussion. The assumptions of that ideology

---

[1] This discussion of language and ideology draws heavily on Volosinov (1973), a little known but very important work, as well as Pitkin (1972).

pervaded the news, and the critical coverage which so galled the administration remained firmly within its bounds. The news in this period often cast doubt on the effectiveness of American policy, particularly the wisdom of supporting Ngo Dinh Diem. It did not cast doubt on the goals of that policy or the world view on which it was based: these were taken for granted. Here, for example, is the lead from a *New York Times* background story on Asia from 1962: "Domestic instability in key non-Communist countries fringing Communist China continues to hamper United States efforts to build up these lands against further Communist penetration into free Asia" (Trumbull, 1962).[2] The headline: "Three Areas of Asia [Laos, South Korea, South Vietnam] Disturb the Free World; U.S. Attempts to Stem Communist Aggression Hampered by Weak Regimes on China's Fringes." The media's focus on the weakness of the Saigon regime was a real political liability to the Kennedy administration. But at the same time, the "framing" of the Vietnam story is as good an example as one could wish of the hegemonic process at work. Ideological assumptions shape the news, and the news in turn reinforces those assumptions, "confirming" them by interpreting a new historical case in their terms.

The contrast between Vietnam and El Salvador coverage is dramatic. To illustrate the extent of the change, I will take as an example a CBS documentary aired in March 1982, *Central America in Revolt*. This documentary is by no means typical of current television coverage. Indeed, it is especially useful for this analysis, because it presses against the furthest political limits of foreign affairs coverage in the American media. It therefore illustrates both the extent to which those limits have changed since Vietnam, and the fact that there remain ideological frontiers which the news does not cross.

Here is the introduction to the section of *Central America in Revolt* dealing with El Salvador:

>This is the war the Reagan administration calls the "decisive battle for Central America." It's a civil war. But we are told the Soviet Union is working through Nicaragua and Cuba to help the insurgents win a victory for Communism. We're told our own security is at stake here.
>
>By now the sights and sounds of the war itself are as familiar as the evening news. But most of us have not seen how the war came about. It did not just happen yesterday. It happened over many yesterdays, all of them filled with violence and terror.
>
>That's the frustrating thing about reporting this story. There is much of it we cannot show you. We cannot show you the Spanish invaders, making slaves of the Indians to begin an era of brutal rule. We cannot show you the big coffee

---

[2] David Halberstam, who was such a thorn in the side of the Kennedy Administration, once wrote (1965, p. 315), "What about withdrawal?...Withdrawal means that throughout the world the enemies of the West will be encouraged to try insurgencies like the one in Vietnam."

growers of a hundred years ago taking the land on which the peasants grew food. And we cannot show you that crucial bloody year of 1932, when the peasants rose up and were slaughtered, thousands and thousands of them, by the dictator who served the ruling class.

Politicization of the Cold War Perspective

The most basic ideological change, reflected in the contrast between this background report and the *New York Times* report quoted above, is that the Cold War interpretation is now no longer assumed, but posed as a particular political position. This is a very new development for American journalism. Even in the later part of the Vietnam war, when journalists were generally disillusioned with American policy in Vietnam, discussion about the origins of revolution or the basic outlines of the U.S. relationship with the Third World were simply not a part of the news agenda. Debate—as represented in the news—concerned the pace and the terms of American withdrawal, not the ideological underpinnings of U.S. policy. It has, in contrast, become common for background reports on Central America to pose the Cold War interpretation as the major political issue to be explored. ABC State Department correspondent Barrie Dunsmore introduced a week-long series of special reports, aired on the evening news on March 9, 1981, 2 weeks after the White Paper was released, with the statement that it would "try to determine if an East-West confrontation over El Salvador is desirable or likely." Note the assumption that confrontation with the Soviets is a *policy,* not an inevitable fact of world politics.

Reporting Internal Causes of Revolution[3]

The "politicization" of the Cold War ideology has been accompanied by a number of other major changes in the presentation of foreign news. The *New York Times* report quoted above said virtually nothing about the specific history or the social or economic structure of South Vietnam, except that there was "domestic discontent" which might render the Diem government ineffective against the Communist threat. This was true of most Vietnam coverage, except during certain periods when policy debate in Washington centered around what to do about the "instability" in Saigon: if the cause of the war was outside aggression, local history was not a significant part of the story. Thus, in the entire corpus of *New York Times* coverage from 1960 through 1963, there were only two references to the problem of land tenure,

---

[3] I mean to include here under "internal" causes of revolution the effects of the world political and economic system on the country concerned. It is important to note that this dimension of the background to revolution is still rarely covered, especially in its economic aspects, although recent coverage of Central America does allude from time to time to the history of U.S. intervention there.

each about a paragraph long. *Central America in Revolt,* on the other hand, began its discussion of each country with an overview of its history. Those histories, moreover, gave considerable attention to certain themes which until recently had been rigidly excluded from foreign policy coverage, including social stratification (not simply "poverty" or "underdevelopment") as a cause of revolution, and the history of U.S. intervention and economic involvement in the Third World. The segment on Guatemala—a particularly striking example of the technique of ironic editing which television news has honed to perfection—centered around the contrast between the sanguine views of an American businessman and the realities of political and economic repression in that country.

Coverage of the "Enemy"
The Cold War consensus, later combined with the involvement of American troops in combat, made coverage of the North Vietnamese and the NLF extremely sensitive politically. Reports from North Vietnam (again, especially on television) usually were heavily laced with warnings about "Communist propaganda;" reports on the NLF were extremely rare.[4] Coverage of the official Nicaraguan position, on the other hand, has become routine in current Central American coverage. In *Central America in Revolt,* Nicaraguan and U.S. officials were "balanced" in the same way Republicans and Democrats are balanced in domestic reporting. Coverage of the guerrillas is also fairly frequent. Most of it is not very substantial; it tends to focus on the reporter's adventure "behind the lines." But the mere fact that the guerrillas appear with a human face, rather than existing purely as they are characterized by Washington, is a significant difference from the Vietnam period. *Central America in Revolt* went further, including clips of interviews with two Guatemalan revolutionaries whose views were presented with some substance, and "balanced" against those of the Guatemalan military.

The "Credibility Gap"
Finally, there has been substantial change in the journalists' attitudes toward political authority. Dan Rather introduced *Central America in Revolt* with three questions: "Are we witnessing another Communist takeover in our hemisphere? Is the United States again becoming hopelessly entangled in another civil war? Is the information that we are getting from our government the truth?" An entire segment of the documentary was devoted to the question of government credibility. Content analysis should show that reporters' statements questioning official information are much more fre-

---

[4] Political sensitivity is only part of the explanation for this lack of coverage. Physical access to the NLF in the field was virtually impossible; in El Salvador, access to the guerrillas is relatively easy.

quent in Central America coverage than in even the later years of Vietnam. An interesting illustration of this skepticism is the use of the term "propaganda." That term, throughout the Vietnam period, was a good example of how "the concept [can] be absorbed by the word, [and lose all] other content than that designated by the word in its...standardized usage," as Marcuse (1964, p. 87) once put it. Throughout the 1960s, the term applied almost exclusively to statements from Communist sources. Today it is not uncommon for journalists to speak of a two-sided "propaganda war" over, for instance, Central America or arms control.

LIMITS OF CHANGE

Would it, then, be reasonable to say that the concept of hegemony is dated —that the hegemonic process so evident in Vietnam coverage was a transitory result of the specific political character of that period? Certainly, if the concept of hegemony is formulated in such a way that it assumes ideological change to be marginal and insignificant, it is of limited use. The fragmentation of the Cold War consensus in the United States is not an event that can be dismissed as historically insignificant. Yet, even in a period of significant ideological crisis, which the current period certainly is for the United States, the media are subject to powerful constraints which limit the impact of change.

It should be noted, first, that defenders of the status quo have not ignored the potential threat to hegemony we have identified here. In the 1970s and 1980s, as ideological strains have affected the media in a variety of ways, a large number of well-financed conservative "media-watch" organizations have been formed in the United States. These groups, along with other conservative organizations and the Reagan administration itself, have focused heavily on Central America coverage, publicizing their criticisms of "unbalanced" reporting and lobbying with media executives. It is difficult to assess the impact of this sort of pressure; if journalists or their supervisors had in fact pulled back from controversial reporting, this is not something they would readily admit. But there are those in journalism who believe the media have pulled back (Hallin, 1983; Massing, 1983). And my own observations suggest—though these are not yet confirmed by content analysis— that there have been significant changes in content since Spring 1982, when the controversy over Central America coverage became particularly intense (note that *Central America in Revolt* aired in March 1982), which are at least consistent with this view. Coverage of the guerrillas and of violence against civilians by Salvadoran security forces, for example, seem to have fallen off substantially since that period.

Nevertheless, it is my view that direct political pressure or control by ruling elites is a relatively small part of the "hegemonic process." (I do not, in other words, subscribe to an "instrumentalist" view of the media, in the sense of Gold, Lo, and Wright, 1975.) So I would like to turn my attention here to two other kinds of limits on ideological change which I believe to be far more significant: those embedded in organizational routines, and those embedded in deeper ideological structures which remain stable while other elements of the dominant ideology are in flux.

THE PERSISTENCE OF JOURNALISTIC ROUTINES

Hegemony, like Weber's authority, is power sustained by ideology. But ideology is not merely a system of symbols. It is embedded in practices, routines, and ways of living and working. To understand hegemony, therefore, it is necessary to examine institutional as well as symbolic structures.

The institutional structure of the American news media has three fundamental characteristics. First, they are privately owned, operated for profit, and legally independent of the state. Second, they have a dual internal structure, very different from other corporations, that gives professional journalists substantial autonomy from the rest of the corporate hierarchy. Third, despite their formal political independence, news organizations have a special working relationship with government officials which dominates the day-to-day production of news. It is this third characteristic that I would like to consider here.

A definitive historical analysis of the relation between the American news media and the state has yet to be written. But in the broadest terms, such an analysis would no doubt show that that relationship gradually became "routinized" over the period from about 1850 to 1950. At the beginning of that period, the news media were partly partisan, partly in transition to the nonpartisan "professional" media of the twentieth century. Their relation to political authority was in flux and often varied from paper to paper and year to year, depending on the party in power. (In 1877, *The Washington Post,* a Democratic paper, said of the Republican Hayes administration, which came to power through a Congressional deal to end Reconstruction, "we do not recognize [it] further than is absolutely necessary to insure peace and tranquility.")[5] By the 1950s, that relationship had become stable and close: the press had become, in Douglass Cater's words (1959), a sort of "fourth branch of government," interacting on a regular basis with government officials whose briefings and press conferences had become the primary source of news.[6]

This relationship has persisted with remarkably little change despite the political conflicts of the 1960s and 1970s (Hallin, 1984). Those conflicts have produced some significant developments. Journalists, as we have seen,

---

[5] Quoted in Roberts (1977, p. 5).
[6] The literature on the working relationship between the media and government is enormous; my favorite study is Sigal (1973).

are more likely to question official information. They are more likely now to discuss the public relations strategy behind official statements. There has been some diversification of sources, as illustrated by the use of Nicaraguan sources in current Central America coverage. And there is now more "investigative journalism" involving an active search for information rather than reliance on information released at the government's initiative. But the basic structure of the media/government relationship remains intact: United States officials remain the basic source of news. This is especially true of foreign policy coverage. For all the increased skepticism of contemporary journalism—and it should be stressed here that most news stories still report official statements at face value—the Presidential statement and the State Department press briefing remain the heart of foreign policy coverage. The persistence of this special relationship between the media and government has blunted the impact of ideological change in several ways, three of which I would like to explore here.

1. Defining the Issue

In the first place, this relationship means that the government is able most of the time to pose the dominant issue around which news coverage will revolve. In the case of El Salvador, this has meant that the Reagan administration has been able to direct media attention heavily toward the Cold War interpretation of the conflict, despite widespread skepticism about that interpretation within the profession of journalism. It will be useful here to review the development of El Salvador coverage, which went through a number of distinct phases.

It is important to emphasize at the outset that, even in questioning Cold War perspectives, the media were following the lead of official policy. Vietnam did not lead directly to a reworking of the "frames" employed in reporting conflicts in the Third World: this change did not occur until the Carter administration, when an alternative *official perspective,* centered around the concept of human rights, had become established.[7]

---

[7] It could be argued that the media's questioning of the Cold War ideology and the Carter administration's formulation of the human rights policy coincided because both were a delayed reaction to Vietnam, a result of a new generation rising to positions of power independently in two institutions. No doubt to some extent that is true. Journalists who were young during the Vietnam era generally say that it affected them greatly, leaving them far more skeptical of political authority than were previous generations. But the media respond so closely to the concerns of officials throughout the development of the Central American crisis, turning their attention to human rights when officials focus on that problem, to the parallel with Vietnam when that is at issue in Washington, and so on, that it seems best to conclude that they were following the official lead. It is worth adding that one independent influence on the attitudes of some journalists—those who cover Central America on a regular basis—was the Nicaraguan revolution, which, because its popular support was so exceptionally broad, shattered many of their previous assumptions about revolution.

The Carter administration itself went back and forth on its emphasis on human rights. In the earliest period of this study, from the October 1979 coup in El Salvador through about October 1980, it supported the military-civilian junta in El Salvador, which it saw as moderate and reformist, and was itself moving in the direction of modest increases in military aid. The news reflected the administration perspective closely. Coverage was sporadic during this early period, but most of it depicted a moderate government trying to mediate between extremists of the right and left.

Then in November-December of 1980 a significant shift of the newsframe occurred. That shift resulted from two events—the election of Ronald Reagan and the murder by government security forces in El Salvdaor of four American religious workers—both of which focused attention on the issue of human rights. The murder of the nuns provoked a temporary cut-off of U.S. military aid, and the election of Ronald Reagan touched off a major conflict over the direction of U.S. foreign policy. Carter officials committed to the human rights perspective began to stress to reporters their philosophical differences with the incoming Reagan regime. By the end of January, when the Reagan administration came to office, the question of human rights had become the dominant theme in news coverage.

The Reagan administration, for its part, was committed to reversing the ideological change we have explored. It sought to restore the Cold War consensus, at the expense of the human rights orientation of the Carter period. Like many political decisions, the decision to "draw the line" in El Salvador had several goals, which can be divided, with some oversimplification, into "instrumental" and "communicative" or ideological goals. The instrumental goal of that decision, and the basis of public justification for it, was to prevent another revolutionary regime from coming to power in the Western Hemisphere. But it was also intended to "send a signal" to the Soviet Union and the world at large that the United States was willing to use military force. And, most important for our purposes, it was intended to achieve the domestic ideological goal of placing the East-West confrontation once again at the center of American consciousness of world affairs.

To accomplish this goal, the increase of American military aid to the Salvadoran regime was accompanied by a public relations campaign designed largely to change the emphasis of news coverage. Like most such campaigns, the strategy was simple. It was to provide a series of public statements which, because they came from high government sources, would automatically meet the media's criteria of newsworthiness, and would thus provide sustained front page coverage centering around the issues the administration wanted to stress. The contents of the White Paper on "Communist Interference" were leaked to the *New York Times* several weeks before its release (Onis, 1981), and, from early February through April of 1981, there was a steady stream of official statements emphasizing Soviet involvement in the Central American conflict.

Journalists, most of whom were much closer to the Carter administration's view of the conflict than the Reagan administration's, were personally quite skeptical of the Reagan position. A wire service bureau chief responsible for Central America coverage describes his reaction this way:

> When the administration came out with this White Paper all the news stories mentioned Communist intervention, Communist intervention. Nobody in Washington bothered to mention that this thing had been going on for years, that the guerrillas have been around for a long time, that the government itself in El Salvador...has been accused of human rights violations, and that is in large part why people are rebelling against it.[8]

Reporters in the field, those who had been covering Central America on a regular basis, were most critical of the Reagan position. But the weakening of the Cold War consensus has been broad enough that they were by no means alone in their skepticism. *National Wire Watch,* for example, the newsletter of an association of "wire editors" who select national and international stories for the "nonprestige" press, criticized the wire services for "heeding in lockstep fashion" "the party-line from Washington on Communist infiltration."[9]

And yet, as both these comments note, it was "Communist intervention, Communist intervention" that dominated the news. The routines of journalism, the practice of assigning central importance to the statements of government officials, overrode the personal beliefs of most of the journalists themselves. The week the White Paper came out, the question of Soviet involvement dominated the news almost totally, while the human rights emphasis essentially disappeared. After that, the administration lost part of its grip on the headlines. Coverage partially shifted from Washington back to Central America itself (which had been its main locus before the administration's public relations "offensive"), and much of it focused once again on human rights and related issues, including the new issue of whether El Salvador would become another Vietnam. But even in this period, with journalists well aware that the administration was making an effort to manage the news to support a particular, controversial interpretation of events in Central America, routine coverage of official statements continued to tilt the balance of news coverage toward the administration's Cold War perspective. Said one correspondent:

> Anybody who'd been to Salvador as much as the people who normally cover it knew [the White Paper] was a pretty simplified view of the situation. But if the

---

[8] Juan Tamayo, UPI, interview, Mexico City, July 15, 1981.

[9] *National Wire Watch,* No. 35, April 30, 1981, p. 2. A survey of editorial comment in 35 newspapers around the United States found that most rejected the Cold War interpretation of the Central American crisis. See "U.S. Press Shines Harsh Light on Reagan's Salvador Policy," by Mary Ellen Leary, Pacific News Service, March 27, 1981.

leader of the Western world makes that statement, it's policy almost. You've got to follow it up... There's always a thing in your mind, "Well, maybe there is something to it!"[10]

2. Setting the Agenda

The media's special relationship with official Washington profoundly affects the news agenda as well; coverage ebbs and flows according to the political rhythms of Washington. This can be an important political resource for the administration in power, since it gives it the ability to choose when public attention will be focused on a given problem and when it will not. It is also of considerable ideological significance, over and above the potential it creates for news management.

The Cold War ideology, as we have seen, deemphasizes the internal causes of political conflicts in the Third World. Part of its power probably lies in its simplicity and economy. It explains all international conflicts in essentially the same, familiar terms, sparing the public the burden of mastering a new set of political intricacies each time a crisis erupts. Rival interpretations generally stress precisely these internal causes of revolution. Journalists, especially those stationed in Third World countries, are aware of this clash of perspectives, and frequently stress, when giving background to political conflicts, the irreducibility of the local political situation. But again, the routines of journalism tend to wash out the effects of changes of consciousness that have occurred since Vietnam. Focus on U.S. officials as the premier newsmakers means that information about the internal politics of Third World countries appears in the news only in a very limited and fragmented form, and is not at all central to the organization of the ongoing news story.

The centrality of Washington to the news agenda can be seen clearly in Central America coverage. Television coverage of Central America averaged about 8 minutes a month from October 1979 through November 1980 (total for the three networks combined); jumped to 37 minutes in December, with the killing of the four Americans, the suspension of U.S. aid, and the conflict between the outgoing Carter and incoming Reagan administrations over human rights policy; and soared to 236 minutes in March 1981, following the release of the White Paper. After April, the administration began to deemphasize Central America, and coverage dropped precipitously, averaging 21 minutes a month from May 1981 through January 1982. Then, at the beginning of February 1982, the administration announced a sharp increase in military aid to El Salvador. This was followed by a series of public statements about Soviet arms shipments to Nicaragua and the announcement of the Caribbean Basin aid plan. Television coverage shot up to 228

---

[10] Ike Seamans, NBC, interview, Miami, July 31, 1981.

minutes in February and peaked at 415 minutes in March, when it centered around the election, which had become the centerpiece of the administration's public justification for further aid to El Salvador. Television coverage has followed a similar up-and-down pattern, closely attuned to the Washington agenda, through the present.

Critical events in Central America itself, on the other hand, have had little independent impact on the news agenda. If Washington was stressing Central America, they might be heavily covered; otherwise, they were likely not to be reported at all. Thus, in January, 1980, when three civilian members of the ruling Junta resigned, signaling the collapse of the political center in El Salvador, the networks did not cover the story. Neither did they report on the formation of the Democratic Revolutionary Front (the political arm of the guerrilla movement in El Salvador) in April 1980, nor the amalgamation in May 1980, of the several Salvadoran guerrilla groups into the Farabundo Marti Front for National Liberation, nor the decision by the rightist-dominated constituent assembly, following the March 1982 elections, to shift to itself much of the power of the Presidency. Those same 1982 elections, along with two sets of elections in 1984, which were heavily emphasized by the administration, were heavily covered by all the media. But intense conflict over El Salvador's land reform program, which began after the 1982 election and led progressively to the demise of land reform, was covered only sporadically in the major newspapers, hardly at all by television. Understanding the politics of Central America from daily news coverage is like trying to grasp the character of Hamlet from Stoppard's play *Rosencrantz and Guildenstern Are Dead*—which puts at a considerable disadvantage any perspective which centers on a socio-political rather than a geo-political interpretation of Third World political conflict.

3. Certifying Legitimate Authorities

The media's reliance on official sources, finally, is an important symbolic acknowledgment of the legitimacy of political authorities. The increased skepticism of foreign affairs reporting since Vietnam may communicate to the public that officials are not as honest or as competent as they once believed. But confidence is not the same as legitimacy. And on legitimacy, the cues are unambiguous: journalists continue to rely routinely on official government pronouncements for authoritative statements about world affairs. No other political actors play this role in the news. If this observation seems trivial, it is only because the institutionalization of the media–government relationship is so strong that we have come to take it for granted.

THE INERTIA OF THE IDEOLOGICAL SYSTEM

> I seem to have had a conception, a diagram, of life, which every new discovery wrecked, or, if it held, had no place for new facts. Facts. It seems to me now that facts have had to beat their way into my head, banging on my brain like

bullets from a machine gun to get in; and it was only by being hit over and over again that I could let my old ideal and college-made picture of life be blown up and let the new, truer picture be blown in. No wonder some men cannot learn; they are subject only to a few shots, not riddled with volleys, daily, all their lives (Lincoln Steffens, 1931, p. 238).

Ideological change is also limited by the inertia of ideology itself. As Lincoln Steffens suggests, ideological presuppositions become so central to the thought-process that they change only with difficulty. An ideological system, moreover, is complex and multi-leveled; the political impact of a change in one element may be blunted by the stability of others.

The Cold War ideology itself, although it has lost its monopoly, retains a good deal of power, not only through the ability of the government to force Cold War themes to the forefront, but through the media's own framing of events. To some degree, different "factions" of the media have been consciously choosing up sides in the emerging ideological conflict. *Time,* for example, reporting on an important Reagan speech in April 1983, took aim directly at what the Reagan administration calls the "Vietnam syndrome":

> Out of fear at repeating that colossal misadventure, Americans have seized hold of its lessons, perhaps inaccurately, perhaps obsessively. There is a strong aversion to undertaking any commitment to shore up threatened pro-American regimes in the third world, no matter how strategically important they are, and a reluctance to believe that the countries of a region could topple like dominoes, no matter how compelling the evidence of spreading subversion (Isaacson, 1983, p. 21).

To a much greater extent however, the Cold War ideology is probably reproduced through a primarily unconscious process, employed by journalists not so much to make a political point as to "package" the presentation of news in terms they assume the audience will find interesting and easy to understand. "It's been one year since the fighting in Nicaragua ended," said ABC's Hugh Downs, introducing a *20/20* segment on the Nicaraguan revolution. "What is the U.S. doing to ensure that the new Nicaragua turns out to be democratic instead of totalitarian?...The Cubans are there and the Russians are coming. But where is the U.S. in Nicaragua's future?" Why the focus on the Cold War angle? "We assume that most of the people we are reaching have 'zero knowledge and zero interest in the subjects we intend to cover,'" explains Av Westin (1982, p. 199), who was then executive producer of the ABC public affairs "magazine":

> There has to be something that will relate the story to the basic concerns of the television viewer....The simplest way is to tie it to American interests.... Central America is just South of our borders; Cuban interests and other dangerous forces are at work there. An understanding of the locale in terms of American national security makes it all the more important for the distracted viewer to pay attention to what is about to come up.

Nevertheless, the weakening of the Cold War ideology is undeniable, and I would like to turn to the second form of limitation mentioned above: I would like to focus on another aspect of American political ideology which has maintained its strength and limits the significance of the fragmentation of the Cold War consensus.

It will be useful here to step back for a moment and make clear how the concept of hegemony applies to foreign affairs reporting, for this is a somewhat complicated case. To say the media play a "hegemonic" role is to say that they contribute to the maintenance of consent for a system of power. The relevant system of power here is the post World War II *"pax Americana"* —the world capitalist system dominated both politically and economically by the United States. The leading power in such a system has to maintain a double hegemony: it has to maintain the consent both of subordinate nations and of its own population. This domestic consent, which we are concerned with here, also has two components. The public has to consent to the domestic system of power—to recognize the legitimacy of foreign policy elites and the institutions of their rule—and also to the international system itself. The Cold War ideology was ideally suited to maintaining this double consent. American dominance of the international system—and the need for domestic sacrifices to maintain that dominance—were justified by the threat of a Soviet-dominated world system; tight elite control of foreign policy was justified by the danger to national security that could lie in any conflict.

As the Cold War ideology weakens, however, other ideological factors serve to maintain consent. These are too numerous to outline exhaustively here. For one example, let us return to *Central America in Revolt,* which illustrated so well the media's turn away from the assumptions of the Cold War. In the conclusion to that documentary, Bill Moyers made the following comment: "My colleagues and I come back from Central America thinking it looks different from up close than from afar, and different if you don't have an ideology to promote or a policy to defend." This seemingly insignificant remark expresses what is in fact one of the most important and pervasive elements of the value system of American journalism: a general distaste for political conflict and partisanship. It was an important underlying theme in *Central America in Revolt,* which presented *all* parties to the conflict in an essentially negative light. American officials were presented as dogmatic; their critics, (who "often sound as though no revolution ever goes sour"), as simplistic. The rulers of Central America appeared as brutal and backward; their opponents as naive (the Catholic missionary) or power-hungry (the revolutionary). Only the journalists themselves, "without an ideology to promote," appeared to possess real wisdom.

As the example of *Central America in Revolt* suggests, distrust of political partisanship is an ideological principle that can cut both ways politically.

But at the deepest level, its implications are conservative; it is at root a preference for order, and it affects most strongly the reporting of those who seek to challenge an established order.[11] Its significance for the maintenance of consent in the field of foreign policy is two-fold.

Distrust of partisanship means, first of all, that, even in periods when the media are not supportive of foreign policy elites, they tend to be at least equally unsupportive of any attempt to challenge established authorities. Indeed, the political opposition faces the special disadvantage that it has no choice but to embrace partisanship and to engage political passion, while elites can often fall back into a quiet "technocratic" or "statesmanlike" posture. (One reason the Reagan administration has had difficulty "managing" the news on El Salvador may be that it took a particularly "partisan" stance initially, attacking the previous administration ideologically and declaring that it sought a basic change in the direction of U.S. foreign policy.)

In their coverage of domestic opposition to U.S. foreign policy, the media have changed little since the later (post Tet offensive) period of the Vietnam war. Coverage of domestic opposition was generally negative, even during the period when the media were most critical of administration policy, often presented more as a threat to public order than as a political statement (Gitlin, 1980; Hallin, forthcoming). In the case of Central America, the domestic opposition has so far appeared in the news only sporadically. Coverage of elite opponents—Congressional critics, former Ambassador Robert White, and to a lesser extent the Catholic church—has been respectful but limited; coverage of more radical nonelite opposition, virtually absent. One important consequence of this limited coverage of domestic opposition is that coherent statements of alternative visions of the world order and of U.S. policy rarely appear in the news. To the extent, moreover, that the media promote the general value of political noninvolvement, they are contributing to a passive form of domestic consent.

Internationally, distrust of partisanship has equally conservative implications. Oppositional political movements in the Third World, especially in areas like Central America where class antagonisms are deep and bitter, necessarily involve levels of political passion quite unfamiliar to most North Americans. With a few exceptions, they appear in the media in a harshly negative light, whether or not they are presented in Cold War terms as agents of Communist aggression.

It is interesting here to consider El Salvador coverage in the period before the Reagan administration came to office. The Cold War framework was

---

[11] Cf., Herbert Gans' (1979) discussion of the importance of order in the journalist's value system. Gans points out that the journalists' value system was formed during the Progressive era. The contrast between politics and professionalism was characteristic of Progressive ideology.

rarely invoked during this period; to the extent that journalists attempted to explain the political conflict, they did so in terms of domestic causes; they were not at all sympathetic toward the established socio-economic order in El Salvador. Yet the opposition to that order appeared in the news as carrier of *irrational* violence, a threat not to the old order but to *order in general*. Here are several excerpts from television coverage.

> NBC, Oct. 30, 1979, a report on political violence the previous day (this is the entire text of the 60-second report, minus personal details on two victims of the violence): "Most people in El Salvador have tried to get on with their daily lives despite political violence off and on for years.... The trouble started with a demonstration by a leftist group, the same group that seized more than two hundred hostages last week in two government buildings. Most of the hostages were freed, but the leftists held on to the government officials they had captured trying to *force* changes here [emphasis from voice inflection]."
>
> CBS, Feb. 13, 1980, a report on the seizure by leftists of the Panamanian embassy and a government building:
>
> Walter Cronkite: "Our Martha Teichner went to the education ministry... and found the militants fresh-faced youngsters who looked as if they were playing some guerrilla warfare game. But it's no game...
>
> Teichner: "Wherever these children go they hear the rhetoric and read the slogans that lead them into leftist groups... Luis is eleven years old. 'I saw the misery of the people,' he says. His words sound like propaganda." [One might imagine here what an eighteen-year-old GI sounded like explaining the War in Vietnam in 1965.]
>
> NBC, April 1, 1980, again a report on political violence:
>
> David Brinkley: "In the tortured country of El Salvador the violence and killing continues every day, and it is random and senseless. It doesn't even have the cold clarity of one side killing those on the other, as Phil Bremen reports from San Salvador."
>
> Bremen (wrapping up): "Before the violence, tourists came to see the ruins of an ancient civilization here. In the face of modern ruins, the United States is urging Salvadorans to bring some civilization to their politics."[12]

If this series of excerpts seems chaotic, it is an accurate reflection of television coverage in this period, which amounted to a set of quickly-passing images centered around the theme of political violence. The violence was

---

[12] The assertion that the violence in El Salvador didn't have "the cold clarity of one side killing those on the other" referred primarily to the assassination of Archbishop Romero, which Breman presented as something that could have been done either by the right (Romero was a strong human rights advocate, and had just shortly before argued that soldiers sometimes had a duty to disobey orders), or by the left "knowing it would be blamed on the right." In December, however, after the American nuns were killed, Bremen reported, "In the struggle for power both left and right burn, kidnap, and kill. But only the right has targeted the clergy" (NBC Dec. 4, 1980)—a good example of the power of the dominant news frame to affect the reporting of particular events.

described most of the time as instigated by "extremists" of both left and right (though the focus, as these examples suggest, was mainly on the left), with the U.S.-backed government caught in the middle. More important than this specific political interpretation, though, is the vague but powerful impression of the "senselessness" of political conflict conveyed by the whole series of images. The ideological deep structure of this coverage is well expressed by Bremen's conclusion. Revolution in the Third World does not appear here as a challenge by the Communist bloc to United States security; but the specter of Communist world conquest is replaced by the specter of world anarchy, the image of a bipolar struggle between democracy and totalitarianism, by the image of "Fortress America," an island of civilization in a sea of political barbarism. It is important here to place Central America coverage in the context of coverage of the Third World generally. In its focus on violence, and in its sporadic, fragmented quality, El Salvador coverage in this 1979/1980 period, before Central America had become a major issue in the United States, was quite typical of Third World coverage generally (Dahlgren, 1982; Morales, 1982; Peterson, 1981); El Salvador stories, in fact, were generally packaged in the news broadcast as part of a series of stories about political violence and terrorism in the Third World, often as a sequel to reports on the seizure of the American embassy in Iran —a fact which substantially enhanced the strength of the image of a world of anarchy. The theme of irrational violence and anti-Americanism continues to run through a great deal of Central America coverage, whether or not that coverage also employs cold war imagery (Hallin, 1983).

CONCLUSION

Gramsci developed the concept of ideological hegemony to explain why revolutionary movements were unable to succeed in Europe in the 1910s and 1920s, despite the deep social and economic crisis of that period. The popularity of the concept with modern Marxism is based largely on its ability to explain the persistent political stability of Western capitalism. But there is an intellectual danger associated with this use of the concept, the danger of assuming that ideology and ideological institutions will always, in one way or another, perform their appointed hegemonic "function." The most extreme example of this sort of functionalism is perhaps Luis Althusser's essay on "Ideological State Apparatuses" (1971, p. 154):

> All ideological state apparatuses [for Althusser all cultural institutions are part of the "state"]...contribute to the same result: the reproduction of the relations of production....Each of them contributes to this single result in the way proper to it....[The] concert is dominated by a single score, occasionally disturbed by contradictions...the score of the Ideology of the current ruling class

Ideology appears here as a sort of *deus ex machina,* standing above and regulating political conflict.

Ideological change of the sort we have explored here tends, from this perspective, to be interpreted as a means of restoring political equilibrium— evidence of the *strength,* not the weakness, of ideological hegemony. There is a good deal of truth to this interpretation. To the extent that the media have abandoned the Cold War perspective, and have adopted a more critical attitude toward official policy, they have done so primarily in response to a growing division *within* the foreign policy establishment. Questioning of the Cold War perspective began, in general, with the articulation of Carter's human rights doctrine; emphasis on human rights in El Salvador coverage began with the debate that accompanied the transition from the Carter to the Reagan administration; emphasis on the parallel between El Salvador and Vietnam, which led the Reagan administration to complain of "excessive publicity" just a few days after it had itself turned the spotlight on El Salvador, followed a bitter debate in Congress which focused precisely on the Vietnam issue. These debates have concerned how, not whether, to maintain U.S. "influence" in the world system. And it is certainly plausible that the ideological changes the media have undergone since Vietnam will prove to be an effective historical adaptation, incorporating the Vietnam experience into the political culture without threatening the established order in any significant way.

But this outcome cannot be assumed a priori. The difficulty that foreign policy elites now have managing public opinion (most polls show about half the U.S. public opposed to Reagan administration policy in Central America and large majorities opposed to sending troops; one poll—taken during the Spring of 1982 when coverage on the model of *Central America in Revolt* was particularly common—found 51% saying they would support young men who refused to be drafted to fight in Central America, e.g., Shribman, 1984,[13] may well have a profound affect on the conduct of American foreign policy and in the long run on the shape of the world system. The Cold War consensus may prove irreplaceable as a source of support for a foreign policy oriented toward preserving U.S. hegemony. Even the "fortress America" perspective seems ambiguous in its political implications, with a potential for isolationism as well as for jingoistic nationalism or for the kind of liberal paternalism implicit in the wrap-up to the Brinkley/Bremen story quoted above. No one planned the fragmentation of the Cold War consensus; if ideology is a symphony, it is a symphony without a conductor. And as for

---

[13] The figure on draft resistance is from an ABC News-Washington Post Poll, reported on ABC *World News Tonight,* March 23, 1982. It is important to add that in many ways the public is extremely ambivalent about Central America policy, and there is evidence that if the administration were able to make a Cold War interpretation of the situation stick, there might be support for more active intervention.

Althusser's "composer," Ideology with a capital "I", it is pure reification to imagine that it stands above the ironies of history.

Once we have set functionalist assumptions aside, however, the hegemonic process can clearly be seen at work, holding communication within limits relatively less threatening to the established order (cf. Paletz and Entman, 1981, Ch. 13). What is perhaps most important about the limits we have explored in Central America coverage is the *relative exclusion of alternatives*. The Cold War perspective, which once organized virtually all foreign affairs coverage into a coherent ideological picture supportive of American world hegemony, now no longer does so. But there is no sign that a coherent *oppositional* ideology is likely to take its place. The media are too closely tied to the established institutions of American foreign policy, and to a culture which is suspicious and uncomfortable with any threat to political order. Critiques of the concept of hegemony often fall into the trap of confronting only the most simplistic version of it. David Altheide, for instance, assumes in a recent critique that journalistic routines must be shown to "negate any journalistic independence" and socialization to mold journalists into a "uniform ideological shape" if the "hegemonic" perspective is to be confirmed (Altheide, 1984, pp. 479-81). But this is to miss the entire intent of the concept of hegemony, as it has been articulated by Gramsci and others, which is precisely to explain how ideological boundaries can be maintained in modern capitalist societies without rigid control of political communication, which is obviously impossible in a liberal democratic political order.

It is always dangerous to speculate about the impact of the media on popular consciousness. But it seems most reasonable to assume that changes in foreign affairs coverage since the Vietnam period would have the affect of creating a sort of ideological vacuum, weakening established assumptions, shattering old myths, but leaving little of any symbolic power in their place. The public might at times react to this vacuum by falling back on the familiar symbols of the Cold War, as a sort of refuge from confusion. It is also possible that a new ideology, presumably a form of defensive nationalism, might develop out of the image of "Fortress America" in a hostile world, particularly if incidents like the Iranian hostage crisis were to become more common. But what seems most likely is an extended period of public confusion and uncertainty about world politics, and a passive, sometimes grudging consent to the decisions of the foreign policy establishment, so long as the costs of those decisions are not extremely high.

REFERENCES

Altheide, D.L. (1984). "Media Hegemony: A Failure of Perspective. *Public Opinion Quarterly* 48, 476-490.

Althusser, L. (1971). "Ideology and Ideological State Apparatuses." *In* L. Althusser, *Lenin and Philosophy and Other Essays* (pp. 127-186). New York: Monthly Review Press.

Anderson, P. (1976-1977). "The Antinomies of Antonio Gramsci." *New Left Review 100*, 5-78.
Cater, D. (1959). *The Fourth Branch of Government*. New York: Vintage.
Cohen, B.M. (1963). *The Press and Foreign Policy*. Princeton, NJ: Princeton University Press.
Dahlgren, P.H., with Chakrapani, S. (1982). "The Third World on TV News: Western Ways of Seeing the 'Other.'" *In* W.C. Adams (Ed.), *Television Coverage of International Affairs* (pp. 45-65). Norwood, NJ: Ablex.
Gans, H. (1979). *Deciding What's News*. New York: Pantheon.
Gitlin, T. (1980). *The Whole World is Watching: Mass Media in the Making and Unmaking of the New Left*. Berkeley, CA: University of California Press.
Gold, D.A., Lo, C.Y.H., and Wright, E.O. (1975). "Recent Developments in Marxist Theories of the Capitalist State." *Monthly Review 27* (No. 5) 29-43; (No. 6), 36-51.
Gramsci, A. (1971). *Selections from the Prison Notebooks*. New York: International Publishers.
Halberstam, D. (1965). *The Making of a Quagmire*. New York: Random House.
Halberstam, D. (1979). *The Powers That Be*. New York: Alfred A. Knopf.
Hall, S. (1979). "Culture, the Media and the 'Ideological Effect.'" *In* J. Curran, M. Gurevitch, and J. Wollacott (Eds.), *Mass Communication and Society* (pp 315-348). Beverly Hills, CA: Sage.
Hallin, D.C. (1983). *The Media Go to War—From Vietnam to Central America. Nacla Report on the Americas*, 17.
Hallin, D.C. (1984). "The Media, the War in Vietnam and Political Support: A Critique of the Thesis of an Oppositional Media." *Journal of Politics 46*, 2-24.
Hallin, D.C. (forthcoming). *The Media, the War in Vietnam and the Crisis in American Politics* [tentative title]. New York: Oxford University Press.
Huntington, S.J. (1981). *American Politics: The Promise of Disharmony*. Cambridge, MA: Harvard University Press.
Isaacson, W. (1983). "Harsh Facts, Hard Choices." *Time 121* (No. 19), 20-28.
Marcuse, H. (1964). *One-Dimensional Man*. Boston, MA: Beacon Press.
Maslow, J.E., and Arana, A. (1981). "Operation El Salvador." *Columbia Journalism Review 20* (No. 1), 52-58.
Massing, M. (1983). "About-face on El Salvador." *Columbia Journalism Review 22* (No. 4), 42-49.
Mecklin, J. (1965). *Mission in Torment*. Garden City, NY: Doubleday.
Miliband, R. (1969). *The State in Capitalist Society*. New York: Basic Books.
Morales, W.Q. (1982). "Revolutions, Earthquakes and Latin America: The Networks Look at Allende's Chile and Somoza's Nicaragua." *In* W.C. Adams (Ed.), *Television Coverage of International Affairs* (pp. 79-113). Norwood, NJ: Ablex.
Onis, J. de. (1981). "Soviet-Bloc Nations Said to Pledge Aid to Salvador Rebels." *New York Times* (Feb. 6), 1.
Paletz, D.L., and Entman, R.M. (1981). *Media Power Politics*. New York: Free Press.
Peterson, S. (1981). "International News Selection by the Elite Press: A Case Study." *Public Opinion Quarterly 45*, 143-163.
Pitkin, H.F. (1972). *Wittgenstein and Justice*. Berkeley, CA: University of California Press.
Roberts, C.M. (1977). *The Washington Post: The First 100 Years*. Boston, MA: Houghton Mifflin.
Robinson, M.J. (1975). "American Political Legitimacy in an Age of Electronic Journalism: Reflections on the Evening News." *In* D. Cater and R. Adler (Eds.), *Television as a Social Force: New Approaches to TV Criticism* (pp. 97-139). New York: Praeger.
Robinson, M.J. (1976). "Public Affairs Television and the Growth of Political Malaise: The Case of 'The Selling of the Pentagon.'" *American Political Science Review 70*, 409-432.

Shribman, D. (1984). "Poll Finds that Fewer than Half in U.S. Back Latin Policy." New York Times (Apr. 29), 1.
Sigal, L.V. (1983). *Reporters and Officials.* Lexington, MA: D.C. Heath.
Steffens, L. (1931). *Autobiography.* New York: Harcourt, Brace and World.
Trumbull, R. (1962). "Three Areas of Asia Disturb the Free World." *New York Times* (Feb. 18) (Pt. 4), 4.
Volosinov, V.N. (1973). *Marxism and the Philosophy of Language.* New York: Seminar Press.
Westin, A. (1982). *Newswatch: How TV Divides the News.* New York: Simon and Schuster.
Williams, R. (1977). *Marxism and Literature.* Oxford, England: Oxford University Press.

Chapter 2
The Media-Policy Connection: Ecologies of News

HARVEY L. MOLOTCH
Sociology Department
University of California
Santa Barbara, CA 93106

DAVID L. PROTESS
MARGARET T. GORDON
Medill School of Journalism
Northwestern University
Evanston, IL 60201

In this paper we examine ways in which the modern practice of journalism affects public policy-making and social problem-solving in the United States. The intellectual context of this inquiry is the long-standing effort of many scholars to understand the impact of mass media on society. We contrast two approaches to this problem: one derived from the traditional quasi-experimental "media effects" paradigm, the other more consistent with recent trends toward an "ecological" orientation toward the media-policy relationship. Using the traditional model as a point of departure, our plan is to show how different types of media-policy connections are better revealed through the ecological perspective.

Traditional effects studies have typically involved measurements—either in laboratory settings or in more naturalistic field situations—of attitude shifts which can be attributed to specific media content. Sometimes, researchers conclude that significant shifts have occurred (Cook et al., 1982; Hovland, Janis, & Kelley, 1953); other researchers and journalists have reported that no such shifts have taken place (e.g. Michelson, 1972). In still other instances, the results are mixed, with efforts made to specify the relevant contingencies of such effects (Comstock, Chaffee, Katzman, McCombs, & Roberts, 1978; Gerbner & Gross, 1976; Klapper, 1960).

This paper grows out of research on mass media and public policy conducted at the Center for Urban Affairs and Policy Research, Northwestern University. A previous version was delivered at the International Association for Mass Communications Research Conference, Paris, Sept. 6, 1982.

These conflicting and mixed results often lead to doubts that media have much of an influence on public policymaking; if effects by media on individual attitudes are so difficult to demonstrate, then the more indirect effects on policy must be even more open to question. In fact, some researchers and journalists themselves (e.g., Greenfield, 1982; Michelson, 1972) have suggested that media do little more than objectively recount events occurring in wholly separate and autonomous policy arenas. In this "mirror model," as one researcher calls it, "news people are merely a conduit for information which is produced by others. They reflect whatever comes to their attention; they do not shape it in any way" (Graber, 1980, p. 58). Journalist-scholar Garry Wills (1982) goes even farther, arguing that "The media's various audiences determine what the media will say, more than do the so-called managers of the media" (see also Michelson, 1972).

Yet elected politicians, other political activists, and agency policy makers usually perceive that media *are* critial to both public attitude formation and to the policy process. This may explain why politicians spend so much time and effort attempting to manipulate media and, on occasion, launching energetic critiques of the way the media personnel do their newswork. As former Senator Adlai Stevenson III put it: "the media makes and breaks the politicians.... It is the nation's most powerful and least accountable institution" (Friendly, 1981). And then there is Theodore White's dictum on elections: "The media *is* the campaign" (cited in Valentine, 1982).

A way of attempting to reconcile such opposing perspectives is to note a critical difference between the "hypodermic" model of influence presumed by much of the research enterprise (see Kraus & Davis, 1976) and the actual world in which media people and political actors live (see: Defleur & Ball-Rokeach, 1975, p. 258). Rather than living in a world in which discrete messages are "injected" into a public world of tabula rosae, such actors participate in an ongoing process of message streams and reactions to those messages. The alternative is, therefore, to presume that media effects, especially in the policy arena, are very complexly determined, and that traditional methodologies and observational stances are not sufficient for discerning them (see Comstock *et al.,* 1978; Gans, 1977, p. 697; Rivers & Schramm, 1980).

This effort to demonstrate the significance of media requires attention to the fact that media, including the agendas reflected in their output, are shaped by "outside forces" such as public bureaucracies (Fishman, 1980), private elites (Gitlin, 1980), and the structure of the news organizations themselves (Tuchman, 1978). Media's need for a "routinization" of news (Tuchman, 1978) promotes the organization of newsgathering into "beats" (Fishman, 1980; Molotch, 1979); which encourages "sweetheart relationships" between journalists and their regular sources (Johnstone, Slawski, & Bowman, 1976), and the development of public relations units or press officers attached to many public officials, agencies and corporations whose job it is to deal with representatives of the press (Fishman, 1978; Gordon, Heinz, Gordon, & Divorski, 1973). Similarly, the same range of important institutions are part of the socialization of journalists (as with most others), thereby shaping the cultural/ideological viewpoints of reporters (their "para-ideology") which then becomes critical to their processing of materials (Gans, 1979; see also Altheide, 1976; Gordon & Heath, 1981).

Such insights point to a need for working models which include, not only ways of understanding how publics and policy actors form *their* agendas and perspectives, but how journalistic agendas are shaped as well, and *how these two sectors of reality-making are interlinked*. Media effects are embedded in the actions of the policy actor, just as the policy actor's own behaviors come to be reflected in journalists' formulations. Media and policy are part of a single ecology in which systemic transfer of cultural materials cumulate and dissipate, often imperceptibly, throughout a media-policy web.

It is our goal in this paper to formulate more systematically connections between media and policy making processes, primarily through attention to contemporary investigative journalism. Our conception of "policy" is quite broad, referring to actions of persons and institutions in political and governmental circles. Our conception of media, for present purposes, encompass persons and organizations involved in generating news—print and electronic. Analytically, we are sensitive to the fact that the role of the media is complementary to those of other institutions, and that media impacts are cumulative, interactive, and subtle. We believe that careful examination of case studies of the media-policy nexus will illuminate why other commentators could come to such mixed conclusions, and also contribute a clearer view of the relationships which make up the media–public-policy system.[1]

We begin with a description of what we regard as the still dominant (although increasingly retreating) model of these relationships, and then, using case studies of contemporary investigative reports, explore iterations of that model. Much of our case material derives from one of the authors' (Protess) direct experience with numerous journalistic investigations during the 5-year period that he was Research Director of the Better Government Association (BGA), a nationwide "watchdog" organization which collaborates with the

---

[1] An ambitious research enterprise has been developed to test in a new way whether or not investigations do have an impact on individual behavior, public attitudes and the policy-making process. Seven faculty from six different disciplines at Northwestern University and the University of California, Santa Barbara, are studying the "careers" of several media investigations and their eventual impact on public policies. The study is being conducted at the Center for Urban Affairs and Policy Research at Northwestern University (see Cook *et al.*, 1982).

news media in disclosing governmental waste and corruption. This provided him with access to original documents, notes, and the accounts of journalistic participants.

THE MUCKRAKING MODEL

In recent years, competition among media has heightened as the fight for economic survival, especially for newspapers, has intensified. Television executives have learned that news programming (and especially news magazine shows) can have important impacts on ratings and profitability. One response to the commercial competition, especially after the publication of the Pentagon Papers and sensational exposures of the Watergate scandal, was the development in many newspapers and television stations of investigative units designed to develop public exposés of wrong-doings.

This contemporary phenomenon is in the tradition of the turn-of-the-century "muckrakers" (Regier, 1930), at least in terms of some of the social goals at work and the romanticism which seems to surround the endeavor. There also lingers the possibility that media–policy relationships implied by the muckraking imagery are also still intact. This imagery implies that muckrakers (*investigative journalists*) unearth evidence of a problem. The exposure (*publication*[2]) of the problem leads to the mobilization of a changed *public opinion,* which in turn is reflected in *policy initiatives* by legislators and administrators, followed by some sort of *policy consequence.* Characteristically, one historian claims that the passage of the Pure Food and Drugs Act in 1906 "may justly be regarded as a product of muckraking, since it was the magazines which aroused the public to support a reform for which medical associations had long been pleading in vain" (Regier, 1930, p. 180; for other examples, see McConnell, 1966, pp. 11–29). Schematically, it looks like this:

Journalistic   Public   Policy   Policy
Investigation → Publication → Opinion → Initiatives → Consequences

This model parallels the "hypodermic" conceptualization which underlies much of the attitude effects research (but adds a few more sequential steps). As such, it suffers from many of the same flaws as the "effects" literatures, and some additional ones as well. A first difficulty with the schema is the implied assumption that, once begun, the presence of the first step in the process (e.g., successful investigation) leads, in some *inexorable* way, to each successive step: i.e., publication of findings, which then gives

---

[2] We use the term "publication" as a proxy for any form of mass media exposure—newspaper, television, or radio. In general, we have used terms commonly associated with print media.

rise to an aroused public, then to fostering policy initiatives. Of course, as any journalist knows, such follow-through does not always happen; the process can be truncated at any point. A related problem is the assumed *linearity* in which A causes B causes C, and so on, rather than, for example, one step being skipped altogether or causal directions being reversed or operating in both directions simultaneously.

Still another problem with the model is that it takes its analytic unit—the "message"—as something relatively *discontinuous*. Such an assumption is incongruent with the fact that news "stories" are frequently not "one-shot" items. More typically, they are an evolving series of journalistic events which continue over substantial periods of time. Indeed, even an apparently discrete message is inevitably embedded in a context of messages which have been transmitted before and others which are envisioned for the future. Commonly, sequences of media items may together produce an effect which cannot be discerned by looking for the impacts of a constituent piece. Sometimes, the only perceptible effect of a given media item is that it facilitates the publication of the next item (as in, for example, reports of "crime waves" (Fishman, 1978). Any effect of a single news item must be understood in terms of its linkages to other such items and their impacts seen in terms of a cumulative force.

Also masking potential media impacts is the fact that a component in the putative muckraking chain (e.g., publication) can persist, even after its apparent role is "finished." When a policy actor takes an action in response to a media report, it may appear that subsequent attitude change is due to the policy action, rather than to the media report. But those policy actions contain, in a sense, the media reports within them. Similarly, a policy action may serve to *remind* the public of a media report (and some of its details) which might have been published long before. That is, media effects (and other effects as well) can persist through various steps of social linkages; there is logical room, not just for a "two-step flow" (Katz & Lazarsfeld, 1955) of effects, but for an N-step flow.

Given the realities of the way modern journalism works, any component of the media-policy process should be viewed as potentially impacting every other component. We see the complex patterns of mutual interaction of components as evolving over time, as different actors with different purposes together determine "the story" and its ultimate policy outcomes.

It is from this viewpoint that we attempt, by drawing upon case studies, to describe some ways in which media play a role in the policy process. In each instance, we provide a name for a specific variation which stands in some degree of contrast to the muckraking "standard." The iterations we present are neither comprehensive nor mutually exclusive, but rather an effort to show concretely how a broad perspective can expose a rich variety of media–policy connections.

TRUNCATED MUCKRAKING

Sometimes the entire muckraking dynamic is stopped because one of the sequential components fails to actualize. We have labeled such instances examples of *truncated muckraking,* and indicate some of their subtypes as follows:

1. Displaced Investigations

Some otherwise "successful" investigative efforts fail to result in media exposure. Completed investigations may result in formulated or fully written stories which are "killed" before publication, thereby preventing the successive steps in the chain from occurring. The classic example of such a displaced story was the *New York Times'* decision to not publish news of imminent invasion of Cuba by U.S.-trained forces at the Bay of Pigs. Because of direct White House Pressure on the *Times'* publisher, the paper altered its news reports on military preparations in Central America to serve what was then seen as the national interest. (For a description of the event from a *Times'* editor's perspective, see Catledge, 1971,p. 264). Without exposure, there could be no advance public outcry, no policy intervention, and hence, no policy consequence. We speak of the investigation as "displaced" (cf. Sills, 1957), rather than just aborted, because it was eventually transformed into a different kind of story: the responsibility of the press to expose improper government activity. We usually learn of such killed stories only if other published accounts eventually displace them.

Displaced investigations, as a variant of the muckraking model, can be represented hence:

$$\text{Investigation} \nrightarrow \text{Publication} \rightarrow \text{Opinion} \rightarrow \text{Initiatives} \rightarrow \text{Policy Consequences}$$

2. Uneventful Exposures

In this variant of truncated muckraking, there is indeed publication of investigatory results, but there is no discernible response anywhere along the rest of the media-policy chain. Typically, no other media "pick up" the story; no interest groups come forth with commentaries; there are no letters to the editor or phone calls to the station; policy makers do not bother to comment during their press conferences; no heads roll. Pollsters do not ask respondents what they think about the issue, and no change in public opinion is (or can be) documented.

One such example involved efforts to provide a definitive exposé of the abuse of power by the Chicago political machine: the use of men and women on the payroll for extensive partisan activity, and the utilization of city facilities and services to sustain the clout of the local partisan apparatus. Although the resultant exposé was widely disseminated through a 1-hour national network television documentary, prominent TV news play, and front page stories in both local Chicago newspapers, there was no evidence of change in public opinion, nor was there a policy response. The TV footage had been dramatic, with filmed records of illegitimate deals with several important people "caught in the act"—but there was virtually no public or policy response. Schematically, this outcome can be described as follows:

Investigation → Publication ≠ Opinion → Initiatives → Consequences

3. Inconsequential Opinion

Public opinion may in some sense "count," but as the gun-control issue has clearly shown, it is not—by itself—a sufficient basis for policy change. Almost nightly, news audiences are exposed to gruesome results of death by fire-arms and details of how "Saturday night specials" easily end up in the hands of criminals and incompetents. Similarly, for many years, public opinion polls have shown that a large majority of Americans favor tougher gun laws (Gallup, 1981, p. 4); but politicians have been *extremely* slow in responding to that fact. This well-known example makes it unsurprising to discover that, in various situations, media exposure can have an impact upon public opinion, but not lead to "corrective" policy formulations.

Returning again to Chicago for recent examples, we offer the case of "The Mirage"—a news investigation managed through the combined efforts of the Chicago *Sun-Times,* CBS-TV's "Sixty Minutes," and the aforementioned Better Government Association (BGA) (Smith & Zekman, 1979). As part of this investigation, the newspaper and the BGA purchased and operated a Chicago tavern ("the Mirage") which was rigged with hidden cameras and bartender-complicitors. The staff of the Mirage then simply waited for the Chicago graft system to come to them. It did; and the results of the careful documentation resulted in a TV broadcast and a month-long series in the local press. The Mirage story was one of the sensational journalistic coups of the decade; it became the staple topic of talk shows, local gossip columns, and cocktail and beer bar banter throughout the metropolitan area. The *Sun-Times* was nominated for a Pulitzer Prize for the series.[3] A scientific public opinion poll taken by the *Sun-Times* in the wake of the scandal showed that the general public overwhelmingly believed and was outraged by what they had learned from the stories. Yet, except for convictions of a few individuals for their wrongdoing, there was no action taken by city officials which would bring about systematic change to deal with the pattern of graft—not even substantial alteration in the organization of the

---

[3] The *Sun-Times* was not awarded the much sought-after Pulitzer after much debate among the contest judges. (See Smith & Zekman, 1979) Their ruling was that the Mirage effort, while legal, enterprising, and for good purpose, involved entrapment.

public agencies involved. Schematically this type of story career can be described as:

Investigation → Publication → Opinion ⇸ Initiatives → Consequences

4. Symbolic Policies

In some instances of truncated muckraking, policy changes are apparently made, at least "on paper," but nothing is really done to affect the original problem. The public is assuaged that "something is being done" when in fact only symbolic gestures are the result.

Edelman's books (1964, 1971, 1977) are replete with illustrations of this sort of "politics of quiescence." Molotch (1970) has documented how, in the aftermath of the 1969 Santa Barbara oil spill, media coverage (local and national) intensely aroused publics, leading to extensive policy discussions (bills, hearings, etc.) but to no substantial changes in federal off-shore policies (see also Cook *et al.*, 1982).

Still another recent example is provided by a team of Northwestern University researchers conducting studies of the effects of media investigative reports on citizen attitudes and public policymaking. Specifically, they found that the television airing of one such story in May 1981, produced a statistically significant attitude change in a random sample of respondents exposed to the program (Cook et al., 1982). Nevertheless, although the U.S. Senate Permanent Subcommittee on Investigations held extensive and widely publicized hearings within a week of the published allegations, legislative or regulatory changes have yet to be formally introduced. (It is now several years after the airing of the investigative report.) In short, policy talk is not the same thing as policy *action* (see also: Protess, Leff, Brooks, & Gordon, in press). Schematically, this truncation may be represented as follows:

Investigation → Publication → Opinion → Initiatives ⇸ Consequences

The Latent Life of Killed Stories

In the examples above we have emphasized the negative. Our attention has been focused on the ways in which truncation results in a "failure" of the muckraking process; that is, on ways the chain may be interrupted. But we do not mean to imply that even these stories were necessarily without effects. Even when an investigation fails to result in publication, the investigators, at least, still know about findings. Such information may influence future choices for stories or inform story angles. Unpublished investigatory findings may live elsewhere in the system, perhaps in the gossip mills of journalists, politicians, or academics. It is even conceivable that a nonstory could have a bigger impact than publication of the original story. For example, in the Bay of Pigs aftermath, newspaper editors may now be more reluctant to kill stories in the name of "national interest."

LEAPING IMPACTS

The capacities for stories to subtly endure, points to the possibility of media-policy relationships characterized by what we call *leaping impacts*. In such instances, one or another "step" in the process is skipped, but the processual impacts are otherwise retained as the other components persist in performing as the model would imply. We do not examine all the logical and empirical possibilities of leaping impacts, but illustrate the idea with relevant examples.

1. Solutions Without Policies

With the aid of media attention, policy problems are sometimes solved without official action. Investigation, exposure, and an outraged public opinion can yield a direct problem solution—with only the passive participation of government or other institutions.

Such an outcome is illustrated by the sensational "Arson and Profit" national television exposé by ABC's "20/20" news magazine show and the BGA. In this case, a 7-month media investigation resulted in stories illustrating how the substantial burn-out of Chicago's Uptown neighborhood appeared to be due not to careless tenants, squatters, or vandals, but rather to a systematic effort by a real estate combine to purchase deteriorating structures, insure them at high rates, and burn them down for large scale profits. These exposés were sufficiently significant that they added the term "arson-for-profit" to the American social problems vocabulary; they also resulted in widespread symbolic assurances from a large number of government officials that "solutions" were in the offing. Nevertheless, despite the fact that the investigations tended to incriminate corrupt or incompetent public officials (e.g., police department inspectors who persistently labeled the fires accidental, and state insurance functionaries who allowed building owners to "over-insure" under public insurance programs), there were no criminal indictments and only minor reforms.[4]

Despite official inaction, however, the rate of fires in the city and particularly in Chicago's Uptown area declined precipitously after the exposé. After a decade of continual increase, insurance payments for "arson-for-profit" dropped by more than 20% in the year after the story aired—the most significant decline of any large city in the U.S. (Metropolitan Chicago Loss Bureau, "Monthly Reports," 1979-1980). Seldom does even active government participation yield more substantial results! Schematically, the "leap" in this case can be represented as:

Investigation → Publication → Opinion —⌒Initiatives⌒→ Consequences

---

[4] Because legal action taken against the owners did not result in indictments, the investigation itself was attacked in a CBS documentary on investigative journalism. It, and the counter-attack by ABC, have led to much self-examination by investigative journalists.

2. Policy Initiatives Without Opinions

In this variant, the leap is over the opinion process. Whether or not there is a change in public opinion becomes irrelevant to the policy outcome. Investigation leads to publication, but the policy change occurs because of a direct impact upon some significant (but small) constituency—either in government or some other important circle. The media function, in effect, as communication conduits between policy makers, sometimes connecting one important policy maker to another through the vehicle of the investigatory report. In such cases, without journalistic intention or public knowledge, the media report itself acts as a catalyst for policy change.

One variant of this phenomenon is illustrated by events following the *New York Times'* publication of the Pentagon Papers in 1971. While the media and the public focused attention on disclosures of governmental deception in the historical conduct of the Vietnam war, the Nixon Administration reacted by holding intense internal discussions about plugging national security "leaks" (Salisbury, 1980). The major policy result of those discussions was the creation of the covert White House "Plumber's Unit," which ultimately burglarized the Democratic National Committee headquarters in the Watergate (leading to even more famous investigative revelations the following year). The *Times'* stories clearly triggered policy consequences that were unintended by the journalists and unrelated to the content of the investigative reports or formulated public opinion.

Schematically:

Investigation → Publication —⌒(Opinion)⌒→ Policy → Consequences

3. Policy Initiatives Without Publication

Sometimes the mere threat of exposure is enough to cause a reformulation of public policy. In these instances, policy changes are sometimes initiated to avoid the pain of "bad publicity" and public controversy. The journalist can act as a type of "blackmailer" (however benign), who has the power to publish such that others may perish. Early twentieth century muckrakers sometimes were able to achieve policy results with only the *potential* for publication (Steffens, 1931). The Watergate journalist-investigators seem to have provided their subjects with numerous opportunities for cleaning "their own house" as a condition for "laying-off;" perhaps it was the Nixon Administration's intransigence that mobilized journalistic efforts to make the investigations a battle to the finish (see below).

On occasion, it is the direct collaboration of news personnel with government officials that can produce intended policy consequences without publication. In 1969, *Alton (Illinois) Telegraph* reporters sent a memo to the U.S. Department of Justice, indicating that their sources had linked a local building contractor to organized crime figures (see Kupferberg, 1981, p. 36). The *Telegraph* never printed a story about the matter, but subsequent action by federal law enforcement authorities and bank regulators led to the collapse of the contractor's businesses.

Schematically:

Investigation—Publication—Opinion—Initiatives→Consequences

4. Opinion Without Exposure

As we have already argued, killed stories can have latent lives. From the memoirs of those living under totalitarian regimes, for example, it seems that journalists' investigations may become a part of "common knowledge" even if they fail to result in published stories. Harrison Salisbury indicates that Soviet citizens were sufficiently adaptive to their country's media system to note that a first-time depiction of Stalin with gray hair was "the first step to prepare us for a change" (Salisbury, 1965, pp. 25-26, as cited in Davison, Boyland & Yu, 1982). Part of this creative work is probably informed by citizens' own direct or indirect contact with practicing journalists who put reports into the gossip mill, which may be as efficacious, in their way, as the accounts which are officially released in formal media. Citizens may be led toward important decisions: a determination to migrate as an individualistic response or, more interesting from our standpoint, a commitment to political movements with alternative strategies (including revolution). Schematically:

Investigation—Publication—Opinion→Initiatives→Consequences

COALITION JOURNALISM

Perhaps we have been misleading in emphasizing the role of journalists as the primary catalysts in the media-policy process. At one time in history, this may have been a reasonably accurate view; it is certainly not at present. The memoirs of journalists and political notables are replete with instances in which *non*journalists took an active role in shaping the journalistic agenda, altering the nature of public issues, and influencing the angle or coverage of reportorial outcomes. Sometimes these are seen as cases in which reporters are "duped;" this seems to be the perspective of Boorstin (1961), who calls attention to media coverage of "pseudo-events" which, in apparent contrast to real ones, are created just for the coverage they might bring. Boorstin's distinction usefully draws attention to the creative work which people do to affect published outcomes, but—in our view—obscures the fact that such "outside" manipulations are the rule and not the exception (see also Lester, 1980). Working as public relations professionals, as savvy politicians, or just as dutiful bureaucrats, the routines of many people are there to structure exposure possibilities.

Ad Hoc Coalition

Less dramatic than Boorstin's illustrations of deliberate event "staging," but essentially corresponding to the same kind of event logic, are the ubiquitous instances in which policy actors find their interests best served by joining in a journalistic investigation. The policy actors' goal is to foster an image of responsiveness, often to head off potentially damaging implications of inefficiency, corruption, or incompetence in agencies for which one has some responsibility. The effort is to "get in front" of the story and start making news oneself. Politicians try to co-opt the scandal to sustain rather than undermine their own public position.

An example of such ad hoc media-policymaker coalition was the 1979 exposé of unsafe, unsanitary, and dangerous conditions in Chicago's local ambulance services. Accounts published in both city dailies were to reveal such abuses as reckless driving habits, untrained "medics," ill-maintained equipment, and overloaded vehicles. The investigation was planned by the *Chicago Tribune* to begin running on a Sunday, but, having heard about it earlier, the *Sun-Times* began a pre-emptive series on Saturday. Relevant city and state officials did not wait for either series to appear; they "initiated" a crackdown on Friday after learning of the forthcoming publications. Significantly, their policy actions were described by each paper as "responses" to *its* series! The Illinois Secretary of State had actually begun a study of the problems two months prior to publication, but his position paper was prepared "during the weekend" in an obvious attempt to dovetail with media schedules. The investigative findings and his "reaction" to them were *both* played on page one of the first day's story.

In a striking illustration of the *quid pro quo* between journalists and politicians, the media attributed blame for the scandal to the greed of private ambulance companies, rather than to governmental regulatory inaction; government officials reinforced this view with their quoted statements, which included the promise of a new bill "in 2 weeks." The Illinois Secretary of State was quoted as crediting the press for performing a "valuable public service by identifying the need for the new law," although his own office's efforts had begun 2 months previously.

Each of the participants seemed to be acting in a way which would "prove" the validity of the traditional muckraking model. Each of the newspapers tried to make it appear as if it *alone* initiated and sustained the investigation, without stimulus from either any policy maker or from any other publication. Further, each presented the story of policy changes as a response to its own *publication,* as if each event had occurred in the temporal order that the muckraking model would specify. Even though it made for some odd exposition, the *Chicago Sun Times* tried to imply, in its subsequent coverage, that the city's initial response, which was reported by the paper to have begun the day *before* the exposé was published, had been a *response* to it.[5] Perhaps such obfuscations of the actual timing were viewed as normative and practical necessities. Journalistic tradition demands independence from government officialdom, and market competition requires self-promotional descriptions of events. Similarly, the policy participants' collusion in this bit of symbiotic deception is consistent with two traditional concerns of elected officials: "responsiveness" to the disclosure of policy problems, and sensitivity to the prerogatives of the press.

Mobilized Coalitions

The sort of logrolling journalism we have been describing seems to be increasing in frequency, and also is tending to become a formalized way of making news and public policy. Two factors help explain this trend. First, with the decline of the urban political machines, political party organizations have decreasingly played a linkage role between public officials and their constituents (Broder, 1972; Crotty, 1980). In the resulting vacuum, the mass media may have come to provide the most effective means for obtaining direct constituent contact (Patterson, 1980). Public officials have thereby *increasingly* found it to be in their electoral self-interest to respond favorably to the demands of the "new muckrakers" in order to project strong leadership qualities to voters, i.e., appearing to "stay on top" of the problems of their constituents. Being a "good (mass media) communicator" becomes, especially under challenging circumstances, a critical resource for politicians everywhere.

From the standpoint of the media, the renewed market for public affairs and news programming has led to increasing media competition for appropriate materials. "Official reaction" is widely perceived as a necessary ingredient to sell such stories—to producers, to sponsors and to audiences. Journalists seeking story credibility and personal recognition have thus found it helpful to obtain such official participation. Among other things, such reactions "dignify" a story's allegations and help to justify follow-up stories, including follow-ups from competing media. Quite paradoxically,

---

[5] These are the verbatim first three paragraphs in the *Sun-Times* follow-up story (emphasis is ours):

City officials disclosed *Saturday* that they have begun making surprise inspections in a crackdown on private ambulances and medicars.

The action was announced after disclosures in *Saturday's* Sun-Times of complaints about unsanitary conditions, unsafe vehicles, careless drivers, and life-endangering service delays.

Board of Health Inspectors hit the street *Friday* night and *Saturday* and made surprise ambulance inspections at...(*Sun-Times,* Mar. 15, 1981, p. 3).

the journalist is led to cultivate the active participation of officials whose failures may quite plausibly be the focus of the investigatory work. It becomes the journalist's "responsibility" to handle the piece in such a way that the role of the cooperative policy actor (who may well be needed on another such occasion) is treated sympathetically.

The growth of television investigative reporting has been particularly important in sustaining this pattern of journalism. Because of the highly transitory (weekly) nature of the TV magazine shows, journalists are forced to build official reaction *into* their stories, and government officials are forced to "respond" in the *context* of the media piece if they are to do so at all. Perhaps TV journalism, lacking the constitutional protections of the print media, finds a degree of security in having such official response as part of a story. Or perhaps it is the very high, "up-front" financial commitments which lead to such a requirement; the presence on tape of important officials implies there will be at least *something* appropriate to show a mass audience. Whatever the reasons, TV news and investigative journalism seems to be playing a leading role in intensifying this symbiotic set of relationships between reporters and policy actors, and in forging this kind of media role in the policy process.

Participation of policy actors in building stories can become a fully conscious effort in which both types of actors form concrete coalition.[6] One clear case of this type of media-policy sector relationship is represented by the workings of Chicago's Better Government Association (BGA). This civic organization carries on investigatory work on various public problems which are brought to its attention by staff, its board of directors, policy actors or concerned citizens. A privately funded organization (founded in 1924) BGA has had a staff as large as 25 (attorneys, researchers, journalists, clerical workers, etc.), a large suite of offices in Chicago, a branch in Washington, D.C., and a substantial track record of consequential "watchdog" activities on both local and national issues. The distinguishing feature of this organization is not, for our purposes, either its reformist goals or its substantial resources, but rather the particular way it puts these resources to work.

Because BGA officials believe the media are critical to the policy process, the organization seeks to develop—at some point early in an investigation—both a "media partner" and —usually at a somewhat later point—a "policy partner." It seeks to join some media organization in a given project, and to

---

[6] Most major journalistic awards committees (including the Pulitzer, DuPont, and Peabody) explicitly evaluate entries in "public service" and "investigative" categories based on the "reforms" they generate.

establish some commonly agreed upon strategy for investigation, publication, and policy response.[7] Media partners often help to support the budgets of agreed upon investigations; these costs can often reach $100,000 for a single exposé; therefore, participation of the major media with their larger budgets has been especially important to the BGA's work. Hence consideration is given, from the beginning, to how the story can be sold to, and effectively played by, the media. The investigation takes its shape, in part, through these perceptions of media needs, just as the media may make their own compromises on matters of story treatment, angle, and timing, to facilitate the BGA's substantive policy goals. Thus, the civic organization and media partner anticipate and negotiate the conditions of one another's work, sometimes over periods of many months for a single piece.

A "policy partner" is usually an administrator or politican who (a) can be apprised of the nature of the developing investigation, (b) can be used as a consultant for informing the investigatory work, and (c) can be relied upon to provide headline-worthy policy initiatives as "response" to the resulting exposés. In return, policy partners gain "insider" access to media coverage in a very advantageous way; they can be "in front" of a breaking story and establish high visibility in a favorable media context. Even though working journalists experience some aspects of this phenomenon quite routinely, the presence of a "policy partner" whose very availability influences the choice of story and gives shape to its treatment is not something envisioned in traditional versions of muckraking. Similarly, the civic organization as an initiating enterprise is not ordinarily given much stress in the scholarly literature on media. Yet such organizations, like other agencies of news promotion (private corporations, chambers of commerce, political parties, social movement organizations, etc.) are critical to the process of inspiring journalists to conduct investigations and to feeding them the information they need to complete such investigations. Their activities, might, as in the BGA case, be sufficiently sophisticated and ambitious to mobilize media and/or policy partners. Common Cause has also been described as working in this fashion (Paletz & Entman, 1981, pp. 124-146), and other organizations such as the various Ralph Nader groups and the Hayden-Fonda Committee for Economic Democracy have developed similar patterns of relating to media personnel.

For other groups and individuals, the program may be more modest; sometimes the role of such actors is only to provide the leaks which their

---

[7] Very rarely, an investigation results in a BGA "white paper" rather than a story published with a media partner. In that event, however, the issue may reach the press as a result of the BGA Director holding a press conference to divulge the content of the white paper.

own proximity to events and powerful people make possible. These "scandals" can be quick and dirty (e.g., Reagan's failure to pay state income tax while governor of California), or lead to long and involved exposés (e.g., Daniel Ellsberg's leak of the Pentagon papers to the *New York Times*). All alert us to the fact that many important investigations do not arise out of media themselves but are, at least in part, the work of some other strategically located actors (Molotch & Lester, 1974).

THE BIG CASE: WATERGATE AS UN-MUCKRAKING

No story of the last decades has been more often cited as an instance of successful muckraking, of effective investigatory journalism, than "the Watergate Story." But a close look at the details of the case indicates that the actual dynamic of the media–policy relationship was different from what the classic muckraking model would have predicted. This giant of a story can be used to illustrate almost all the types of media–policy relationships we have outlined, although no more than certain highlights can be examined within the confines of this paper.[8]

The initial Watergate event, the "break-in," came into print (in *The Washington Post*) as a result of routine policy beat coverage by two novice reporters. In the process of covering the resultant criminal trial (6/18/72), one of these reporters (Woodward) heard, through questioning by the presiding judge, that the organizer of the break-in was a former CIA agent, James McCord. The Justice Department, in response to this information, announced (later the same day) that it would initiate a federal grand jury investigation—a fact which was then the basis of an AP wire story that further incorporated the information that McCord was also an official of the Committee to Reelect the President (CREEP). The direct tie to President Nixon thus become evident without any Woodward-Bernstein investigations (although with some digging by one AP reporter).

Already in the history of the story there is evidence of an evolving mutuality of causal factors: ordinary beat coverage revealed the first bits of big news to the reporter, made possible by the police department's own internal record keeping and external record provisions (see Fishman, 1980). In a similar routine way, the mechanics of the trial revealed still other information to the reporter on duty. But, because of the cumulating exposure (we

---

[8] Our anlaysis of the Watergate affair rests primarily (but not exclusively) on the description provided by Bernstein and Woodward (1974), the two reporters most responsible for developing the story. For a more recent, comprehensive accounting of Watergate news coverage, see Lang and Lang (1983).

presume), the Justice Department was induced to make its move, which then generated still more stories and the first evidence of independent journalistic investigation (the CREEP connection in the AP report).

The battle to control this dynamic of policy-bureaucracy-media interaction was clearly under way. The Nixon Administration attempted to deprive the dynamic of vitality by refusing to play its part—by refusing to dignify the story with "official reaction." In response to a press query, the President's Press Secretary (Ronald Ziegler) called the whole affair a "third rate burglary attempt not worthy of further comment" (Bernstein & Woodward, 1974, p. 26)." He was stating, in effect, that the story should follow the career of other stories routinely gathered through the mundane police-beat duty, and that he would not provide the government "reaction" that would be necessary to sustain a story beyond that point. The strategy seemed to work, for the moment; Woodward went on vacation and Bernstein was "shipped back to Virginia politics." The story had stalled, "maybe even died" (Bernstein & Woodward, 1974, p. 35).

This 1-month lull in investigating activity ended with the *Post* story on the CREEP slush funds. Several more such stories followed, but prominent newsplay and public controversy about these stories was pre-empted by the breaking news (developed by GOP activists) regarding the Democratic Vice Presidential candidate's past history of mental therapies (see Altheide, 1976). Despite the relatively weak newsplay given to the slush fund stories, they prompted a GAO audit of CREEP financing. Several weeks later (8/22/72) the GAO's preliminary findings (the existence of an illegal cache of $500,000 which became known as the "plumber's" fund) made front page news in the *Post* and generated prominent coverage throughout the country.

In retrospect, we observe a sequence of events in which the outcome of a government action—the important GAO investigation—seems out of proportion, in its significance, to the rather subdued coverage and controversy which prompted it. Even without the benefit of a widespread coverage or major shifts in agendas or opinions, there is a "leaping" impact upon the policy sector—a change which much *later* was to have substantial media and opinion consequence.

For the next 2 months, the *Post* kept at its investigations and continued publishing stories about the secret funds, including Senator George McGovern's sharp reactions to them. However, other media outlets failed to pick up this new round of material or to publish it with very much prominence. This illustrates another departure from the assumptions of a simple muckraking model: publication in one place must be followed by confirmatory publication in other places; reaction from one policy actor may not be consequential enough if that actor is marginal in the "hierarchy of credibility" (Becker, 1967). Without such a pattern of imitative coverage and comment, a newspaper is out on a dangerous limb and a press report may be without apparent consequences.[9] We are left with Uneventful Exposure.[10]

The tide turned somewhat when the *Post* published (Oct. 9–10, 1972) evidence of a link between former Attorney General Mitchell, the secret fund, and a nationwide campaign of espionage and political sabotage directed by the White House and CREEP. This time around, "stonewalling" (the term used for a strategic unwillingness to dignify a story with official reaction) was more difficult. The heat from the *Post* stories, and the inability of the Administration to deal with them, apparently provided the necessary encouragement for the first legislative probe of Watergate. Republicans rejoined by vociferously attacking the *Post* for its "political motives."

There is ample evidence that the *Post* was indeed affected by these attacks —both in terms of its institutional health and in the content of its coverage over the next several months. The paper's Managing Editor, Benjamin Bradlee, is quoted by Bernstein and Woodward (1974, p. 152) is saying that "our cocks are on the chopping block now" (genitalia figure frequently in Watergate discourse). Although additional investigatory work was authorized, the stories were to slack off because, in Bernstein's and Woodward's account (1974, p. 224), "the election was too near" and it was regarded better to wait until a time when "the White House would be forced to abandon the line that the *Post* was working for the election of McGovern."[11] (The *Post* was to be one of the few U.S. papers editorially to support McGovern.) The displacement of this phase of the Watergate story (displaced toward a later, less strategic date and replaced with routine election coverage material), may indeed have changed the course of the election and of history. Because the timing of a story is a critical feature of its reality, a postponement does not mean that the same story happens, but only later. It means a *different* story happens later.

When the election was over, the *Post* took up the story once again. Part of the *Post*'s motivation for pursuing Nixon "to the end" may have come from challenges to the licenses of the *Post*'s broadcasting properties. Such

---

[9] Perhaps this is what Attorney General Mitchell had in mind when he warned Woodward that his boss, *Post* publisher Katharine Graham, was risking getting "her tits caught in the ringer." (Quoted from a Woodward speech at University of California, Santa Barbara, Oct. 14, 1976).

[10] To see this point demonstrated in regard to a very different kind of case, see Morentz's excellent study of the nonlinear dynamic of the African Sahel drought story (Morentz, 1980).

[11] In terms of attitude effects, Watergate had no significant impact on the 1972 election. After five months of stories, Nixon won by the highest electoral margin in American history thus far. Some studies (Weaver, McCombs, & Spellman, 1975) of voting behavior did find Watergate opinion effects, but only among very specialized population groups.

threats involved the potential for multi-million dollar losses, providing the *Post*-Nixon conflict with some of the qualities of a contest for survival. Again, the threats display the policy sector's influence on media, even though the effort turns out to have backfired in terms of intended effects.

The most important breakthrough among all of the Watergate events came as a delayed, but spectacular, policy-sector response. Senator Sam Ervin (Democrat, North Carolina) convened the now famous Watergate Hearings, after first sending for Woodward to "pick his brain" on sources and leads (Bernstein & Woodward, 1974, pp. 275-277). Through his access to Ervin, journalist Woodward could have direct impact on the policy sector by providing the Senate Committee with materials (hunches, rumors, unsubstantiated accounts, unverified documents) which were useful for the Committee but insufficiently documented for meeting the high publication standard which the *Post* had established for Watergate stories. Moving far beyond "Deep Throat"[12] as a policy partner, the press had moved toward coalition with some of the most powerful officials and diligent investigators in the land.

Once the hearings were in progress, all Watergate-related occurrences became part of the routine beat structure of the world news system. This was especially facilitated by the controlling Committee Democrats who set agendas and witness lists to maximize the opportunities for making the hearings into a series of media events. As soon as a wire story reported that Watergate burglar McCord had sent Judge John Sirica a letter which revealed that high level pressure had been placed upon him to plead guilty and to commit perjury, the Counsel to the Committee Majority (Sam Dash) held a news conference to announce that McCord would appear before the Committee and name names. The matter was then headlined everywhere. Bernstein and Woodward (1974, p. 306) ruefully state: "the days when the *Post* had dominated the Watergate story was over." By then, the government bureaucracies (via the hearings and the courts) were doing most of the investigating, and some of the most sensational revelations (e.g., the existence of tape-recorded White House conversations and their contents) came about through routine institutional functioning. Each successive breakthrough occurred on live television before millions of viewers. The ultimate fusion of policy and media roles was approached: daily hearings constituted the successive big news stories, while each day's media coverage (and feeding of new angles to Committee interrogators) shaped and gave texture to the next day's hearings.[13]

---

[12] "Deep Throat" is the term used by Bernstein and Woodward to designate their key informant.

[13] Although their book reached us too late to enrich the Watergate analysis we provide, certain of the arguments of Lang and Lang (1983) parallel our own.

WATERGATE AND THE MEDIA POLICY CONNECTION

One of the most striking impressions we are left with after our examination of the Watergate and other instances of the press-policy connection is the fragility of media projects, given the ongoing dependence of journalists on symbiotic actions from prominent actors in other realms. When investigations are first conceived, they compete with other stories (especially those vigorously promoted by such "outside" sectors); at any point along the way, they may be interrupted, and hence transformed. Even if brought to fruition through competent publication, there may be no impact, no change.

But it is also clear that the policy actors' dependence on media induces them toward actions which facilitate the development and sustenance of stories—including stories which investigate wrong-doing in high places. This can mean that, while one group of policy actors are attempting to kill a story through nonparticipation, another group—perhaps emboldened by previous media exposures which have weakened their policy adversaries—take official actions aimed at achieving the opposite consequence. Hence, even the results of thwarted, muted, or displaced investigations can eventually have some impact, as the conditions for the release of their results come to be seen as appropriate, given the goals, however constrained (Ewen, 1976; Mueller, 1973; Schiller, 1971), of policy actors.

This is not to argue, of course, that the Watergate history shows that such consequences must inevitably flow, that investigations always bear fruit. Indeed, the sustenance of the Nixon presidency past its first term, and the eventual Nixon resignation-in-disgrace, was a very different historical outcome than, say, a McGovern electoral victory. That Nixon "got it" in the end does not mean that it doesn't matter when the end came, or how it came. The point is that there were many different potential Watergate stories, including no story at all; the particular one which unfolded was determined by the very special mix of intersecting conditions present during its life course.

We therefore disagree with those who would assign "credit" for the Nixon exposures to the media, just as we would disagree with those who would assign it to the Congress. Nor should the credit go, in some acontextual, additive sense, to both of these sectors. Instead, the Watergate "correction" was the result of the ways in which news of the Nixon scandals fit the goals and strategic needs of important media and policy actors. All of these actors, each with some degree of "relative autonomy" (Dreier, 1982), are best seen not as a series of discrete forces which can be allotted partial variance in some static modeling of influence. Instead, they are a part of an evolving "ecology of games" (Long, 1958), part of a "dance" (Gitlin, 1980; Molotch, 1979) in which actors have, by virtue of their differential skills and status positions, varying access to participate. Because they so continuously anticipate each other's moves, their activities are, *as a matter of course,* mutually constituted.

This more ecological view of the media–policy process loses the advantage of neat research designs characteristic of the effects studies, and substitutes the less exact methods of ethnography and history. We give up testing the proposition that, *as a general rule,* media reports cause or do not cause opinion or policy consequences. Nor do we try to explain the lack of a given effect in terms of specific flaws in a story, or errors in a certain public opinion, or incapacity in a given official. We don't look for the cause of a story's failure *within* the story, the opinion, or the politician. The critical issue is not so much the technical and substantive nature of a given message (although such things do matter), but how that message relates or fails to relate to the practical purposes—at that time point—of actors in a number of other significant realms. Media "effects" on policy (as on anything else) come from the capacity of journalists to play a role (delimited, but omnipresent) in this larger ecology of individual and institutional practices.

REFERENCES

Altheide, D.L. (1976). *Creating Reality.* Beverly Hills, CA: Sage.
Becker, H. (1967). "Whose Side Are We On?" *Social Problems 14,* 239-247.
Bernstein, C., and Woodward, R. (1974). *All the President's Men.* New York: Warner Books.
Boorstin, D.J. (1961). *The Image: A Guide to Pseudo-Events in America.* New York: Harper & Row.
Broder, D.S. (1972). *The Party's Over: The Failure of Politics in America.* New York: Harper & Row.
Catledge, T. (1971). *My Life and the Times.* New York: Harper & Row.
Comstock, G.A., Chaffee, S.H., Katzman, N.I., McCombs, M.E., and Roberts, D.F. (1978). *Television and Human Behavior.* New York: Columbia University Press.
Cook, F.L., Tyler, T.R., Goetz, S.G., Protess, D., Gordon, M., Leff, D.R., and Molotch, H.L. (1982). "Media and Agenda-Setting: Effects on the Public, Interest Group Leaders, Policymakers, and Policy." *Public Opinion Quarterly 47,* 16-35.
Crotty, W.J. (Ed.). (1980). *The Party Symbol.* San Francisco, CA: W.H. Freeman.
Davison, W.P., Boyland, J., and Yu, F.T.C. (1982). *Mass Media: Systems and Effects* (2nd ed.), New York: Holt, Rinehart and Winston.
Defleur, M., and Ball-Rokeach, S. (1975). *Theories of Mass Communication.* New York: Mckay.
Dreier, P. (1982). "The Position of the Press in the U.S. Power Structure." *Social Problems 29,* 298-310.
Edelman, M. (1964). *The Symbolic Uses of Politics.* Urbana, IL: University of Illinois Press.
Edelman, M. (1971). *Politics as Symbolic Action: Mass Arousal and Quiescence.* Chicago, IL: Markham.
Edelman, M. (1977). *Political Language: Words that Succeed and Policies that Fail.* New York: Academic Press.
Ewen, S. (1976). *Captains of Consciousness.* New York: McGraw-Hill.
Fishman, M. (1978). "Crime Waves as Ideology." *Social Problems 25,* 531-543.
Fishman, M. (1980). *Manufacturing the News.* Austin, TX: University of Texas Press.
Friendly, F.W. (1981). "Media Power: Why the Press Must Begin Reporting on Itself with the Same Aggressive Vigor It Applies to the Coverage of Congress." *Gentlemen's Quarterly 51* (No. 11), 216-217.

Gallup, G.H. (1981). *The Gallup Poll: Public Opinion 1972-1980.* Wilmington, DE: SR Scholarly Resources.
Gans, H.J. (1977). "The Famine in American Mass-Communications Research: Comments on Hirsch, Tuchman, and Gecas." *American Journal of Sociology 77,* 697-705.
Gans, H.J. (1979). *Deciding What's News.* New York: Random House.
Gerbner, G., and Gross, L. (1976). "Living with Television: The Violence Profile." *Journal of Communication 26* (No. 2), 173-199.
Gitlin, T. (1980). *The Whole World is Watching: Media in the Making and Unmaking of the New Left.* Berkeley, CA: University of California Press.
Gordon, A.C., Heinz, J.P., Gordon, M.T., and Divorski, S.W. (1973). "Public Information and Public Access: A Sociological Interpretation." *Northwestern University Law Review 68,* 280-308.
Gordon, M.T., and Heath, L. (1981). "The News Business, Crime and Fear." *In* D.A. Lewis (Ed.), *Reactions to Crime.* Beverly Hills, CA: Sage.
Graber, D.A. (1980). *Mass Media and American Politics.* Washington, DC: Congressional Quarterly Press.
Greenfield, J. (1982). *The Real Campaign: The Media and the Battle for the White House.* New York: Summit Press.
Hovland, C.I., Janis, I.L., and Kelley, H.H. (1953). *Communication and Persuasion.* New Haven, CT: Yale University Press.
Johnstone, J.W.C., Slawski, E.J., and Bowman, W.W. (1970). *The News People: A Sociological Portrait of American Journalists and Their Work.* Urbana, IL: University of Illinois Press.
Katz, E., and Lazarsfeld, P.F. (1955). *Personal Influence.* New York: Free Press.
Klapper, J.T. (1960). *The Effects of Mass Communication.* New York: Free Press.
Kraus, S., and Davis, D. (1976). *The Effects of Mass Communication on Political Behavior.* University Park, PA: Pennsylvania State University Press.
Kupferberg, S. (1981). "Libel Fever." *Columbia Journalism Review 20* (No. 3), 36-40.
Lang, G.E., and Lang, K. (1983). *The Battle for Public Opinion.* New York: Columbia University Press.
Lester, M. (1980). "Generating Newsworthiness." *American Sociological Review 45,* 984-994.
Long, N.E. (1958). "The Local Community as an Ecology of Games." *American Journal of Sociology 64,* 251-261.
McConnell, G. (1966). *Private Power and American Democracy.* New York: Knopf.
Michelson, S. (1972). *The Electric Mirror.* New York: Dodd, Mead.
Molotch, H.L. (1970). "Oil in Santa Barbara and Power in America." *Sociological Inquiry 40,* 131-144.
Molotch, H.L. (1979). "Media and Movements." *In* M. Zald and J.D. McCarthy (Eds.), *The Dynamics of Social Movement* (pp. 71-93). Cambridge, MA: Winthrop.
Molotch, H.L., and Lester, M. (1974). "News as Purposive Behavior: On the Strategic Use of Routine Events, Accedents and Scandals." *American Sociological Review 39,* 101-113.
Morentz, J.W. (1980). "Communication in the Sahel Drought: Comparing the Mass Media with Other Channels of International Communication." In *Disasters and the Mass Media, Proceedings of the Committee on Disasters and the Mass Media Workshop* (Feb. 1979) (pp. 155-183). Washington, DC: National Academy of Sciences.
Mueller, C. (1973). *The Politics of Communications.* New York: Oxford University Press.
Paletz, D.L., and Entman, R.M. (1981). *Media Power Politics.* New York: Free Press.
Patterson, T.E. (1980). *The Mass Media Election: How Americans Choose Their President.* New York: Praeger.
Protess, D.L., Leff, D.R., Brooks, S.C., and Gordon, M.T. (in press). "Uncovering Rape: The Watchdog Press and the Limits of Agenda Setting." *Public Opinion Quarterly.*
Regier, C.C. (1930). *The Era of the Muckrakers.* Chapel Hill, NC: University of North Carolina Press.

Rivers, W.L., and Schramm, W. (1980). *Responsibility in Mass Communication.* New York: Harper & Row.
Salisbury, H.E. (1965). *Russia.* New York: Atheneum.
Salisbury, H.E. (1980). *Without Fear or Favor.* New York: Ballantine.
Schiller, H.I. (1971). *Mass Communications and American Empire.* Boston, MA: Beacon Press.
Sills, D.L. (1957). *The Volunteers: Means and Ends in a National Organization.* Glencoe, IL: Free Press.
Smith, Z.N., and Zekman, P. (1979). *The Mirage.* New York: Random House.
Steffens, L. (1931). *The Autobiography of Lincoln Steffens.* New York: Harcourt, Brace.
Tuchman, G. (1978). *Making News: A Study in the Construction of Reality.* New York: Macmillan.
Valentine, D. (1982). "Is TV Trivial?" *Nation 235,* 85–86.
Weaver, D.H., McCombs, M.E., and Spellman, C. (1975). "Watergate and the Media: A Case Study of Agenda-Setting." *American Politics Quarterly 3,* 458–472.
Wills, G. (1982). "Comments on the Media-Policy Connection," Remarks to the Media Cluster Roundtable, Center for Urban Affairs and Policy Studies, Northwestern University.

Chapter 3
The Publicity of State Subjects

GRAHAM KNIGHT
Sociology Department
McMaster University
Hamilton, Ontario
Canada L85 4144

BRUCE CURTIS
Department of History and Philosophy
Ontario Institute for Studies in Education
Toronto, Ontario
Canada, M59 1V6

Critical analysis of the news discourse has frequently pointed to its preoccupation with the state. News prioritizes the state and its agents, treating even minor state activities as inherently newsworthy, viewing agents of the state as "reliable" sources and as interesting speakers, and portraying the visible aspects of relations among states. A facile critique of news discourse would point to this fascination with the state as an instance of "news bias," and would suggest a redistribution of news coverage.

The preoccupation of news with the state is a necessary feature of news as a public discourse. News production is a form of social labor which operates in the "public realm," drawing its material from events and figures in this realm. Yet the public as such is a terrain constituted by the state, and continually ordered and organized by the administrative labor of the state. As a public discourse, the conditions of possibility of news are the conditions of possibility of the realm in which it operates, and hence, ultimately are the conditions of existence of the state itself. News appears then, as a reproductive discourse, a discourse which constantly presents and represents social reality in forms and categories generated by the state. News has a political content, not simply because it prioritizes some categories of public speakers and events over others, but rather by virtue of the fact that it is a *public* discourse.

On the one hand, this means that news as a discourse shares the general features of the public realm; it is massified, universally distributed, and shares certain conceptions of social totality. More important, as a form of social labor, news discourse tirelessly reproduces the conditions of existence of the sphere in which it operates. Since the public sphere is an internally contradictory political form, news labor is forced continually to re-work and to re-present social contradictions. The simple fact of this constant re-working and re-presentation gives to these contradictions a naturalness which mystifies them.

To elaborate this position, it is first necessary to present an analysis of the state and of the relations of subjects and objects formed by it. We will point to the contradictions inherent in the political organization of subjects and objects in bourgeois society, and we will conclude with an examination of some specific features of news discourse.

I

The development of the political state, the constitution of a public sphere, and the emergence of a distinction between state and civil society were questions which interested the young Marx. These processes have been reexamined in detail more recently by Geoffrey Kay and James Mott in *Political Order and the Law of Labor* (1982). We follow their analysis closely here.

The material life of bourgeois society is based upon the production and exchange of commodities, which in its intensified form is capitalist accumulation. Commodity exchange as a general form assumes a threefold social separation: of subjects from objects; of subjects from subjects; and of objects from objects. This implies historically, the breakdown of community and of directly communal forms of appropriation, the development of the division of labor, and the transformation of the products of labor into objects of exchange. The existence of objects in general as objects of property, and of subjects in general as potential owners of property, implies the existence of abstract and general rights to property. Actual exchanges in bourgeois society takes place in a context of universal rights of ownership applicable to any social object. This, as Kay and Mott point out, assumes the existence of a particular form of state:

> for it is only through the medium of a state that persons and things can be formally constituted as subjects and objects prior to their actual collisions (Kay & Mott, 1982, p. 5).

As many writers have pointed out (e.g. Bendix, 1964, p. 175), the general and undifferentiated right to property is the basis of citizenship in the political state. The constitution of this right by the state (which is at the same time the creation of the state itself) creates a condition of universal political subjectivity in which all subjects appear as formally equal citizens of the state. It is this general right, which creates a type of formal social universality, which forms the basis of the "public realm."

It must also be pointed out that right is force. My right to appropriate, possess, alienate, or consume an object exists (in principle if not in practice) as a forceful exclusion of the rights of others. A generalized right to property presupposes the existence of generalized force, the state. Citizenships in principle a forceful relation between the state and universal political subjects. In practice, this forceful relation exists as administration (cf. Weber, 1958, pp. 196-244). The state is a general force as the guarantor of abstract right, but also, insofar as it is separated from civil society, it is a special or particular force.

While the public realm is a social sphere created by general relations of property and populated by formally equal and undifferentiated citizens, it is also a sphere constantly riven by contradiction. While simple exchange is the basis of the state and universal political subjectivity, it generates a curious reversal which constantly threatens to burst its own structure. This reversal is the appearance of capital and labor power. In these relations, the subject of property becomes its object; the object of property becomes its own subject.

As Kay and Mott (1982) point out, commodities as capital become enmeshed in a process of accumulation wherein the self-expansion of value operates as a motor force. The means of production transformed into property threaten to burst the forms which first generated them. The subject of property—the capitalists—find their will subordinated to economic conditions quite beyond their control. The dictates of the market and the conditions of existence of capital as a totality shape and propel the capacity of the individual capitalist to possess. With the development of the process of accumulation, the self-expansion of value becomes the objective of social activity and the object of property—capital—increasingly operates as an independent and abstract social subject.

On the other hand and at the same moment, the will of some citizens is transformed into an object of property. As workers, the subjects of property alienate their own capacities and, in the practical consumption of these capacities in the productive process, their will is subordinated to that of capital. Here the reversal is complete: subjects become objects, and objects become subjects.

What is important for our purposes is the contradictory nature of bourgeois society and its political forms. We wish to stress that the antagonistic class division between capital and labor is produced and reproduced through universalistic political forms. It is through the formal equality of all citizens of the state, and the existence of general and undifferentiated rights to property, that substantive inequality and real propertylessness are reproduced. The formal universality and political equality of the public realm coexist uneasily alongside the increasing power of activated objects and the increasing subordination of individuals.

The state as the general force which organizes abstract right is increasingly enmeshed in a process wherein the defence of the general right to property is a substantive defence of the domination of labor by capital. The defence of universality is at once the defence of an antagonistic condition of particularlity. As an administrative force, the state is constantly faced with the problem of containing this basic social contradiction. As Marx noted in his early essay "On the Jewish Question" (1975a), the state at once unifies and particularizes empirical interests. And, later, he also points out that this administrative labor attempts to portray social contradictions as natural and inevitable, or attempts to locate them outside the public realm.

> Insofar as the state admits the existence of *social* defects, it sees their cause either in the *laws of nature,* which no human power can command, or in *private life,* which does not depend on the state, or in the *inexpedient activity of the administration,* which does not depend on it (Marx, 1975b, p. 197, emphases added).

Below, we will suggest that news as discourse accepts these fundamental aspects of administrative labor.

We have examined political subjectivity thus far as an abstract form, deriving from exchange and intensified by the development of capital. Political subjectivity also has an empirical and historical dimension.

In a recent work, Michel Foucault (1983, pp. 208-228) points to three dimensions of social subjectivity. Social subjects exist in part as objects of administration. As much of Foucault's own work has documented (e.g. Foucault, 1978), state institutions such, as prisons, mental hospitals, and schools, attempt to construct particular kinds of subjectivity by arranging individuals and their activities in time and space through the selective development of capacities. The reality of the social subject is in part a product of this administrative labor. Again, Foucault points out that subjectivity exists as a more or less developed capacity for meaningfulness. Recent research (Curtis, forthcoming) shows that this capacity is developed in particular ways and acquires particular forms through activity in state institutions. Hoskin (1984) for instance, details an important eighteenth century shift in the pedagogy of reading whereby the objective of reading instruction became the transmission of and verification of particular kinds of meaning. Finally, Foucault notes that subjectivity exists in part as a capacity—again more or less developed—for reflection, criticism, and initiative directed at the processes of subjectification themselves.

The historical development of subjectivity as an empirical phenomenon, we wish to argue, is strongly influenced by the administrative labor of the state. Administrative labor is a never-ending round of attempts by the state to undercut the threats to generalized political subjectivity existing as substantive inequality and fragmentation of the body politic, which at the same time enforces the separation of subjects and objects which generates this same inequality and fragmentation. Administrative labor is never-ending in that its success in the large sense would be its own elimination. But its effectiveness and powerfulness should not be gauged by its general failure. Administrative labor is particularly a labor of containment which attempts to transform and neutralize the structural antagonisms of bourgeois relations by situating them in constraining categories and institutions.

In general, this labor involves the organization of social divisions in forms capable of adopting a public existence. It seeks to transform structural antagonisms like that between capital and labor into managed conflict between public "interest groups." Administrative labor seeks to assert the universality of the public realm against the particularity of "private interests." Paradoxically, this "totalizing" activity often proceeds by the fragmentation of the public sphere. Kay and Mott (1982, pp. 137-146), for example, detail one of these processes of administration in their discussion of the appearance of "unemployment" as a public category.

Public categories, which we argue are generated primarily by the administrative labor of the state, are vertical categories which cut across class lines and collapse antagonisms into manageable, discrete conflicts. In order to do this, the universality of political subjectivity requires a consensual foundation opposed to the antagonism of class relations. This foundation is the category of population, and the practices of the administrative state revolve around its management. As opposed to class, which is finite and determinate, population gives us a world of subjects that is infinitely reproductive and reproducible. Population is subdivisible into a limitless array of subjects who circulate in a field of events and actions that is contingent and abstracted.

What this points to is the positivism of the commodity form and the categories of administrative subject that flow from it. Just as extended commodity exchange necessitates the abstraction of objects as exchange values from the conditions of social labor that produced them, so the extension of the state as generalized force requires the abstraction of real persons from their conditions of life and struggle, and their formalization into administrative state subjects. Abstraction and formality, then, are the real historical substance of the state; the state is the idealization of "ideology," just as labor-power is its materialization. It is abstraction and formality which detach subjects and objects from their relations to one another. Through this positivism of subjects, the state attempts to close off and regulate the real struggles and collisions that, in many cases, formed these subjects anterior to its interest in them.

II

As a daily document of politics and law-and-order, news is the publicity of the subjects of state administration. More so than other discourses, news operates to inform the public realm and reproduce the public subject. In doing this, it appropriates, for the most part uncritically, the public categories of the state, and draws heavily upon the discursive forms in which those categories are inscribed. The critical capacity of news is limited chiefly to the redistribution of these subjects to a broader field of substantive questions than that of the official discourses in which they are embedded. In this respect, news remains secondary (it abides by a code of meta-representation), dependent, and official-like in its concerns.

The dependency of news is historical; it is related directly to the development of professional journalism in tandem with the expansion of the administrative state. This dates from the last quarter of the nineteenth century and the crisis in the international economy of capital (cf. Hobsbawm, 1968). This crisis was resolved by the large scale consolidation of capital (concentration and centralization), together with the growth of bureaucratic organization (administration) which intensified further the separation of absolute property and real propertylessness. The growth of administration, within the corporation and the state, realigned the class structure by promoting the growth of what has variously been called a "new middle class" and new middle class strata of "intellectual labor" composed of salaried professionals, managers, and officials in general: those for whom the production discourse has become the dominant mode of livelihood (cf. *inter alia,* Ehrenreich & Ehrenreich, 1978; Nobel, 1977; Weber, 1978).

Dating back to Weber, the rise of the new middle class, professionalism, and bureaucratic organization have been associated not only with each other but also with the spread of rationalism and the application of rational principles to social administration. In the case of news, as both talk and institution, this has taken the form primarily of the decline of overt political partisanship in favor of a commitment to "objectivity" realized through empiricism (fact-fulness), impartiality and the balancing of accounts (cf. Elliott, 1978; Rutherford, 1978; Schudson, 1978; Smith, 1978). This has reinforced the dependence of news on the political and juridical models of official discourse, by incorporating the need and desire to give "both sides" the right and opportunity to speak and be recorded accurately, a model derived fundamentally from the equivalence of commodity exchange (Knight, 1982). This has intensified further the positivism of administrative subjects as news has continued to detach them from their real historical relations and conditions in the interests of representational balance and the facts of the immediate moment. As in the marketplace, equivalence in discourse masks real inequality and fragmentation.

A common academic criticism of news is that it is restricted to the interests and perspectives of this new middle class (cf. Gans, 1979; Tuchman, 1978). What we would emphasize here is that these main elements of practical news-talk, as part of the rationalist ideology of intellectual–administrative labor as a whole, represent a fundamental class contradiction, and cannot be explained away simply in terms of the empiricism of attitudinal socialization. The new middle class exercises power and enjoys privilege, yet it is essentially propertyless. In this respect, the condition of possibility for the new middle class, as for the state and corporate capital, is that it fulfills the separation of absolute property and real propertylessness, and thus realizes the ideological subordination of the latter to the former (formalization and abstraction). Unlike the "old" petit bourgeoisie of independent commodity producers, whose existence as such resided in real property, the new middle class must attempt continuously to replace the latter with its own knowledge and discourses. Those who talk for a living not only depend in large measure upon the state for their employment but also, more generally, depend upon it for the certification, and thus exclusivity, of their knowledge and talk. Unlike real property, whose exclusivity rests on its privative character, knowledge and discourse can be reproduced without alienation (and normally are), but cannot be alienated through direct reproduction. There is no better example of the paradoxes of the spiral of certification and exclusivity than modern journalism, which requires ever more extensive forms of rational training in order to be able to talk to as many people as plainly as possible. In this respect, even those sections of the new middle class employed by private capital still depend closely on the administrative state for the conditions of their own existence and reproduction.

The dependency of news is also substantive. In its daily accounts of political initiative and opposition, the disruption and restoration of order, and the endless parade of personalities, some more evanescent than others, news reproduces the universalizing and particularizing forces of the state as the latter strives to contain the basic contradictions that are its condition of existence. News is consensual, a labor of consensus-making and consensus-management. While it cannot deny the separation of universality and particularity, totality and individuality, it attempts to suppress their *dialectical* relationship by subordinating the latter term of each pair to the former. In this suppressive role must be situated the much observed tendency for news to transform contradiction into conflict, change into novelty, history into timeless nature, resistance into deviance, structure into personality, the continuous into the discrete, the determinate into the contingent: in sum, the finite reality of class into the infinite realism of population (cf., *inter alia,* Altheide, 1976; Fishman, 1980; Gans, 1979; Glasgow Media Group, 1976, 1980; Hall, 1978; Knight, 1982; Tuchman, 1978). These transformations speak of the positivism of subjects that news appropriates from administration, and internalizes as epistemology.

In practice, the consensual labor of news is implicit and indirect. To reproduce consensual space, official discourses, political and juridical, exclude, marginalize, and stigmatize certain categories as they define the boundaries of normal sociality. The concern of news with deviance, disorder, and the breakdown of normality publicizes this field of exclusion and devaluation in a reflexive way. The public subjects of bad news—deviants, criminals, terrorists, protesters, strikers, foreign "strongmen," etc.—inscribe an idealization, a mythology, or normality more deeply in the social consciousness and the plays of popular talk. They do so, however, only by perpetuating external particularity that not only makes consensus incomplete, but also, correlatively, makes consensual discourse continuous. The contradiction of the administrative state, that its condition of existence is at once the problem it must contain, is here mirrored back upon itself as the persistence of a discourse that can never fulfill itself. Consensualism must continually defer its objective; "bad news" as talk of order and normality makes sense only in a society whose real principle is chaos (cf. Kay and Mott, 1982).

In the democratic society of capital, the separation of particularity and universality is institutionalized in the formal separation of the political and juridical state. The former consists in the management of legitimated opposition and dissent, usually with respect to the plurality of means addressing consensual goals. The juridical state consists of the imposition and reimposition of order through the operationalization of universal legal subjectivity—the system of police, courts, prisons, etc.—which then admits empirical particularity. In the abstract, the juridical state is subordinate to the political; in real practice, the relationship becomes reversed. This contradiction threatens continually to collapse their separation, and thereby generates a torsion whose real substance is administration, its discourses, and their reproduction as news.

This is illustrated by the way news talks about collective violence and the overt disruption of public order. Juridical discourse of law-and-order invokes a universal, consensual appeal to immediacy which is distributed through the empiricist narratives of news. This is the sense of urgency conveyed in the descriptions of rioting, etc., and in the statements of police and other officials of the need to act "now" to contain disruption and harm to persons and property, and to restore universal order (cf. Wren-Lewis, 1981). The immediate power of talk of acting now by no means closes off the ability of news to offer critical balance. But this is normally directed in a way that accepts as natural the separation of law-and-order from political discourse and action. The balancing of accounts, in any extensive way, normally takes place in the realm of institutionalized politics where opposition and counter-initiative are legitimated. As such, the focus of critical balance then shifts away from the agents who acted "now" to restore the consensual formality of dissent. Here the discourse of law-and-order submits itself to the political, the practical to the abstract, which is able to transcend the strictures of the here-and-now and enter a discursive space of past and future where it argues about such things as the "roots" and "underlying causes" of disorder, and the possibilities of "long-term solutions." In this abstract discursive space, disorder may well be attributed publicly to social problems and inequalities, and oppositional political voices given their say; but what is now immediate is the desire to "speak now" rather than "act now" (even when such talk is about the exhaustion or redundancy of talk).

The particularity of political subjectivity is managed back into a universality of forms so long as it is contained within the state's administrative field. This universality of form is expressed in those abstract subjects to which news so commonly resorts—the average person, the citizen, the voter, the nation, the electorate, etc. They express the universality of individuality in that they are spoken of as definite, unitary, singular subjects: not voters or citizens but *the* voter, *the* citizen. They are the discursive form within which difference, and thereby critical self-subjectification (Foucault's third sense), are ordered. Even when news stresses the radical character of political opposition and dissent, it does so within this consensual form. In its coverage of the 1983 British general election, for example, CBC television news stressed again and again the divisiveness of the contest, but came back to the dominance of this consensual subject: "some members of the British electorate" we were told on the evening of June 5, 1983, "call Mrs. Thatcher's policies extreme" (Knight & Taylor, 1984).

This consensual subject is the point of opening as well as closure for the discourses of population. It is the point from which (administrative) subjectivity is subdivided into its fragments—women, Blacks, ethnics, labor, consumers, the private sector, the economy, criminals, and so on—which are abstracted from their real historical relations and the conditions of their possibility as such. News appropriates the idealism and positivism of administration, and parades these subjects before us as fixed and objective in their realism. Their real particularity is collapsed into the universality of abstract equivalence: they become functional. Real difference is undone in the face of the ceaseless modernization of the world that news achieves. Talk of "community" and "life-styles", for example, the former with its connotations of shared ideas and beliefs, the latter of a deliberate, almost contrived, "stylization" of behavior, illustrate this homogenization. Moreover, their popularity comes precisely at a moment of real historical crisis, when the contradictions of administration threaten to burst their bounds, and the work of consensualism is re-intensified as new forms of meaningfulness emerge.

The modern moment of this intensified consensualism is a humanism of individual rights and choices. It regards collective subjectivity as the (temporary) means to achieving the goal of universal individuality; and it takes these rights and choices (which remain formal and abstract), like subjectivity in general, as naturally given, not as the product of social material process. Humanism is the generalized ideology of the "new" middle class. It is a simulation or modelling of the world at large according to the interests, perspectives, and experiences of that class.[1] Humanism is the "ideology" of the radical separation of absolute property and real propertylessness: the individual as full possessor of his/her own person and capacities. It fulfills the personalization of power's positivities: right as the universal entitlement to expand individual forces and capacities, not as a dialectic of particular claim and force.

Humanism nonetheless displays its powerful character in the discourses it inhabits, real social divisions appear through it in mediated form. News, for example, has often been criticised for personalization and naturalism, reducing its accounts to the ascertainable, immediate motives of individuals on the one hand, and to abstract, objectified forces of naturalistic proportions on the other (cf., *inter alia,* Knight, forthcoming). This dualism is an inscription of administrative power. It is particularly significant of the subjects of bad news—the oppressed, the marginal, the deviant, etc—who are at once reinforced in their exclusion and recuperated by humanization. Particularity is fed into universality as the subjects of bad news are detached from their practices by depicting them in emotional and naturalistic ways. Strikers and demonstrators, for example, are "angry," "frustrated," "defiant," or "militant," the poor live in a "climate of hopelessness and fear;" violent disruptions of public order "erupt," "break out" or "flare up;" and so on.

Humanism is exclusive in that it alienates the subjects of bad news from the (self-) power of rationality. In this way, it inscribes them as the objects of public regard and fascination. The separation of these subjects and their practices de-politicizes them as it saturates them with the objectivity of administrative power. At the same time, it reembraces them as it internalizes all subjects within the circuit of administration and its discourses. All this talk of emotionalism and naturalism incites the reader to enter the text, and, whether with sympathy or distaste, to do so with the interest, concern, and reflection of the universal subject of the state. The reader inscribes him/herself as an administrative subject (the informed citizen, member of the general public, etc.) whose "patience" is encouraged by an abstract system that defies unitary understanding (for objective method dictates a plurality, usually duality, of "perspectives"). The reader must take sides for unity.

Particularity is fed into universality as subjects are detached from each other, from their social-historical relations. News has no difficulty in portraying many of its subjects as victims. The poor, the unemployed, immi-

---

[1] For Baudrillard (1975, 1983), modern society is the society of perpetual simulation in which the referent has been absorbed into the signified and the latter overwhelmed by the signifier. Everything is now internalized within the circuit of value; everything is now valuable and exchangeable as commodity and/or sign; this, we would add, is administration.

grants, minorities, for example, are now commonly spoken of as the subjects of forces beyond their control, as the vulnerable victims of systems at fault (an uncaring state, an impersonal marketplace, etc.). Such talk, however, not only implies their solution by further administration, but also contains the representation of their real conditions by positioning them against abstract models of universality. Particularity is set against universality, not against other particularity. In their study of Canadian television coverage of the 1983 British election, for example, Knight and Taylor (1984) show how the absence of "positive" balance restricted the critique of Thatcherism undertaken by the news reports. The unemployed were presented in evocative humanistic terms which spoke of suffering and ruined and shattered lives, and which attributed some measure of blame to the Thatcher government. The balance to this, however, was framed at an abstract and institutional level. There was no talk of definite individuals or groups, such as professionals or businessmen, whose real conditions had improved because of Thatcherism, only of the benefits to the "average man" and "those still working" and of the "signs" of an economy on the mend. The *relational* particularities of class society were evacuated of their contradictory force, and repositioned in terms of some more or less abstract sign of society as a whole. The absence from the news text of Thatcherism's real beneficiaries denied talk of its victims a point of real reference and contextuality.

When news speaks openly of the "disadvantaged," the "powerless," even the "oppressed," it is administration talking. Power is personalized as possession (to *have* power) and instrument (to wield *it*), and abstracted from social relationality. Administration seeks to saturate the "powerless" with power as objects; humanism with power as subjects. Both operate through a mythology of positivism that strives to manage "limit and lack" (Foucault) *without* loss (Baudrillard). Both seek a world of separated subjects and objects charged to the fullest with power as formal equals, a world of uncontradictory contradictions where absolute property *is* real propertylessness.

III

To confront critically administration and its public discourse, we must engage form as well as substance. Discourse that restricts itself to the latter contents itself with a redistribution of given subjects and an expansion of fields whose structure is already there. Critical discourse must extend beyond attempts to get across to the dominant media "alternative views of the facts or events." This reproduces the model of ceaseless discursive balance in which administration consists. It reproduces the forms of administrative subjectivity as it seeks to expand their empirical content. Strategy of this kind restricts itself to an ideology of formal equality under conditions of real inequality. Critical discourse, rather, must seek also to open up the forms of subjectivity that administration and official-like discourse objectify.

In the society of universal value (as commodity and/or sign), criticial discourse must be relentlessly 'impatient' and reflexive. It must confront the separations, appropriations, and distributions of its own talk as well as that of its object. Most especially, it must confront critically and noisily its own possibility as a publicity of state subjects.

REFERENCES

Altheide, D.L. (1976). *Creating Reality: How Television News Distorts Events*. Beverly Hills, CA: Sage.

Baudrillard, J. (1975). *The Mirror of Production*. St. Louis, MO: Telos Press.

Baudrillard, J. (1983). *Simulations*. New York: Semiotext(e).

Bendix, R. (1964). *Citizenship and Nation-Building*. New York: Wiley.

Curtis, B. (forthcoming). "The Speller Expelled." *Canadian Review of Sociology and Anthropology*.

Ehrenreich, B., and Ehrenreich, J. (1978). "The Professional-Managerial Class." In P. Walker (Ed.), *Between Labour and Capital*. Montreal: Black Rose Books.

Elliott, P. (1978). "Professional Ideology and Organisational Change: The Journalist since 1800," In G. Boyce, J. Curran, and P. Wingate (Eds.), *Newspaper History from the Seventeenth Century to the Present*. London: Coustable.

Fishman, M. (1980). *Manufacturing the News*. Austin, TX: University of Texas Press.

Foucault, M. (1978). *Discipline and Punish: The Birth of the Prison*. New York: Pantheon.

Foucault, M. (1983). "The Subject and Power", and "On the Genealogy of Ethics: An Overview of Work in Progress." In D. Dreyfus and P. Rabinow, *Michel Foucault: Beyond Structuralism and Hermeneutics* (2nd ed.). Chicago, IL: University of Chicago Press.

Gans, H.J. (1979). *Deciding What's News*. New York: Pantheon.

Glasgow Media Group. (1976). *Bad News*. London: Routledge and Kegan Paul.

Glasgow Media Group. (1980). *More Bad News*. London: Routledge and Kegan Paul.

Hall, S. (Ed.). (1978). *Policing the Crisis: Mugging, the State and Law and Order*. London: Macmillan.

Hobsbawm, E.J. (1968). *Industry and Empire*. Harmondsworth, England: Penguin.

Hoskin, K. (1984). "Cobwebs to Catch Flies." Unpublished paper, Joint Department of Classics, University of Warwick.

Kay, G.B., and Mott, J. (1982). *Political Order and the Law of Labor*. London: Macmillan.

Knight, G. (1982). "News and Ideology." *Canadian Journal of Communication 8* (No. 4), 15–41.

Knight, G. (forthcoming). "News of Talk, News of Riot." In S. Thomas (Ed.), *Culture and Communication: Methodology, Behaviour, Artifacts, and Institutions,* Norwood, NJ: Ablex.

Knight, G., and Taylor, I. (1984). "CBS Television News and the 1983 British Election. A Study in 'Foreign News' and the Reconstruction of Political Consensus." Unpublished paper, Department of Sociology, McMaster University, Department of Sociology and Anthropology, Carleton University.

Marx, K. (1975a). "On the Jewish Question." In K. Marx, *Collected Works,* Vol. 3 (pp. 146–174). Moscow: Progress Publishers.

Marx, K. (1975b). "Critical Marginal Notes by a Prussian." In K. Marx, *Collected Works,* Vol. 3. Moscow: Progress Publishers.

Noble, D.F. (1977). *American by Design.* New York: Knopf.
Rutherford, P. (1978). *The Making of the Canadian Media.* Toronto, Ontario: McGraw-Hill Ryerson.
Schudson, M.S. (1978). *Discovering the News.* New York: Basic Books.
Smith, A. (1978). "The Long Road to Objectivity and Back Again." In G. Boyce, J. Curran, and P. Wingate (Eds.), *Newspaper History from the Seventeeth Century to the Present.* London: Coustable.
Tuchman, G. (1978). *Making News.* New York: Free Press.
Weber, M. (1958). "Bureaucracy." In H.H. Gerth and C.W. Mills (Eds.), *From Max Weber: Essays in Sociology.* New York: Oxford University Press.
Weber, M. (1978). "Socialism." In W.G. Runciman (Ed.), *Max Weber: Selections in Translation* (pp. 251-262). London: Cambridge University Press.
Wren-Lewis, J. (1981). "The Story of a Riot: The Television Coverage of Civil Unrest in 1981." *Screen Education 40,* 15-33.

Chapter 4
The Influence of Camera Perspectives on the Perception of a Politician by Supporters, Opponents, and Neutral Viewers

HANS MATHIAS KEPPLINGER
WOLFGANG DONSBACH
Institut für Publizistik
Johannes Gutenberg Universität
Mainz, Federal Republic of Germany

INTRODUCTION

In television coverage of political campaigns, candidates are shown from various camera angles. Because these candidates are filmed so often in so many different situations, it might be assumed that, overall, they would be presented on television in nearly the same way. Nevertheless, in practice candidates are sometimes presented differently. In the television coverage of West Germany's Parliamentary Elections of 1976, Helmut Kohl, the leading candidate of the opposition party, was shown significantly more often from low- or high-positioned camera angles than was Chancellor Helmut Schmidt, who more often was shown at eye level (Kepplinger, 1979, 1980, 1982). It has also been true that candidates in debate have been presented differently. In the 1980 U.S. Presidential primaries, during a debate with George Bush, Ronald Reagan was constantly filmed from below while Bush was shown at eye level (Hellweg & Phillips, 1981). In the 1976 Presidential campaign, during the second debate between Gerald Ford and Jimmy Carter, one camera angle used frequently made it appear as if the slender and smaller challenger was larger than the athletic President (Tiemens, 1978).

Do such television portrayals affect viewers' images of the candidates? Perhaps not, but it is at least conceivable that camera angles affect viewers' perceptions. Television is a medium that communicates with both sight and sound, and there is strong evidence that viewers are particularly attuned to what they see. Not all camera angles may equally flatter a candidate, thus affecting viewers' perceptions of the candidates' style and appearance.

The experiment was carried out with a grant from the German Science Foundation (Deutsche Forschungsgemeinschaft). It was first reported in W. Schulz and K. Schönbach (Eds.), *Massenmedien und Wahlen*. Munich: Ölschläger.

There have been experimental studies of the influence of camera angles, but their results have been contradictory or inconclusive (Mandell & Shaw, 1970; McCain, Chilberg, & Wakshlag, 1977; Tiemens, 1970). A possible reason is that camera angles were not precisely controlled. Conceivably, minor adjustments in camera angles may stimulate major differences in perceptions (Kepplinger & Donsbach, 1981). Perhaps a larger problem of these studies is that the test films have shown politically neutral speakers, and thus do not adequately simulate the actual conditions of an election campaign. The perception of a politician most likely will be influenced not only by camera angle, but also by the political distance between the politician and the viewers. It is unreasonable to presuppose that supporters and opponents are affected equally by the way a candidate appears.

In the following study the influence of camera angles and political distance on the perception of a speaker are examined.

Two null hypotheses were formulated:

1. Camera angles have no influence on viewers' perception of a politician. Personality and statements alone are decisive.
2. Neither supporters nor opponents of a politician are influenced by shots taken from unfavorable angles. Their political opinions override their perceptions (McGrath & McGrath, 1962; see also Sigel, 1964).

EXPERIMENTAL DESIGN

For the study, six test films were produced. Each test film portrayed a politician being introduced by a journalist. The politician was filmed simultaneously by three cameras mounted 0.85 meters above each other. The middle camera was placed at eye level of the speaker, the other two above and below. The camera angles were $-18°$ (clear bottom view); $0°$ (eye level); and $+18°$ (clear top view). The films showed the head and upper torso of the politician, slightly from the side and at a distance of about 2.50 meters.[1] The politician stood at a lectern equipped with microphones which did not obstruct his face. The background was a blue poster with the partially legible title, "Energy Forum." The politician was a man of about 45 years who gave a speech on problems of energy supply. The content of his speech was politically neutral, i.e., he did not represent the opinions of a particular political party.

The journalist was filmed at eye level and gave two different introductions of the speaker. In the first version, the journalist introduced the speaker as the "energy spokesman for the CDU/CSU parliamentary fraction" (conservative version); in the second version, he was presented as the "energy spokesman for the SPD parliamentary fraction" (liberal version).

---

[1] The camera angles were tuned to the content analysis categories of the television news coverage of the parliamentary elections of 1976. (See Kepplinger, 1979, 1980, 1982.)

Table 1. Experimental Design

Camera Angle	Political Distance		
	Supporters	Neutral Subjects	Opponents
Clear Top View (+18°)	N = 13	N = 9	N = 13
Eye Level (0°)	N = 16	N = 12	N = 12
Clear Bottom View (−18°)	N = 16	N = 11	N = 14

The introduction lasted approximately 15 seconds, the speech about 90 seconds. Both the politician and the journalist were unknown to the subjects. To produce the six test films, the two introductions and the three shots of the politician were combined with each other.

The experiment was carried out with a test audience of 122 subjects from a state police school. Nearly all subjects were men (118), of whom the majority were aged between 20 and 34 (101). Although the subjects could not be randomly assigned to the six test conditions, no significant differences between the six viewing groups were found. Variables examined included age, sex, and political attitudes. After the subjects had viewed one of the six test films, their perceptions of the speaker and their political positions were measured on a 7-point scale whose end points were designated with "liberal" and "conservative." Test subjects who placed themselves on the liberal or conservative side of the middle were classified respectively as "liberal" or "conservative." Subjects who marked the middle point were classified as "neutral." Subjects who viewed a film with the speaker introduced as from their own political camp were classified as "supporters." Subjects who viewed a film with the speaker from the other political camp were classified as "opponents." Subjects who classified themselves in the middle of the scale, regardless of which film they viewed, were considered to be "neutral viewers."

The subjects' perceptions of the speaker were measured with a 20-scale semantic differential. The positive and negative marks of the end points of each of the 20 scales were randomly ordered from left to right, with the most positive value always scored as 7, the most negative value always scored as 1. Therefore, the higher the value, the more positive the evaluation; the lower the value, the more negative the evaluation.[2]

RESULTS

General Impressions

Both camera angle and political distance affected, independently of each other, the perception of the speaker: significant ($p < .05$) main effects were

---

[2] This procedure was possible because all terms could be clearly evaluated as positive or negative.

found for camera angles on 11 of 20 scales, and for political distance on 6 of 20 scales. Significant interaction effects were found only on one scale: the nonviolent/violent scale.[3]

Initial results on the type and strength of camera angle influence and political distance on the perception of the speaker thus provided the analysis of 15 scales on which at least one significant main or interacting effect was found. These 15 scales were then used to create indicators of the *tendency* and *homogeneity* of subjects' perceptions.

Tendency of perception refers to the degree of the subjects' positive or negative judgment of the speaker. It is measured as the mean of subjects judgment on the 15 scales remaining in the analysis. The higher the mean, the more positively the speaker was perceived, independent of the particular characteristics evaluated. As Table 2 indicates, most favorable impressions are obtained from shots taken at eye level. In comparison, filming from a clear bottom or clear top view resulted in less favorable impressions. There were also considerable differences between shots taken from a clear bottom or clear top view: the latter stimulated a poorer general impression.[4]

The influence of political distance on the tendency of perception was unexpected. Neutral subjects expressed more favorable judgments than either supporters or opponents of the speaker.[5] The relationship between political distance and tendency of perception proved to be curvilinear. A possible explanation comes from the fact that the speaker's statement was neutral in content. As a result, subjects who classified themselves as politically liberal or conservative perhaps missed the arguments of their political camp, and therefore judged the speaker less positively than expected.

Homogeneity of perception refers to the similarity of evaluations of the speaker with regard to various characteristics. This measure was calculated from the standard deviations of the judgments of each test subject on the 15 scales in the analysis. The smaller the standard deviation, the more uniform are the positive or negative evaluations of the speaker on the various scales. The larger the figure, the more diverse are the judgements. For example,

---

[3] In the first analysis phase, all results were subjected to a factor analysis, which led to a five-factor solution. The individual scales which constituted a factor measured various characteristics, which in part possessed totally diverse political relevance. For this reason, the analysis was based upon the individual scales and not on the factors.

[4] An inquiry of camerapersons has already indicated that shots taken from a clear top view obtain a poorer impression than shots from a clear bottom view (Kepplinger, 1979, 1980, 1982). An eta value of 0.14 was ascertained for the relationship of camera angle and perception for all 15 scales. This implies that 14% of the perceptions can be explained through camera angles. For several scales, the variance was considerably greater: active/passive: 27%; violent/nonviolent: 21%; relaxed/tense: 22%; reserved/obtrusive: 19%; weak/aggressive: 26%.

[5] An eta value of 0.09 was ascertained for the relationship between political distance and perception. Thereby, camera angles influenced perceptions more strongly than political distance. Those expectations expressed in the text are based on "perceptual balance principle" studies. (See McGrath & McGrath, 1962).

Table 2. Influence of Camera Angle and Political Distance on Tendency of Perception—Mean Values of the Mean Values of the 15 Significant Scales

	Political Distance		
Camera Angle	Supporters	Neutral Subjects	Opponents
Clear Top View (+18°)	3.73	3.85	3.50
Eye Level (0°)	4.56	4.69	3.79
Clear Bottom View (−18°)	4.10	4.52	4.09

Two-way-analysis of variance: p   eta^2
camera angle   <.001   0.14
political distance   <.005   0.09
No significant interaction effects

one subject might have perceived the politician as very aggressive (1 on the scale) and very expert (7 on the scale); another subject might have perceived him as medium aggressive (4 on the scale) and medium expert (4 on the scale). This would result in identical means but different standard deviations: person one got a contradictory impression, person two a homogeneous one. From the individual standard deviations, the mean was calculated for each test group. This provides information on the average homogeneity of perceptions of the test subjects under the diverse conditions. Independently of political distance, camera angles significantly ($p < .001$) influenced the homogeneity of the perception of the speaker (see Table 3). Filming at eye level essentially resulted in a smaller distribution and thereby a considerably more homogeneous perception of the speaker than did filming from a clear bottom or clear top view. No differences existed between shots taken from clear bottom or clear top view.[6]

Theoretically, the tendency and homogeneity of perception are independent of each other. However, a close empirical relationship between the two was found. Filming at eye level not only obtained a more positive, but also a more homogeneous, overall impression than did shots taken from a clear bottom or clear top view.[7] This result points to the conclusion that filming at eye level created an image of the speaker that conforms to the "Gesetz der guten Gestalt": it was harmonious, simple, and impressive (Köhler, 1933, 1958; Kohler, 1963).

Perceptions of Individual Characteristics

The perception of the speaker when filmed from eye level and clear top view, as well as from eye level and clear bottom view, were compared with

---

[6] This confirms the results of an experiment on the influence of seven camera angles on the perception of a neutral speaker (See Kepplinger, Donsbach, 1981.)

[7] These results confirm the study by Tiemens (1970), Kepplinger and Donsbach (1981), and contradict the study of McCain et al. (1977).

Table 3. Influence of Camera Angle and Political Distance on Homogeneity of Perception—Mean Values of Individual Standard Deviations

Camera Angle	Political Distance		
	Supporters	Neutral Subjects	Opponents
Clear Top View (+18°)	1.79	1.66	1.77
Eye Level (0°)	1.51	1.24	1.33
Clear Bottom View (−18°)	1.71	1.68	1.68

Two-way-analysis of variance: p eta^2
camera angle <.001 <0.16
political distance n.s.
No significant interaction effects

each other (t-test).[8] The analysis of individual scales resulted in two general conclusions: camera angles inconsistently influenced the tendency of perception of individual characteristics, and they influenced supporters more strongly than neutral subjects or opponents. With regard to the first conclusion, in comparison with other angles, shots taken from eye level gave positive impressions of eight characteristics, and negative impressions of four characteristics (see Table 4). When filmed at eye level, the speaker appeared as meek, nonviolent, reserved, natural, likeable, intelligible, expert, and substantial; however, at the same time, the speaker was seen as passive, tense, insensitive, and inaccessible.

The perceived characteristics can be grouped into two types, corresponding to the direction of the effects (see Table 4). Type A is comprised of the eight characteristics that are positively accentuated from shots taken at eye level. Type B is comprised of the four characteristics that are negatively accentuated in shots taken at eye level. Supporters, neutral subjects, and opponents showed the same reaction patterns, so that the scales could be classified in the same way.[9] The existence of type A and type B is the reason why the homogeneity of perception was greater when the speaker was filmed from eye level then from clear bottom or clear top view; shots taken from the latter perspectives resulted in contradictory judgements on the scales from type A and type B.

---

[8] Formally considered, the data could be examined with a simple variance analysis. However, because the difference between shots taken from a clear bottom view and eye level are smaller then the difference between eye level and a clear top view, on numerous scales this would yield no significant values, with the present level of significance. The pair-wise comparison of mean values with t-tests is therefore a more reasonable procedure.

[9] In 9 of the 12 scales, the classification is in agreement with the results of a prior study. For only three scales are differences found. Therefore, the classification of scales and characteristics to types A and B seem to be quite stable for the presented speaker (Kepplinger & Donsbach, 1981.)

Table 4. Perception of Individual Characteristics of a Speaker by Supporters, Neutral Subjects, and Opponents when Filmed from Various Camera Angles—Mean Values

Characteristics	Supporters			Neutral Subjects			Opponents		
	CB	EL	CT	CB	EL	CT	CB	EL	CT
TYPE A									
meek/aggressive	2.5	4.8	2.4	2.6	5.1	2.4			
non-violent/violent	3.9	5.9	3.1	4.2	5.6	3.3			
reserved/obtrusive	2.5	4.5	2.2		3.8	2.3			
natural/cramped		3.9	1.7		4.2	2.1			
likeable/unlikeable	2.8	4.6	2.9					3.3	1.9
intelligible/unintelligible	5.0	6.0	4.9					5.6	4.2
expert/inexpert								3.5	2.5
substantial/insubstantial								4.3	3.1
TYPE B									
active/passive	6.3	4.6	6.2	6.5	5.4		6.0	4.4	6.2
relaxed/tense	6.3	4.6	6.2	6.4	5.3	6.7	6.5	5.4	6.5
sensitive/insensitive	4.5	3.2	4.5						
frank/inaccessible							5.2	3.9	

CB = Clear Bottom View; EL = Eye Level; CT = Clear Top View
The mean values of the shots taken at eye level vary significantly from the mean values of shots taken from clear bottom view and a clear top view ($p < .05$)

The negative influence of shots taken from clear top view was almost equally strong among supporters, neutral subjects, and opponents. The negative influence of shots taken from clear bottom view was more marked among supporters than among neutral subjects or opponents. In other words, shots taken from clear top view gave all subjects a negative impression of the speaker, while shots taken from clear bottom view gave only supporters that impression.

A change in camera angle from eye level to clear bottom or clear top view influenced between 20 and 40% (from eta values) of the perception of most of the individual characteristics in a positive or negative direction (Table 5). In some cases, however, even stronger effects were identified. For supporters and neutral subjects, changes in camera angle from eye level to clear top view yielded eta^2 values between 0.35 and 0.67 on the peaceful/aggressive, nonviolent/violent, and reserved/obtrusive scales. Shots taken from various camera angles influence the perception of supporters more strongly than that of neutral subjects and opponents. This might be explained by the dispositions of the subjects. Supporters were more likely to be interested in the speaker, and more likely to pay attention to him. Therefore, it is probable that they responded more sensitively to a positive or negative depiction of his personality by various camera angles. Following this explanation, one

Table 5. Perception of Individual Characteristics of a Speaker by Supporters, Neutral Subjects, and Opponents when Filmed from Constant Camera Angles—Mean Values

Characteristics	Clear Bottom View (−18°) Supporters	Clear Bottom View (−18°) Neutral Subjects	Clear Bottom View (−18°) Opponents	Eye Level (0°) Supporters	Eye Level (0°) Neutral Subjects	Eye Level (0°) Opponents	Clear Top View (+18°) Supporters	Clear Top View (+18°) Neutral Subjects	Clear Top View (+18°) Opponents
meek/aggressive				4.8*	5.1	3.3			
nonviolent/violent				5.9*	5.6	4.3			
reserved/obtrusive				4.5		3.1			
natural/cramped					4.2	2.8			
likeable/unlikeable	2.8	4.1		4.6		3.3			
expert/inexpert					4.1	3.5	3.7*	3.9	2.5
sensitive/insensitive				3.2	4.9				
graceful/clumsy	2.6	3.4					4.5		2.9
interesting/uninteresting			3.4						
differentiated/undifferent.	4.8		3.7	4.6		3.4			
successful/unsuccessful		4.9			5.5	4.1			
distinct/indistinct									
Quantity of significant mean value differences:		4			11			3	

The mean values vary significantly from each other (p < .05).
* Supporters vary significantly only from the opponents.

can assume that the greater the viewer's ego involvement (Irle, 1976, pp. 292–294) or level of activation, the greater the camera angle effect should be.

The impact of specific shots on different categories of viewers was also examined, and the analysis can be summarized in two general statements. First, shots taken at eye level created extremely diverse perceptions by supporters, neutral viewers, and opponents, while, in comparison, shots taken from clear bottom or clear top view created very similar perceptions among all viewers. In the first case, there exist 11 statistically significant differences, compared with only four and three statistically significant differences for bottom and top view, respectively. Therefore, shots taken at eye level created differences in perceptions of supporters, neutral subjects, and opponents. In comparison, shots taken from clear bottom or clear top view leveled the perception of the three categories of viewers. Second, the presentation of the speaker from clear bottom and clear top view reduced the advantage which a speaker normally enjoyed among supporters and neutral subjects when viewed at eye level. When filmed from eye level, the significant perceptual differences between supporters and opponents measured on the 15 scales added up to 7.0 scale points. When filmed from below or above eye level, it added up to only 2.8 and 1.4 scale points, respectively. When viewing shots taken from clear top or clear bottom view, supporters perceived the politician nearly as negatively as his opponents.

Although leveling of perception is not identical to the homogeneity of perception, there exists a close relationship between the two effects. Homogeneity of perception deals with a tendency for extensive perception conformity of the various speaker characteristics by the viewer, regardless of the political opinions he possesses. In comparison, the leveling of perception deals with a tendency for perception conformity of an individual speaker's characteristics by numerous viewers with diverse or even opposing political opinions. Although both situations are influenced by camera angles, the effects were not the same. Filming from clear bottom or clear top view led to less homogeneity and greater leveling, while shots taken at eye level led to greater homogeneity and more limited leveling.

SUMMARY AND DISCUSSION

The results of the experiment can be summarized in five statements:

1. Camera angles and political distance had, independent of each other, an influence on the *tendency of perception* of the speaker. Subjects who viewed shots taken from eye level judged the speaker more positively than subjects who viewed shots taken from a clear bottom or clear top view.
2. Camera angles had an influence on the *homogeneity* of the perception of the speaker. Subjects who viewed shots taken from eye level evalu-

ated various characteristics of the speaker more similarly than subjects who viewed shots taken from a clear bottom or clear top view.
3. Camera angles influenced the perception of supporters more strongly than the perception of neutral viewers or opponents. This effect was found on many scales and for many pairs of camera angles. It applies especially to shots taken from a clear bottom view.
4. Camera angles influenced the perception of two categories of characteristics which, corresponding to the scales by which they were measured, can be designated as type A and type B. Shots taken from eye level positively influenced the perception of eight characteristics belonging to type A, and negatively influenced four characteristics belonging to type B.
5. Shots taken from clear bottom or clear top view leveled the perception of supporters and neutral subjects on one hand, and of opponents on the other. Supporters and opponents perceived the speaker almost equally. Thereby, the speaker lost the bonus which he normally enjoyed as a result of his affiliation with a particular political party.

The results of this experiment refute the hypothesis that camera angles have no influence on viewers' perception of a politician. Camera angles do influence these perceptions, particularly among a politician's supporters. The fact that the perceptions of supporters were more strongly influenced by camera angles than the perceptions of neutral subjects or opponents was explained by their greater ego involvement. Possibly, the supporters paid closer attention to the speaker and, therefore, responded more sensitively to the influence of camera angles. One can regard supporters as potential voters of a politician. Camera angles therefore influence just those viewers who are of special importance for the politician presented.

REFERENCES

Hellweg, S.A., and Philips, S.L. (1981). "A Visual Analysis of the 1980 Houston Republican Primary Debate." Paper presented at the International Communication Association Convention, Minneapolis.
Irle, M. (1975) *Lehrbuch der Sozialpsychologie*. Göttingen: Verlag für Psychologie Hogrefe.
Kepplinger, H.M. (1979). "Ausgewogen bis zur Selbstaufgabe? Die Fernsehberichterstattung über die Bundestagswahl 1976 als Fallstudie eines kommunikations-politischen Problems." *Media Perspektiven 11,* 750-755.
Kepplinger, H.M. (1980). "Optishe Kommentierung in der Fernsehberichterstattung über den Bundestagswahlkampf 1976." In T. Ellwein (Ed.), *Politikfeld-Analysen 1979* (pp. 163-179). Köln: Westdeutscher Verlag.
Kepplinger, H.M. (1982). "Visual Biases in Television Campaign Coverage." *Communication Research 9* 432-446. (Reprinted in *Mass Communication Review Yearbook 4,* 391-405, 1983.)
Kepplinger, H.M., and Donsbach, W. (1981). "Der Einfluss von Kameraperspektiven auf die Wahrnehmung eines Redners." (Manuscript.)
Kohler, I. (1963). "Wahrnehmung." In R. Meili and H. Rohracher (Eds.), *Lehrbuch der experimentellen Psychologie* (pp. 53-102). Bern: Huber.

Köhler, W. (1933). *Psychologische Probleme.* Berlin: J. Springer.
Köhler, W. (1958). *Dynamische Zusammenhänge in der Psychologie.* Bern: Huber.
Loderhose, W. (1980). "Eingluss von Kameraleuten auf Fernseh- und Film-producktionen." Unpublished master's thesis, Johannes Gutenberg-Universität, Mainz.
Mandell, L., and Shaw, D.L. (1973). "Judging People in the News—Unconsciously: Effect of Camera Angle and Bodily Activity." *Journal of Broadcasting 17,* 353–362.
McCain, T.A., Chilberg, J., and Wakshlag, J. (1977). "The Effect of Camera Angle on Source Credibility and Attraction." *Journal of Broadcasting 21,* 35–46.
McGrath, J.E., and McGrath, M.F. (1962). "Effects of Partisanship on the Perception of Political Figures." *Public Opinion Quarterly 26,* 236–248.
Sigel, R.S. (1964). "Effect of Partisanship on the Perception of Political Candidates." *Public Opinion Quarterly 28,* 483–496.
Tiemens, R.K. (1970). "Some Relationships of Camera Angle to Communicator Credibility." *Journal of Broadcasting 14,* 483–490.
Tiemens, R.K. (1978). "Television's Portrayal of the 1976 Presidential Debates: An Analysis of Visual Content." *Communication Monographs 45,* 362–370.

PART II
STUDIES

Chapter 5
The Role of Private TV Stations in Italian Elections

GIANPIETRO MAZZOLENI

Department of Sociology
University of Milan
20122 Milan, Italy

Most of the research on media and elections focuses on national television channels and disregards local stations. There are obvious reasons for this: in many countries local, private TV stations are not allowed; where they exist (e.g., in the U.S.), they are usually part of large networks; moreover, local politics is often seen as "minor," unworthy of attention by political and social scientists, who are very busy studying national and/or presidential politics.

Nevertheless, local electoral contests (state, county, province, city, and the like) and the use that local candidates make of locally based broadcasting media, as well as the interest of local radio and TV stations in local campaigns, deserve closer attention.

Observation of changes in the interaction between politicians and media in local elections may lead to a better understanding of analogous trends on national levels. Furthermore, the impact of local media on voters, hence the results of the election, have an undeniable—even if delayed—repercussion on national politics. Finally, although one cannot speak of the "central role" of local TV stations, it is no exaggeration to say that, in the countries where they exist, they can be an independent variable in the electoral process.

This is a hypothesis applicable especially to the Italian case, following the consolidation of a system of several TV stations broadcasting in limited urban and rural areas. The "ethereal revolution," as this phenomenon is commonly called, could bring extreme changes to the traditional relations between media and the political system. To begin with, it is bringing about a new kind of "electoral television,"[1] quite different from the existing one.

This paper is based mainly on the findings of a pilot study conducted in the metropolitan area of Milan (Italy) during the campaign for administrative

---

[1] By "electoral television," we refer here to the complex of mutual relationships between TV and election campaigns. It is something different from "political television," by which we mean the treatment by TV of political events other than elections (e.g., political news, current affairs, etc.).

(regional, provincial, town) elections in June 1980 (Mazzoleni & Boneschi, 1980). The study attempted to identify indicators of the new trend in the relations between local, private TV stations and candidates for local offices.

"ELECTORAL TELEVISION" IN ITALY

The Italian experience with television regulations, especially "electoral television," is halfway between the system of public control on broadcasting existing in many European countries and the system of free enterprise typical of the United States. Beginning in 1976, Italy has possessed a "mixed system" in which public radio and television and a number of private channels coexist. The pattern public/private is reflected also in "electoral television." Here we find, on one side, a parliamentary ruling requiring party access to public broadcasting and free air time; on the other, an unrestricted free market.

The Election Tribunes

The two elements now making up Italian "electoral television" are: the long-established national TV series of "Political Tribunes," and the expansion of private TV stations.

The "tribunes" are periodic television broadcasts in which parties or trade unions present statements, engage in debate, or ask for support. This arrangement was started in the 1960 administrative election. It was a historic event. Before that time, any form of political communication via radio and television was strictly controlled by the Christian Democratic Party, a private monopoly within a public monopoly. For years, other parties excluded from government alliance, and from access to public broadcasting, claimed the right to make their voices heard. "The televised tribune," observed a politician 10 years later, "was the concrete translation of a generally shared demand, that is, to give the country the largest possible opportunity to express all the opinions represented in and out the Parliament: in other words, to open to the attention and interest of public opinion doors kept tightly closed until then." The parties of the Left, that is, the parties always kept far from the studios and the attention of RAI (Italy's Radio-TV Public Service), were the ones that benefitted most by this liberalization of access.

This positive experience brought other initiatives. In 1961, the "Political Tribune," reserved for the debates between parties outside electoral periods, was broadcast for the first time. The "Trade Unions' Tribune" followed in 1968, and the "People's Tribune" in 1970. All these tribunes still broadcast today; the significant exception is the "People's Tribune" which lasted only one season. Despite the screening of people directly addressing politicians, the political parties did not like this kind of live confrontation, and forced RAI to drop the program.

In 1970, Italy was the first Western country in which parties and trade unions could have television time at their disposal and could use it at their discretion. However, only the parties represented in Parliament had access, and the air time was proportional to their voting strength, e.g., 1 hour for the largest parties, a half hour for those of medium size, and 15 minutes for the smallest ones. Since the campaigns of 1979 (general election, European election), this restriction has been rescinded: all parties, large and small, participating in the election, are now granted the same amount of air time.

The feature that distinguishes Italy's "Election Tribunes" from similar programs in other countries is the privileged position of parties as subjects of political action in the Italian electoral system. Moreover, in Italy, public life and social relations appear more "politicized" than in neighboring countries. These structural characteristics are represented in "electoral television." It is the party or its spokesperson that addresses the voters, not the candidates. The trend toward some "personalization" of political communication is limited to a handful of top party leaders already familiar to the national audience.

Furthermore, the television tribunes have not transformed Italian election campaigns into "image" campaigns. That is to say, the phenomena observed in the United States or in France, (see, for example, McGinniss, 1969; Nimmo, 1970; Patterson & McClure, 1976; Schwartzenberg, 1977; Wyckoff, 1968), are not typical of Italian political contests. Political leaders so far, have not used television effectively. The speech of Italian politicians is strongly ideological, abstract, generally obscure, specialistic, and mainly addressed to élites. It lends itself far more to press and radio then to television.

Given these circumstances, it is no wonder that, as recent studies have confirmed, Italian voters dislike and avoid televised political communication. Asked whether the election tribunes were boring and difficult to understand, 64% of a panel of Roman voters answered yes (see Santoro Libri, 1980). Research sponsored by RAI, based on a national population sample, found that 60% of Italians pay little or no attention to election campaigning. The same study observed that election tribunes have bored the voters and turned them away from any kind of interest in campaign issues (see "Ricerca sal palinsesto tadioteleviso," 1980).

The Private Television Stations

Before 1972 there existed in Italy a radio and television monopoly. Parliament (formerly the Government) had full authority in the field. Every 6 years it contracted the management of the service with RAI, a state-controlled company, and established a permanent parliamentary committee that controlled the legitimacy of RAI's activities. This was the official structure of the system, a strong monopoly of public broadcasting, the only one allowed by existing laws.

Private enterprises always tried—unsuccessfully—to break this monopoly. However, in 1972 the establishment of the first private cable-TV in a small town gave rise to a harsh dispute with RAI, and a long debate in the press on whether the monopoly was legitimate and consistent with Article 21 of the Constitution defending the free expression of thought. The debate and the law suits against the many "pirate" cable and air TV stations that followed this first experiment brought the Constitutional Court to declare in 1974 and 1976 that the national monopoly was legal according to the fundamental charter. But the court also ruled that private radio and television broadcasting enterprises on the *local* level were constitutional. The RAI was assured the operation of the public service throughout the country; the private stations were allowed to establish coverage in local areas only.

This ruling provided sufficient incentive for the birth and proliferation of private stations: in 1980, about 2,000 radio and 500 television stations were counted by the Ministry of Telecommunications. The number is astonishing, if one compares it to the 750 stations existing in the U.S., where the population is four times as large!

The explosion of private TV broadcasting is something peculiar to the Italian social, cultural, and economic situation. It is rooted in the liberal philosophy of the Constitution, in the political balances of the post-war period, in the structure of the advertising market, and in the organization of Italy's cultural industry.

The intent of private entrepreneurs, at the beginning, was not to be an alternative to the public service. They aimed at filling those spaces that the state TV could not or would not fill, given its national requirements. Theirs was just a local interest, limited to participating in the local advertisement business, to giving information on local events, to broadcasting quizzes and games conducted by local showmen, and the like.

Since 1980, that is, after the pioneering period, the trend has changed. A period of settlement or rationalization of the field is under way.

Now, there is a movement toward the concentration of TV stations, the creation of networks crossing local boundaries, and the demand for access to satellite facilities. Behind all this one finds big entrepreneurial groups that have enough power to influence political parties and to create nationwide oligopolies.

Such maneuvers are possible because there has been no legislation in this area, despite several attempts by the various governments. Without legislation, the stronger groups have declared war on RAI. Their goals are to:

1. withdraw as much audience as possible from RAI. (The audience share of private TV stations in 1980 was about 25 to 30% of the total audience);
2. buy films and serials with high audience potential;
3. establish micro-wave bridges all over the country;

4. produce better programs;
5. increase advertising income.

With respect to advertising, the total income of private TV stations increased from 50 million dollars in 1979 to 80 million in 1980.

To summarize, private TV stations appear on the way to assuming a key place in Italy's broadcasting landscape, despite the uncertainties represented by the "mixed system" and by unpredictable legislation yet to come.

THE PRIVATE TV STATIONS IN THE 1980 LOCAL ELECTIONS CAMPAIGN

In Western democracies, elections are periodic competition between political subjects for power. This competition is rooted in the economic system from which electoral contests have borrowed many methods and practices. Elections are a market where, instead of private material goods, collective moral goods are offered, negotiated, and exchanged: a good administration, social reforms, and welfare on one side; vote support on the other. The selling strategies are substantially the same; both the political and economic spheres resort to the boosting power of the mass media, especially television.

This is clearly shown by the American experience. Now there exist indications that it may become typical of the Italian political arena as well, despite the past rigidity of the media-politics relationship.

Here are some explanations.

As observed, private TV stations are already important outlets of the advertising market. No wonder they turn into channels of political communication and are used in electoral battles. Italian parties have already moved in three directions to gain advantages in the local media markets. These are:

1. establishing and directing their own stations;
2. giving support to those stations in their area of influence;
3. buying air time during campaigns.

I will focus on the third strategy.

The 1979 national and European campaigns showed the keen interest with which politicians look at private stations as propaganda vehicles. In fact, the first moderate "assault" on private broadcasting took place in 1979. The total expenditure for political ads was about 1.5 million dollars. According to an IIC survey, all of the 120 stations of the sample sold or offered free air time (about 1 hour per day) for political propaganda ("Le televisioni private," 1981). Moreover, the RAI voter survey found that private broadcasts came third, after public television and the press, as a channel for campaign information.

The 1979 campaign was the first test of a new campaign style in Italy. This development provoked controversy among politicians, political analysts, and voters. The leftist parties spoke of the danger of an "Americanization" of Italian political customs. Other commentators were, on the contrary, happy with the end of dull television campaigning; they welcomed the birth of modern political communication.

The 1980 administrative campaign provided an interesting opportunity for a closer observation of the new trends. The local nature of these electoral contests, in contrast to national elections, allowed for viewing the private stations' impact more directly. In these elections, there is a heavier concentration on local issues, interests, and candidates. The private television stations satisfy the demands of such local election campaigns better than other media.

Study Design and Findings
The role played by local TV stations during the 1980 campaign, the extent of their involvement in the game, and the implications of the resort to local media are the aspects that this pilot study analyzed. Our hypothesis foresaw an intensification of the use of private broadcasting resources as primary channels of electoral propaganda, and the improvement of the presentation strategies of candidates' messages.

Given the large number of small stations spread around the country, and the difficulty of obtaining reliable data directly from a large sample of station managers, we preferred the method of a pilot study that offered the possibility of an immediate cross-control of the information gathered from a small but significant sample of local TV stations. The cross-control was carried out as follows. The managers were interviewed in the first week of the campaign about their stations' initiatives, types of broadcasts, types of contracts with political candidates, daily amount of political broadcasting, and budgets. This information was checked again in the last week. Reliability was further assessed by direct viewing of election programs, and by interviewing the advertising companies that were intermediaries between candidates and stations.

The metropolitan area of Milan (with a population of about 3,500,000) was chosen as the test area for the study. Its social and political characteristics are fairly representative of the mostly urban milieu in which the private TV enterprise was born and developed, and where "electoral television" has the best opportunities for fulfillment.

Nine stations (out of a total of 14 in the area) were included: five commercial stations with the highest audience indexes:

ANTENNA NORD
CANALE 5
CANALE 51
TAM
ANTENNA 3

There were two with medium audience indexes that had distinguished themselves in the 1979 campaign by the number of election broadcasts:

TELENORD
TL 1-2

Finally, there were two stations clearly bound to ideological groups:

TRM 2
TELENOVA

All these stations (with the exception of TELENOVA) had also broadcast some campaign messages in the national and European elections of 1979.

Access Criteria
On the whole, the commercial stations did not discriminate against political parties. Only the communist TRM 2 excluded neo-fascist communication from its broadcasts. The commercial ANTENNA NORD, owned by a moderate-right publisher, vetoed the participation of "extremist parties." Interestingly TL 1-2 had forbidden access to both the communist and the neo-facist parties in 1979 but gave them airtime in 1980. The majority of stations appeared fairly independent, thanks to their prevailing commercial philosophy.

Actually, despite the large access opportunities, not all the parties were able to exploit the air time put at their disposal by the stations, the smaller parties in particular could not afford it.

In brief, certain parties and candidates were advantaged by the money shortage of other parties, or by the sometimes declared preference of certain station managers for some candidates. In fact, the Socialist Party turned out to be the most favored party (in frequency of broadcasts) by TL 1-2, ANTENNA 3, ANTENNA NORD, TAM, and TELENORD; the Christian Democratic Party by TELENOVA and CANALE 51; and the government coalition by CANALE 5.

Types of Campaign Broadcasts
Three communication strategies were followed by political candidates and by the stations.

1. A *notoriety-confirming* strategy was implemented by incumbents already well known in the Milan area, who were running for re-election. This strategy was carried out by means of TV *spots* produced by advertising firms, and broadcast repeatedly by the stations as normal commercial ads. The spots turned out to be the most used type of political communication in the 1980 campaign. The candidates resorted to them more than the parties.

2. An *image* strategy was implemented by local candidates who were little known to the voters and were seeking office for the first time. These candidates attempted to build their personal and political image by means of TV

shorts (3 to 10 minutes long) in which they either appeared alone, exalting their attributes and credits; appeared with their families in their living rooms; appeared in an interview format with pseudo-journalists; or appeared in a group with other candidates of their party, presented by well known party leaders. The content of these shorts was candidate-oriented; there was a strong emphasis on personal traits and style. The shorts were inserted as programs in the daily timetable of TV programming, usually before popular serials or movies.

Another part of the image strategy was the paid participation of candidates in popular entertainment programs, like quizzes or cabarets. Limited to one station, this might become a common feature in future campaigns.

3. A *confrontation* strategy. This was implemented by the stations themselves. Political candidates or party leaders were invited to participate in debates and phone-ins moderated by nonpartisan people. Participation in these broadcasts was free and open to almost all parties. The few refusals usually came from certain parties that did not want to appear on the screen with their traditional enemies.

The length of these *telecasts* was from 10 to 60 minutes, and they were an almost daily feature of all stations. Compared to the spots and shorts, the content of the telecasts was more issue-oriented and stressed the role of the party rather than candidates.

One might expect an "information" strategy through newscasts and reports on the campaign. Strangely enough, we did not find much interest by the stations in campaign news. The reason was that only three stations have their own news departments. Some just broadcast the news of local newspapers. Other stations broadcast no news. During the 1980 campaign, one station (TELENORD) produced a pseudo-evening news program in which a speaker read campaign news packaged and furnished by the parties.

Intensity of Campaign TV Broadcasting

The rate of election TV broadcasting was quite significant (see Table 1). TELENORD reserved 21% of its total daily broadcasting time for campaign spots, shorts, and telecasts; TL 1-2 and TRM 2 were second with 11%; and CANALE 5 designated 1 hour of its 14-hour broadcasting time. The daily average per station was about 50 minutes, an increase of some 40% over 1979.[2]

Of great interest for our intensification hypothesis are the figures on the number of spots broadcast, although a comparison with 1979 is impossible because of lack of data for that year.

According to the stations' managers there was an upward trend. In 1980, the commercial stations that broadcast more spots in the month-long campaign were CANALE 51 (about 200), TELENORD (100), and CANALE 5 and ANTENNA NORD (80).

---

[2] Based on data in the Progress Report of the quoted IIC survey.

Table 1. Daily Average of Campaign Broadcasting Times

Stations	Daily Broadcasting (minutes)	Campaign Broadcasting (minutes)	%
ANTENNA NORD	720	14	2
CANALE 5	840	60	7
CANALE 51	900	40	4.4
TAM	720	53	7.3
ANTENNA 3	720	30	4
TELENORD	720	150	21
TL 1-2	540	60	11
TELENOVA	600	8	1.3
TRM 2	420	45	11

Note: The figures are comprehensive for the 30 to 60-minute spots.

A significant exception was TRM 2 (communist). It did not accept paid political ads, since its managers were critical of what they considered a negative innovation in election campaigns.

Financial Aspects

The figures regarding the financial aspects are a bit complicated because of the several formulas and combinations used by the various stations and because of some understatement by the managers. The answer to the question, "What are the rates for political spots and shorts?" was usually, "The same as for commercial ads." Such information was misleading, for we found that the official rates underwent variations because of two factors: the audience index of each station, and the special treatment for campaign propaganda.

As far as the first factor is concerned, the rates varied greatly: from 150 dollars for a 30-minute spot on TELENOVA, to 450 dollars on CANALE 51. Moreover, stations had different rates depending on the hour of broadcasting: higher rates during prime time, lower rates earlier or later in the evening.

The second fluctuating factor in prices (and budgets) was frequent discounting: often, a candidate was charged 250 instead of 300 dollars. TAM, CANALE 51, ANTENNA NORD, and TELENORD "helped a few friendly candidates" through big discounts and even by offering free advertising spaces.

Even if this is limited to four stations, it is a salient feature of the peculiarity of Italian "electoral television." The relations between private TV stations and political clients are, of course, fairly business-like; however a large part is left to "informal negotiations" according to the best good-neighbor tradition between the entrepreneurial world and the political establishment.

The data in table 2 only partially indicate the budget story. For instance, CANALE 51 had the biggest budget, but was also the commercial station

Table 2. Amounts Private TV Stations Collected for Political Broadcasts (thousands of US dollars)

CANALE 51	100	(36.5%)
TELENORD	50	(18.3%)
ANTENNA NORD	42	(15.3%)
TL 1-2	30	(11.0%)
CANALE 5	22	(8.0%)
ANTENNA 3	15	(5.5%)
TELENOVA	7.8	(2.9%)
TAM	7	(2.5%)
Total	273.8	(100.0%)

Note: The figures are estimates.

allowing the largest discounts. Moreover, according to its managers, the 1980 budget was 50% smaller than that of the 1979 campaigns; TL 1-2 also announced a 20% decrease from 1979.

Despite these facts, and keeping in mind that, since 1979, the rates have risen 20 to 30%, it is reasonable to assume that the 64 TV stations of the entire Lombardy region managed a budget very close to one-half million dollars; this is equivalent to one-eighth of the total 4 million dollars of TV campaign advertising spent for the entire country in 1980.

DISCUSSION

The analysis of private TV stations' involvement in the 1980 local elections supports the hypothesis of a gradual change in Italy's election campaigns toward a morphology of imported and national features fairly well.

The study has found three partial indicators of this process: the *intensification* of the use of local TV stations, and the *spectacularization* and the *personalization* of political communication. These are "partial" indicators because, according to the existing empirical evidence, the three phenomena are still in an initial phase, compared to the sophisticated developments in other countries.

1. *Intensification.* The 1980 campaign showed a decrease of campaign broadcasting compared to that of 1979 for only three of nine stations; those worried about the risk of losing audience if too much politics was broadcast. Marketing research has demonstrated that people turn to private stations mostly to satisfy entertainment needs. Nevertheless, the majority of stations increased political air time (some started to broadcast campaign materials in 1980), and political candidates resorted massively to the stations, exploiting the free and paid facilities put at their disposal.

The general data, therefore, confirm the trend toward an increase in the political use of private television.

2. The *spectacularization* of political communication is structurally bound to the specificity of television language. Spectacularization refers to the same idea as "image campaign," where media attention is focused on the "spectacular" aspects of the electoral race and of candidates' actions.

The election programs broadcasted by private TV stations were distinguished by immediacy, liveliness, attention to image, and by imagination, compared to the stiff and boring programs aired by RAI. Even though a few stations repeated the traditional scheme of the RAI, "Political Tribunes," we noted in general a search for new formulas, at times very unusual ones, of election communication.

A moderate spectacularization of Italian campaigns is not necessarily as negative a phenomenon, as some commentators hold. The RAI survey pointed out the audience's lack of interest in TV political programs. The wide process of estrangement of voters from party politics under way in Italy, as well as in other countries, certainly accounts for the indifference. However, a part of the responsibility rests on the Italian politicians' incapacity for making more interesting—and thus more digestible—the contents and the issues of the political debate. Private television offers an opportunity for the politicians to win back at least the attention of their potential supporters.

3. The *personalization* in television campaign propaganda was remarkable. This phenomenon is attributable, as noted above, to the local nature of the administrative election. In the past it brought an emphasis on personal attributes and style in the traditional media: posters, leaflets, and the like. Now, such transformation can be observed on television. Because of its peculiar nature, this medium is becoming the crucial factor for the increase in the degree of personalization in local and national election campaigns. One can even find evidence in public television itself. It has contributed to the diffusion of some star-system values and methods on the national political stage.

Such built-in power has practically doubled because of private TV broadcasting, which, in the present period of easy access, is an effective springboard for obscure candidates looking for publicity and supporters.

Personalization also means the increasing independence of the single candidates from their parties. Similarly to what happened in the U.S. (Nie, Verba, & Petrocik, 1976, p. 346), there has been a decline in the role of the party and of its organization. In the 1980 campaign, candidates conducted their *personal* campaign, directly resorted to the media's services, and personally contacted voters. All this, in a country where parties control almost everything, was something unforeseeable until 1979.

Can we say at this point that the private TV station plays an important role in Italy's election campaigns? A duly cautious look at the empirical evidence gathered in our study evokes a positive answer. In particular, the critical place that the preferential ballot has in the Italian electoral system can help to make private television a new, decisive arm of the traditional campaign weaponry.[3]

It may be of interest to underline the wide success of the Socialist Party and of its leading candidate (Mayor of Milan) in the mayoral contest: both of them "stole the show" with heavy advertising on all private TV stations. We do not have enough evidence to explain their success, based only in terms of TV propaganda. Many other factors are involved. But, certainly, a reasonable hypothesis is that the use of private television significantly influenced the results.

However, the over-all picture is incomplete, for it does not take into account the effect that the present process of concentration of stations may have on media-political relations.

As observed earlier, the 500 stations, following the golden period of enthusiastic pioneering, are now suffering financial difficulties. Many of them; especially the smallest ones, are about to close. The stations tied to big industrial and publishing companies, that is, those with strong political connections, are finding larger audience and advertising budgets by strengthening their operations, absorbing small stations, and creating nationwide networks. The private television landscape is rapidly changing. By 1980, only 40 stations held 90% of the total advertising investment! Observers predict that, in a few years, out of the 500 stations only a limited number will remain.

This trend will have repercussions on televised political advertising. The existence of private TV oligopolies will mean higher advertising rates. The first immediate effect will be to increase the cost of access to broadcasting for political candidates.

The following are a series of general implications of the above analysis.

To begin with, political life is increasingly dependent on the rhythms and technical requirements of television. For example, the Council of Ministers' meetings usually end in time for the late night newscasts. Party conventions and campaign events are strongly influenced by the presence of TV cameras.

Moreover, both the success and the failures of parties and candidates are moderately tied to the effective use of television.

---

[3] Italy's electoral system is based on the proportional distribution of vote. Political parties, at the beginning of the campaign, present a list of their candidates (8 to 40 names). The leading names in the list are of those candidates that the party wants to be elected to office. The remaining candidates have less chance to be elected, unless they engage in well-organized personal propaganda and succeed in making their names familiar to voters. Voters, when casting their ballots, after marking the party's symbol can write in up to 4 candidates' names, thus changing the final results, often in contrast to the party's indications.

Future electoral competitions will be increasingly based on what has been called "electronic campaigning."

In Italy, as has happened elsewhere, we see the signs of a gradual transformation of traditional campaign customs.

One worrisome trend is the impoverishment of the "policy issues" in favor of excessive attention to the "campaign issues," (Patterson, 1980), in other words, to an "image campaign."

However, the riskiest development is that "electoral television," as carried by private stations, may start a process of forced arrangement of the Italian political system.

If it is true that television is destined to become a crucial instrument in election campaigns, if it is true that private TV stations are turning into additional gatherers of the consensus of larger voters' quotas, it is also true that the use of television is increasingly costly.

Moreover, the massive resort to private TV broadcasting observed in 1979 and in 1980 shows that political candidates are not content with the *hours* of free air time that the public television service grants to them.

The expenses for paid propaganda on private TV and radio stations are becoming an important item of the parties' and candidates' budgets.

If the Parliament does not regulate the matter, the present system of a wild market will favor only the strongest parties and the richest candidates, with the effect of bringing about substantial changes in the power balances between political forces and a margination of the smallest and weakest ones.

The political arena might even appear in future less crowded with hardly imaginable consequences for Italian democracy.

REFERENCES

Mazzoleni, G., and Boneschi, M. (1980). "Televisioni Private ed Elezioni." *Problemi dell 'Informazione 5*, 397–430.

McGinniss, J. (1969). *The Selling of the president, 1968*. New York: Trident Press.

Nie, N.H., Verba, S., and Petrocik, J.R. (1976). *The Changing American Voter*. Cambridge, MA: Harvard University Press.

Nimmo, D. (1970). *The Political Persuaders*. Englewood Cliffs, NJ: Prentice-Hall.

Patterson, T.E. (1980). "The Role of the Mass Media in Presidential Campaigns: The Lessons of the 1976 Election." *Items 24* (No. 2), 27–28.

Patterson, T.E., and McClure, R.D. (1976). *The Unseeing Eye*. New York: G.P. Putnam's Sons.

"Ricerca sul palinsesto radiotelevisivo e sul-l'offerta culturale, informativa, di svago o di partecipazione in periodo preelettorale. (1980). Rome: Segreteria del CDA, RAI.

Santoro Libri, M.A. (1980). "Il Pubblico e le Tribune." *Tribune e Accesso 5* (No. 66), 17.

Schwartzenberg, R.-G. (1977). *L'etat spectacle*. Paris: Flammarion.

Le televisioni private in Italia. (1981). Rome: FNS-RAI.

Wyckoff, G. (1968). *The Image Candidates*. New York: Macmillan.

Chapter 6
Journalism Versus Public Relations: Determination of Latent Interaction Through Analysis of Patterns of Influence

BARBARA BAERNS
Sektion für Publizistik und Kommunikation
Ruhr-Universität Bochum
Bochum, Federal Republic of Germany

THE PROBLEM

Investigations of the treatment of reality by the news media, mainly comparisons between events as presented by the media and what "in fact" happened, are criticized as unjustifiable in their premises and impossible: "Objective" reality—theoretically conceivable in its complex entirety, but in practical terms only selectively perceivable and thus objectively impossible to reconstruct—is always a question of ideological approach or Weltanschauung (Schulz, 1976, pp. 25-34). Proceeding from this, a newer theoretical approach involves deducing journalistic criteria of selection and interpretation of reality from the elements of the image of reality that mass media present. Because journalistic hypotheses, irrespective of their relationship to the "real" event or process, are perceived as guaranteed statements of fact by the recipient, they are equivalent to reality in their effects. It is these effects that matter in research. The criteria that news media employ defining reality are assessed empirically, isolating selected characteristics, news factors,[1] in news items of high or low news value.[2] Here, several German authors follow the internationally discussed attempts further to develop a typology of news bias.

Within the context of criticism concerning the value of content analysis, it has to be questioned whether the restriction of research to characteristics

---

Based on a paper presented at the International Association for Mass Communication Research Conference, Paris, 1982.

[1] The following were considered to constitute news factors: duration, thematic treatment, geographical proximity, political proximity, cultural proximity, relevance, regional centrality, national centrality, personal influence, prominence/status, unexpectedness, structure, conflict, crime, damage, success, reference to persons, ethnocentricity.

[2] The degree of prominence, i.e., the placing and the length of an item, characterizes news value.

of media content is an adequate precondition for either well-founded propositions concerning typical rules of "journalistic" selection or insights into the effects upon the recipient. It is on this basis that Rosengren, whose work has prompted such theoretical considerations, suggested that, through taking extra media data into consideration and comparing these with intra media data taken from media content, it was possible to go beyond describing and classifying content and to create possibilities of comparison with perceptions of reality independent of the media. Rosengren selected the following indicators, geographical distance, population size, as well as import and export statistics, as reference points for his politico-economic interpretation of foreign news coverage (Rosengren, 1971, 1974, 1975, 1980; Rosengren & Rikardsson, 1974).

The consideration of "public relations" as a possibly determining factor might enable us to find a way out of the theoretical dead-end without recourse to fruitless approaches involving nothing more than a traditional media-centered orientation. The simple question of whether that which purports to be "journalistic" news is in fact "public relations" indicates an approach transcending media content.

Following the paradigm that media content can be described as "results of a whole series of selections" (Lippmann, 1922, p. 354; in the same sense, Luhmann, 1975, p. 21), it should prove fruitful to analyze just this process of selection and distribution in order to determine its structure. In this context, I am not concerned with the actual content of news and its controversial relationship to "objective" reality—nor with stereotypes implying prejudice, but with the sequel of production, which could also be stereotyped. Thus, the question of which elements *characterize* news is replaced by the question of how information enters news agency services, radio, and television programs, as well as newspapers, and thereby *becomes* news. This approach is all the more sensible in view of the fact that, in the field of journalism, misunderstandings and misinterpretations occur all too easily, because one is dealing, not with a static phenomenon, but with a dynamic process which Tuchman (1973, p. 110) called "routinizing the unexpected" and which, continuously and without stronger frictions, is experienced and exercised by journalists as their every-day work. "Public relations" in its context, must first be noticed, and then its effects must be determined.

Several studies examining the internal structure of media institutions, and thus revealing the conditions of production in large scale media enterprises, in which division of labor, specialization, technology, and economics not only govern the purely technical aspects of production but also their intellectual aspects, contain important insights. Furthermore, a number of studies of the flow of news, following the classical gatekeeping approach and its developments, have observed in passing that restriction of space and schedules govern the content of media coverage as well. Judged as a whole, however, there are shortcomings. "In terms of a time-oriented approach, for instance, there is little known about public coverage of an event from the moment of occurrence of the event itself, or from the moment of initiation of a piece of information via possible intermediary stages, to potential processing into the mass media as news. In terms of the process of editing, for instance, the activities in the phases of information gathering and/or recording as a pre-condition for its distribution and dissemination are in the main opaque" (Baerns, 1979, p. 309). It is these procedures, however, that convert reality into media reality. My special interest in this field focuses on interactions of "public relations" and "journalism" in the selective opening up of reality. At the same time, my reflections upon problems concerning the origin of *public* media coverage, and upon how *public* information is supplied and disseminated, allow a reexamination of fundamental questions indicated by the classic model of "Publizistikwissenschaft."[3] (see also Ronneberger, 1978 b, p. 16.)

A study of latent relations, which have hitherto escaped attention, requires a reasonable framework for the purpose of delineation. For this reason, the examination assumes two syntactically similar,[4] semantically nonequivalent systems of information that are less partners (Wagner, 1974) than competitors. Public relations, first, may be described as "self-perception and presentation of one's own particular interests via information, whereby the instruments used may include all techniques and forms of written, oral, photographic, film, and audiovisual public messages and interpersonal communication" (Baerns, 1981 b, p. 262).[5] Second, journalism may be considered as a function of the general interest. Journalists, working for both primary and secondary media (news agencies, daily newspapers, radio, and television), in contrast to "political parties and interest groups, for instance, but also State leadership, which have to work for the achievement of particular objectives which derive from their programs and ideologies," are required to "collect and publish differing and controversial views," to "compare the aims and demands of the political and public authorities,

---

[3] "Publizistikwissenschaft" in Germany has mainly dealt with media messages and the public. There was little interest in interpersonal relations and "communication."

[4] Rühl, in proceeding from one system and its relationships with the relevant environment, will no longer be able to differentiate between public relations and journalism at a functional level. He chooses this approach in order to avoid the danger of ontologizing he otherwise fears (cf. Rühl, 1980, p. 173f). My own approach is not concerned with "ontical" differences between the two. Two systems are assumed, and both treated as starting points, in order to deduce and determine the relationships between their respective activities. At a higher level of abstraction, they can, of course, be integrated into a single system again, one that is albeit a more accurate representation of what, in fact, happens.

[5] Public relations is not confined to briefing the media. This activity, however, which is of prime concern in the context of the present study, is particularly important in terms of the amount of time devoted and the value attached to it (Wilke & Müller, 1979, p. 129; also Deutsches Institut für Public Relations, 1973, pp. 9–11).

question them on the basis of new conditions and point to the necessity of adapting accordingly." They are, furthermore, required to "observe and critically portray the way in which organizations make decisions" and "thereby give the members of such organizations the opportunity of checking their own positions, of getting to know other points of view and of orientation" (Ronneberger, 1978 a, p. 161).

In the formal language of systems theory, journalism may be considered to be a sub-system of the media system. Public relations, on the other hand, may be considered as a sub-system of any other system outside the media system. Their activities, however, and herein lies the similarity, are both directed towards the media system and make their impact accordingly. Their purpose is the presentation of reality via selection, i.e., information.

The differentiation presented above fits in well with the way in which the respective professional groups perceive their own roles. This is reflected in professional codes of conduct. The German Public Relations Association, founded in 1958, binds its members to the following norm: "to keep clear of all attempts at improper influence directed towards the public and to respect the freedom and independence of the Press" (Deutsche Public-Relations Gesellschaft, 1964).[6] On the other hand, the Press Codex adopted and published in 1973 by the German Press Council in association with the press associations' appeals to the journalists to pursue their duty of serving the public without regard to personal advantage, the private and commercial interests of third parties, and other extraneous motives (Deutscher Presserat, 1976). Hence, an attempt to outline the interdependencies between public relations and journalism involves taking the content of ethical codes of conduct into account.

Following the assumptions of the American political scientist, Dahl, on which he bases his empirical findings with respect to the distribution of power in the social system as a whole, interactions between public relations and journalism will be described in terms of influence (Dahl, 1957, pp. 202–203, 1968, p. 407, 1976, p. 29). The term "influence" is used here to denote a connection between actors in which one actor can get the other to behave in some way he would not otherwise. Applied to the relationships in this study, one could, on the one hand, say that public relations activities have exerted influence successfully if the result with respect to media coverage would otherwise have been different. On the other hand, journalism has successfully exerted influence if the result would have been different without its own investigative activity (search for information). Assuming the absence of other factors, mutual dependency may be postulated as: the more influence public relations activities exert, the less this is so of journalism, and vice versa. Dahl's suggestion of seeing influence in terms of the

---

[6] A similar expression of intent is also to be found in the internationally recognized Code of Athens, paragraph 11 (text reproduced in Baerns, 1981b: 270–272).

probability of particular decisions can be operationalized by looking for the sources of news coverage.

This approach seems to be particularly fruitful for two reasons; first, it is possible to specify the object of study without paying attention to what is called the advertising or indoctrinating character of public relations information. Second, the concept of *relative* influences is appropriate in that a decision for an item of information is always one against another in the media and their products, limited in time and space as they are. "In view of the sheer amount of news that could be published, every item which is actually published will take the space for another item away....The truth as presented by the Press can in its very nature and techniques be nothing more than 'truth to measure'" (Steffens, 1971, pp. 22-23).

Media performance, thus apparently limited and, in terms of production techniques, depending on investments in time, resources, and coordination via organization, may be discussed at three different levels: At the level of the individual medium (e.g., the daily newspaper, "Neue Ruhr Zeitung"; the news agency, dpa; the television program, "Hier und Heute"; the radio program, "Forum West"), at the level of a media type—as defined by certain characteristics (e.g., primary and secondary media, print and broadcast media, privately and publicly owned media), and at the level of the media system (e.g., North-Rhine Westphalia) as a whole.

Up to this point, the chronology of the processes to be analysed may follow the schemes suggested by gatekeeping and diffusion research,[7] the least prejudicial of incompatible models treating the emergence, transmission, and dissemination of an item as a process of selection and mediation over a chain of successive selection systems connected by channels. The systems of selection reduce reality: "spectrum of occurrences" (Reimann, 1968, p. 168), "objects of orientation" (Westley & MacLean, 1957), "interests" (Ronneberger, 1973); via binary choice (selection). The selections present themselves for further selections via transmission channels (mediation). Nevertheless, such presentations are strangely imprecise in interpreting some analogous concept of active "search for information," if the communication paradigm does not account for shortcomings. Although not elaborated sufficiently in the available process diagrams, the underlying explanatory design is principally in a position to translate the problem of differentiation, since it could assume an endless expansion of the bounds within which information is obtained (Deutsch, 1966, pp. 128-142).

I believe that we can improve our understanding by reducing complexity in raising the single question of the indeterminacy of choice and how it is

---

[7] "Gatekeeping" is the term employed for the process of selection on the part of the communicator (cf., for the current state of research: Arbeitsgemeinschaft für Kommunikationsforschung, 1977.) "Diffusion" research is concerned with the sequence in which information is distributed, ideas are adopted and methods are emulated among individuals, in groups or in organizations (cf., for state of research: Schenk, 1977, 1978).

related to the concrete sociohistorical context. The decision to combine a sociotechnical approach of selection and mediation models with historical hermeneutical orientations as cognitive elements of a systematic historical matrix opens the way for a renewed discussion of the central theoretic concept of "the public," from the perspective of the central question of freedom of choice under a hitherto neglected aspect—"availability of information" (Lerg, 1977, p. 19) and "free access to the place of the event" (Clausse, 1962, p. 13). Hence, the concepts of influence, selection, and performance need no longer be treated in a "formal syntactic way," but should become more concrete in their "social semantic context" (Rühl, 1980, p. 173).

This approach would be misunderstood if it were insinuated that it tries to adopt a "complete, particular, or any concept of order" which restricts the perspective from the very start (Saxer, 1978, p. 73). In order to expand material understanding such an approach, is not only open to assets and liabilities but also to deficits and interpretative latitude in the reflection on norms. It is its purpose as an analytical tool to lead them to the category framework.

METHODS

Consequently, a structuralizing principle emerges which embraces the concept of public performance and perception, literally differentiating between public events accessible to everyone and nonpublic events,[8] to which access is restricted. Between these extremes, an indeterminate area of potential public participation or lack of such is considered, which at the same time constitutes an arena within which both public relations and journalism operate under equal conditions. The effects of the two acting together, among others, objectify themselves as published by the media. Regarding media content as a "patterned distribution" or a "patterned relationship between events" (Deutsch, 1966, pp. 82, 146), dominant configurations will be subject to analysis as soon as the sources are under control.

---

[8] The concept of recourse to public access as an option is expanded at length elsewhere (Baerns, 1981a, pp. 17-31). In this context here, it is sufficient to note that the activities carried out on behalf of various political, economic, and individual interests described as public relations are largely identical in terms of organization and the activities they embrace. However, differences can be ascertained when the question of the extent to which journalists enjoy a right of access to information as a conceivable corrective to self-presentation is put. This is because the current Federal Republic's information order ensures that the mainly political public sector —and not the private sector, which predominantly comprises economic and individual interests —is open to investigative journalism. One may thus assume that differing performance in news coverage is intentional. The demand for an extension of the journalist's right to information does not figure as a possible variable. This is perhaps due to the fact that journalists are able to assert themselves in other ways. It is also conceivable that they make little use of the right to information. A further possible explanation is the assumption that public relations activity neutralizes the necessity for investigation at the very outset by voluntarily providing information.

North-Rhine Westphalian political affairs as a system, a deliberate choice, recommends itself as an extensive but, at the same time, manageable "natural" unit; its media infrastructure should facilitate the falsification of the central hypothesis.[9]

The study embraces the daily mass media, news agencies, the regular state press conferences and press information offices as institutions of selection, mediation, dissemination, and multiplication. Because the chosen subject area of political affairs is one in which journalists enjoy an indisputable right of access, one may legitimately assume that public relations activities will not overinfluence the news activities of the primary and secondary media in this particular sphere. On the other hand, public relations will dominate news if journalists neglect independent inquiry and investigation. Over and above this, there is also a network of varied noninstitutionalized and irregular relationships to consider, which result in the information exchange properly called communication. The effect of this should be a further contribution on the part of journalists to the news material disseminated by the agencies and mass media.

The study is devoted exclusively to daily information. It was designed to include all relevant news agencies and the daily news media. In order to ensure that the performance of the publicly and privately organized mass media could be compared, the local pages of the dailies examined were ex-

---

[9] Indicators of media performance, which could be employed to analyze actual performance in a consistent and systematic manner, cannot be extrapolated from the constitution of the Federal Republic of Germany. Because it guarantees freedom of opinion and expression and freedom of the media, normative prescriptions concerning the nature of content are out of the question. Instead, proceeding from the assumption that, on the contrary, the precondition for an independent formation of opinion is the variety of views expressed deriving from differing perspectives and convictions, it also refers judgements on questions of purpose and value to the market of controversy. Free competition, independent of central state control and interference, is regarded as a basic precondition, if an optimal structure is to be ensured (*Bundesverfassungsgericht,* Federal Constitutional Court, 1962, pp. 262-263, 1972, p. 325). The Federal Constitutional Court gives priority to the maintenance of competition between the print media, which "operate according to the principles of free enterprise and in the private sector," which "compete intellectually and economically," and "in which public authority must not intervene under any circumstances" (*Bundesverfassungsgericht,* 1967, pp. 162-163), and to a decentralized system of electronic media in the hands of public broadcasting authorities obliged to ensure that the diversity of standpoints is reflected in their respective program schedules. It makes the guarantee of the *structural* preconditions conditional upon the fulfilment of the task of public opinion formation it expects (*Bundesverfassungsgericht,* 1962, p. 263, 1972, p. 326). The different way in which the press and broadcasting sectors are organized also leads to competition between these sectors, a further element characterizing the way in which the system functions. The mass media system of the Federal Republic of Germany is thus conceived and organized as a well balanced, self-regulating and controlling system which, precisely because of the different constitution of its various elements, aims at a total picture, total value, and total performance, which individual units cannot achieve but which crystallize only through the total activity (colligative properties, using the terminology of systems theory) of its elements (Baerns, 1981a, pp. 32-36).

cluded from the analysis. The analysis of relevant coverage in radio and television is not restricted to daily news programs, but also includes scheduled current affairs programs covering day-to-day affairs. The term "information" is used with respect to written or spoken text, and not to other auditory or visual components (music, sound effects, etc.) which are typical of radio and television and are of little relevance for the study.

With the help of a practically comprehensive survey encompassing the comparable, daily and thematically specific[10] output of the individual agencies,[11] daily newspapers,[12] and radio[13] and television[14] programs, the study attempts, at a microlevel, to assess the daily amount and impact of standardized sources made available, particularly by public relations activities, as well as the characteristics of reproduction. Through aggregation and overall analysis of the findings relating to individual media and media types, conclusions may also be drawn at the macro-level concerning the additive performance of the system and the characteristics specific to the system as a whole.

Because the study compares editorial items[15] with the potential source[16] material available, a continuous time sample is necessary. The decision

---

[10] The term "State (or North-Rhine Westphalian) political affairs" is used in this study to denote all source material and items containing information on legislative and executive organs and their activities at the state level in North-Rhine Westphalia, also in connection with organized and single constituent elements of the political system such as public services, parties, interest groups and associations, business enterprises, civic action groups, and single citizens classified in terms of public access and/or in terms of journalists' right to acquire informations or not.

[11] lnw, (dpa), ddp, ap.

[12] Twenty-seven editorial units in North-Rhine Westphalia.

[13] The regional radio program "Echo West" (WDR I), "Zwischen Rhein und Weser" and "Nachrichten aus NRW" (WDR II), "Forum West" (WDR III), as well as news broadcasts covering federal and international affairs: 5.00 p.m. (WDR II), 7.00 p.m. (WDR I, WDR II), and 8.00 p.m. (including a commentary) (WDR III).

[14] The regional television programmes, "Hier und Heute" (first service), "journal 3", "Letzte Nachrichten" (third service), as well as the national news programmes, "Tagesschau": 5.50 p.m.; "Tagesschau", 8.00 p.m.; "Tagesthemen" (first service); "heute": 5.00 p.m. and "heute-journal" (second service).

[15] An "item," the term used to denote the "natural" unit editors working the various media employ in order to structure the material they present, is characterized by thematic unity and certain formal distinguishing features such as a headline, in the case of the print media and intermissions, introductions and the like in radio and television programs. In the case of the latter, introductions and concluding remarks between the items themselves was excluded when the material was coded.

[16] The term, "source," denotes the text supplied by sources of information, whether presented orally or in written form and in its entirety in terms of both content and its formal features. The information supplier, although the initiator of relevant source material, is not necessarily directly involved in the respective issue concerned as an actor. With respect to items disseminated by the media, the source which determines the headline and lead indicating the item's subject matter is regarded as the primary source. All further (second to fifth) sources used are regarded as secondary sources.

against a synthetic time sample is also justifiable in theoretical terms; the stochastic character of the object of study has to be tested, and not simply assumed. The choice of at least two comparable sample periods allows more insight into whether the results are representative or not. The sample periods of 4 weeks each (press: 2 weeks), separated by a period of 6 months, the first month of the second and fourth quarters of 1978 respectively, correspond well with the rhythm of parliamentary work. The year of study, moreover, the middle of the 5-year electoral period, ensures the absence of extraordinary conditions with respect to media coverage caused by elections. On the other hand, there was little in common between the topics of public discussion and/or those on the parliamentary agenda. Certain correspondents' and press officers' posts changed hands and considerable changes took place within the Executive.

PATTERNS OF INFLUENCE WITHIN THE MEDIA SYSTEM[17]

The data on the performance of the individual media—irrespective of their categorization as primary or secondary, print or broadcast, or public or private—reveal a consistently high proportion of items based on public relations source material. Approximately two out of every three items are, on the basis of their respective primary sources—and the subject matter which is thereby determined—the outcome of press releases and conferences, whereas the rest may be traced back to public events, journalistic investigation, or nonpublic events to which journalists were invited. Public relations as the primary source of information is almost uniformly distributed throughout news coverage. This applies to both periods of investigation (cf. Figure 1). Hence it may be concluded that the greater the number of items presented by any individual medium on State political affairs, the greater the number of press releases and conferences reproduced; the less the number of items, the less the number of press releases and conferences reproduced.

If these findings are interpreted against the background that the print and broadcast media are differently organized, misgivings as to the efficiency of both the private (print) and public (broadcast) media systems emerge. Seen in this light, there is no basis for the argument that, if measurement shows that organization under private law does not lead to the fulfilment of certain set objectives, "the logical consequence would be the consideration of new forms of organization, such as those applicable to broadcasting, as a means of accomplishing postulated aims" (Knoche, 1980, p. 134). At the same time, the results suggest that a further, albeit economic aspect, that of the costs involved in news investigation, is also worthy of consideration.

---

[17] Presented here are selected results of empirical studies financed by the German Research Association ("Deutsche Forschungsgemeinschaft") (Baerns, 1981a).

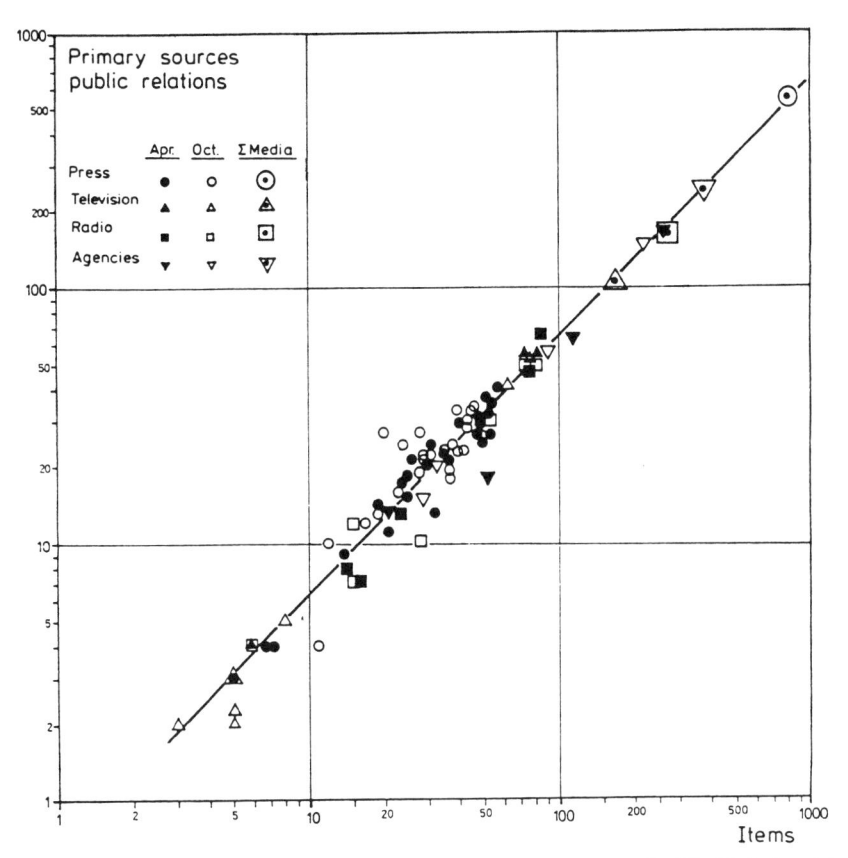

Figure 1. The Distribution of Standardized Primary Sources (Public Relations) in the North-Rhine Westphalian Media System

Apparently, the media, in disseminating as news that which they have obtained in the form of free information, pass on a large proportion of such costs to the public relations sector.

While the results do not indicate that media play no role at all, investigative journalism only accounted for a negligible proportion of items (slightly less so in October than in April: in the case of news agencies, around 8%, the secondary media, approximately 11%). Furthermore, follow-up and supplementary investigation in journalism was in itself not very pronounced (in the cases of the news agencies, 18%; daily newspapers, 21%; radio, 17%; and television, 13%).

Dissemination via integration of different source material, frequently characterized as the media's central role, accounts only for a relatively small proportion of news coverage (only 16% of all agency items, 17% of all newspaper items, 15% of radio items, and 13% of television items rely upon more than one source). What could perhaps otherwise be interpreted as a coding effect in the case of news agencies because, apart from corrections, every text and text sequel has been accorded a separate reference number, in fact proved to be a characteristic of all news coverage irrespective of the medium involved (cf. Table 1).

On the other hand, if one looks beyond an exclusively source-oriented approach, it becomes apparent that the media do have a particularly significant role to play, principally in the form of rapid processing via selection and subediting (cf. Table 2). These findings could allow one to assume that this activity absorbs work capacity in such a way that journalism, as an autonomous system in the gathering of information, loses relevance in relation to self-presentation via public relations. Thus, diversity of information tends to be the result of differing criteria of selection and/or interpretation of the items supplied by the public relations sector, as well as media-specific processing of material in technical and dramaturgical terms.

Table 1. Structure of Media Items in Percentages (Total Period of Investigation)

	Primary Media	Secondary Media		
	Agencies	Press	Radio	Television
One source only	84	83	85	87
Two or more sources	16	17	15	13
Number of items	826	1,768	562	347

Table 2. The Formal Reproduction of Primary Standardized Sources (Public Relations) in Media Items in Percentages (Total Period of Investigation)

	Primary Media	Secondary Media		
	Agencies	Press	Radio	Television
Full text, word for word reproduction				
Shortened text		1		
Content in full	12	5	6	3
Shortened content	83	88	87	92
With reference to...	5	6	7	5
Number of standardized primary sources	491	1,132	340	218

$p < 0,001$.

Table 3. Explicit Reference to Standardized Sources (Public Relations) in Media Items (in Percentage Terms) (Total Period of Investigation)

	Primary Media	Secondary Media		
	Agencies	Press	Radio	Television
Reference	55	28	33	17
No reference	45	72	67	83
Number of standardized primary sources	491	1,132	340	218

$p < 0.001$.

Newspaper readers, radio listeners, and television viewers can hardly be aware of the enormity of dependence on standardized sources in daily news coverage—because omissions of explicit references to sources are not infrequent. Whereas news agencies name their sources in 55% of all relevant items disseminated, the proportions in the cases of radio, newspapers, and television are only 33, 28, and 17%, respectively (cf. Table 3). This omission is probably one reason why, thus far, even researchers have all too readily ascribed to journalism what is in fact a product of public relations activities.

PATTERNS OF INFLUENCE ON THE MEDIA SYSTEM AS A WHOLE

Systems analyses follow the assumption that, generally speaking, collective entities have two sets of properties: first, the properties of their elements and, second, those of a global and contextual kind which do not apply to the separate elements unified within a system (Hummell, 1972, p. 91). Expectations concerning the Federal Republic of Germany's media system involve such contextual properties, since they are based on the assumption that the combined activity of various media units and types results in a sum performance of new quality not attained by that of any single medium. In contrast, however, the evidence, which has demonstrated the close relationship between individual and collective media performance with respect to the influence of public relations, discounts any existence of such supplementary or compensatory properties in this case. The influence is homogeneous. Despite the fact that optimal conditions exist in North-Rhine Westphalia for free competition, the influence encompasses not only individual news agencies or the agencies as such, individual newspapers or the daily press as such, individual radio and television programs or broadcasting as such, but the entire system.

From a systems perspective, it was also apparent that, on the one hand, the supply of standardized source material was diminished by selction: of 159 press releases and conferences originated by the Legislature and Executive,[18] 134 were selected for use and processed. On the other hand, the supply was increased through the effect of multiplication; the 159 items of standardized source material resulted in a total of 1,189 items based thereon in 47 separate media.

Whereas, for instance, Nissen and Menningen (1977, pp. 160–161) focused their interest on the similarities and differences among single media units with respect to the processing of information in terms of reduction, the present study is primarily concerned with similarities and differences arising from an increase in supply via multiplication. Twenty-eight percent (in absolute terms: 38) of the source material provided by the Legislature and Executive are reproduced in one medium only. At the other end of the spectrum, 2% (3 items) were reproduced in one way or another in at least 40 media units. A large number of press releases and conferences were used minimally; a few releases and conferences were used extensively by the media (cf. Figure 2). Incidentally, the same relationship can be shown to exist in the case of source material deriving from journalistic investigations, insofar as these were made available, mainly via press agencies, to other newspapers and broadcast media.

The mechanism of multiplication also has a time dimension. Not all standardized source material is processed and disseminated with the same speed. News agencies, newspapers, radio, and television reproduced an average of 67% of the source material selected within the first day possible. A relatively small proportion took longer to reproduce, the number of items decreasing with time (cf. Figure 3). This same phenomenon also applies to comparable source material deriving from investigative journalism.

The multiplication and circulation processes presented are synchronous. Their *overall* effect is comparable to qualitative effects of the process of shortening, subediting, and placing of items by the editorial staff of an individual medium. And if the media system as a whole offered few obstacles to the influence of public relations, the system as such diminished or enhanced its influence through the profiling effected by the dimensions of time and channel availability.

---

[18] Because the respective dates of press conferences and press releases were known, reference points existed with respect to the dimension of time. Furthermore, in as far as the total volume of standardized sources offered was known, a condition that, because of the design of the survey, was fulfilled in the case of the sub-sample, Legislative and Executive sources, quantitative reference points existed outside the media system as well (cf. Appendix: Method and Procedure of Analysis). The observations made in this section of the paper refer to the time-spans covered by the study including the press. The data for the two separate periods are presented in amalgamated form.

CONCLUSIONS

The results of the present study do not falsify the central hypothesis that public relations determines the content disseminated by the news media. What is more, the findings support the assumption that the influence is relatively strong, contrary to the express understanding the professional groups concerned have of their role, to the scope provided for by legal norms and to societal expectations. The findings may be summarized as follows:

1. The public relations sector has the topics of news coverage under control. The disposition of information, the initiation of news, the pressing of certain topics, and, hence, the shaping of reality as presented by the news media, may thus, on the basis of empirical evidence, be attributed primarily to this sector and not to the autonomous activities of journalists. The findings suggest that those who do not make use of the instrument of public relations have little chance of access to media reality. In view of the fact that

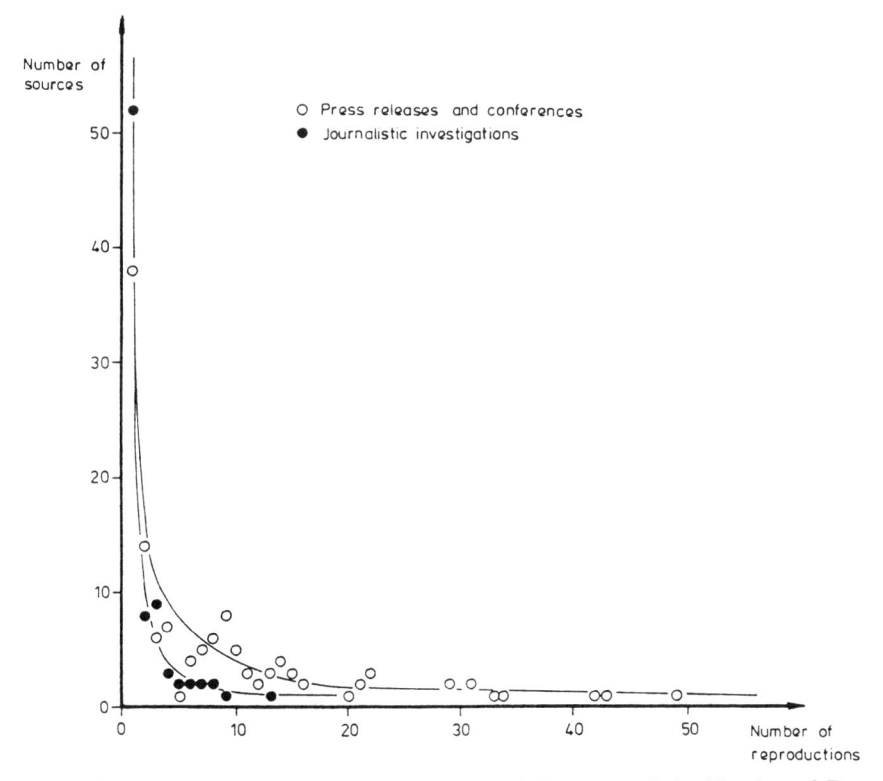

Figure 2. Relationships between the Number of Sources and the Number of Reproductions (Primary Sources: Press Releases and Conferences and Journalistic Investigations)

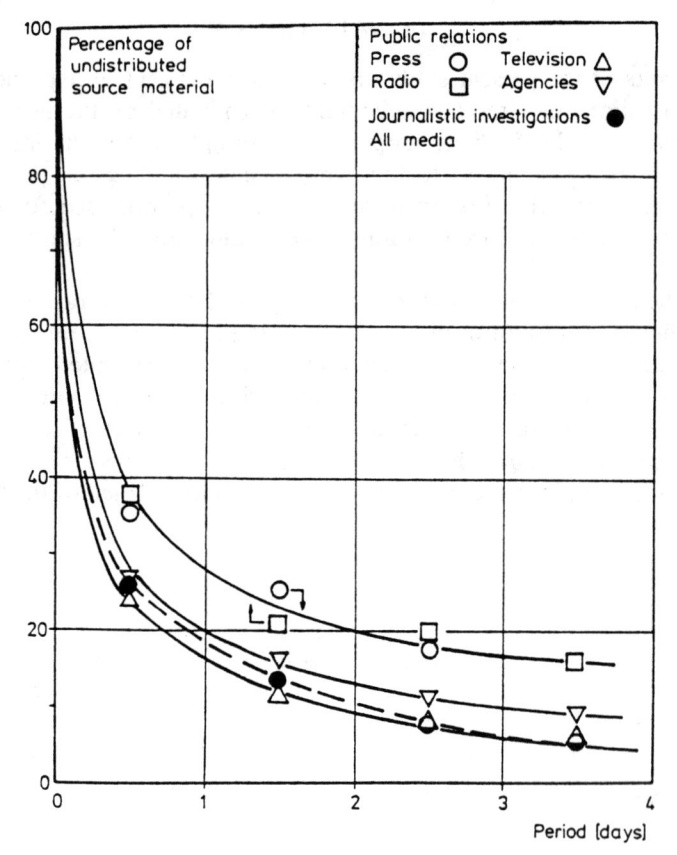

Figure 3. Time Taken to Redistribute Source Material (Primary Sources: Press Releases and Conferences and Journalistic Investigations)

most topics are predetermined, journalistic investigation is for the most part ex-post-investigation.

2. The public relations sector also has timing under control; for press releases and conferences directly induce news coverage. If the intrinsic value of certain themes and events or journalistic criteria determine news coverage, it remains to be explained why press releases and conferences do the same irrespective of the dimensions of subject matter and time. The fact that not all standardized sources available are processed is of little consequence in this connection. That the public relations sector is flexible enough to adapt itself to journalistic maxims, media constraints, and what is known of individual and variable preferences and emphases should not necessarily be discounted. Nevertheless, the sequence of interrelating steps observed already indicates, at least to a certain extent, "who plays the tune."

3. The "interdependent" relationships did not prove to be dynamic. Those who accept the nonvariable results of two periods of investigation

can describe the phenomena found to exist just as well, if not better, in terms of a vertical information gap than in terms of various communication models. There is little evidence of the "indispensible dynamic moment" the press supposedly embodies, and which is so important "for social progress" (Löffler, 1968, p. 77), to be derived from the observations concerning collaboration between public relations and journalism and its consequences. The findings, moreover, concern relationships in the public sphere of political affairs, one which is, per se, open to investigative journalism.

4. If the introductory question concerning the mutual dependence of public relations and journalism is raised once more, this time against the background of the evidence presented here, it could be asked whether there are links between the strong influence of the former, and the relatively small influence of the latter. Assuming that journalism *did* at one time generally —and not only in specific cases—match the role it is assigned, the findings here suggest that public relations activities are in a position to cripple investigative journalism and neutralize the predisposition to act in the public interest. Because information is tailored to the requirements of the media anyway, there is little or no "external" pressure to ensure that motivation is given the necessary backing in terms of competency and resources, and thereby translated into activity. Journalists can look for information, but the media are not necessarily dependent upon this. Since those who do not look do not come across obstacles, a lack of reflection on the question of applicable norms can thus also be explained.

On the other hand—thus returning to basic considerations—the more it is realized that "the system of mass communication (in its present form) is becoming more and more unsuited to the task of tackling growing deficits in information and of preserving the communicative interdependencies between the various social units without public relations" (Nahr, 1977, p. 47), the greater the flood of public relations information confronting the media every day. The journalistic notion that facts should guide thought and behavioral routines is of little help in the development of appropriate strategies to tackle the problems caused by public relations' ability to adapt. Furthermore, research, if it continues to devote itself to superficial phenomena, does not count in their solution. Journalism would continue to be replaced by public relations, and, whether projected or not, a revision of norms would continue to be anticipated: "Information is not the duty of demand but of supply" (Schmidt, 1979, p. 31).

REFERENCES

Arbeitsgemeinschaft für Kommunikationsforschung e.V. (AfK). (1977). Schlussbericht. Synopse Journalismus als Beruf. Erarbeitet für das Presse- und Informationsamt der Bundesregierung (Project Management: Hans-Jürgen Weiss), München.

Baerns, B. (1979). "Öffentlichkeitsarbeit als Determinante journalistischer Informationsleistungen. Thesen zur realistischeren Beschreibung von Medieninhalten." *Pulizistik 24,* 301-316.

Baerns, B. (1981 a). "Öffentlichkeitsarbeit und Journalismus. Zur Notation und Interpunktion latenter Beziehungen. Ein Versuch empirisch-analytischer Annäherung durch Ermittlung von Einflüssen ins Mediensystem. Inaugural Dissertation, Bochum.

Baerns, B. (1981 b). Public Relations, Öffentlichkeitsarbeit." In K. Koszyk and K.H. Pruys (Eds.), *Handbuch der Massenkommunikation,* pp. 262–272. München: Deutscher Taschenbach Verlag.

Bundesverfassungsgericht. (1952-). Entscheidungen des Bundesverfassungsgerichts. Edited by the Members of the Federal Constitutional Court, Tübingen.

Clausse, R. (1962). *Publikum und Information. Entwurf einer ereignisbezogenen Soziologie des Nachrichtenwesens* (Kunst und Kommunikation, 6). Köln: Westdeutscher Verlag.

Dahl, R.A. (1957). "The Concept of Power." *Behavioral Science 2,* 201-215.

Dahl, R.A. (1968). "Power." *International Encyclopedia of the Social Sciences 12,* 404-415.

Dahl, R.A. (1976). *Modern Political Analysis.* Englewood Cliffs, NJ: Prentice-Hall.

Deutsch, K.W. (1966). *The Nerves of Government: Models of Political Communication and Control,* New York: Free Press.

Deutsche Public-Relations-Gesellschaft e.V. (DPRG). (1964). *Grundsätze dur Deutschen Public-Relations-Gesellschaft.* Köln: DPRG.

Deutscher Presserat. (1976). *I. Publizistische Grundsätze (Pressekodex) vom Deutschen Presserat in Zusammenarbeit mit den Presseverbänden beschlossen und Bundespräsident D. Dr. Dr. Gustav W. Heinemann am 12. Dezember 1973 in Bonn überreicht. II. Richtlinien für die redaktionelle Arbeit nach den Empfehlungen des Deutschen Presserates. Stand: 16. Juni 1976.* Deutscher Presserat.

Deutsches Institut für Public Relations (DIPR). (1973). *Primärerhebung. Berufsbild Public Relations in der BRD.* Köln: DIPR.

Hummell, H.J. (1972). *Probleme der Mehrebenenanalyse* (Studienskripten zur Soziologie, 39), Stuttgart: Teubner.

Knoche, M. (1980). "Die Messbarkeit publizistischer Vielfalt." In S. Klaue, M. Knoche, and A. Zerdick (Eds.), *Probleme der Pressekonzentrationsforschung.* Ein Experten-Colloquium an der Freien Universität Berlin (Materialien zur interdisziplinären Medienforschung, 12). pp. 127-138. Baden-Baden: Nomos Verlagsgesellschaft.

Lerg, W.B. (1977). "Pressegeschichte oder Kommunikationsgeschichte?" In E. Blühm (Ed.), *Presse und Geschichte. Beiträge zur historischen Kommunikationsforschung.* Referate einer internationalen Fachkonferenz der Deutschen Forschungsgemeinschaft und der Deutschen Presseforschung/Universität Bremen, 5.-8. Oktober 1976 in Bremen (Studien zur Publizistik. Bremer Reihe. Deutsche Presseforschung, 23). München: Verlag Dokumentation.

Lippman, W. (1922). *Public Opinion.* New York: Harcourt, Brace.

Lisch, R., and Kriz, J. (1978). *Grundlagen und Modelle der Inhaltsanalyse. Bestandsaufnahme und Kritik* (rororo studium, 177), Reinbek bei Hamburg: Rowohlt.

Löffler, M. (1968). *Presserecht. Kommentar, 2,* München: Beck.

Luhmann, N. (1975). "Veränderungen im System gesellschaftlicher Kommunikation und die Massenmedien." In O. Schatz (Ed.), *Die elektronische Revolution. Wie gefährlich sind die Massenmedien?* pp. 13-30. Graz: Verlag Styria.

Nahr, G. (1977). "PR zwischen Journalismus und Marketing?" *PR-magazin 7*(65), 46-49.

Nie, N.H., Hull, C.H., Jenkins, J.G., Steinbrenner, K., and Bent, D.H. (1975). *SPSS. Statistical Package for the Social Sciences.* (2nd ed.). New York: McGraw-Hill.

Nissen, P., and Menningen, W. (1977). "Der Einfluss der Gatekeeper auf die Themenstruktur der Öffentlichkeit." *Publizistik 22,* 159-180.

Riemann, H. (1968). *Kommunikations-Systeme. Umrisse einer Soziologie der Vermittlungs- und Mitteilungsprozesse* (Heidelberger Sociologica, 7). Tübingen: Mohr.

Ritsert, J. (1972). *Inhaltsanalyse und Ideologiekritik. Ein Versuch über kritische Sozialforschung.* Frankfurt a.M: Athenäum.

Ronnenberger, F. (1973). "Leistungen und Fehlleistungen der Massenkommunikation." *Publizistik 18,* 203-215.

Ronneberger, F. (1978 a). *Kommunikationspolitik I. Institutionen, Prozesse, Ziele* (Kommunikationswissenschaftliche Bibliothek, 6). Mainz: v. Hasse und Koehler.
Ronneberger, F. (1978 b). "Zur Lage der Publizistikwissenschaft. Ein Essay." In: G. Steindl (Ed.), *Publizistik aus Profession. Festschrift für Johannes Binkowski aus Anlass der Vollendung seines 70. Lebensjahres.* (Journalismus N.F., 12), pp. 11-19 Düsseldorf: Droste.
Rosengren, K.E. (1970). "International News. Time and Type of Report." In H.-D. Fischer and J.C. Merrill (Eds.), *International Communication; Media, Channels, Functions,* pp. 74-80. New York: Hastings Houser.
Rosengren, K.E. (1974). "International News: Methods, Data, Theory." *Journal of Peace Research 11,* 145-146.
Rosengren, K.E. (1975). "International News: Four Types of Tables." In *Der Anteil der Massenmedien bei der Herausbildung des Bewusstseins in der sich wandelnden Welt.* Konferenzprotokoll, Internationale wissenschaftliche Konferenz, Sektion Journalistik, VDJ der DDR, AIERI. IX. Generalversammlung der AIERI, Leipzig, DDR, pp. 281-288.
Rosengren, K.E. (1980). "Bias in News. Methods and Concepts." *Mass Communication Review Yearbook 1,* 249-263.
Rosengren, K.E., and Rikardsson, G. (1971). "Middle East News in Sweden." *Gazette 20,* 99-116.
Rühl, M. (1980). *Journalismus und Gesellschaft. Bestandsaufnahme und Theorieentwurf.* (Kommunikationswissenschaftliche Bibliothek, 9). Mainz: v. Hase und Koehler.
Saxer, U. (1978). *Publizistik und Gesellschaft I,* Zürich.
Schenk, M. (1977). "Strategische Positionen in Informationsnetzen." In H. Reimann and H. Reimann (Eds.), *Information* (Soziale Probleme, 6), pp. 101-127. Münchon: Goldmann.
Schenk, M. (1978). *Publikums- und Wirkungsforschung. Theoretische Ansätze und empirische Befunde der Massenkommunikationsforschung* (Heidelberger Sociologica, 16). Tübingen: Mohr.
Schmidt, H . (1979). "Information als Bringschuld. Nur wer Sorgen und Angste ernst nimmt, kann Vertrauen zurückgewinnen." *Communication 1* (No, 3), 31 et seq.
Schulz, W. (1976). *"Die Konstruktion von Realität in den Nachrichtenmedien. Analyse der aktuellen Berichterstattung."* (Alber-Broschur Kommunikation, 4), Freiburg: Alber.
Steffens, M. (1971). *Das Geschäft mit der Nachricht. Agenturen, Redaktionen, Journalisten.* München: Deutscher Taschenbach Verlag.
Tuchman, G. (1973). "Making News by Doing Work: Routinizing the Unexpected." *American Journal of Sociology 79,* 110-131.
Wagner, H. (1974). "Die Partner in der Massenkommunikation. Zeitungswissenschaftliche Theorie der Massenkommunikation." Inaugural dissertation, München.
Westley, B.H., and MacLean, M.S., Jr. (1957). "A Conceptual Model for Communication Research. *Journalism Quarterly 34,* 31-38.
Wilke, J., and Müller, U. (1979). "Im Auftrag. PR-Journalisten zwischen Autonomie und Interessenvertretung." In H.M. Kepplinger (Ed.), *Angepasste Aussenseiter. Was Journalisten denken und wie sie arbeiten.* (Alber-Broschur Kommunikation, 8), pp. 115-141. Freiburg: Alber.

APPENDIX: METHOD AND PROCEDURE OF ANALYSIS

The process of data collection, coding, and analysis, carried out separately for each of the two periods under examination, consisted—despite overlapping between some of the steps—of five distinct phases.[a]

---

[a] After a similarly conceived preliminary study, no need for a pretest was felt (cf. Baerns, 1979, p. 310 et seq.).

Phase 1

Daily determination and collection of source material (written press releases from official information offices of the Legislature and the Executive; records deriving from participant observation of the scheduled State Press Conferences, and further events open to journalists; official minutes of the State Parliament's activities and official parliamentary publications).

Daily gathering of news agency output, cumulation of the daily newspapers produced by North-Rhine-Westphalia's editorial units, recording[b] of the relevant daily radio and television programs as scheduled by the Broadcasting authorities.

Phase 2

Systematization and numerical coding[c] of the original source material—texts of press releases and material gathered at press conferences and other relevant news briefing events—chronologically and with regard to information suppliers.

Precoding of agency output, and newspaper, radio and television coverage of State-bound affairs (degree of correlation between the four coders with respect to categorization: 0.99[d]).

---

[b] Transcripts were made of the radio recordings for April. However, it proved that the procedure's possible advantages did not justify the effort involved. Hence recordings were analyzed "directly."

[c] Each item of source material was accorded a separate code number composed of respective figures indicating the type of source, the information supplier, the data of dispatch or of the relevant event and the running case number. The categorization and tagging was undertaken and cross-checked by a single coder.

[d] The degree of correlation between the coders may constitute a criterion for assessing the reproducibility of the study's results using the same survey techniques. The reliability test carried out immediately after the training of the coders comprised 122 randomly selected agency, radio, television, and newspaper items taken from both periods of observation. The coders were required to process every item independently. Reliability was measured using an index, created by Spiegelmann, Terwilling, and Fearing, and regarded as being particularly stringent in this respect by Ritsert (cf. Ritsert, 1972, pp. 65 et seq.). The index defines reliability as the proportion of matching pairs achieved in relation to the total number possible. Because a maximum of six matching pairs are attainable in a coding team consisting of four persons for every item, the total number of matching pairs—including cases in which items were not coded—possible was $122 \times 6 = 732$. 720 were achieved. The coefficient of correlation was thus $720 : 732 = 0.99$. (For noncoding and the problems caused thereby with respect to coefficients of reliability, cf. Lisch & Kriz, 1978, pp. 95-99). The items classed as covering State affairs numbered a total of 44. These were then processed further. Because 27 separate coding possibilities were available for each item, $27 \times 6 \times 44 = 7128$ matching pairs could potentially have been achieved, had each coder been in agreement with every one of his colleagues with respect to every item. In fact, the number of matching pairs was 6373 and the resulting coefficient of reliability $6373 : 7128 = 0.89$. In summary: in 99% and 89% of the text codings, matching results were obtained. The procedure selected, inevitably passes inconsistencies in the first phase on to the second. Thus the test conditions were the same as these of the study proper.

Phase 3
Comparison of media coverage with pre-structured source material. Analysis of the material and classification of the resulting data in line with the study's central hypotheses (degree of correlation between the four coders: 0.89).

Phase 4
Follow-up and supplementary investigation,[e] and correction of the coded survey data.

Phase 5
Computer processing and analysis of the data using a slightly modified version of the SPSS-package.[f]

---

[e] If a media item referred to a standardized source not included in the collection of source material, since the information supplier had not been observed, the likely originator was contacted in order to ascertain whether the text was distributed to the media via a press conference or press release, and when. All items which could not be traced back to one of these possibilities or invitations to journalists to nonpublic events were regarded as originating in investigatory journalism.

[f] Cf. Nie et al (1975). The data analysis was primarily comparative. Furthermore, in order to assess whether levels of variation were significant or not, the chi-square was employed. The tests allowed for a maximum error of 5%.

Chapter 7
Media and Conscientious Objection in the Federal Republic of Germany

HANS MATHIAS KEPPLINGER
MICHAEL HACHENBERG

Institut für Publizistik
Johannes Gutenberg Universität
Mainz, Federal Republic of Germany

The following investigation analyzes developments in the phenomenon of conscientious objection to participation in military service from the time period 1961 to 1975 in the Federal Republic of Germany. Our goal is to present data useful in establishing general regularities rather than to chronicle the individual events of the period. We focus on the following kinds of events and patterns: (a) the press' legitimization of behavior as legal or illegal, (b) the spread of certain behaviors among those who are about to become subject to compulsory military service, and (c) changes in the laws intended to define what behaviors are legal.

Data on the behavior of the press are drawn from quantitative content analysis of the reports of 10 important daily newspapers, one weekly, newspaper, and one weekly magazine.[1] Information on the behavior of those in the military is drawn from official statistics (Bundesminister der Verteidigung, 1972, 1974; Deutscher Bundestag, 1969, 1970, 1975). Changes in the law are drawn from historical reference works (Archiv der Gegenwart, 1956).

The four-nationally distributed newspapers traditionally represent the political spectrum of regionally distributed newspapers, radio, and TV in West Germany. Their coverage is typical in this regard, and can be taken as indicative of the coverage of all media. Therefore, the analysis concentrates on them. A four-step model is outlined: small group activities stimulated the coverage of press, radio, and TV. This was especially true for liberal or

---

An extended version of the study was first published in *Kölner Zeitschrift für Soziologie und Sozialpsychologie 32,* 1980.

[1] The following newspapers and magazines were analyzed: *Frankfurter Rundschau* (FR), *Frankfurter Allgemeine Zeitung* (FAZ), *Süddeutsche Zeitung* (SZ), *Die Welt, Berliner Morgenpost, Kölnische Rundschau, Kölner Stadtanzeiger, Westdeutsche Allgemeine Zeitung, Bild-Zeitung, Abendzeitung Munchen, Die Zeit,* and *Der Spiegel.*

progressive media. The coverage of press, radio, and TV caused the formation of larger reference groups which legitimated conscientious objection. The legitimation of conscientious objection by these reference groups influenced the behavior of an increasing number of draftees who became conscientious objectors. The increasing number of conscientious objectors and the public criticism of the legal system caused a decision of the federal government which was itself partly illegal.

HISTORY

The constitution of the Federal Republic of Germany, dated May 23, 1949, contains the following provision in article 4, paragraph 3: "No one shall be forced against his will into armed military duty. Details are dealt with in a Federal law." However, the basic right to object for reasons of conscience can only be claimed if and when such reasons or scruples exist. Individuals refusing to serve in the military for any other reasons cannot refer to the constitution.

The Compulsory Military Service Law of 1956 introduced general military conscription into the Federal Republic of Germany and simultaneously regulated conscientious objection. This military law confirmed a procedure by which conscientious objectors were to be recognized, and prescribed that they must participate in an alternative civilian service program. Those liable for compulsory military service who for moral or religious reasons refuse to participate in armed military service must fill out an application affirming that they conscientiously object to such service. An examining committee decides on the case at a hearing which determines whether or not the applicant is acting on moral or religious grounds.

In 1960, the Federal Constitutional Court in a major constitutional decision, established what was to be understood by the term "moral decision" for conscientious objectors, the court declared that moral decisions generally are absolute decisions against any form of military service involving the use of a weapon. This must arise from a principled, morally or religiously based refusal to use force of arms in fighting against nations or countries. Therefore, the Basic German Law allows for conscientious objecting only when there exists a complete objection to war in general. This law does not permit topical, situationally based objections to a war.

According to the 1956 law providing for Compulsory Military Service, the alternative civil service should deal with problems that concern the general well-being of the population; for example, jobs in hospitals. This alternative civilian service program should take the same length of time as is taken by basic military service and by the military exercises of draftees. In 1960, the law pertaining to the alternative civilian service determined the rights and duties of those involved in alternative civilian service, and which social and charitable organizations, such as the German Red Cross, were to be the recipients of the services of conscientious objectors in this program.

THE CONSCIENTIOUS OBJECTOR MOVEMENT

The Evangelistic Church of Germany had defended individual's right to object to military service even before the introduction of the general compulsory military service. It also had called for the possibility that one might refuse participation in the military service for political reasons. After the introduction of the general compulsory military service, several regional churches provided information-centers for conscientious objectors. The activities were coordinated by a working group. The call for a full-time church commissioner to represent conscientious objectors was made as early as 1964. However, it was not until 1969 that this was realized. Indeed, during the early 1960s, the conscientious objectors in the Federal Republic of Germany had no independent and efficient organization.

The Student Movement, in about 1968, changed the character and the political meaning of conscientious objection. The general political goals of the conscientious objectors were combined with the political goals of the Student Movement. Thus, resonance with conscientious objectors increased among the youth, and also in the mass media. In addition, conscientious objection was now employed as an instrument to help direct the struggle against the Vietnam War, the National State of Emergency Laws, and the German Army (Seidler & Reindl, 1971, p. 186) among others. Conscientious objectors founded their own regional associations, which were joined together as the Federal Office for Conscientious Objectors in Frankfurt in 1971. The political consciousness of conscientious objectors rose as the number of eligible draftees who applied to become conscientious objectors rose (Bundesminister der Verteidigung, 1974, p. 57). This development resulted in a lack of sufficient vacancies for recognized conscientious objectors. As a result, grievances arose in alternative civilian service.

The increased political consciousness of the conscientious objector, and the grievances in the alternative civilian service, led to latter's politicization. The alternative civilian service personnel reacted to an attempt to force them to live in barracks with an illegal country-wide strike in January and February of 1970. In March 1970, their representatives sought a new goal: the alternative civilian service should offer conflict-solving alternatives to the compulsory military service. The German Peace Society also rejected the organizational format of the alternative civilian service, and requested self-reorganization of alternative service personnel to bring about a change in society. In November 1970, the alternative service personnel requested, by means of a new illegal strike, the resignation of the Federal Commissioner responsible for the Alternative Civilian Service. In March 1971, they proclaimed an illegal strike nation-wide.

RESULTS

The newspapers and magazines we examined published, from 1961 to 1975, a total of 904 articles on conscientious objection. The various individual newspapers and magazines characteristically treated the topic differently, and gave it different amounts of coverage. The four nationally distributed newspapers we sampled published 651 articles (72% of the total); in comparison, the four regionally distributed newspapers with comparable circulation published only 179 articles (20%). A weekly newspaper and a weekly magazine published 62 articles (7%), even though they were issued less often. Two daily newspapers published, in comparison, only 12 articles (1%). The four nationally distributed newspapers and the two intensively read weekly magazines would have to be the source of any agenda-setting on the subject of conscientious objection. In this respect, a nationally subscribed newspaper played a special role: The "Frankfurter Rundschau" published 236 articles—that is 26% of the reports in all examined newspapers and magazines, and 36% of the reports in the four national distributed newspapers.

The newspapers and magazines under investigation presented the motives and goals of the conscientious objectors in a predominantly positive or neutral light.[2] Their motives and goals were justified 157 times, they were treated neutrally 167 times, and were only criticized 67 times. Even though the Federal Constitutional Court declared the political motives and goals of the conscientious objectors for the most part illegal, the newspapers and magazines we examined justified them. This legitimization was opposed only by weak criticism of the political goals and motives.

The presentation of the motives and goals of the conscientious objector showed a definite connection to the political tendencies of the newspapers. The more left-wing the newspapers were, the more often they displayed the motives and goals of the conscientious objector positively. The further right-

---

[2] Positive presentations were coded as: explicit positive value judgements on motives and goals; explicit justifications of motives and goals; statements on the ethical, altruistic character of motives; statements on the honesty of motives and goals. Negative presentations were coded as: explicit negative value judgements on motives and goals, explicit criticism of motives and goals; statements on the unethical, egoistic character of motives and goals; statements on the dishonesty of motives and goals.

Table 1. Presentation of the Motives and Goals of Conscientious Objectors in the German Press—All Newspapers Under Investigation

	Statements			
	Positive	Neutral	Negative	Total
Political motives, goals	62	60	23	145
Religious motives, goals	48	47	2	97
Moral motives, goals	37	39	1	77
Unselfish motives, goals	9	10	1	20
Egoistical motives, goals	1	11	40	52
Total	157	167	67	391

wing their political views, the more often were these motives and goals presented negatively (see Table 2).

The consequences of conscientious objection were not presented as positively as the motives and goals of the conscientious objector. Nevertheless, the positive statements greatly outweighed the negative ones. The newspapers we examined published particularly important arguments with the following frequencies: (a) alternative civilian service would improve the social conditions of many people—90 times, (b) the defense willingness of the troops would be weakened—46 times, and (c) troop discipline would be endangered—38 times. The various individual newspapers presented the results of conscientious objection in very different ways. With regard to the total number of statements made, the weekly newspapers and magazines very frequently published the argument (85% of all arguments), that alternative civilian service would improve the social conditions of many people.

However, the two negative statements more or less predominated in the nationally distributed newspapers (49%), the regionally subscribed newspapers (46%), and in newspapers sold on the street (17%). The presentation of results of conscientious objection within the separate types of newspapers was again clearly connected to the political stance of the newspapers: The more left-wing oriented the newspapers, the more frequently they assumed that conscientious objection would improve the social situation of many individuals.

In sum, one can see that the nationally distributed newspapers in particular, as well as both weekly publications, presented the goals and motives of conscientious objectors positively. Goals and motives were justified in terms which, according to the Federal Constitutional Court, were an insufficient basis for conscientious objection. In particular, two national newspapers and both weekly publications presented conscientious objection as behavior with positive social consequences. Conscientious objection thus enjoyed a change of its image, from legally possible to socially desirable behavior.

Table 2. Presentation of Motives and Goals of Conscientious Objectors and the Social Consequences of Conscientious Objection in National Newspapers with Various Political Standpoints

	Newspapers*				
	FR	SZ	FAZ	WELT	TOTAL
Positive					
Motives, Goals	41	29	15	8	93
Consequences	21	14	12	5	52
Subtotal	62	43	27	13	145
Negative					
Motives, Goals	4	8	7	19	38
Consequences	11	6	19	20	56
Subtotal	15	14	26	39	93
Total	77	57	53	52	238

* From left (FR) to right (WELT) political standpoints

THREE PHASES

There were three phases to the positive presentation of the motives and goals of the conscientious objectors. The first phase started in 1963, the second in 1965, and the third in 1968/69. Each later phase received more media attention than its predecessor. An increase occurred over this period in the intensity with which the motives and goals of the conscientious objectors were justified. Before 1969, the newspapers under investigation rarely presented the goals and motives of conscientious objectors negatively. The number of positive statements clearly outweighed the number of negative statements. Not until 1969, during the third phase of positive reporting, did the criticism increase so much that one could speak of manifest conflict concerning the motives and goals of conscientious objectors. In the following years, more negative and fewer positive statements about motives and goals were published. However, the total number of value-judgment statements pertaining to motives and goals diminished greatly in comparison to previous years. The critics of these motives and goals reacted very late to the activities of the supporters of conscientious objection. They only achieved a majority after this topic had almost completely disappeared from political discussion, thereby making their belated victory in the press Pyrrhic. It possessed absolutely no value for them.

At the beginning of the movment we have described, these newspapers depicted the conscientious objectors' moral and religious motives and goals

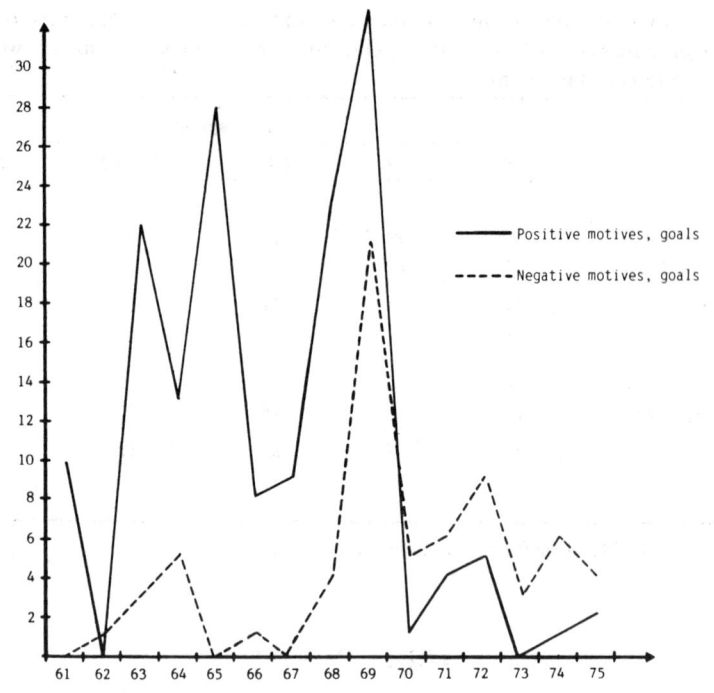

Figure 1. Positive and negative presentation of the goals and motives of conscientious objectors

in an especially positive light. The number of positive statements concerning moral and religious motives and goals was therefore much greater than the number of positive statements concerning political motives and goals. However, parallel to the previously described publication phases, the number of positive statements pertaining to political motives and goals increased greatly after 1963, and in 1968 it even exceeded the number of positive statements pertaining to moral and religious motives. In the following years, approximately the same number of positive statements concerning political and moral or religious motives were published. Thus, the justification of the motives and goals of conscientious objectors changed over a 6-year period from moral and religious justifications to, at least partially, political justifications. In this process, the newspapers we examined increasingly justified behaviors which were in conflict with the current laws, or which were only compatible in a limited sense.

At the onset of the previously described development, these newspapers most often reported positive consequences of conscientious objection. Conscientious objection thus appeared to be a behavior which improved the social situation of many people. On the other hand, the negative aspects of

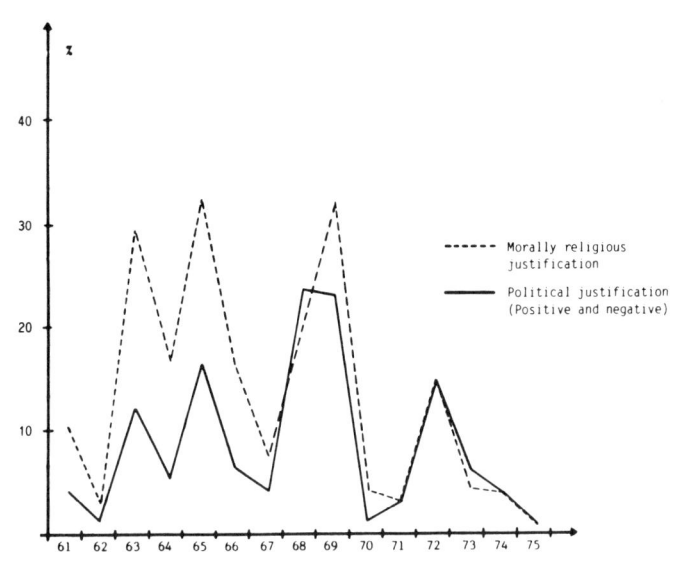

Figure 2. Morally religious and political justification of conscientious objectors

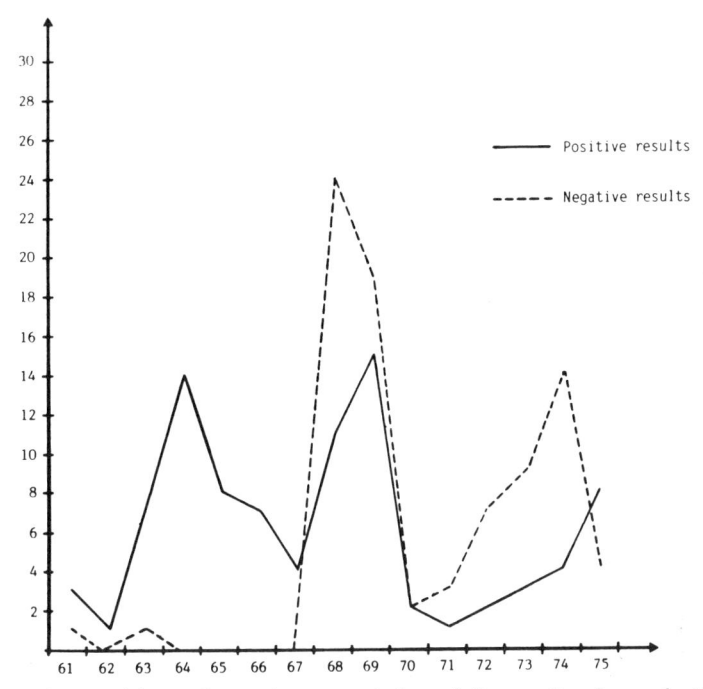

Figure 3. Positive and negative presentation of the results of conscientious objection

conscientious objection, as related to troop discipline and the defense readiness of Germany, were hardly ever mentioned. This situation suddenly changed in 1968. From this period onward (with the exception of 1970) considerably more was published on the negative consequences vis-à-vis the positive consequences of conscientious objection. The critics of conscientious objection also reacted very late here. However, they clearly were able to succeed in the fight against the supporters.

The positive representation of the motives and goals of the conscientious objector, and the positive representation of the consequences of their behavior, can be considered a legitimization of behavior for conscientious objectors. It provided a social motive for putting the behavior into practice. The newspapers we investigated have, in this sense, legitimized the behavior of conscientious objectors in three phases and thereby have caused an increase in this behavior by providing social support for it. The first phase lasted from 1963 to 1965. In these 3 years, most statements favored legitimizing the behavior. Statements which criticized it were almost completely nonexistent. Their portion of the total number of all value-judgments concerning motives, goals, and results, amounted to only 9%. The second phase

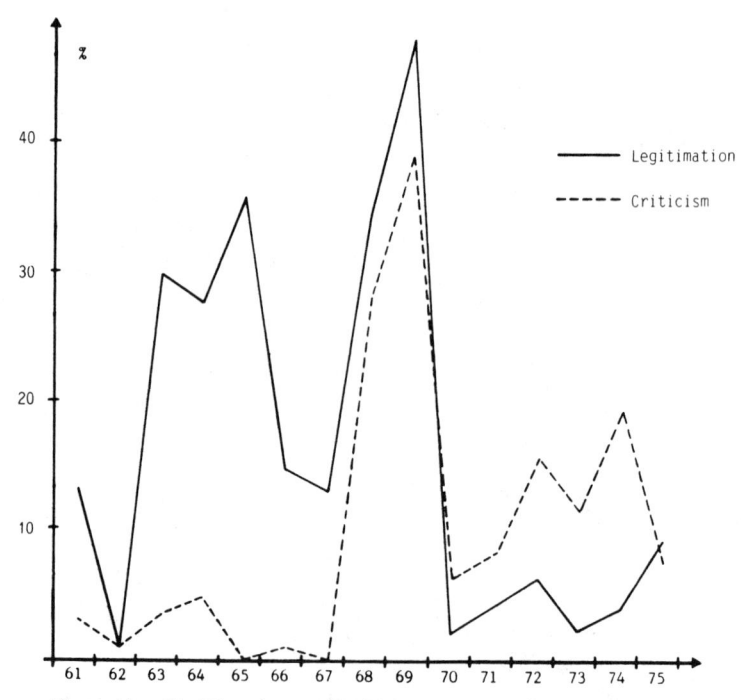

Figure 4. Legitimation and criticism of conscientious objection

lasted from 1968 to 1969. It was a shorter, but more dramatic period. Also, in both of these years more statements appeared legitimizing behavior than criticizing it. However, the portion of all statements which criticized behavior was larger than before. It amounted to 45%. In the following 5 years, many more critical than legitimizing statements were published. However, in the meantime, discussion of the motives, goals, and results had exceeded its highest point in the press. It was transferred to another level.

INCIDENCE OF OBJECTION

In 1961, 5 years after passage of the law on Compulsory Military Service, and 1 year after passage of the law on alternative civilian service, conscientious objection legal, although highly unconventional, behavior. In 1961 contrary to the expectations of the government, which had anticipated 25-30% conscientious objectors, only 3,804 people submitted an application declaring themselves conscientious objectors. That was less than 0.5% of the age group eligible for compulsory military service. In the following year, the number of applications increased somewhat, but it decreased in 1963, and in 1964 it fell even further. In other words, the conscientious objectors made up only a small minority of the people eligible for compulsory military service, even though the compulsory military age-group experienced the Second World War as children. From 1965 to 1967, the number of those subject to compulsory military service who applied for exemptions as conscientious objectors rose slightly. From 1968 to 1972, it increased greatly at a steady rate each year of approximately 6,000 (with the exception of 1972), and reached its temporary high point in 1973.

The curve which describes the development of the practice of applying for conscientious objector status resembles the curve which describes the diffusion of an innovation (Rogers & Shoemaker, 1971). However, it is not an ordinary sort of diffusion curve because it does not follow the *same people* over time but rather depicts the level of a behavior's incidence among 15 different groups of people over 15 years, each group being in a position to exhibit that behavior as it reached the critical age of becoming subject to military conscription. Those subject to conscription in 1972 who applied for conscientious objector status cannot be called "laggards," since the fact that they engaged in the behavior then, rather than in 1962, reflects the fact that they were born 10 years later, not that they took longer to reach a decision to adopt an innovation or were possessed of more conservative points of view. Those who applied for conscientious objector status in the years 1961 to 1964 were certainly avant-garde or innovative, however, since their behavior placed them in a tiny minority (see Figure 7).

PUBLIC OPINION

In the latter part of the summer of 1968, the discussion concerning conscientious objection was reaching its highest level. Simultaneously, the population of the Federal Republic of Germany judged draftees more positively than conscientious objectors. In August, 52% admitted that in their eyes it was considered a "plus" for a young man to have actively discharged his military duty. Only 27% disagreed with this view. At the same time, 45% felt "much respect" for conscientious objectors, who acted as they did for reasons of conscience. In contrast, 33% explicitly stated that they had little respect for a conscientious objector. The act of conscientious objection was thus criticized more often than was the act of serving in the military. Furthermore, those willing to serve in the military were more often approved of than those serving in the civilian alternative service.

In 1968, the majority of the population, as shown in Table 2, had a positive opinion of draftees, judging them, indeed, more positively than they did conscientious objectors. When asked what they thought other people's evaluation of the draftees was, only 22% correctly believed that the public in general respected those who served in the military more than they did those who did not serve. In fact, fully 59% believed that the public did not approve of those who served in the military. The majority of the population considerably underestimated the predominantly positive public evaluation of those who served in the military. The public overestimated disapproval by 32% and underestimated approval by 30%.

Table 3. Social Evaluation of Compulsory Servants and Conscientious Objectors by the Public of West Germany in April of 1968

Question 1: "Assuming you hear that a young man has completed his draft time; do you consider this a plus or not?"

Question 2: "Assuming the case of a young man who is a conscientious objector for moral reasons; would you respect such a person or not?"

	Compulsory Servants %	Conscientious Objectors %	Difference %
Positive (a plus, much respect)	52	45	+7
Negative (not in my opinion, no respect)	27	33	−6
Undecided, no opinion, other answers	21	22	−1
Total	100	100	

Source: Jahrbuch der öffentlichen Meinung 1968-1972. Hrsg. v. E. Noelle-Neumann und E.P. Neumann, Bonn 1974, S. 499; Allensbach Archives, IfD-Survey 2043.

Table 4. Actual and Assumed Social Evaluation of Compulsory Service by the Public of West Germany in August, 1968

Question 1: "Assuming you hear that a young man has completed his draft time; do you consider this a plus or not?"

Question 2: "Do you believe that a young man who has served his draft time, is more greatly respected by the public than one who has not, or do you not believe this?"

	Actual Evaluation %	Assumed Evaluation %	Difference %
Positive (a plus, more greatly respected)	52	22	+30
Negative (not in my opinion)	27	59	−32
Undecided (no opinion)	21	19	+2
Total	100	100	

Source: Jahrbuch der öffentlichen Meinung 1968-1972. Hrsg. v. E. Noelle-Neumann und E.P. Neumann, Bonn 1974, S. 498; Allensbach Archives, IfD-Survey 2043.

One reason for the public's mistake in assessing public opinion may well have been the media coverage given the subject. After the newspapers under investigation, and surely other publications, had reported positively about conscientious objectors for several years, the majority of the population obviously believed that this press coverage reflected the generally accepted attitudes prevailing in the population. In light of what they assumed was a widespread positive opinion of conscientious objectors, the public generally guessed that their own opinions were in the minority.

The social evaluation of conscientious objectors was clearly dependent upon the age of the person questioned. The younger the persons questioned, the more likely they were to have "much respect" for a conscientious objector. In August 1968, 54% of those in the youngest aged category (16 to 29 years) held this opinion. In comparison, only 38% of people in the oldest age category (60 and over) shared this opinion. On the other hand, the older the person questioned, the more frequently he or she held "little respect" for conscientious objectors. In the eldest aged category, 39% voiced this opinion, compared to only 26% in the youngest age category. Thus, conscientious objectors received the greatest amount of respect from their own age group, the reference group for whom the decision which a young man has to make to render military duty or civil service work, plays the most important role. Therefore, the decision itself was in many cases practically dictated.

After 1968, the newspapers under investigation reported in an increasingly critical manner on conscientious objection. The following years, however,

Table 5. Social Evaluation of Conscientious Objectors by Various Age-groups in August of 1968

Question 1: "Assuming the case of a young man who is a conscientious objector for moral reasons; would you respect such a person or not?"

	Age-groups			
	16–29 %	30–44 %	45–59 %	60+ %
Great respect	54	45	41	38
Lack of respect	26	31	38	39
Other answers	5	5	6	4
No answers	15	19	15	19
Total	100	100	100	100

Source: Allensbach Archives, IfD-Survey 2043

showed that the majority of the 16 to 29 age group, nevertheless, had "much respect" for conscientious objectors.

In particular, adolescents with secondary education showed increasingly positive and ever-decreasing negative opinions of conscientious objectors. However, adolescents with a lower educational background showed a contrary development.

The greatest number of applicants for exemptions were students (54%) and college students (12%), even though they represented only a small segment of people liable for military service. Among the students, the secondary school pupils dominated (94%) (Krolls, 1977, p. 70). Therefore, one could refer to the act of conscientious objecting as a "basic right" of the highly educated. These facts reflected the wide-spread positive evaluation of conscientious objectors among adolescents with secondary education, as well as the wide-spread negative evaluation among those adolescents with a lower level of education. The decisions made by the members of both groups followed the different behavioral expectations of their reference groups, and in turn led to the decision either backing conscientious objection or serving in the military. In other words, the divergent behavior patterns were based upon identical kinds of causes.

On the basis of the data now available, the development of this viewpoint among educated youth can be reconstructed as follows. The mass media had circulated a misleadingly positive account among the public by reporting on the activities of relatively small groups of conscientious objectors, thereby giving the impression that conscientious objectors were highly respected. Relatively homogeneous groups, expecially among adolescents with higher education, came into existence during the development of this widely-held opinion. These groups, in opposition to the general public, actually judged conscientious objectors positively. After these groups reached

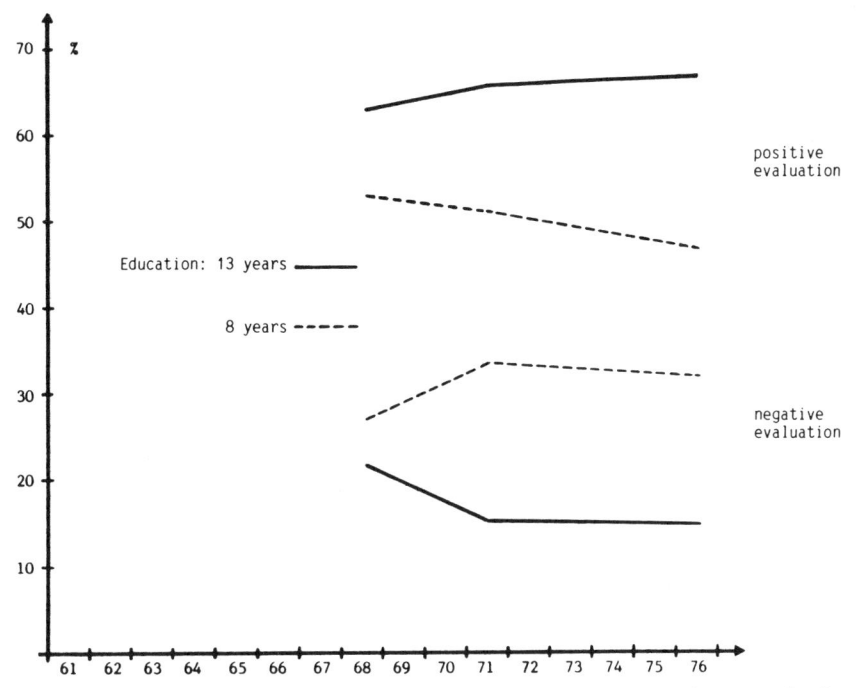

Figure 5. Social evaluation of conscientious objectors by men and women in the age of 16–29 years with different levels of education

a certain size and number, they cut themselves free from the increasingly critical reporting by the mass media. The number of groups increased and became more homogeneous. Groups created in this manner became reference groups for perspective draft candidates with similar education and social status.

GOVERNMENT ACTION

The German Government adopted several measures in order to increase the number of job-openings for recognized conscientious objectors and also to do away with the grievances in the alternative civilian service. In April 1970, it created a Federal Commissioner, responsible for alternative civilian service, that informed Parliament about the situation of the alternative civilian service personnel. In October 1971, the civilian service school was founded, which prepared recognized conscientious objectors for their jobs. In July 1973, a law came into force newly to regulate the duties of conscientious objectors. In November of the same year, the Federal Office for Conscientious Objectors was organized; it centralized the administration and fundamentally reorganized the alternative civilian service.

The conscientious objector procedure recognized only those applicants who refused to serve in the military with a weapon, for moral and religious reasons. It, therefore, served as an instrument for controlling and directing behavior. The procedure for the recognition of conscientious objectors has been increasingly criticized, even as the number of applicants applying to become conscientious objectors has increased greatly. The reasons for this seemingly paradoxical behavior are to be found in the fact that conscientious objection, because of its many years of legitimization, was rated rather positively, whereas the procedure which controlled the applications contained serious deficiencies. The Evangelical Church of Germany (EKD) played a particularly active part in these discussions.

The EKD was already skeptical of the test of conscience before the procedure for recognition of conscientious objectors was introduced. After its introduction, Präses Beckmann, an important church leader, criticized the composition of the board of examiners. In 1969, the synod of regional churches of Hessen and Nassau demanded the abolition of the procedure. In 1970, the German Peace society—War Resisters' International—and the German Federation of Trade-Unions repeated this demand. Two years later, the Social Democrats (SPD) made it part of their platform. In April 1973, the SPD decided to abolish the procedure for recognition of conscientious objectors. The prerequisite for abolition was to be a sufficient number of openings created for civilian service personnel. A short while later, the 5th Synod of the EKD repeated the demand first made by the regional churches, and made it part of the program of all German Evangelistic Churches. In the following year, the Catholic working group for conscientious objectors and civilian service personnel endorsed this position, in a joint decision with the Evangelical working group responsible for conscientious objectors. This created a large common front of opponents against the procedure for recognition of conscientious objectors. Simultaneously, discussions reached a new political dimension.

In 1974, the two political parties in power, the Social Democrats (SPD) and the Free Democrats (FDP), each independently submitted bills to abolish the procedure. It was proposed that, instead of the procedure of recognition for examining eligibility, a registration procedure should exist. Applicants would simply inform the local military service office that, due to moral or religious reasons, they refused to participate in the military service with a weapon. Before representatives of both parties were able to work out a joint draft of the bill, the Federal Minister of Defense, Georg Leber, himself a member of the SPD, submitted his own reform plan providing for the suspension of the recognition procedure. The Federal Government was authorized once again to introduce a modified procedure for recognizing conscientious objectors in case of dangerously low number of personnel in the military service. However, the initiative of the Federal Minister of Defense could not effectively bring the activities of both parties in power to a halt.

PRESS COVERAGE

The newspapers we investigated published 107 value judgments concerning the legality and legitimacy of the procedure for recognizing conscientious objectors. They published 153 demands to abolish and/or change the procedure, and another 67 value judgments concerning the types of changes planned. The nationally distributed newspapers composed by far the most important sources of information. They published 71% of the arguments. Clear connections existed between the political position of the newspapers and their judgments concerning the legality and the legitimacy of the procedure, and the type of changes planned.

The two politically left-oriented nationally distributed newspapers clearly rejected the procedure for recognizing conscientious objectors. Their criticism was directed almost completely against the legitimacy of the procedure, while its legality was little argued. This result suggests that the criticism of this procedure stemmed, for the most part, from political and not legal motives. The two politically right-oriented nationally distributed newspapers took few steps to defend the existing procedure. Rather, they left the battlefield to the opponents of this procedure, with almost no fight.

The two left newspapers published one-half of the calls made by all newspapers under investigation, in favor of the abolition of the procedure, and they published more than two-thirds of all such calls in the nationally subscribed newspapers. The two politically right-oriented nationally distributed newspapers published far fewer calls for a change in the procedure. The proportion of calls for a change of the procedure was, at the same time, smaller; it amounted to only 44% of the total or 60% for the national papers. The powerful and concentrated call to abolish the existing procedure was not opposed by a similar call for reform of the existing procedure.

The two politically left-oriented nationally distributed papers criticized the planned reform of the procedure of recognition as not being far-reaching enough. The two politically right-oriented nationally subscribed newspapers criticized the planned reform for being too far-reaching. The degree of conservative criticism greatly exceeded the degree of progressive criticism. It was stronger and more concentrated.

The reporting of the procedure of recognition of conscientious objectors thereby follows the same pattern as that concerning the goals, motives, and the results of conscientious objection. The progressive newspapers, here represented by two nationally subscribed newspapers, supported a change in the status quo. The conservative newspapers, also represented by two nationally subscribed newspapers, defended only weakly, or not at all, the status quo, and only half-heartedly pleaded for reform. Only after the status quo had changed did they criticize these changes. They did not act, but rather reacted. The conservative newspapers had previously left the field to the progressive newspapers, without a battle. The criticism by the conserva-

Table 6. Value Judgements Concerning the Legitimacy and Legality of the Procedure, the Planned Changes in the Procedure, and Demands in Favor of the Abolition of the Procedure in Nationally Subscribed Newspapers with Various Political Standpoints

	Newspapers*				
	FR	**SZ**	**FAZ**	**WELT**	**TOTAL**
Positive					
Procedure is legal, legitimate	3	2	6	3	14
Changes are too far-reaching	5	7	11	10	33
Minor changes accepted	6	4	11	4	25
Subtotal	14	13	28	17	72
Negative					
Procedure is illegal, illegitimate	30	19	7	5	61
Changes are not far-reaching enough	8	2	1	4	15
Demands for abolition	33	26	10	18	87
Subtotal	71	47	18	27	163
Total	85	47	18	27	235

* From left (FR) to right (WELT) political standpoints

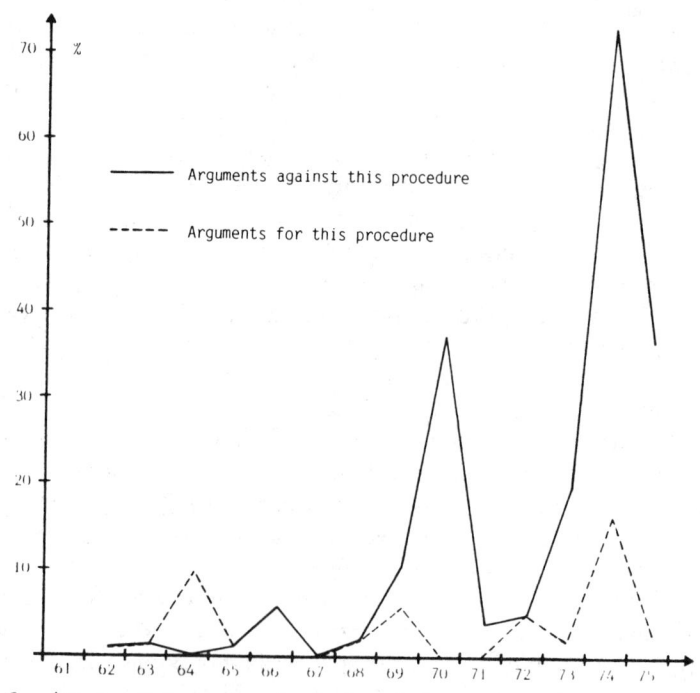

Figure 6. Arguments for and against acknowledgement of conscientious objectors

tive newspapers, therefore, came much too late to be able to halt the changes. However, the progressive and conservative newspapers reflected only the activity, or the passivity, of the opponents and supporters of the existing circumstances.

The criticism of the existing procedure and the demands for its abolition, which both reached their climax in 1974, placed considerable political pressure on political parties and the government.

RESOLUTION?

In July 1975, the fractions of SPD and FDP presented the Parliament with a joint draft which would change the Compulsory Military Service Law and the Civil Service. This draft represented a compromise between the conceptions of the parliamentary coalition groups and the Federal Minister of Defense. It was met with sharp criticism because, as with the Leber plan, it subordinated military interests to the recognitions procedure. In October 1975, the CDU/CSU (Christian Democratic Union/Christian Social Union) Opposition presented the Parliament with their own draft of a bill which fundamentally provided for the retention of the existing procedure of recognition.

In April 1976, the SPD/FDP coalition's draft, intending to change the Compulsory Military Service Law and the Civil Service, was adopted by means of SPD/FDP votes, even though the government, which consisted of members of SPD and FDP, still had doubts. At the same time, the draft drawn up by the CDU/CSU was rejected, thereby causing judicial and political controversies lasting for 2 years.

In July 1976, the Senate, consisting of the representatives of the Bundesländer, defeated the draft with the votes cast by the CDU/CSU governed Bundesländer. Before this, settlement had failed in the Arbitration Commission, which is composed of members of the Parliament and Senate. After the Parliament had passed the bill with a simple minority, Walter Scheel, President of the Federal Republic, announced in November that he would not sign the bill in the form submitted because he doubted its constitutionality. Thereupon, the draft was reformulated no longer to require the endorsement of the Senate. In July 1977, the President of the Federal Republic signed the law after detailed examination. The parliamentary group CDU/CSU instituted proceedings against this at the Federal Constitutional Court, and applied for an interlocutory decree to prevent the law from being enacted before the court decision was announced. After the Federal Constitutional Court had declined to issue an interlocutory decree, the law was put into force on August 1, 1977. Thereupon, the examining procedure was replaced by a simple registration procedure.

Those who intended to refuse to be drafted into armed military service now only had to give the Local Military Service Office a written notice;

thus, the number of applicants increased sharply (Deutsche Presse-Agentur, 1977, p. 6). The increase was so great that even the worst fears of the Federal Ministry for Defense were surpassed. It led, after only a few months, to the danger of a critically low number of personnel in the German Army in the future. Six months later, the Federal Constitutional Court announced its decision on the suit filed by the CDU/CSU Parliamentary Group. The court ruled that the suit was justified in most instances, and the law was found in its major parts to be unconstitutional (Bundesverfassungsgericht, 1978). Thereupon, the former, slightly modified procedure of recognition of conscientious objectors was once again enforced until a new, final ruling could be made.

SUMMARY AND INTERPRETATION

The legitimization of the behavior of conscientious objectors by the press can be seen as one of several causes of behavior, and as an indicator for the legitimization of behavior by other groups. It led to the establishment of an avant-garde of conscientious objectors, who organized their interests and became a reference group for potential conscientious objectors. They were able to develop their own dynamic, quite independent of legitimization by third parties, i.e., the press or church. Unconventional behavior became conventional. Once conscientious objecting became recognized as a conventional type of behavior, the standards which limited this behavior were attacked. The result was the change in the existing laws by the Parliament (see, for comparison, Zucker, 1978). Figure 7 shows the connection between the most important phases of this development.

The summarized presentation of the various developments show some regularities which can be combined in five points:

1. The behavior changes of draftees and the decisions made by the Federal Government were legitimized in all cases under investigation.
2. In all of the investigated cases, the originators of the legitimization were relatively small groups to begin with, i.e., they consisted of only a few newspapers. These groups created an "insisting minority."
3. In all investigated cases, the insisting minority, for the time being, was able to publish its arguments without opposition. As a rule, the opponents of the insisting minority did not oppose it until the legitimization of the behavior was followed by the actual behavior itself.
4. The illegal behavior was, at least in regard to certain social groups, simultaneously legitimate behavior. In other words, in reference to legitimacy, no difference existed between legal and illegal behavior. Therefore, illegal behavior probably had the same causes as legal behavior: conformity to the behavior expectation of the reference groups.

MEDIA AND CONSCIENTIOUS OBJECTION IN WEST GERMANY

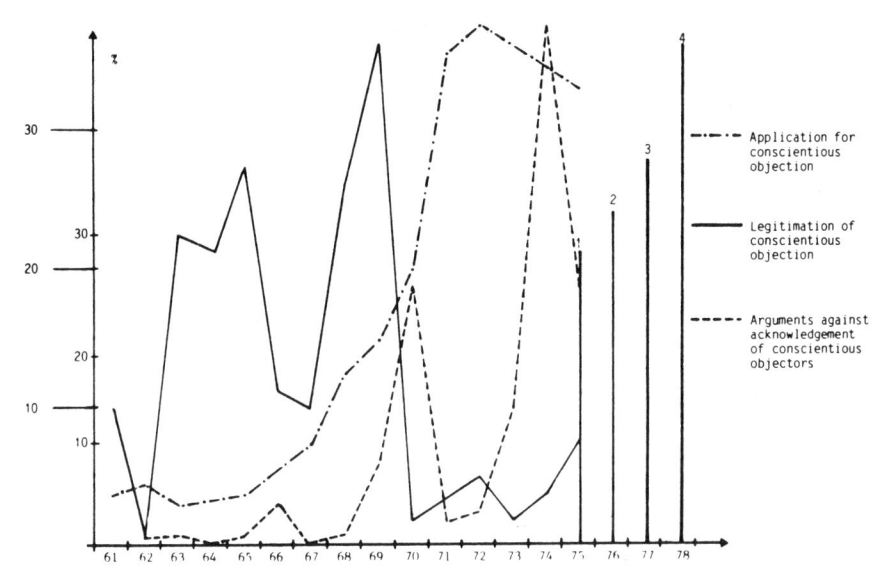

Figure 7. Legitimation of conscientious objection, applications for conscientious objection, demand for abolition of the testing procedures, political activities for the abolition of this procedure.

1. Presentation of a joint draft concerning the Compulsory Military Service Law and the Civil Service by the fractions of SPD and F.D.P. to the parliament.
2. Adoption of the law by the lower house.
3. Effective date of the law.
4. Decision of the Federal Constitutional Court.

5. The social changes, which had their peak in the law amendments of the Parliament, were the result of the radicalization of controversies and behavior. The existing norms were criticized at first, and the violation of norms was then legitimized. The norm was increasingly broken down until it was finally abolished. The entire process of social change lasted from its intellectual origin to its judicial culminating point, a total of 15 years. Approximately half of this time period passed before the opponents of change began seriously to defend the existing situation.

One must conclude, that even relatively small social changes emerge slowly and continually. Many of these changes exist in the intellectual legitimization of future changes. This legitimization takes place in public. However, it is ignored by the majority of individuals or not taken seriously. Public attention towards the changes only takes place when the changes in behavior become manifest. This could well be the reason why social changes, even though they have such long warming-up periods, are perceived as sudden and dramatic occurrences.

REFERENCES

Archiv der Gegenwart. (1958). Bonn, Wien, Zürich.
Beniger, J.R. (1978). "Media Content as Social Indicators. The Greenfield Index of Agenda-Setting," *Communication Research 5,* 437-453.
Bundeminister der Verteidigung. (1972). *Weissbuch 1971/72.* Bonn. Unpublished material.
Bundeminister der Verteidigung. (1974). *Weissbuch 1973/74.* Bonn. Unpublished material.
Bundesverfassungsgericht. (1978). *Urteil vom 13.4.1978.* (2 BvF 1, 2, 4, 5/77.)
Burstein, P. (1979). "Public Opinions, Demonstrations, and the Passage of Antidiscrimination Legislation." *Public Opinion Quarterly 43,* 157-172.
Deutscher Bundestag, 5. Wahlperiode. (1969). *Jahresbericht 1968 des Wehrbeauftragten des Deutschen Bundestages.* (Bundestags-Drucksache V/3912.) Bonn.
Deutscher Bundestag, 6. Wahlperiode. (1970). *Jahresbericht 1969 des Wehrbeauftragten des Deutschen Bundestages.* (Bundestage-Drucksache VI/453.) Bonn.
Deutscher Bundestag, 7. Wahlperiode. (1975). *Unterrichtung durch den Wehrbeauftragten. Jahresbericht 1974.* (Bundestage-Drucksache 7/3228.) Bonn.
Deutsche Press-Agentur. (1977). *Hintergrund. Archiv- und Informations-material.* Hamburg. Unpublished material.
Krolls, A. (1977). *Kriegsdienstverweigerung. Grundrecht zwischen Gewissensfreiheit und Kriminalität.* Leverkusen: W. Hubner.
Rogers, E.M., & Shoemaker, F.F. (1971). *The Communication of Innovation: A Cross-Cultural Approach.* New York: Free Press.
Seidler, F.W., and Reindl, H. (1971). *Die Wehrpflicht. Dokumentation zu Fragen der allgemeinen Wehrpflicht, der Wehrdienstverweigerung und der Wehrgerechtigkeit.* München: Olzog.
Zucker, H.G. (1978). "The Variable Nature of News Media Influence," *Communication Yearbook 2,* 225-240.

Chapter 8
Changes of American News Coverage in Two Chinese Newspapers: A Comparison

KUAN-HSING CHEN
School of Journalism and Mass Communication
University of Iowa
Iowa City, IA 52242

INTRODUCTION

The extent and content of foreign news coverage in the Chinese press has been relatively unexplored, perhaps because the analysis of the media in what seems a tightly controlled communist country would seem to yield little of interest. However, the Chinese press has experienced some unprecedented changes in recent years. These changes are the direct consequences of a drastic realignment in China's internal politics and international relations, which have led to a shift in Communist Party policies. The United States started to normalize relations with the People's Republic of China in early 1972. Since then, the radical leftist "Gang of Four" was overthrown, ending the "Cultural Revolution;" Mao Tse-Tung and Chou En-lai died in 1976; the pragmatic faction led by Deng Xiao-ping came into power; and the United States formally recognized the Peking regime by the end of 1978.

To explore the extent to which news coverage of the United States has changed in the Chinese press since 1978, the present study is a comparative content analysis of two Chinese newspapers, *Jen-Min-Jih-Pao (People's Daily)* and *Kuang-Ming-Jih-Pao (Enlightenment Daily)*, of the years 1971 and 1981, representing the year before the "normalization" and 2 years after the United States' recognition of China.

The Functions of the Press and Its Relations with Foreign Policy
Propaganda, as prescribed by the Chinese Communist Party, is the fundamental function of the press in the struggle for the materialization of socialism and the consolidation of a proletarian dictatorship to carry out the highest form of communism.

Comments on earlier drafts of this paper by professor Hanno Hardt are gratefully acknowledged. A previous version was presented at the Conference on Culture and Communication, Philadelphia, 1983.

Experts on the Chinese mass media identify several specific functions of the press. Yu indicates that "Mao Tse-Tung has assigned five major functions to the press: to organize, to stimulate or encourage, to agitate, to criticize and to propel" (Yu, 1963, p. 274). Mobilization, information, power struggle, and ideological reform have been functions of the Chinese press in the current structure, according to Chu (1979). Moreover, the essential role of the press became "the most powerful weapon to educate the population in socialist thought, to propagandize the Communist Party's plans and policies, and to tighten the close relationship between party and the masses" (Markham, 1967, p. 350).

A synthesis of these contentions reveals that the functions of the press in China have been to propagate the policies, to educate and organize the masses, and to attack the enemy. To carry out these functions, information in Chinese journalism is always subject to political objectives. Factual information only enhances the aims of Party policy. As Yu concluded, "This is not to say that the Chinese Communists are not interested in news. It is only to suggest that to Chinese Communists, news can be only one thing: the process of developing socialism and eventually communism" (Yu, 1963, p. 275).

The relationship between the press and Party policy is such that the press not only propagates the policy, but also advocates changes of policy (Pye, 1978); in Lee's words, "the media mirror the ruling ideology and usher in power/policy shifts" (C.-C. Lee, 1981, p. 93). Concerning the relationship between the press and foreign policy issues, the press must, then, reflect Party policy. Therefore, previous research tends to analyze the Chinese press as a gauge of Chinese foreign relations with other nations. And the findings seem to confirm the theoretical observations.

Historical Context

The Sino–U.S. relationship has gone through several stages since 1949. During the period before President Nixon's trip to China, the relationship had been unexplored, and the United States had been consistently labeled the first enemy of the communist world. Edelstein and Liu (1963), in their study of the *People's Daily,* argue that the condemnation of "American imperialism" served a functional purpose. It was an instrument for internal social control. Externally, it was a strategy to achieve ideological leadership within the communist world and among the revolutionary nations.

Oliphant (1964) analyzed the *Peking Review* for the period of 1958 to 1963, and found the use of distortions, misinterpretations, and quotations out of context. Imperialism had been the Chinese image of the United States. The problematic economic situation and the high ratio of crime were the emphases of reportage. The purpose behind this effort, Oliphant argues, was to shape the world image of the United States, and, in turn, favor Communism.

Having investigated the *Peking Review* during 1966 to 1969, Tretiak (1971) discovered that Chinese hostility toward the United States had been softening, while the Soviet Union became a new target.

Wang and Starck's (1972) analysis of China's external propaganda materials indicated a temporary suspension of its belligerency toward the United States during the "ping-pong" diplomacy period.[1]

The second stage in the process of "normalization" started with President Nixon's trip to China and ended with President Carter's recognition of the Peking government. During this period, the Sino-U.S. relationship was quite ambivalent. The Chinese were uncertain about the new direction of their policy, since it might be seen as contradicting past strategy and influencing their leadership in the Communist world. Furthermore, the "Taiwan controversy" could not be negotiated by both sides. Another variable was the conflict between China and the Soviet Union which threatened China. Liu's (1974) content analysis of the *People's Daily* showed the United States was still seen as "imperialist," and that social and economic crises were reported as problems of capitalist America.

Y.L. Lee's (1981) investigation of the *People's Daily* during 1975-1976 shows a rise in positive coverage of the United States. His findings indicate a shift in the portrayal of the United States, when compared to Liu's 1974 analysis.

The third stage has been the period since President Carter's recognition of the Peking government until the present time, when the Sino-U.S. relationship arrived at a new point. Y.L. Lee (1981) discovered that positive coverage of the United States dramatically increased in the *People's Daily*.[2] He suggested that this friendliness is based on the idea that it is advantageous for China to construct a broad "United Front" strategy to challenge Soviet expansionism. C.-C. Lee's (1981) study of the *People's Daily* during 1979-1980 further confirms the previous findings that the United States had come to be favorably portrayed. He agreed with Y.L. Lee that this happened at the expense of the Soviet Union.

The previous research suggests a consistency between Chinese foreign policy and what has been portrayed in the Chinese press. Thus, the Chinese press reflects the directions of the policy. However, there are some problems with this research. These studies seem to presuppose a homogeneity of the Chinese press, when only the official *Peking Review* and *People's Daily* were examined. Furthermore, no comparison has been made among Chinese

---

[1] On April 6, 1971, China invited the American table tennis team to visit Peking. On July 15, President Nixon announced his intention to visit China. Therefore, this period of time was called "ping-pong" diplomacy.

[2] Lee Yuet-lin, a student at the Chinese University of Hong Kong, content-analyzed the *People's Daily* by comparing the years 1975-1976 and 1979-1980. He points out, "But most interesting of all was the jump in the positive coverage of the United States from a low of 8.3% (1975-76) to a high of 82.8% (1979-80)" (Lee, 1981, p. 34).

newspapers to verify the implicit assumption—the homogeneous nature of reporting in a highly controlled Chinese press system. Second, the measurement of attitudinal trends in these studies was ambiguous. For instance, most studies, except Wang and Starck's (1972), did not specify indicators in determining the coverage of American news as favorable or unfavorable, thus yielding impressionistic findings.

Research Problem

The post-Mao regime, to a large extent, has seemed to re-examine its long standing cultural isolation and radical leftist position, and has started initial contacts with the outside world. The "Four Modernizations"[3] have now been recognized as a reaction to the failure of the long-term "closed-door" policy; and the Soviet Union has also been adding pressure upon the PRC, which intensified after the "Soviet-Vietnam Treaty of Cooperation." The result was an increased need for American assistance to fulfill the "Four Modernizations," and to receive military aid to resist Soviet expansionism. Deng Xiao-ping, the leader of the pragmatic faction, started seeking the normalization of relations with the United States actively, culminating in Carter's formal recognition of Peking on December 15, 1978.

Due to the changing situations of China's internal politics and international political environment, the policies of the Communist Party have had to shift. Simultaneously, the function of the press, as a tool of the party, and the propagation of party policies, also had to change. Based upon this assumption, this study investigates how Chinese newspapers cover American news and the extent of changes in the coverage of American news after the development of closer Sino-U.S. relations. Furthermore, the study investigates whether or not there exists the type of homogeneity of the press supposed by earlier research.

Two nation-wide newspapers were selected for examination: *Jen-Min-Jih-Pao (People's Daily)* and *Kuang-Ming-Jih-Pao (Enlightenment Daily)*. These are the only two nation-wide newspapers with regular coverage of foreign news. For their American news coverage, they relied on the New China News Agency (NCNA). Both published 7 days a week. However, *People's Daily* published six pages in 1971 and eight pages in 1981, whereas *Enlightenment Daily* published four pages during both years.

The *People's Daily* is the mouthpiece of the Communist Party under the jurisdiction of the Party Central Politburo. It has been the most powerful Chinese newspaper; it is always the first to stress the significance of Party policy or important issues from the Marxist-Leninist point of view. There is

---

[3] Since 1976, when the pragmatic faction came into power, they developed a plan to modernize China. The modernization of agriculture, science and technology, industry, and national defense has become not only a party policy but also a political slogan.

an unspoken law that other news media should reprint its editorials (Yu, 1963). It is the largest newspaper, with a circulation of 6 million.[4]

The *Enlightenment Daily*, formerly the voice of the Democratic Alliance, was taken over by the Communist Party in the 1957 "anti-rightist struggle" and became a nation-wide government newspaper. It is presently run by the Party Central Department of Propaganda. This paper focuses on propaganda pertaining to cultural, educational, and scientific issues (Liu, 1971).

The New China News Agency (NCNA) is the only news agency in China supplying international information (Liu, 1971). All foreign news distributed to the news media, with the possible exception of radio short-wave, is provided by NCNA. Therefore, the function of NCNA is not only to provide news, but also to act as a prime instrument for the control of media content (Hinker, 1966). The agency is operated on territorial levels, according to the organization of the state and the Party (Yao, 1963). With its headquarters in Peking, the NCNA is supervised by the administrative hierarchy, operates under the State Council, and its work is supervised by the Culture-Education Office. Decisions on distribution of news content are made and controlled by the Department of Propaganda of the Central Committee of the Party (Markham, 1967).

The years 1971 and 1981 were chosen because they mark the beginning and ending point of the normalization process. The period includes Nixon's trip to China and the subsequent Shanghai Communique in 1972 and Carter's formal recognition of the People's Republic of China (PRC) at the end of 1978. In 1971 no significant sign of normalization had occured, and the relations between the United States and China had remained relatively unexplored. By 1981, 2 years had elapsed since China and the United States had entered into a new relationship. By comparing the American news coverage in 1971 and 1981, this study centers on changes over time. The specific subjects examined are the quantity of news items, news sources, news content, and the hostile-friendly attitudes expressed toward the United States as covered in these two Chinese newspapers.

METHODOLOGY

Content analysis was the technique used in this study. Thirty issues for each paper in both years were randomly selected.[5] The single news story, regardless of the length, was chosen as the unit of analysis.

---

[4] According to *Ta Kung Pao,* the circulation of *People's Daily* was six million in January 1980.

[5] The specific dates in both years were: January 5, 12, 18; February 10, 26; March 8, 17, 30; April 3, 29; May 11, 20; June 11, 24; July 9, 19, 23; August 14, 15; September 6, 14; October 16, 28, 31; November 7, 28, 31; and December 1, 13, 23.

The coding technique was more "pragmatic" than "mechanistic," because of the special characteristics of the Chinese press;[6] for instance, news content was not coded as political or economic but as specific topics. The major subject in each story was recorded first. When the coding was completed, similar subjects were grouped together to establish specific content categories.

American news coverage was defined as the reporting of news events happening outside of mainland China and having to do with the United States. It included the United States as a political entity, the U.S. government, U.S. officials, and American people in general. Since "news" was the focus, the study was not concerned with editorials, commentaries, or special reports.

Attitudinal Directions

Attitudes toward the United States were coded according to terminologies or words used in news items, regardless of whether or not those were the attitudes of the Chinese press. This decision was made under the presupposition that the adoption of news stories in the Chinese press should be consistent with Party policy, since the function of the press is to propagate the official policy. This is especially the case for China's foreign policy toward the United States. Thus, the terminologies used in the headline or the lead (first paragraph) of each news story were the indicators for determining attitudinal directions.[7]

Three categories were developed to chart attitudinal directions toward the United States: positive, negative, and neutral.

A positive attitude was defined as the terminology and/or word used in the news content with a sense of approbation or favorable disposition toward the United States. For example:

> The Foreign Affairs Ministry of the United Kingdom has declared to advocate US policy on the issue of El Salvador.

Other terms, such as "agree," "welcome," "strengthen the cooperation with the United States" were coded as positive.

---

[6] In the pretest, some problems emerged showing that the traditionally developed categories for studying the news content of "western" news media could not apply to Chinese newspapers. For instance, in 1971 American domestic events seemed not to be the major concern of the news coverage; most coverage of American news was in an international context. Also, classifications of news stories as political, economic, social, literary, or diplomatic did not work, since all news stories seemed to be political in nature. Furthermore, it was hardly possible to identify value judgements by Chinese reporters or editors, since a great many of the stories were adopted from other countries; reflecting their attitudes toward U.S. policies or positions.

[7] I feel safe and comfortable in doing this, since the terminologies and/or words used by these Chinese papers were consistent, especially during these 2 years.

A negative attitude was defined as the terminology and/or word used in the news content with a sense of enmity and any other unfavorable disposition toward the United States. For example:

> It is ridiculous and stupid that Reagan's administration maintains contacts with the Taiwanese so intimately.

Other terms, such as "anti-American," "anti-American imperialism," "anti-American capitalism," "American imperialistic invasion," "brigandish behavior," or "provocative behavior" were also coded as negative.

A neutral attitude was defined as the term or word used in the news story with no judgemental disposition; it was "objective" toward the United States. For example:

> President of Mexico visits the United States.

Content Categories

Three general categories were developed to study the news content:

1. International: news stories in which the United States was the "object" discussed by other nations. For example: other nations' reactions to the U.S. position, policy, or action on certain, specific issues. Therefore, persons who were not Americans, but visiting the United States and making comments on the United States, were coded in this category.
2. Sino-U.S. relationship: events inside the United States having to do with China, or Chinese persons. Thus, the news of Chinese officials visiting the United States was coded in this category.
3. Domestic: with the exception of the events classified in the above two categories, any event inside the United States, and, in addition, Americans travelling or making statements outside the United States. In other words, whenever the United States was the "subject" and not the "object," the news story was coded in this category.

The specific news content was further classified according to the major subject of each news story. This is illustrated in Table 1.

Coding Steps and Reliability

In summary, coding consisted of the following steps: (a) summarizing the subject of the news story; (b) identifying the key word or terminology to determine the attitudinal directions as positive, negative, or neutral; (c) determining the general content category as international, Sino-U.S. relationship, or domestic; (d) grouping similar topics together; (e) coding the news sources.

The coding was done by the author, following a pre-testing of instructions involving four randomly selected issues and three other coders. Results indicated 89% agreement among three coders on identification of attitudinal

Table 1. Number, Content, Attitudinal Directions of American News Items in *People's Daily* and *Enlightenment Daily* in 1971 and 1981

	1971 People's Daily No. of Items	1981 People's Daily No. of Items	1971 Enlightenment Daily No. of Items	1981 Enlightenment Daily No. of Items
I. INTERNATIONAL (total)	121	11	73	0
A. Positive	0	7	0	0
1. advocate U.S.' Russian policy	0	5	0	0
2. advocate U.S.' other policies	0	2	0	0
B. Negative	121	2	73	0
1. oppose U.S. invasion of Indo-China	49	0	30	0
2. U.S. failure in Indo-China	25	0	11	0
3. oppose U.S. invasion in Korea	11	0	11	0
4. anti-U.S. capitalistic domination in international economy	8	0	2	0
5. anti-U.S. militarism and expansionism	14	0	4	0
6. oppose U.S. brigandish action	6	0	7	0
7. anti-U.S. colonialism	5	0	1	0
8. oppose U.S. China policy	2	0	4	0
9. anti-U.S. cultural invasion	1	0	0	0
10. USSR oppose U.S. position	0	2	0	0
C. Neutral	0	2	0	0
1. Compare the military strength of U.S. and USSR	0	1	0	0
2. foreign leader visit U.S.	0	1	0	0
II. Sino–U.S. (total)	0	11	0	4
A. Positive	0	0	0	0
B. Negative	0	4	0	1
1. oppose U.S Taiwan policy	0	4	0	1
C. Neutral	0	7	0	3
1. development of Sino–U.S. relations	0	2	0	1
2. Chinese officials visit U.S.	0	3	0	0
3. cultural activities	0	2	0	2

continued

Table 1. (Continued)

	1971 People's Daily No. of Items	1981 People's Daily No. of Items	1971 Enlightenment Daily No. of Items	1981 Enlightenment Daily No. of Items
III. DOMESTIC (total)	11	46	7	13
A. Positive	0	0	0	0
B. Negative	11	0	7	0
1. anti-war (anti-invasion in Indo-China)	4	0	4	0
2. strike (anti-capitalist monopoly)	1	0	2	0
3. crisis of capitalism	3	0	1	0
4. demonstration (anti-discrimination, minority oppression)	3	0	0	0
C. Neutral	0	46	0	13
1. U.S.–USSR conflict	0	18	0	3
2. U.S. foreign policies and foreign relations	0	18	0	0
3. political problem	0	2	0	0
4. social problem	0	1	0	1
5. strike (economic problem)	0	1	0	0
6. scientific report	0	5	0	8
7. human interest story	0	1	0	1
TOTAL NEWS ITEMS	132	68	80	17

trends, 92% agreement on classifications of three general categories, and 92% agreement on the coding of news sources.

RESULTS

Table 1 presents an overall comparison of the American news coverage in *People's Daily* and *Enlightenment Daily* in the years 1971 and 1981, in terms of the quantity of the news items, news content, and attitudinal directions toward the United States. Tables 2 and 3, derived from Table 1, illustrate special aspects of the findings.

Quantity of News Items

Table 2 indicates the changes in the number of American news items in both newspapers. The total number of American news items decreased in 1981. However, the number of domestic news items increased significantly. In *People's Daily*, the total number of American news items decreased from 132 items in 1971 to 68 items in 1981. It also decreased from 80 items to 17 items in *Enlightenment Daily*.

In the international context, both papers covered over 90% of the total items in the year 1971. It declined radically in 1981 for both papers—*People's Daily* with 17%, and *Enlightenment Daily* with 0%, of the total American news items. However, both in Sino-U.S. and Domestic categories the number of the news items greatly increased. There was no American news coverage in the Sino-U.S. category in the year 1971. In 1981, 11 news items (17% of the total number) in *People's Daily*, and 4 items (24% of the total number) in *Enlightenment Daily* appeared in this category.

Domestic news coverage in *People's Daily* increased from 11 items (8% of the total number) in 1971 to 46 items (68% of the total number) in 1981. In *Enlightenment Daily*, it jumped from 7 items (10% of the total) in 1971 to 13 items (76% of the total) in 1981. This also indicates that the overall

Table 2. Changes in the Number of American News Items in *People's Daily* and *Enlightenment Daily**

	1971 People's Daily No. of Items	%	1981 People's Daily No. of Items	%	1971 Enlightenment Daily No. of Items	%	1981 Enlightenment Daily No. of Items	%
INTERNATIONAL	121	92	11	16	73	91	0	0
SINO-U.S.	0	0	11	16	0	0	4	24
Domestic	11	8	46	68	7	9	13	76
TOTAL	132	100	68	100	80	100	17	100

* x% = (number in one category)/(total number). For example, in 1971 *People's Daily*, 121/132 = 92%.

American news coverage had changed from an emphasis on the international context to one on domestic events.

Of the two papers, *People's Daily* covered more American news than *Enlightenment Daily* in both years. The size of these two papers might be the reason for this difference. *People's Daily* gave two pages to covering foreign news in both years, whereas *Enlightenment Daily* had only one page of foreign news per issue in both years. Therefore, in terms of American news coverage in the Chinese press, *People's Daily* provided the most information.

Moreover, in 1971 these two papers showed a certain degree of homogeneity in their emphasis on the American news coverage. For *People's Daily*, 92% of the total news items fell in the international category, 8% in the domestic category, and 0% in the Sino-U.S.; whereas *Enlightenment Daily* covered 91% of the news in the international, 9% in the domestic, and 0% in the Sino-U.S. category. However, in 1981 some slight differences began to show up. *People's Daily* covered 16% of the total American news in international context; on the other hand, *Enlightenment Daily* covered none of the news in this category. With regard to the domestic news coverage, 76% of the news covered by *Enlightenment Daily* fell in this category, compared to a comparatively low 68% in *People's Daily*.

News Content and the Attitudinal Directions

Since news content and attitudinal trend are two tightly related topics, they are discussed together in this section. The changes of attitude toward the U.S. are presented in Table 3.

The attitude toward the United States shifted from a 100% negative to a *neutral* coverage in both papers. For *People's Daily*, 100% of the total news items reflected a negative attitude in 1971, which decreased to 9%, with 11% positive, and 81% neutral views in 1981. For *Enlightenment Daily*, 100% negative attitude in 1971 also decreased to 6%, with no positive, and 94% neutral views.

With regard to the news content in 1971, 100% of the coverage in both papers was explicitly against the United States. In the international context, 49 news items in *People's Daily* and 30 in *Enlightenment Daily* condemned the US "invasion" in Indo-China. Similarly, 25 news stories in *People's Daily* and 11 in *Enlightenment Daily* reported the failure of "American imperialism" in the Indo-China war. Other negative coverage included opposition to U.S. military and political intrusion in Korea, blaming U.S. capitalism for dominating the international economy, anti-U.S. militarism and expansionism in the rest of the world, and condemnation of American brigandish behaviors, colonialism, cultural invasion, and inappropriate China policy. In brief, the news contents in both papers in 1971 were chosen from those countries which held a negative attitude toward the United States on certain issues.

Table 3. Changes of Attitude Toward the U.S. in *People's Daily* and *Enlightenment Daily* *

	1971 *People's Daily* No. of Items	%	1981 *People's Daily* No. of Items	%	1971 *Enlightenment Daily* No. of Items	%	1981 *Enlightenment Daily* No. of Items	%
INTERNATIONAL	121	92	11	16	73	91	0	0
a. positive	0		7		0		0	
b. negative	121		2		73		0	
c. neutral	0		2		0		0	
SINO-U.S.	0	0	11	16	0	0	4	24
a. positive	0		0		0		0	
b. negative	0		4		0		1	
c. neutral	0		7		0		3	
DOMESTIC	11	8	46	68	7	9	13	76
a. positive	0		0		0		0	
b. negative	11		0		7		0	
c. neutral	0		46		0		13	
TOTAL	132	100	68	100	80	100	17	100
a. positive	0	0	7	10	0	0	0	0
b. negative	132	100	6	9	80	100	1	6
c. neutral	0	0	55	81	0	0	16	94

* x% = (number of news items in each category)/(total number of news items).

Furthermore, the negative views appeared in the coverage of domestic events in 1971, although only around 10% out of the total coverage fell into this category. Four news items in both papers were about the demonstrations against United States' involvement in the Indo-China war. One story in *People's Daily* and two in *Enlightenment Daily* were about the labor strike against capitalist monopoly of the economy, and the deprivation of labor interests. The rest of the news stories were devoted to the coverage of the crisis or problems of the American economy, and anti-discrimination or racist movements.

The news coverage in 1981 noticeably shifted toward a neutral stance: the critical, derogatory, and condemning terminologies frequently used in 1971 no longer existed. The only exception was the "Taiwan issue." Four items in *People's Daily* and one in *Enlightenment Daily* stated that the U.S. position on the Taiwan issue was ridiculous, stupid, wrong, and should be changed.

Another tendency suggests that much of the news covered expressly served the purpose of "using" the United States to oppose the Soviet Union. Five of 11 stories in the international category of *People's Daily* concerned the support of U.S. policy in negotiating with the USSR through high government officials of West Germany, the United Kingdom, and France. A similar trend became evident in the domestic category. In 18 of 46 news stories in *People's Daily*, and 3 of 13 in *Enlightenment Daily*, U.S. government officials publicized their country's policies or opinions on the issue of dealing with Soviet expansionism.

With the development of closer Sino-U.S. relations, there was some news covering the activities between the two nations in the year 1981. This was unlike the situation in 1971, where no news coverage in this category could be found.

Following the changes of attitude in 1981, all news on domestic American events in both papers was neutral. The negative implications behind the news stories, however, were still present to a certain extent. Two political problems, i.e., the conflict between Secretary of State Alexander Haig and national security advisor Richard V. Allen, and Allen's apparently taking what could be construed as bribes, were covered by *People's Daily*. The increasing rate of divorce and young people's materialism as a social problem (by Chinese standards) were also reported in both papers, as were the economic problems of workers' strikes. Nevertheless, unlike the completely negative coverage of 1971, these news stories, even those carrying certain negative implications, were presented without any satirical or condemning terminology.

Worth noting is the proportion of "scientific" news in the Chinese press. Eight out of a total of 17 news stories in *Enlightenment Daily* pertained to science and technology, and *People's Daily* also featured 5 such items during 1981.

In comparing the two papers' news content and attitude toward the United States, the views were consistently negative in 1971. However, this situation changed in 1981. While no positive view was found in *Enlightenment Daily*, *People's Daily* carried 7 positive items (11% of the total). Likewise, *Enlightenment Daily* seemed to be moving toward an "apolitical" position, emphasizing the coverage of science news and cultural, educational, and even some human interest stories. Fifty percent of the total news items (8 out of a total 17) were science news; two were about the cultural activities between the United States and China. However, both papers had adopted a similarly neutral attitude toward the United States.

News Sources
Since the New China News Agency (NCNA) was the only news agency in China in direct contact with foreign news media or news agencies, most sources of foreign news in these two papers were provided by the NCNA. Therefore, most foreign news appearing in the newspapers would begin with NCNA information, followed by an indication of a specific place, news media, or a news agency from which NCNA received the news. Table 4 indicates the news sources identified in these two papers.

An increasing number of specific news media and news agencies were clearly identified by both papers in 1981, as the sources of information, whereas such specific sources were rarely indicated in the papers in 1971.

The adopted news sources had shifted largely from the Asian area to the United States and certain European countries. Those adopted by *People's Daily* tended to come from countries with close U.S. contacts. For *Enlightenment Daily*, all news sources in 1981 supplied by the American news media or other agencies came through the NCNA.

In comparing these two newspapers in 1971, the adoption of news sources in *People's Daily* and *Enlightenment Daily* was extremely similar; in 1981 they were quite different.

Table 4. Comparison of News Sources in *People's Daily* and *Enlightenment Daily*

	1971 *People's Daily* Number of Items	1981 *People's Daily* Number of Items	1971 *Enlightenment Daily* Number of Items	1981 *Enlightenment Daily* Number of Items
Asia				
S. Vietnam Liberation News Agency (Vietnam)	14	0	6	0
Hanoi (Vietnam)	9	0	8	0
Vietnam News Agency (Vietnam)	4	0	4	0
Saigon (Vietnam)	2	0	2	0
Vietnam People's Daily	1	0	1	0
Cambodia	0	0	2	0
Cambodia News Agency	6	0	3	0
Phnom Penh (Cambodia)	1	0	0	0
Laos News Agency	4	0	4	0
Laos Radio-network (Laos)	7	0	3	0
Pyongyang (Korea)	6	0	3	0
Labor News (Korea)	5	0	5	0
Korean Central News Agency	4	0	4	0
Eastern News Agency (Japan)	6	0	1	0
Tokyo (Japan)	5	0	2	0
Japan	0	0	1	0
People's Star Daily (Japan)	1	0	0	0
Manila (Philippine)	1	0	0	0
Jakarta (Indonesia)	1	0	0	0
People's Voice (radio network in Thailand)	3	0	5	0

continued

Table 4. (Continued)

	1971 People's Daily Number of Items	1981 People's Daily Number of Items	1971 Enlightenment Daily Number of Items	1981 Enlightenment Daily Number of Items
Middle East				
Bagdad (Iraq)	1	0	0	0
Damascus (Syria)	1	2	0	0
Egypt Pyramid Daily (Egypt)	0	1	0	0
Cairo (Egypt)	0	1	0	0
Kuwait	0	1	0	0
Beirut Daily (Lebanon)	0	1	0	0
Tehran (Iran)	0	1	0	0
Central and South American				
Tokusiaba (Honduras)	1	0	0	0
Havana (Cuba)	1	0	0	0
Panama	2	0	1	0
San Juan (Puerto Rico)	2	0	0	0
Jida (Ecuador)	1	0	1	0
San Diego (Chile)	0	0	2	0
Peru	0	0	1	0
Lima (Peru)	4	0	2	0
Red Flag News (Peru)	1	0	0	0
Africa				
Busaka (Angola)	1	0	0	0
Malaguy	1	0	0	0
Australia				
Pioneer News Daily (Australia)	0	0	1	0
Europe				
San Clemente (Spain)	1	0	0	0
Stockholm (Sweden)	1	0	0	0
Paris (France)	2	0	1	0
Red Humanist News (France)	0	0	1	0
London (United Kingdom)	2	3	0	0
Reikjavik (Iceland)	1	0	0	0
Brussels (Belgium)	1	2	0	0
West Germany	0	1	0	0
Bonn (West Germany)	0	1	0	0
Geneva (Switzerland)	0	2	0	0
Moscow (USSR)	0	1	0	0
TASS (USSR)	0	1	0	0

continued

Table 4. (Continued)

	1971 People's Daily Number of Items	1981 People's Daily Number of Items	1971 Enlightenment Daily Number of Items	1981 Enlightenment Daily Number of Items
N. America				
Ottawa (Canada)	1	2	0	0
Global News (Canada)	1	0	1	0
United States				
Washington (DC)	6	24	4	5
New York	2	0	0	0
Los Angeles	1	0	0	0
Rhode Island	0	1	0	1
AP	0	2	0	0
UPI	0	1	0	1
New York Times	0	3	0	0
Washington Post	0	1	0	1
Wall Street Journal	0	1	0	0
Newsweek	0	1	0	0
Science Digest	0	1	0	1
US News & World Report	0	0	0	1
New York Daily News	0	0	2	1
Long Island News Daily	1	0	1	0
United Nations	1	0	0	0
New China News Agency	17	7	10	6
Jen-Min-Jih-Pao	0	4	0	0
TOTAL	132	68	80	17

DISCUSSIONS AND CONCLUSION

There have been significant changes in the Chinese press and its coverage of American news. The quantity of news items covering domestic American events and the Sino-U.S. relationship increased significantly; those in the international category decreased drastically. The increasing coverage of activities between China and the United States indicates the changes in the development of the relationship between the two countries. The shifting emphasis from international to domestic events suggests that the Chinese press has become more interested in covering American domestic news, and more concerned with the internal situations of its new friend.

The attitude toward the United States had also shifted from a negative to a neutral orientation in both papers. Therefore, previous findings cannot be supported by this study. Y.-L. Lee's analysis of the *People's Daily* (1981) shows a highly positive coverage of the United States. C.-C Lee (1981) also indicates a favorable portrayal of the United States. However, their favorable-unfavorable or positive-negative dichotomy leaves no room for neutrality. Furthermore, to suggest a shift toward a favorable attitude is, at least at this stage, simply a myth. Unless China fully abandons the communist system, the positive portrayal of capitalism would contradict fundamental principles of the Communist Party. The evidence shows that the emphasis upon domestic political, social, and economic problems of the United States reported by both papers in 1981, although stated fairly, is still present. No matter to what extent the Sino-American relation had changed, the United States was still seen as a capitalist country. In order to attain the "highest form" of communism, the deficiencies of capitalism must be continuously indicated, if not attacked.

Another tendency found in the news content of 1981 is the use of information about the United States to combat the Soviet Union. This tendency can be explained by China's problematic relation with the Soviet Union since the mid 1970s. The subsequent change in China's foreign policy in pursuing normalization with the United States was to "use" the United States to "threaten" the Soviet Union. This does not, however, necessarily indicate a more favorable attitude toward the United States; instead, the Chinese seemed to have taken advantage of antagonisms between the USSR and the United States. Also, with the exception of elements in news items disclosing other nations' support of U.S. policies, it was never explicitly indicated that the Chinese would fully advocate any U.S. policy against the Soviet Union. Thus, political concerns remained implicitly behind the stories, although the attitude may seem neutral.

The frequent coverage of "scientific" news in 1981 reflected a call for the press to "serve the Four Modernizations,"[8] begun in 1976. Science and technology are among the most important assets China wishes to acquire from the United States. Thus, if we were to interpret this phenomenon from the angle of a changing policy, this type of nonpolitical coverage of science would still be "political" in nature. Nonetheless, the increased coverage of science news provided more diversity in the news stories.

More significantly, the nonbiased terminologies used in the news contents, and the increasingly precise indications of news sources, suggest a tendency toward a more "objective" and "responsible" journalism. The antagonistic and overwhelming anti-American voice in the news had nearly

---

[8] Since 1976, there has been a call for the press to enhance the development of modernization programs. Four basic objectives are agriculture, science and technology, industry, and national defense.

disappeared. it was replaced by seemingly neutral political news and certain scientific, cultural, educational, and even human interest stories.

In comparing *People's Daily* and *Enlightenment Daily*, the high degree of homogeneity in 1971 in news content and news sources was no longer found in 1981. *Enlightenment Daily* had obviously been moving toward the coverage of scientific, cultural, and educational stories. Although this was probably due to changes in the press policy, since different newspapers have been assigned to serve different functions, the homogeneity of the Chinese press, as presupposed by the previous research, no longer seems to be confirmed.

In sum, this study shows that the change of coverage of American news in these two Chinese papers has been the direct consequence of the changing situation of China's internal politics, its international politics, and subsequently, the new direction of its media policy. Although these changes have retained their inherently political nature, they have provided the "people" with a more varied and relatively less biased reportage. This has been an experience for the Chinese press unprecedented since the beginning of the Communist regime. The general availability of several other publications, including one in English, indicates an increasing interest in "foreign" news and suggests the need for further research.[9]

---

[9] There are several suggestions for further research. The *Reference News (Tsan-Kao-Hsiao-Hsi)*, a semi-public, quarto-sized paper has been published since the early 1950s by NCNA. In the very beginning, it was restricted to high-level party cadres leadership, but was later gradually expanded to more than 10 million copies by 1977 and 1978. By then it had become the largest newspaper in China.

Keng, a former journalist in China, who later moved to Hong Kong, identified the *Reference News* as the most popular paper in China, with a circulation of more than 10 million. The function of the *Reference News*, as suggested by Chou En-lai, is to maintain an "open-door" policy and let people "open their eyes a little bit". Its content consists mostly of reprints, without interpretation, of news dispatches and excerpts from foreign news agencies, and of some commentaries from foreign newspapers. The *Reference News* has recently begun to publish more information on Chinese internal events. Through foreign articles and commentaries, it reveals many more details and evaluations than the regular news media. "Since all the materials covered in any newspaper should be consistent with the position and policy of the Communist Party, this paper could not be formally published as a regular newspaper", according to Liu Bing Yan, a journalist from *People's Daily*, who was interviewed while in the United States. Therefore, in terms of readership and potential influence of the image of foreign countries in general, and the United States in particular, the *Reference News* is a worthy source for a detailed analysis.

In June, 1981, *China Daily* started publishing for the specific purpose of "letting foreign friends know more about China". (Premier Chao Tze-young made this statement to congratulate the establishment of this English language newspaper. *People's Daily*, June 1, 1981.) *China Daily* is the first English language newspaper published in China. Thus, an ideal study of the Chinese press' coverage of foreign news or American news should include: *People's Daily, Enlightenment Daily, Reference News,* and *China Daily*. A comparison of these four papers could produce an accurate measurement of the foreign news coverage in China.

REFERENCES

Chu, G.C. (1979). "The Current Structure and Functions of China's Mass Media." In G.C. Chu and F.L.K. Hsu (Eds.), *Moving A Mountain: Cultural Change in China* (pp. 57-77). Honolulu, HI: University of Hawaii Press.
Edelstein, A.S., and Liu, A.P.-L. (1963). "Anti-Americanism in Red China's *People's Daily:* A Functional Analysis." *Journalism Quarterly 40,* 187-195.
Hinker, P.J. (1966). "The Effects of Mass Communications in Communist China". Unpublished dissertation, Massachusetts Institute of Technology.
Lee, C.-C. (1981). "The United States as Seen Through the *People's Daily.*" *Journal of Communication 31* (No. 4), 92-101.
Lee, Y.-L. (1981). "Changing Faces of China's Press." *Asian Messenger 5* (No. 3), 32-35.
Liu, A.P.L. (1971). *Communications and National Integration in Communist China.* Berkeley, CA: University of California Press.
Liu, A.P.L. (1974). "Control of Public Information and Its Effects on China's Foreign Affairs." *Asian Survey, 14,* 936-951.
Lu, K. (1980). "The Chinese Communist Press as I See It." *Asian Messenger 4* (No. 2), 44-53.
Markham, J.W. (1967). *Voices of the Red Giants.* Ames, IA: Iowa State University Press.
Oliphant, C.A. (1964). "The Image of the United States Projected by *Peking Review.*" *Journalism Quarterly, 41,* 416-420.
Pye, L.W. (1978). "Communications and Chinese Political Culture." *Asian Survey 18,* 221-246.
Tretiak, D. (1971). "Is China Preparing to 'Turn-Out?': Changes in Chinese Levels of Attention to the International Environment." *Asian Survey* 11, 674-678.
Wang, K., and Starck, K. (1972). "Red China's External Propaganda During Sino-U.S. Reapproachment." *Journalism Quarterly 49,* 674-698.
Yao, I.P. (1963). "The New China News Agency: How It Serves the Party." *Journalism Quarterly 40,* 83-86.
Yu, F.T.C. (1963). "Communications and Politics in Communist China." In L.W. Pye (Ed.), *Communication and Political Development* (pp. 259-297). Princeton, NJ: Princeton University Press.

Chapter 9
The Press and Redemocratization in Brazil

CELINA R. DUARTE
Institute of Economics, Sociology and Politics
São Paulo, Brazil

This paper deals with the liberalization of the press, as part of the decompression of the Brazilian political regime undertaken from 1974 onwards by the Geisel administration. My conclusion, expanding on politico-institutional analyses of the process of *abertura* ("opening up") carried out by Lamounier (1979), Lafer (1975), and Souza and Lamounier (1980), is that the liberalization of the press during this period was fundamental to the *abertura* process, giving it real viability enhancing the state's capacity to govern, and strengthening the Geisel group then in power. It also seems clear that the press played a major role in lending impetus to the rearticulation and political reactivation of civil society. This role, however, was limited by the actual structure of the newspaper publishing business, on the one hand, and by the indirect mechanisms for controlling the press in the hands of the state, on the other.

In the first section of this paper, I review the main hypotheses. I then deal with the limits to freedom of the press, and finally show how the liberalization of the press became a major instrument in the efforts of the Geisel group to neutralize the military and civilian radicals, with the aim of making viable the implementation of that group's political project.

THE ROLE OF THE PRESS AT THE OUTSET OF THE POLITICAL DECOMPRESSION PROCESS IN BRAZIL (1974–1978)

The liberalization of the press was an integral part of the process of *abertura* from its very origins. Lamounier, Lafer, and Souza clearly show that, although there was pressure for democracy from civil society and foreign

---

Based on a presentation to the panel on "The Media, Politics and Redemocratization" at the XIIth World Congress of the International Political Science Association, Rio de Janeiro, Brazil, Aug. 9-14, 1982. A version in Portuguese was published in *Dados*, vol. 26 (no. 2), 1983.

The author wishes to acknowledge the financial support of FAPESP, through Project no. 10-HS-80/0734-9.

sources, the decompression process was in fact defined and decided upon by the administration itself, or by specific factions within it, and identified with the group around Geisel which at that moment was striving to ensure its hegemony in the command of the political process. "Slow, safe, and steady decompression" was the strategy adopted by this group with the aim of controlling a number of disfunctions arising from the very struggle to consolidate authoritarian rule. Among these were the loss of legitimacy, the lack of genuine feedback channels, the imminent paralysis in decision making due to the administration's excessive centralization, and the existence of a polarized opposition.

The government's main sources of legitimacy—the fight against communism and the promise of economic growth—were now discredited. The economic and social distortions, caused by the economic model and aggravated by the international crisis, broadened and intensified discontent among the middle and lower classes. The entrepreneurial elites, shaken by the reduction of surplus to be shared, began to demand greater participation in the decision-making process. The excesses of violence committed in the fight against communism had also begun to displease the elites, the middle classes, and even segments of the armed forces, who felt that this slide into barbarity was a threat to the dignity of the Brazilian military. For all these reasons, many of those who had hitherto supported the regime now began to join the ranks of opposition protest. The administration thus realized the need to invest in legitimacy in order to restore its basis for support and ensure a minimum of trust and credibility.

The second disfunction arose out of the country's rapid development, the complexity and diversification of which had led to sweeping changes in society. This, in turn, created the need for the state to extend its ability to obtain the knowledge of reality required for a more efficient peformance of its role as administrator of society. The government's plans began to consider the possibility of unblocking some feedback channels in order to incorporate at least one or two outside elements into the decision-making process.

The concentration of power was producing paralysis in this process since it permitted the creation within the power system of radical pressure groups. These groups tended to grow stronger and more autonomous, thus weakening the administration's ability to absorb tensions and implement decisions. On the other hand, the isolated nature of the government and its rapidly deteriorating legitimacy prevented it from setting up valid interlocutors who could identify alternatives, sustain them in serious negotiations, and assume responsibility for them on behalf of those they represented.

An equally important development was the formation of a polarized opposition: on the right, a radical group linked to the security apparatus and opposed to the decompression policy, and on the left a broad front encompassing a variety of ideological tendencies, ranging from the mildest dissidents to the extreme left. This obstructed negotiations and hindered cooptation. Decompression was designed to weaken the radicals and contribute towards a recomposition with the moderates, thus strengthening the center.

The way out of this impasse required the revival of a number of mechanisms of political action. In this context, the press was an efficient instrument, among other reasons, because it was the only one which could recover its former role rapidly, and because it was a potential catalyst for the others. Let us examine how this came out.

1. Since democracy was the new banner through which the government intended to recover the basis for its legitimacy, the liberalization of the press was a means to enrich the credibility of this project. At the same time, it permitted the immediate renewal of support on the part of newspaper proprietors, who, even though they were not opposed to the regime on matters of principle, formed the entrepreneurial group which had been most harmed by authoritarianism, through the use of censorship. The certainty that a hostile press would not result from this liberalization is clearly expressed by General Golbery do Couto e Silva, considered the main architect of the decompression policy: "If *Estado de S. Paulo* is no longer censored, the newspaper which emerges will be neither left-wing nor hostile to the regime. What emerges will be the conservative newspaper it really is. More conservative than me. At the moment *Estado* publishes poetry by Camões instead of the articles cut by the censors, which the readers then think must have contained some major protest. But that's not always so" (from *Veja* magazine, no. 602, March 19, 1980).

2. The press is an important source of feedback, above all when society's other major channels of communication are controlled or still debilitated. During this first stage, then, it was to be society's main sounding board.

Along with this role, the press can encourage a more authentic reorganization of various groups within civil society. In the search for news, it ends up forcing incumbent leaderships to take a clear stand, and they can then be judged by the rank and file. By further giving the latter a hearing, it also paves the way for the emergence of new leaders. This, for example, is what happened with the entrepreneurs from late 1976 onwards: As soon as some of them started speaking out on political matters, the press undertook a survey of the whole stratum; round tables were organized, individual opinions requested, and articles commissioned. The *Gazeta Mercantil,* for example, a business newspaper which had hitherto specialized in economic affairs, opened its pages to politics. Indeed, it went even further. In 1977, it organized a poll of 5000 entrepreneurs. They were asked to name those colleagues they considered most representative of the profession. It is significant that, of the 10 names placed at the top, not one was a president of a professional association. The results of the poll were published, together with a summary of the political and economic views of each chosen entrepreneur. Since then, the same newspaper has regularly repeated this type of poll, with results published in a special supplement, known as *Balanca Anual* ("Annual Balance Sheet"). One concrete result of this political dynamization was the election held by the São Paulo State Federation of Industry in 1980, the first to be hotly disputed for many years. The opposition slate won.

3. As regards the tactical aim of splintering the opposition, the press could use the same mechanism as outlined above to inform the government of the manner in which the political and ideological realignment was taking place, as well as indicating with which groups negotiations could be undertaken. It could also help to assess groups, and help to predict their political behavior.

4. The liberalization of debate and criticism concerning the economic situation not only permitted the incorporation of outside elements as an aid in formulating new policies, but was fundamental in reversing popular expectations created by the "economic miracle." By publishing the facts of economic reality, the press was preparing society for the difficult times ahead.

5. Through the expectations of democratization it contains, the liberalization of the press acts as a neutralizing factor in the face of pressure, thus permitting the postponement of some stages in the process of political decompression (Linz, 1974). In the Brazilian case, it was especially efficient in neutralizing pressure in *opposition* to the decompression process. By making this pressure public, it hindered the organization of conspiratorial groups. This point is dealt with in greater detail in the last section.

A "FREE BUT CONTROLLED" PRESS

The liberalization of the press, as a first step in the decompression policy, thus appeared as the main instrument to trigger the political changeover. The press found itself, as a result, at a turning point in its history; as one journalist, Alberto Dines, wrote at the time: "The press in Brazil has almost always trailed in the wake of politics and ideas. But fate and President Geisel's reluctance to limit its action have determined that it should now occupy a unique position in anticipating, directing and commanding Brazilian political thought" (*Folha de S. Paulo,* May 1, 1977).

However, the press was unable to take full advantage of this opportunity, owing to the limiting effects of the country's information industry itself, plus the instruments of control in the hands of the state and the vestiges of the authoritarian situation which had previously prevailed and which eventually solidified. These factors provided the government with ample resources to control and manipulate the press, thus preventing it from acquiring sufficient autonomy to determine how best to use its freedom. At the same time, as the liberalization of the press in Brazil permitted the advance of the democratic process and of political gains by civil society, it also allowed the Geisel group, through its skillful manipulation of freedom and control mechanisms, to succeed in reinforcing its own power and imposing its political project on public opinion and the press itself.

When the administration was not able to obtain press support through conviction or seduction, both widely employed methods, it turned to the whole arsenal of available authoritarian mechanisms. The matter of the press during this period takes on a seemingly contradictory appearance. The greater the freedom formally granted the press, the more intense the mechanisms for bringing pressure to bear on it. This contradiction became even more acute once the internal division in the power bloc had emerged, with the right-wing radicals pressuring the government and taking parallel action against the press. It is how this contradiction came into being and ended up being resolved to the benefit of Geisel's political plans that we shall examine, starting with the analysis of the mechanisms of control.

The very way in which press liberalization came about, through gradual and uneven application of measures to different newspapers, was in itself a stimulus to self-censorship. While some newspapers continued to be subject to censorship, those for which it had begun to be lifted feared that the slightest excess would bring the censors back into their offices.[1] Moreover, all the official notifications that prior censorship had been lifted were accompanied by recommendations that excesses be avoided. So much so that even though *Estado de S. Paulo* had been relieved of prior censorship in January 1975, it was only in August 1976 that this newspaper published a series of articles on corruption and special privileges within the state bureaucracy, a scoop which caused considerable turmoil in political circles —a reaction which undoubtedly would not have been anything like as intense at a time of full democracy. Indeed, there is even evidence that Geisel himself might have been interested in clamping down on a number of the malpractices brought to light.

During the whole of the Geisel administration, all the arbitrary measures affecting the press remained in force: the 1969 Constitution, the 1967 Press Law, the 1970 Decree-Law no. 1077 (banning publications considered obscene and a "threat to morality"), Ordinance 11-B (which brought in prior censorship in 1970), Institutional Act no. 5, and the National Security Law. It should also be mentioned that the coercive nature of this legislation is ag-

---

[1] The first formal act issuing from the new freedom of the press was the lifting of the prior censorship of *Estado de S. Paulo* in January 1975. It was only 1 year later (June 1976) that the magazine *Veja* was similarly benefitted, while the newspapers *Movimento* (a member of the "alternative" press), *Tribuna da Imprensa* (Rio de Janeiro), and *O São Paulo* remained censored until June 1978. (The latter is published by the São Paulo Archdiocese.)

gravated by the fact that there is no unifying code to bring together these scattered rules. Rather there are a number of decrees, in addition to countless subordinate provisions which specify the scope of the law down to the smallest detail, as well as helping to promote deep-seated psychological insecurity regarding the range of applicability of prohibitions and punishments.[2]

Beyond all this, there are extra-legal mechanisms which are often more efficient than the rest owing to their subtlety, and the tendency for many of them to become permanent. They can be classed in four groups: informal measures, bureaucratization of information, self-censorship, and economic pressure.

1. *Informal measures.* These include all unofficial pressure brought to bear by groups linked to the power structure, whether openly or not. The most frequent are "recommendations" and censorship orders transmitted by telephone to the newsrooms, or passed on during conversations with journalists and newspaper proprietors. A greater threat was posed by the actions of right-wing terrorist groups aimed at journalists, newspaper head offices and branches, press unions, etc., in addition to a large number of accusations of communist infiltration in the press. These methods arose more frequently and more violently between 1976 and 1977, when the internal struggle reached its peak and the press liberalization process was furthest advanced.

2. *Bureaucratization of information.* The militaristic view of information, whereby it is directly linked to the concept of National Security, led the military governments after 1964 to attempt the strictest possible control over the copy published by newspapers.[3] To do so, it gave considerably greater weight to its press offices (*assessorias de imprensa*), which were bureaucratized and multiplied throughout the administration. This also led to the institutionalization of the press release, and these devices as a whole began to operate as genuine "gatekeepers" of information. A further measure was the accreditation of the journalists in charge of covering official circles, a system which is not immune to ideological discrimination.

Within this context of limited access to information, the value of off-the-record statements became greatly reinforced and enhanced. As the government usually comes down hard on anyone found responsible for news leaks, relationships between journalists and their sources now became somewhat embarrassing. With this dependence on sources, and even the possibility of being used by them; "it is basically through the eyes of his source that a journalist may gaze upon the powerful," as journalist Luis Nassif put it in *Estado de S. Paulo* (December 15, 1979). In the same article, where he attempts to remove the veil from the relations between the press and power,

---

[2] For the Brazilian legislation on the press, see Chagas (1979); Marconi (1980); Breguês (1978); and Costella (1970).

[3] On military thinking concerning the media, see Mattelart (1978) and Marconi (1980).

Nassif warns of the dangers of the relations between the press and the official bureaucracy in Brasilia. Moreover, permanent contact with government officials may over the long run give journalists the mistaken impression that they have been allowed into the social hierarchy and inner circle of political power, thus exposing them still more to techniques of persuasion.

There are, of course, a number of journalists who have already made a name in the profession, thus forming an independent group whose comments and articles have a certain influence on the government.

The position occupied by Brasilia itself within the Brazilian political system is a further major factor when analyzing governmental interference in the country's political news columns. The growing weight of the federal government in the country's social and political life is alone enough to lead to the overestimation of the importance of official news and news related to political activities in the federal sphere. This shows that the government has effectively influenced the journalists' agenda, if not the content of what they write.[4] The peculiar characteristics of Brasilia, a city entirely centered on the life of the governmental bureaucracy, oblige the journalists living there in constant contact with the powerful—as in the case with all the major political reporters and analysts—to lose touch with the rest of the country's social and political reality. This tendency to overestimate the political affairs of federal government circles is thus reinforced.

3. *Self-censorship.* The liberalization of the press led to the reinforcement of self-censorship, further bolstered by the maintenance of the whole legal arsenal of arbitrary measures, and the memories of recent abuses committed against the press. Two other factors were also important in this sense. The first was the crisis in the labor market. In Brazil today, there are few newspapers which can afford to give their journalists professional status and pay them well. Moreover, since the 1970s the number of schools of journalism has multiplied, pouring hundreds of fresh professionals onto the market every year. Job security thus became even more dependent on behaving in accordance with the employers' expectations.

The second factor can be said to be a case of political tactics. Despite the softening of censorship, there remained the fear, encouraged by the government itself, that any aggressive attitudes on the part of the press might endanger the whole decompression process. People linked to the administration have often leaked information regarding the possibility of a political backlash. The majority of the opposition groups, including the press, were quite aware that the struggle for democracy, which had to be based on the political tactics of the possible, meant that, at that precise moment, it was safer to let sleeping dogs lie on the political scene in order to smooth the way for the implementation of the decompression policy, rather than taking more

---

[4] See Scavone et al. (1975) on this subject.

aggressive stands which could provide the occasion for more decisive interference by the radical military groups. There was a more of less universal awareness that the best political position for the time being was, if not to support, at least to take care not to make things difficult for President Geisel's political project. As we heard a renowned political reporter stationed in Brasilia put it: "During the crisis which placed Geisel and General Ednardo in opposite camps there was plenty of information we didn't publish because we knew that Geisel was on the right side, and that we had to take care not to aggravate the military situation so far as to lead to a breakdown in all the liberalization effort then in progress."

4. *Economic pressure.* This became highly effective owing to the changes which took place in the newspaper industry over the two preceding decades and the growing state intervention in the economy. The modernization of the industry and its consolidation along highly sophisticated industrial lines led to a purge of economically weak and politically inconvenient newspapers.[5] Today the Brazilian market is monopolized by a handful of newspapers, with production centered on the Rio-São Paulo axis. The five major newspapers are: *O Estado de S. Paulo, Jornal da Tarde, Folha de S. Paulo,* in São Paulo; *Jornal do Brasil* and *O Globo* in Rio de Janeiro. Two of them belong to the same company *(O Estado de S. Paulo* and *Jornal da Tarde).* There are two big publishing houses (Editora Abril in São Paulo, and Editora Bloch in Rio) which bring out magazines with a nationwide readership and thus the ability to influence public opinion, including the centers of power. A further publication to be considered is the *Jornal de Brasilia,* which is read every day by the governmental bureaucracy. These major vehicles exert a strong influence on the regional press. Through the distribution of copy by means of their news agencies, as well as the sale of syndication rights to their articles,[6] not to mention the solidity of their reputation, they are basically responsible for setting the tone for the rest of Brazilian journalism. This form of organization seems to make it easier for the state to control and manipulate the industry, as the number of enterprises with which it has to negotiate is limited.

On the other hand, the insertion of newspapers into the world of big business led them to undertake swift de-politicization. This went against the prevailing tradition of the Brazilian press, which at least until the mid-1960s had been essentially political. Today the newspaper publishing enterprises have big diversified economic interests which have to be preserved to the

---

[5] In Rio de Janeiro, for example, there were 26 dailies in 1952, including morning and evening newspapers. Today there are no more than 10. (See *Boletim da ABI,* Rio de Janeiro, October 1952, and *Anuário Brasileiro de Mídia,* 1979, 1980.)

[6] The column signed by Carlos Castelo Branco for *Jornal do Brasil,* the most important of its kind in Brazilian political journalism, is reproduced in over 20 regional newspapers.

detriment of political interests and ideals. This situation leads proprietors to prefer defending their exclusivist interests through individual and informal contacts with the government.

Operating within the principles of mass communication, newspapers now have to serve a more and more diversified readership, as sectoral distribution for the different kinds of public can no longer be practised. They have to take into account the interests of distinct economic groups, both Brazilian and foreign, and on whom they depend economically. Faced with the excessive concentration of power in the hands of the state, which is, moreover, one of the main advertisers, they can hardly fail to consider the opinions of the men in government.

This situation has led newspapers to set up a kind of pendulum. Some times they take the side of the national bourgeoisie, while at others they defend international interests; one day they defend liberal positions in order to win over their readers, but the next they engage in the purest official journalism. Yet this does not represent a neutral policy, given that, in the last analysis, the major newspapers still give priority to serving the more general interests of the ruling class, while those of the subordinate classes are left out of this pendulum-like fluctuation.

The main challenge now facing the press in Brazil is the solution of these contradictions. The most important element, moreover, is that the state has begun to play a more and more influential role within it. The government virtually monopolizes economic decisions, and can thereby reward or punish newspaper proprietors according to its interests. During the Geisel administration, for example, as recounted by a journalist working for *Jornal do Brasil,* the *Jornal* and *O Globo* simultaneously requested authorization from the Industrial Development Council to import the same type of plant. *O Globo* received permission in under 2 months, but *Jornal do Brasil* had to wait more than six.

The newspapers are almost solely dependent on their advertising revenue, and, owing to the heavy state control of the economy, along with the increase in government advertising campaigns, they can be seriously damaged if official advertising is cut. Early in 1977, *Jornal do Brasil* was forced to give way to government pressure after a 3-month boycott on advertising by official agencies. It is also important to mention the large degree of dependence on the part of those enterprises which also hold licenses to operate radio and television broadcasting stations.[7] This is the case specifically of the Rio newspaper *O Globo,* whose owners are the holders of

---

[7] The Brazilian radio and television system is based on the granting of precarium licenses— i.e., the government can withdraw the license at will for any reason, as well as having the right, at the executive level, to choose the licensees.

the license to run the country's major television station. This newspaper is seen by many as a genuine mouthpiece of the federal government.

A further means of strengthening the dependence of the newspaper publishers on the state is the opening of joint ventures between them and the state. Most now have this kind of relationship, some with very strong ties, such as Editora Abril and Organizacões Globo.

The fragility of these enterprises is enhanced by the financial and economic crisis they are undergoing. With the benefits of the "economic miracle" at the end of the 1960s, they invested heavily in the construction of luxurious office complexes and imports of sophisticated machinery, thus contracting large debts and operating with very high costs. On the other hand, the consumption of newspapers in Brazil represents, not only one of the world's smallest markets, but also shows a minute rate of growth. In the advertising market, newspapers are losing ground to television.

It should also be mentioned that most of the newspaper publishers are in arrears with the Social Security authorities, with the biggest deficit being that of the *Folha de S. Paulo*.

All these factors throw light on this comment by journalist Hamilton Almeida Filho: "I think that over the last 15 years a highly intelligent form of censorship has been developed, because to start with it was done by force, and it stayed that way until 1975.... From then on (the government) realized it held sway economically over the whole of the press and no longer needed to censor it" (Marconi, 1980, p. 189).

FREEDOM OF THE PRESS: A WEAPON USED BY GEISEL TO FIGHT THE MILITARY OPPOSITION

Precisely because he could control the press indirectly, President Geisel had no qualms about lifting censorship, making this the starting point for the implementation of his political project aiming at steady but safe decompression. There is a great deal of evidence that the President in fact intended to improve the hitherto strained relations between the government and the press.

Before Geisel took office, his main advisors held a number of meetings with influential journalists, to whom they presented the new government's political project, with assurances that censorship would shortly be lifted, creating an atmosphere of intense expectation. In the months immediately preceding Geisel's investiture, in late 1973 and early 1974, several previously "unmentionable" subjects were already being brought out into the open, such as the economic situation, the question of democracy, and the use of more stinging types of satire and irony. *Veja* magazine, for example, launched a series of articles in a metaphorical language, in which the main characters were angels and devils. The former clearly represented the Geisel group, and the latter stood for the administration which was at the end of its term. The issue which dealt with Geisel's investiture included a suggestive documentary-style article on the ritual of exorcism, in which the magazine rejoiced in the "return of the angels" and the expulsion of the devils. Even the "alternative" press, which had suffered most at the hands of the censorship, was carried away by this optimism, as shown in the words of Fernando Gasparian, director of the weekly *Opinião:* "There was a wave of rumors that censorship would be lifted for our paper. And in actual fact, compared with the difficult times we'd been through under the Médici administration, there was more freedom to deal with certain subjects in the paper" (Pinheiro Machado, 1978, p. 86).

A number of concrete steps were taken at once. As soon as the new government took office, censorship was lifted from *O Estado de S. Paulo,* as well as the weekly *Pasquim* and *Veja* magazines. It was soon brought back again, however. It seems the government was unable to resist the first wave of press criticism, such as *Veja*'s articles on the tenth anniversary of the 1964 "Revolution," another on the situation of the Brazilian exiles, and, above all, a cartoon by Millor Fernandes on torture, which annoyed the military groups linked to the security agencies. The same was true of a number of critical articles signed by Carlos Chagas in *O Estado de S. Paulo.* It should also be remembered that, during these first days and weeks, the Geisel group was still unsure of its ground relating to the more radical, pro-censorship segments of the regime. After the setback mentioned above, press liberalization followed an irregular rhythm, oscillating between moments of freedom and moments of repression. This seesaw process closely accompanied the internal struggle for power. The "hard line" was sometimes kept quiet by punishing the press, but at the same time Geisel encouraged the breaking of the vicious circle of censorship. On occasion he acted directly, such as when he literally tore up the dossier against the journalist Carlos Chagas presented to the National Security Council by members of a group centered around the Army Minister, Sylvio Frota. At other times he was more subtle, such as when he expressed his opinion on the work of reporters: "Reporters should 'act natural' and go about their work as if the times were normal" (*Folha de S. Paulo,* Jan. 16, 1977, column titled "Jornal dos Jornais"). Two facts give irrefutable support to the view that Geisel intended to improve the relations between the press and the government, in addition to neutralizing military influence in this field. One was the appointment of his "protegé," Humberto Barreto, as press attaché to the President, clearly showing that this post was to be considered most important by the incoming administration. The other was the closing down of the Special Public Relations Office of the Presidency (AERP) and its incorporation into the Press Office. The significance of this measure becomes clearer if it is understood that the AERP was directly subordinated to the *Casa Militar*, while the Press Office was controlled by the *Casa Civil*.[8]

As part of its preparations to govern with a considerable amount of press freedom, the administration used techniques of persuasion in an attempt to obtain the spontaneous support of a large part of the press. Even before the investiture, General Golbery do Couto e Silva began a series of meetings with top-ranking journalists. The upshot was the formation of a group of journalists with a great deal of influence in the main papers of Rio de Janeiro and São Paulo, where the government's political project was believed in. General Golbery had already amassed vast experience in this kind of strategy, since the time when he was head of the Public Opinion Group of IBAD (see Dreifus, 1981, p. 192), an agency entrusted with working on the mass media in order to swing public opinion against Jango Goulart's administration. It can be said that General Golbery was successful on both occasions.

In my opinion, the Geisel group made use of press freedom primarily to reduce internal pressure. "He [Geisel] would often have news leaked to the papers in order to confront the various groups in power," as one journalist put it. With the liberalization of the press, the field of what was permissible for these groups was limited. According to one journalist involved in Golbery's scheme, press liberalization was decided on "when the government was reeling from its first clash with the military," during the attempt to investigate the case of the 30 members of the Brazilian Communist Party killed at the start of the Geisel administration. "I know that the government was anxious to investigate but the military apparatus prevented it."

The first major endeavor by the government to avoid suppression of news of torture occurred during the crisis centered on the 2nd Army in São Paulo, after the deaths of the journalist Vladimir Herzog and the worker Manuel Fiel Filho, on the premises of the DOI-CODI (Army Intelligence).[9] The newspapers (except those still subjected to censorship) gave wide coverage to Herzog's death, and this undoubtedly contributed to the mass attendance at protest demonstrations. It must not be forgotten, however, that the São Paulo State Journalists' Union, where recent elections had seen the victory of the opposition slate, played a fundamental role in the episode. The atmosphere set up by the crisis allowed President Geisel to begin something like a "mopping-up" operation in the strategic areas of military com-

---

[8] In 1976, Geisel revived AERP, according to our information, owing to pressure from military groups concerned with the government's image, but also because 1975 saw the first elections held since the government party's resounding defeat in 1974. The AERP continued, however, incorporated into the *Casa Civil*.

[9] The journalist Vladimir Herzog, then director of journalism at TV Cultura, the State television station, had been charged with having connections with the PCB. He was found dead in his cell on October 25, 1975. In January 1976, the worker Manuel Fiel Filho was found dead under the same circumstances.

mand and make sure that the key posts were given to commanders in his confidence. After the death of Fiel Filho, General Ednardo D'Avilla de Mello was removed from the command of the 2nd Army in São Paulo and replaced by General Dilermando Gomes Monteiro. Humberto Barreto himself gave the news and conspicuously failed to avoid establishing a link between the two episodes.

From then on, in addition to news on torture, the press earned the right to mention another major aspect of the treatment of political issues: conflict within the Armed Forces.[10] The conflict became steadily worse until the decisive battle (involving the question of the presidential succession) between President Geisel and the Army Minister.

In this battle, the press acted as the main instrument of the Geisel group and the main target for criticism from the Frota group. While the former attempted to improve relations with the press and gain its support, the latter employed all available weapons in order to try to neutralize press strength. In an action unprecedented since 1964, General Dilermando Monteiro, Commander-in-Chief of the 2nd Army, paid a visit to the São Paulo Journalists' Union; meanwhile, the Frota group was unleashing a series of accusations of communist infiltration in the press, along with direct acts of repression. This period also saw the beginning of right-wing terrorist activity against the press. As one journalist put it, "It was not a debate conducted by the regime as to how to define press freedom, but rather the use by groups within the system of one another's weak points." The upshot was a sizeable advantage to the Geisel group. As the journalist Alberto Dines said at the time: "The relative press freedom we enjoy today is the great achievement of decompression, and perhaps the present government's major political base. If it were not for the newspapers' capacity to expose pressure and activities by hard-line groups within government circles, their influence would be fatal. Once opportunely denounced, their action is contained. When they are exposed to the public eye, they withdraw" (*Folha de S. Paulo,* July 24, 1977).

The choice of President Geisel's successor was made in an unusual manner, compared to procedures in force since 1964. Whereas the preceding successions had been decided behind closed doors—indeed, some newspapers were actually submitted to prior censorship in order to avoid a discussion of the succession of President Médici—the reverse was now the case.

In order to guarantee that its favorite would be chosen and to avoid being surprised by a military coup, the Geisel group decided to anticipate

---

[10] The press wormed its way slowly into the politico-military question, culminating with the series of articles entitled "Encruzilhada Brasileira" ("Brazil at the Crossroads") published by *O Estado de S. Paulo* from March 16, 1977 onwards. For the first time, at least since the Institutional Act no. 5 was issued in December 1968, the press managed to enter the barrack rooms in order to hear the military's opinions on political affairs.

the debate on the succession and open it up to public opinion.[11] For the first time since 1964, the Brazilian public was able to follow all the moves of a process, in which, however, it was prevented from participating. According to Stumpf and Pereira Filho (1979), it all began with an article by Villas-Boas Corrêa in the magazine *Isto É* (June 21, 1977), in which the writer stated that the succession game involved "two teams warming up on the field": Figueiredo/Golbery versus Frota/Hugo Abreu. The organizers of Figueiredo's candidacy saw this as "a sign that the succession campaign must begin at once." There are even those who believe that the Frota candidacy may well have been pressed harder by journalists linked to Golbery, in order to alert President Geisel to the danger ahead and force him to take a stand (Abreu, 1979; Stumpf and Pereira Filho, 1979). Golbery and Heitor de Aquino began to work on Figueiredo with the aim of having him pay more attention to the press (Stumpf and Pereira Filho, 1979). On July 6, the *Jornal de Brasilia* published an interview with Figueiredo in which he confirmed his candidacy "providing President Geisel supports me." On July 20, Humberto Barreto, who was no longer at the Press Office, told *Veja* magazine that he supported Figueiredo.[12] Given Barreto's closeness to the President, it was thus clear that this was also Geisel's candidate. Shortly afterwards, Major Heitor Aquino, Geisel's private secretary, began to distribute biographic sketches and photographs of General Figueiredo to the press in his own name; this material had been prepared at the offices of *Manchete* magazine (Editora Bloch) in Brasilia. The dispute on the succession was on the front pages of the newspapers, which presented General Figueiredo as the candidate of the "*abertura*," in opposition to General Frota, the candidate of a "return to a hard-line regime." Once the debate had begun, relations grew worse and worse between Geisel and his Army Minister. Until the latter's dismissal, on October 12, 1977, the press remained the main target of this conflict. A month before the dismissal, a series of publications, some on the subject of Soldier's Day and others on torture of political prisoners, led General Frota to issue a press release accusing the press of acting as an instrument of the communists to destabilize the regime. According to Walder de Góes (1978), General Frota, without Geisel's authorization, requested the taking of legal proceedings against the newspa-

---

[11] It had already been decided to make General João Baptista Figueiredo president as successor to Geisel before the latter took office. A number of journalists who had established close relations with General Golbery and Major Heitor Aquino were let into the secret from the start.

[12] Humberto Barreto left the Press Office early in 1977 and took up the presidency of the Federal Savings Bank (Caixa Econômica Federal). Some believe that this move was engineered by Geisel himself, to preserve Baretto from a number of arbitrary measures to be introduced by the government, the so-called "April package" (*pacote de abril*). Others link the episode to a dispute between Humberto Barreto and Golbery for ascendency over the President.

pers *Folha de S. Paulo, O Globo,* and *Jornal do Brasil.* Geisel considered the Minister's attitude "impertinent" and ordered the Minister for Justice to move proceedings taken only against the journalist Lourenco Diaféria, of the *Folha de S. Paulo,* because of an article considered offensive to the image of the Duke of Caxias, patron of the Brazilian Army. In his investiture speech when taking Frota's place as Army Minister, in October 1977, General Belfort Bethlem made a point of mentioning his sympathies for the press, perhaps in an effort to reconcile the two institutions.

There can be no doubt about the skill with which most of the press took advantage of this conflict. When freedom increased, it pursued the issue of human rights and the need for redemocratization of the regime. Moreover, this campaign was timely, at least at that particular moment, for the Geisel group. According to one political analyst with good credentials in government circles, many attacks on the security agencies' abuse of power were in fact encouraged by Geisel, "precisely in order to give him room to manouver against the radical pockets." The same source relates a personal experience: "In the case of Frota, I can quote an actual fact. One of Geisel's direct advisors called me and asked me to publish Frota's letter of resignation without any omissions."[13] After Frota's fall, the issue of the succession and its treatment by the press changed its character, and the government was obliged to resort more directly to those journalists felt to be identified with it.

A further aspect which linked press liberalization to the conflict between the Geisel administration and the military was the fact that it was a means of eliminating the military's monopoly over the means of information which influenced the government's decision-making procedures. Until then, the main channels of information which generated decisions at all levels of government had been the synopses and reports prepared by the National Intelligence Service (Servico Nacional de Informacões, or SNI). The diversification of information sources, including unofficial ones, provided not only major alternatives for an improved critical vision of reality but also forestalled the risk of manipulation of information on the part of groups in power.[14]

REFERENCES

Abreu, H. (1979). *O outro lado do Poder.* Rio de Janeiro: Nova Fronteira.
Breguês, S.G. (1978). "A Imprensa Brasileira Após 64." *Revisita Encontros com a Civilizacão Brasileira,* Rio de Janeiro, Aug., (No. 2).

---

[13] In this letter, Frota accused the government itself of having been infiltrated by communists.

[14] On the decision-making process in the Geisel administration, See Góes (1978).

Chagas, C. (1979). *A Censura e a Liberdade.* Paper delivered at Symposium on "Censorship: Background, situation and solutions," held by Communications Committee of Federal Chamber of Deputies, May 16.

Costella, A. F. (1970). *O Controle da Informacão no Brasil.* Petrópolis, Rio de Janeiro: Editora Vozes.

Dreifus, R.A. (1981). *1964: A Conquista do Estado, Acao Política, Poder e Golpe de Classes.* Petrópolis: Editora Vozes.

Góes, W. de. (1978). *O Brasil do General Geisel.* Rio de Janeiro: Nova Fronteira.

Lafer, C. (1978). *O Sistema Político Brasileiro,* (2nd ed.). São Paulo: Perspectiva.

Lamounier, B. (1979). "O Discurso e o Processo." In H. Rattner, (Orig.) *Brasil 1900: Caminhos Alternativos do Desenvolvimento.* São Paulo: Brasiliense.

Linz, J. (1974). "Opposition to and under an Authoritarian Regime: The case of Spain." In R.A. Dahl (Ed.), *Regimes and Oppositions.* (2nd ed.) New Haven, CT: Yale University Press.

Marconi, P. (1980). *A Censura Política na Imprensa Brasileira, 1968-1978* Colecão Passado e Presente no. 14). São Paulo: Global Editora.

Mattelart, A. (1978). "Ideologia, Información y Estado Militar." In A. Mattelart and M. Mattelart, *Comunicación y Ideologia da la Seguridad.* Barcelona: Editorial Anagrama.

Pinheiro Machado, J.A. (1978). *Opinião x Censura: Momentos de luta de um jornal pela liberdade,* Porto Alegre: L&PM Editores.

Scavone, L., Belloni, M.L., and Garbayo, C. (1975). *A Dimensão Política da Comunicacão de Massa: um estudo exploratório do caso brasileiro.* Rio de Janeiro: Editora da Fundacão Getúlio Vargas.

Souza, A. de, and Lamounier, B. (1980). *Escaping the Black Hole: Government-Labor Relations in Brazil in the 1980's.* (mimeograph.)

Stumpf, A.G. and Pereira Filho, M. (1979). *A Segunda Guerra: Sucessão de Geisel.* São Paulo: Brasiliense.

PART III
ASSESSMENTS

Chapter 10
Election Communication and the Democratic Political System

JAY G. BLUMLER

Centre for Television Research
University of Leeds
Leeds LS2 9JT, England

This paper amounts to a plea to political communication scholars to "go back to first principles" in our field more often, aiming to develop, in additin to the many other things that they do, the principles, considerations, and issues of debate and analysis that would form part of a political philosophy of mass communication. Such an effort would involve an attempt to work out a tenable notion of political democracy and to derive from it a view of the part that communication could play in realizing or promoting democratic values, including the generation of fresh statements about the standards that political journalism should serve when presenting election campaigns specifically, and the world of political affairs more generally. My approach to this theme divides into two parts. In the first, I aim to justify my plea for "going philosophic" in this manner, for it is not at all self-evident that we should do so. In the second, I aim to illustrate what such an approach might look like in personal, albeit sketchy, terms.

I

The justification for going back to first principles may be presented from four angles. The first refers to a paradoxical gap in the media and politics literature. Without the effort I have in mind, much of our work is liable to remain unbalanced, unconstructive, even impotent from the sidelines, as it were. Reading what we write, you could almost imagine that we aspired to be the Cassandras of election communication—crying woe over a cumulation of misfortunes that cannot be averted. In fact, much election communication scholarship could be described as anomic: short on standards but long on criticism.

First published in W. Schulz and K. Schönbach (Eds.), *Massenmedien und Wahlen*. Munich: Ölschläger.

On the one hand, the inadequacies of media performance and role in election campaigns that have been cataloged in our writings add up to an impressive indictment. They include: undue concentration on the campaign "game" at the expense of substantive issues and policies (Patterson, 1980); encouraging the reduction of political argument to such nuggets, slogans, and one-liners that can be squeezed into a television news item (Blumler, Gurevitch, & Ives, 1978); conveying a Presidential impression of even Parliamentary political systems through near-exclusive attention to top party leaders (Harrison, 1982); projection of an unduly narrow set of contestants and issues (Seymour-Ure & Smith, 1982); narrowing choice to one between what Nelson Polsby (1980, p. 65) has called "heroes and bums," through disproportionately savoring campaigners' inevitable mishaps and fumbles, as in the case of President Ford's East European gaffe in 1976; exerting pressure on the parties themselves to run their campaigns by media premises (Siune, 1982); so routinizing campaign coverage patterns into a number of repeated rituals that chances of exciting audience interest and involvement are missed (Gurevitch & Blumler, 1982); an events orientation encouraging a flow of essentially irrelevant political material from campaigners—as when, in 1980, Ronald Reagan steered a steamboat on a less than steady course down four miles of the Mississippi River, and when, in 1979 in Britain, Margaret Thatcher (as described by David Butler and Dennis Kavanagh, 1980, p. 172):

> in particular spared no trouble to help the photographers. She was shown waving her shopping basket, or swinging a broom in one factory and tasting tea in another, or in the most extreme and most satirised case, cuddling a newborn calf, which in fact she held for thirteen minutes until every cameraman was satisfied.

On the other hand, ever since publication of the last chapter of *Voting,* the book on the 1948 Presidential election race by Berelson, Lazarsfeld, and McPhee (1954), classical notions of democracy, and of the place of the interested, informed, and rational elector in it, mostly have been abandoned as unrealistic, while few principled alternative conceptions of democracy have been proposed to replace them. That is why we often seem prepared heavily to criticise journalistic failings but unprepared openly to articulate the criteria according to which we reckon that it would be fair to hold the news media to account for their political performance.

A second prong of this case stems from several signs that the legitimacy of the journalistic function, as traditionally or professionally defined, is no longer so widely and unreservedly accepted as it once was. Political television, for example, has been exposed to an increasingly hostile barrage of criticisms and pressure. In Britain, whose experience is not atypical, the discontented have ranged "from standard-bearers of social causes, such as racial equality and the feminist movement, to inverterate wielders of pressure, such as the main political parties, to even well-entrenched Establishment sectors such as the police, the trade unions and the medical profession" (Blumler, 1981, p. 259)—and latterly the government of the day itself. Managers of the medium hardly know how to respond: when graciously to concede fault, when cautiously to trim sails, when boldly to fly the flag of independence. And although they can draw some comfort from continuing widespread audience support, as well as occasional splits in their critics' ranks, the broad spread of complaining voices suggests that it may not be the particulars so much as the principles of journalistic practice that require attention.

In such an atmosphere, the time may be ripe for reappraisals and fresh statements of the purposes and standards of political journalism. This need is further accentuated by widening disparities between what professional journalists claim predominantly to be doing—that is, providing informative snapshots of newsworthy external events—and academic accounts of newswork, which are increasingly describing it in terms of reality *construction* by newsmen (not *representation*); evidence of audience members' uses of the news (who seem more attuned to its thematic "music" than to its factual "words"); as well as what key élites expect to find in the news.

Third, there is a philosophic justification for going back to first principles of democratic political communication. This pivots on what political theorists term the problem of political obligation: Why should the citizen abide by the laws of his state? Different regimes may rest their claims to allegiance on different grounds—for example, theocratic, ideological, meritocratic, traditionalistic, or Hobbesian ones. But democracy is the only form of regime the legitimation of which *necessarily* involves communication. This is because liberal theory traces the citizen's duty to obey government back to a sense in which it could be said that he or she has consented to be ruled by it—which in modern democracy is supposedly embodied in the act or opportunity of voting. But (as Carole Pateman, 1979, p. 88, has argued), this implies that citizens should "be able to ascertain" through communication "what kind of commitment they are undertaking [when they vote] and whether good reasons exist for them to do so." Of course, for such a political theory the backers of losing parties, causes, and policies present a difficulty. To what might they have consented? And again the solution turns in part on communication. The obligation of the momentarily vanquished stems, first, from their acceptance of the integrity and fairness of communication processes in which they could have carried the day, and second, from the fact that, with further access to media channels, they stand a reasonable future chance of minimizing, making endurable, and even reversing their temporary subservience. Distortions of election communication, then, ultimately undermine the very authority of the democratic state.

Finally, the case for airing questions about the political responsibilities of journalists seems stronger and more urgent the more we stress the pivotal place that the mass media now occupy in democratic political systems. As I understand it, what Elisabeth Noelle-Neumann (1973) has called our "return to the concept of powerful mass media" has been propelled by two quite profound forces (in addition to the findings of particular communication effects studies).

First, at a time when the public's confidence in many social and political institutions has steeply declined, both parties and voters have become more dependent on media resources, the former for means of access to the electoral audience, as their own channels have started to wither and lose credibility, the latter for impressions of what is at stake, as previous suppliers of guiding frameworks have lost their authority (Ball-Rokeach & De Fleur, 1976). At election time, not only is the vote more volatile and unpredictable, with more footloose voters for parties and candidates to woo through media appeals; but the outcome is also "more sensitive to short-term influences.... which are transmitted largely by the media" (Patterson, 1980, p. 6).

Second, our sense of the potency of the mass media has been strengthened by a growing awareness that all news has a normative component (Alexander, 1981), stemming ultimately from the need to make stories relevant as well as comprehensible to audience members. The media, then, do more than just provide channels of advocacy and accounts of environmental events; they continually imply standards as well, by which society at large might make sense of what it hears and vicariously experiences. Of course this was always so, but the normative function of the news has become much more noticeable—and more contentious—as our societies have become more fractious and splintered. And whereas Marxists maintain that, as a result, mass communications monolithically support the status quo, other scholars discern much scope for disorder and de-legitimation (Robinson, 1976) in the flow of negative news stories that continually report institutional failures and shortcomings against a backcloth of presumed societal norms.

There would be little point in proposing new guidelines for political coverage, however, if, as Thomas Patterson argues in *The Mass Media Election* (1980), eloquently fortified by the ghost of Walter Lippman (1922), journalism is essentially incorrigible. Partly this is because (he maintains), "The press is not a political institution and has no stake in organizing public opinion" (p. 173). Partly it is due to lapses from democratic grace of the average audience member—lacking time, energy, and motivation to become well-informed—for whom the press caters. The news, then, is simply "not an adequate guide to political choice," and, "The press cannot be expected to organize political information in a meaningful way" (pp. 175-6). Political communication arrangements can be improved only by restoring the lost coherence of political party institutions, not by striving to make reporters change their workways.

Such a formidable challenge may be countered along four lines. First, election communication involves a close interaction and mutual interdependency between party spokesmen and media professionals, in the course of which the two sides may be said to constitute a subtly composite unity. This is not to say that they merge to form a new organic whole in which their separate identities are lost. On the contrary, each side to some extent retains its separate purposes, its distance from the other, and, occasionally, even its oppositional stance toward the other. Nevertheless, the political messages which emanate from the dominant patterns of interaction between both sides are in a sense traceable to a composite source (Blumler & Gurevitch, 1981). And it follows from this diagnosis of election communication that one-sided approaches to its reform, tackling it solely from the political end and ignoring the journalistic end, cannot suffice. This is not to deny that reforms intended to strengthen the internal articulating capacities of the parties would be beneficial in their own right.[1] But by themselves, they would not improve politicians' standing with voters by a single jot. Consequently, few of the pressures on campaigners to mount appeals of certain kinds through the mass media, which ultimately stem from our current volatile and sceptical opinion climates, would be countered by such an approach to reform. Moreover, no changes made in political institutions can alter the fact that, in the end, those leaders and policies that emerge from them will have to be presented to electorates through the mass media. And if *their* ways of presenting campaigns are not modified, competing politicians will continue to adapt their behavior to them.

Second, political journalism is not a homogeneous entity. Since it evidently varies across media, organs, genres, time periods, and cultures, it is presumably open to change—and potentially for the "better." For example, even television news coverage of a British election campaign is less riveted by the horse-race element and more attuned to substantive issues than are its American counterparts.

Similarly, third, so far as receptivity to political communication is concerned, there is no standard audience member nor some predominant type of audience response that overshadows all others. Rather are ambivalence and complexity, typical characteristics of audience attitudes toward political messages. "Uses and gratifications" studies of audiences for election television, for example, typically suggest, not that electors are merely bored, cynical, or uninterested, nor that they invariably divide up neatly into the

---

[1] Alexander (1981, p. 37) also deplores, as a "peculiarly American" weakness, the inability of "institutions that should produce self-conscious political norms" to "provide certain kinds of competing inputs to the media."

politically-minded and the apathetic. It is rather that the same individual can be both attracted to ways in which television can serve his or her political needs and repelled by less appealing elements, such as the predictability of party positions, boredom with what is over-familiar or superfluous, or lack of constructive nourishment.[2] Such a mixed pattern offers a paramount reason for not giving up the quest for more valid ways of presenting elections to the public through the mass media. For if many voters are indeed poised to be either engaged or "turned off," then the quality of the campaign communications they receive could well help to determine in which way their ambivalence will for the time being be resolved.

Fourth, we should not forget that, in the medium of television especially, despite all its weaknesses, we have at our disposal, not merely an admittedly tightly constrained vehicle of daily journalism, but also in its numerous discussion and current affairs programs, a more ample "national debating chamber," in which the juxtaposed views of many major social and political interests are often relayed to heterogeneous audiences. It is, therefore, still meaningful, presumably, to direct some of our expectations of a democratic communication service to the controllers of such a public asset.

II

To do so coherently, however, we need to draw on a principled yet realistic conception of democracy and to spell out some of its possibly neglected journalistic implications. Elsewhere, I have argued that "a democratic test of a political communication system would be how far it enabled people to make choices in accord with the politics they wished to support" (Blumler, 1981, p. 270), a proposition which closely followed in turn from John Plamenatz's (1973, p. 186) view that:

> If there is to be democracy, citizens when they make political choices must have intelligible, relevant and genuinely different alternatives to choose between, and the men who put the alternatives to them must have sufficient motives for putting alternatives of this kind.

From such a notion, perhaps five priority guidelines for the enhancement of political journalism might be proposed:

First, in media coverage of politics (and especially of election campaigns) there should be more invitations to choose than to kibbitz. This is not to

---

[2] Recent research into audience reactions to parliamentary reporting on British radio and television has yielded a similarly mixed picture. Many people seemed to respond to extracts of House of Commons proceedings along several different dimensions of perception and evaluation, while parliamentary stories were more likely to be judged important, and worth including in TV news bulletins, than to be judged interesting. Thus, Parliament was apparently regarded as an institution that *deserved* attention, even if what goes on there was thought less interesting than many other events.

deny that politics is about power plays as well as policy differences. But when journalism treats the latter as mere playthings of the former, it encourages electors to become detached spectators rather than involved "problem-solvers" (Bauer, 1973).

Second, more credible and valid formats of political advocacy should be devised and introduced. As framers of options, takers of initiatives, and seekers of electoral support, what the parties (and other opinion sources) wish to tell voters in their own way deserves pride of place in a democratic communication system. But, too often, the formats through which this principle is implemented (e.g., political commercials and party broadcast rations) seem at best to have earned a grudging tolerance, and at worst to have invited much ridicule and disbelief. Yet several ways of improving the conditions of media access for political spokesmen, without undermining the journalistic function of independent scrutiny of what they say, have been proposed in the literature (cf. Seymour-Ure, 1974; Blumler *et al.* 1978; Walden, 1982) and by now deserve some trial.

Third, some reinterpretation of the impartiality norm may be called for by the striking unevenness of news treatment that seems to be allotted to the various contenders for citizens' ears and affections. At present, certain institutions are almost always accorded respect, even reverence (e.g., the Royal Family in Britain). Some often enjoy a benign sort of neglect (e.g., industrialists or the Supreme Court in the United States). Some evoke a mixture of symbolic deference and pragmatic exploitaton (e.g., the British Parliament). Some mainly suffer the slings and arrows of straight news-value fortunes (e.g., trade unions). Some can only get attention if they stir up trouble (many deviant minorities). Without enshrining a mathematical equality, blandness, or uncritical acceptance of publicity handouts, it should, nevertheless, be possible for all major opinion and interest groupings at least to recognize in the coverage of their affairs the essential elements of what they believe.

Fourth, in addition to the more adversarial qualities of challenge, vigilence, and exposure, a rounded political coverage would also occasionally acknowledge the difficulties involved in shouldering political responsibility and trying to implement policies. This is not a matter of looking up deferentially to office-holders or of turning a blind eye to their peccadilloes and errors. It is rather one of avoiding an overly simplistic view of the political vocation.

Finally, ways might be explored of occasionally expressing explicitly those normative guidelines that so often shape political stories implicitly at present. Such a tack, especially if it was pursued in the pluralistic spirit of appreciating that most events may be interpreted through more than one set of norms, could help to counter pressures toward media consonance and pack journalism; weaken the incentives of opinion spokesmen to try to manipulate news frameworks to their advantage; and inject more islands of order into the seeming atomism of daily news flows.

It may be that something like a paradigm shift in our way of conceiving the central function of political news is implied in much of the preceding analysis. There is certainly room for debate over how far the balance should be tilted in the proposed directions. But I do wonder whether, in the 1960s, many of us were too quick to accept journalists' own views about their political task at face value, when we said that they were essentially involved in pumping out information and providing the basis for public cognitions (Becker, McCombs, & McLeod, 1975). In what sense, I now find myself asking, is issue salience, for example, a *cognitive* dependent variable? After all, it reflects a person's priorities, not a matter of fact that he could grasp either correctly or incorrectly. And in that sense, the agenda-setting function of the press may be more like persuasion, even if unintended, than like learning, with which we have tended recently to classify it.

At any rate, it is as if when viewed from the standpoint of democratic criteria, the mirroring of fact and the dissemination of sheer information become rather less important than the projection of possible goals and values. The task of journalism is then seen less in terms of representing reality than of conveying alternative ways of coping with it. And the news becomes (or is recommended to become) less a record of events and more an exchange of ideas, less a knowledge test that everybody is bound to fail, than an agenda of priority concerns that are open to pursuit in a variety of ways.

REFERENCES

Alexander, J.C. (1981). "The Mass News Media in Systemic, Historical and Comparative Perspective." In E. Katz, and T. Szecsko (Eds.), *Mass Media and Social Change* (pp. 17-52). London: Sage.

Ball-Rokeach, S.J., and De Fleur, M.L. (1976). "A Dependency Model of Mass-Media Effects." *Communciation Research 3* (No. 1), 3-21.

Bauer, R.A. (1973). "The Audience." In I. de S. Pool, F.W. Frey, W. Schramm, N. Maccoby, and E.B. Parker (Eds.), *Handbook of Communication* (pp. 141-152). Chicago, IL: Rand McNally.

Becker, L.B., McCombs, M.E., and McLeod, J.M. (1975). "The Development of Political Cognitions." In S.H. Chaffee (Ed.), *Political Communication: Issues and Strategies for Research.* Beverly Hills, CA: Sage.

Berelson, B.R., Lazarsfeld, P.F., and McPhee, W.N. (1954). *Voting: A Study of Opinion-Formation in a Presidential Campaign.* Chicago, IL: University of Chicago Press.

Blumler, J.G. (1981). "Political Communication: Democratic Theory and Broadcast Practice." In H. Baier, H.M. Keppelinger, and K. Reumann (Eds.), *Public Opinion and Social Change* (pp. 258-272). Köln: Westdeutscher Verlag.

Blumler, J.G., and Gurevitch, M. (1981). "Politicians and the Press: An Essay on Role Relationships." In D.D. Nimmo and K.R. Sanders (Eds.), *Handbook of Political Communication,* (pp. 467-496). London: Sage.

Blumler, J.G., Gurevitch, M., and Ives, J. (1978). *The Challenge of Election Broadcasting.* Leeds: Leeds University Press.

Butler, D., and Kavanagh, D. (1980). *The British General Election of 1979.* London: Macmillan.
Gurevitch, M., and Blumler, J.G. (1982). "The Construction of Election News: An Observation Study at the BBC." In J.S. Ettema and D.C. Whitney (Eds.), *Individuals in Mass Media Organizations: Creativity and Constraint* (pp. 179-204). London: Sage.
Harrison, M. (1982). "Television News Coverage of the 1979 General Election." In R.M. Worcester and M. Harrop (Eds.), *Political Communications: The General Election Campaign of 1979* (pp. 68-77). London: Allen and Unwin.
Lippman, W. (1922). *Public Opinion.* New York: Macmillan.
Noelle-Neumann, E. (1973). "Return to the Concept of Powerful Mass Media." *Studies of Broadcasting* (No. 9). 67-112.
Pateman, C. (1979). *The Problem of Political Obligation: A Critical Analysis of Liberal Theory* New York: John Wiley and Sons.
Patterson, T.E. (1980). *The Mass Media Election: How Americans Choose Their President.* New York: Praeger.
Plamenatz, J. (1973). *Democracy and Illusion.* London: Longman.
Polsby, N.W. (1980). "The News Media as an Alternative to Party in the Presidential Selection Process." In R.A. Goldwin (Ed.), *Political Parties in the Eighties* (pp. 50-66). Washington, DC: American Enterprise Institute for Public Policy Research.
Robinson, M.J. (1976). "American Political Legitimacy in an Era of Electronic Journalism." In D. Cater and R. Adler (Eds.), *Television as a Social Force: New Approaches to TV Criticism* (pp. 97-139). New York: Praeger.
Seymour-Ure, C. (1974). *The Political Impact of Mass Media.* London: Constable.
Seymour-Ure, C. and Smith, A. (1982). "Prophets and Wildernesses, Press Coverage of Minor Parties: A Study of the Boundaries of the 1979 Campaign." In R.M. Worcester, and M. Harrop (Eds.), *Political Communications: The General Election Campaign of 1979* (pp. 88-102). London: Allen and Unwin.
Siune, K. (1982). "Parties and Journalists in Election Broadcasts." Paper presented to International Congress on Mass Media and Elections in Democratic Societies, Munster.
Walden, B. (1982). "Broadcasting and Politics." *Independent Broadcasting* (No. 31), 11-15.

Chapter 11
Media Agenda-Setting and Elections: Assumptions and Implications

DAVID WEAVER
Bureau of Media Research
School of Journalism
Indiana University
Bloomington, IN 47405

There seem to be two basic assumptions underlying media agenda-setting research:

1. The press does not serve as a simple conduit or as a *mirror* held up to the world. In other words, the press does not *reflect* reality, but rather *filters* and *shapes* it, much as a kaleidoscope filters and shapes light.
2. Concentration by the press over time on relatively few issues and subjects, and certain aspects of those subjects, generally leads to the public perceiving these issues and subjects as more salient, or more important, than other issues and subjects.

Most of the work on agenda-setting in the United States during the past decade or so has focused on testing the *second* assumption—that media emphasis on certain subjects results in public concern about these subjects. There has been relatively little agenda-setting research concerned with the first assumption—that the press actively shapes and filters reality rather than acting as a transmission belt or as a mirror of society.

And yet, in some ways, the first assumption is just as crucial to the idea of media agenda-setting as the second, for even if there is a correlation between what the press emphasizes and what people are concerned about (and numerous studies done in the past decade suggest there is, and several of them suggest that there is a causal relationship between media emphasis and public concern), it is not quite accurate to speak of the press *setting* agendas if it is mainly passing on priorities set by other actors and institutions in the society. In other words, if the press is acting mainly as a mirror or a transmission belt for various segments of the society, then it is not setting any agendas—it is simply passing on agendas set by others.

First published in W. Schulz and K. Schönbach (Eds.), *Massenmedien und Wahlen*. Munich: Ölschläger.

There have been some attempts to test the assumption of an active press that filters and shapes. A recent study (Gilberg, Eyal, McCombs, & Nicholas, 1980) shows that prior press coverage seemed to have more influence on President's Carter's issue agenda in his second State of the Union address than this speech had on the subsequent press issue agenda. Although this research is certainly a step in the right direction, it does not systematically compare the agendas of various news sources as compared with those of various media, to see whether news source priorities are substantially filtered and shaped by the media, or passed on to audiences largely intact.

In the 1976 Three Sites election study, reported in our book, *Media Agenda-Setting in a Presidential Election* (Weaver, Graber, McCombs, & Eyal, 1981), we made some attempts to compare the issues that were being stressed by political parties and front-running candidates with the issues that were being emphasized by newspapers and television, but these comparisions were not as rigorous and systematic as they should have been, mainly because the main thrust of our study—like almost all other agenda-setting studies—was in testing the second assumption that increased media emphasis on certain subjects over time results in increased salience of these subjects among the public. Because our study did focus on the media—audience link rather than on the source—media relationship, we limited our data collection mainly to the content of the media (newspapers and television) and to the concerns and interests of voters. We did not make much of an effort systematically to collect and analyze transcripts of candidates' speeches and press releases, or political party announcements and platforms.

But there is some evidence from our study that not all of the issues being emphasized by the Republican and Democratic candidates and party platforms were being heavily covered by the press. In another major year-long study of the 1976 election of political scientist Thomas Patterson (1980), it was found that the issues which the candidates stressed most heavily were *not* the same as those displayed most prominently in the news. Patterson found that, in their campaign speeches and television political advertising, the candidates talked mostly about "diffuse" issues—broad policy proposals, such as the commitment to maintain a healthy economy. In contrast, the media stressed what Colin Seymour-Ure (1974) has called "clear-cut" issues—those which neatly divide the candidates, provoke conflict, and can be stated in simple terms, usually by reference to shorthand labels such as "busing" and "detente."

One of Patterson's (1980) major conclusions regarding issues in the presidential campaign is that the issue news reflected the interests of the press more than the candidates' interests. This suggests support for the assumption that the press is more a kaleidoscope filtering reality than a mirror reflecting it; that the press is a more active interpreter than a passive transmission belt. Still, more needs to be done to compare systematically the agendas of various candidates, parties, and other news sources with media agendas.

In raising this concern about the relationship between news source agendas and media agendas, I do not want to imply that we have done all we need to do in studying the media agenda—audience agenda link. There is still considerable debate about whether media content does indeed tend to shape our perceptions of what is important and thus tell us what to think *about,* if not what to think. It seems to me that, after a decade or so of empirical studies on this subject, the debate is centered not so much on whether there *is* media influence but rather on the *contingent conditions* that make for more or less of this influence. There seem to be three positions emerging from the various studies conducted thus far:

1. The media are both necessary and sufficient in setting public agendas.
2. The media are necessary, but not sufficient, in setting public agendas.
3. The media are neither necessary nor sufficient in setting public agendas.

I. The first and most widespread position—that media are both necessary and sufficient in setting public agendas—seems now to hold true only with regard to certain *groups* of people (rather than individuals), to certain kinds of issues or subjects, to certain periods of time, to certain media, and to certain societies. The 1976 election study, and others, suggest that, with regard to *issues,* media agenda-setting varies according to the time period of the campaign, the kind of news medium being considered, the nature of the issues, and the orientation of the voters.

Put very briefly, the influence of both newspapers and television on public concern over issues seems to be greatest during the spring and summer, and least during the final few months of an election campaign. And this media influence seems to be confined mainly to those issues *least* likely to have a direct impact on most voters' daily lives—those we called *"unobtrusive,"* such as foreign affairs, government credibility, government spending and size, crime, and the environment and energy. MacKuen (in MacKuen & Coombs, 1981), in an analysis of the relationship between news magazine emphasis on issues and public concerns measured by Gallup surveys from 1960 to 1977, found the same thing—considerable support for media agenda-setting for the relatively unobtrusive issues of race relations, campus unrest, environment, the Vietnam war, crime, and energy, but very little support for media agenda-setting with regard to the more obtrusive issues of employment and inflation.

We also found that the distinctions between newspapers and television as issue agenda-setters became *less* pronounced as the campaign wore on. During the primary elections in the spring of 1976, we found evidence of a "two-step flow" of media agenda-setting, with the newspaper issue agenda remaining very stable over time, the television agenda changing to become generally more similar to the more stable newspaper agenda, and the voter agendas of issues becoming more similar to the television issue agenda. But after the summer political party conventions, the newspaper and television issue agendas became nearly identical and changed little.

In contrast to the declining importance of newspapers and TV as issue agenda-setters later in the year, the orientations of voters seemed to become *more* important as the election campaign drew to a close. Although levels of motivation to follow the campaign had fairly minor effects on voter issue agendas during the spring and summer seasons, this was not true during the fall period. Those voters with a high need for orientation (high interest and high uncertainty about whom to support) had issue agendas in the fall that were substantially *more similar* to the media agendas than did other voters. MacKuen (in MacKuen & Coombs, 1981), also found, in a separate analysis of Michigan's Center for Political Studies election study data from 1964 to 1976, that those most educated and most politically interested had issue agendas most similar to the media's. Thus motivation to follow the campaign was most important in the agenda-setting process near the *end* of the race, when the need for information was greatest for the still-undecided voters.

With respect to candidate images, our election study suggests that the press plays a major role in making some candidates, and certain of their characteristics, more salient than others. Warren Miller, in the Foreword to MacKuen and Coombs' (1981, p. 12), supports this finding in writing that "with candidates for public office, even more than with the public policy issues of the day, it is the content of the mass media that necessarily shapes impressions, understandings, and evaluations that constitute a citizen's response to a candidacy." In fact, this kind of agenda-setting probably has more influence on the voters' early perceptions of the campaign, and the final choices available at election time, than does issue agenda-setting. Like issue agenda-setting, however, image agenda-setting appears to be neither simple nor direct. It varies according to a number of contingent conditions, including media exposure patterns of voters, interpersonal communication patterns, prior knowledge and attitudes, and levels of motivation to follow the campaign. We found, for example, that prior knowledge, high interest, and high media exposure were all linked positively to learning about the personality traits and campaign styles of the candidates and, to a lesser extent, their job qualifications and ideological positions. Overall, though, our data suggest that the press, especially newspapers, played an important role in setting the agenda of candidates during the primary elections and the agenda of image characteristics for Carter and Ford later in the campaign.

Of course, it must be remembered that the evidence of issue and image agenda-setting supplied by our 1976 study, and by nearly every other study of agenda-setting I am aware of, is based on a comparison of media rankings of issues, or topics, with rankings of similar issues or topics by *groups* of respondents, not by individuals. Typically in such studies, randomly-selected individual voters or members of the public are asked about the issues of most concern to them, and, typically, they mention one or two such issues. These responses from individuals are then aggregated into a ranking of issues which reflects no single individual, but rather a group, or groups, of individuals. Thus, in nearly all agenda-setting studies, it is *not* accurate to speak of the media influencing individuals' agendas, but rather of the media influencing the *distribution* of the top one or two concerns among representative groups of voters or citizens. Even though this is not as dramatic an effect as some advocates of agenda-setting might hope for, it is still an important phenomenon, I believe, for it suggests that the relative amount of emphasis on various subjects by the press determines, and/or is reflective of, the size of various groups of individuals in a given community or society who are most concerned about these same subjects. And evidence collected over time, at least in the early periods of the 1976 U.S. Presidential campaign, suggests that the direction of influence is mostly from the press to the voters, rather than the other way around, a conclusion at least somewhat supported by other studies of agenda-setting across time using data from a 1972 U.S. election study (Shaw & McCombs, 1977; Weaver, McCombs, & Spellman, 1975), and by another study based on the 1976 U.S. election (Eyal, 1979).

The few studies which have been conducted at the individual level have produced very limited, or nonexistent, findings of media agenda-setting (Erbring, Goldenberg, & Miller, 1980; McLeod, Becker, & Byrnes, 1974; Siune & Borre, 1975). My own reaction is to interpret the data gathered thus far as indicating some support for the proposition that media emphasis on certain subjects over time does influence the number of citizens concerned about these subjects. This is, of course, not the same thing as saying that the press sets an agenda of issues or subjects for the individual citizen or voter, but it comes down more on the side of a macro-level, or societal level, agenda-setting process than does Becker's (1982) sceptical conclusion. I do agree with Becker, however, that media agenda-setting is a complex process, and that the media probably do not act alone in providing cues to audience members about issues. I also agree that the uses made of the media, as well as the social situation within which audience members reside, have a lot to do with how people assess issues. And I agree that the media may have more influence at one stage of issue development than at others, and more influence with respect to some kinds of issues than others.

Having said all this, however, my answer to the question of the existence of media agenda-setting is still a qualified "yes." In other words, I would conclude that there is evidence to suggest that media emphasis on certain issues and subjects over certain periods of time does influence which issues and subjects become of most concern to certain groups of people in an industrialized democracy such as the United States. Moreover, our data from the 1976 election study suggest that, by concentrating on certain attributes of candidates Carter and Ford and downplaying others, the *Chicago Tribune* did contribute to voter *evaluations* of these candidates as well as to voter images of them.

Put another way, I would conclude, *with regard to public agenda-setting,* that mass communication ordinarily functions among and through a nexus of mediating functions and influences, but that it often does serve as a necessary and sufficient cause of audience effects.

II. But not all researchers would agree with the position that the media often serve as a necessary and sufficient cause of public agendas. Some, like Gladys and Kurt Lang (1981) and Erbing et al. (1980), would be more comfortable with the second position—that the media are necessary, but not sufficient, in setting the public agenda. In their study, the Langs (1981) argue that Watergate did not become a highly salient issue by virtue of heavy media coverage alone. Rather, they maintain that, although media attention was a necessary condition for the emergence of the Watergate issue, it was not sufficient, because media coverage alone could not convince the public of the truth of the changes, or their seriousness. It took the participation of other institutions, such as the courts and the Congress, and the involvement of other political elites, to make Watergate highly salient as an issue. The Langs, and some political scientists such as Cobb and Elder (1972), refer to this as an *agenda-building* process, where the media are highly important, but function in concert with other institutions to create issues of public concern.

While I have little disagreement with this concept of agenda-building, it strikes me that, for many members of the public, the frequency and kind of messages are still the determining factors with regard to the public salience of an issue. Rather than seeing agenda-building as a new conceptualization of the media—audience relationship, I see it as pertinent mainly to the news source—media relationship. In other words, it seems to me that the agenda-building process as characterized by the Langs and others is more concerned with the assumption that the media filter and shape reality, than with the assumption that media emphasis on a topic leads to public concern with that topic. Agenda-building research seems to be mostly concerned with how issues *originate* or how topics of news coverage becomes issues, and with the relationships between media organizations and other actors and institutions in the society, than with the relationships between media content and audience perceptions.

Erbring et al. (1980), on the other hand, argue that exposure to media content is a necessary but not a sufficient condition for increased individual concern over certain issues, because such concern is contingent upon people's pre-existing issue sensitivities and their discussion of issues with others. They argue that their data, primarily from the 1974 Michigan National Election Study, suggest that media coverage of a new issue provides the impetus for increased interpersonal communication of the issue, but that, over time, this interpersonal discussion dominates the effects of media exposure and real-world conditions (as measured by unemployment and crime rates). And they find that for people not discussing politcs often, issue salience becomes "doubly dependent" upon media channels and environmental cues. Based on these findings, they argue that the "social processes of secondary diffusion and reality testing ultimately control the impact of the media" (Erbring et al., 1980, p. 46).

It seems to me that *in the early stages* of the emergence of an issue, Erbring et al.'s findings could be interpreted as supporting the position that the media are *both* necessary and sufficient in setting public agendas for those who frequently discuss politics and for those who do not. This interpretation would be consistent with the results of our year-long election study (Weaver et al., 1981), which suggested greater media influence early in the campaign. But *over time,* this media influence seems to give way to the influences of interpersonal communication and real-world cues. MacKuen in MacKuen and Coombs (1981) finds that dramatic events are more important than the amount of media coverage in agenda-setting, suggesting again that media impact is greatest during the early stages of issue formation and that the weight of media coverage over time does not automatically determine levels of public concern. In the end, MacKuen (1981, p. 141) concludes that "the shape of citizen agendas clearly reflects the editorial judgments defining news coverage, but is also sensitive to the real world independent of the media's orientations." His findings, like those of Erbring et al. (1980), could be interpreted as supporting the necessary and sufficient position in the early stages, and the necessary, but not sufficient, position in the later stages.

In short, with regard to the relationships between media organizations and sources of news, *agenda-building* research suggests that the media are often necessary, but not sufficient, in the creation of issues. With regard to the relationships between media and public concerns, *agenda-setting* research suggests that the media may be both necessary and sufficient in the early stages of public awareness of an issue, especially a more unobtrusive one, but that, over time, interpersonal discussion and real-world experiences make the media less sufficient, if not less necessary.

III. The third and least popular position—that media are neither necessary nor sufficient in setting public agendas—has received support from only a few studies, or parts of studies, dealing with individual persons' agendas and with *obtrusive* issues—those directly experienced by many people in their everyday lives. (See, for example, McLeod et al., 1974; Siune & Borre, 1975; and Weaver, Stehle, Auh, & Wilhoit, 1975). These studies suggest that the relative salience of individual-level day-to-day concerns is not greatly influenced by media news priorities, whereas the salience of more remote, more general public concerns is. They suggest that personal experience with day-to-day problems is a much more powerful teacher of perceived importance than are the media of communication. Most people, for example, do not need media coverage to tell them that inflation is a problem (although such coverage may reinforce their personal experiences), or that unemployment or energy prices are problems. But most people *do* need the media to perceive foreign policy or government credibility as important problems.

Thus, the power of the media alone to influence the perceived salience of a problem seems positively correlated with the remoteness of that problem from day-to-day experiences. And the ability of the media to influence the relative salience of such problems seems confined to a few leading ones, rather than to an entire agenda of eight, ten, or more. At least, this seems true for the *ranking* of such issues by each person, as compared with the media *ranking* of issues. But if one simply compares *which* issues are likely to appear on individual persons' agendas with those on the media agendas, there is more support for media influence than if only the rank orderings of these issues are compared. And as Nord (1981) notes, some political scientists interested in studying community power would maintain that which issues get on the public agenda (and which do not) is a more important question than the precise ranking of those issues.

To conclude, there seems to be most support from the research for the position that the media are often both necessary and sufficient for increasing the salience of just-emerging issues for *groups* of the general public, at least with regard to subjects that are outside that public's personal experience. There is also considerable support for the idea that the media are necessary, if not sufficient, in generating new issues. There is least support for the position that media are neither necessary nor sufficient in setting public agendas.

IMPLICATIONS

There are important implications of these conclusions for elections in industrialized democracies, for the role of the press as a guide to informed political choice in such elections, and for future research.

Elections and the Political System. Although the relative salience of issues, candidates and their image qualities, and politics in general is but one of a number of possible media effects on election campaigns and voter choices, it seems to be a highly important effect, possibly the most important effect, in elections. As Barber (1978, p. 156) puts it, "Attention is one of our polity's scarcest resources; so agenda-setting is powerful decision-making...deciding who's serious—bounding the universe of inquiry—may be journalism's most influential decision."

But simply deciding which issues, which candidates, and which qualities of candidates are the most important is not the same thing as deciding which party, which platform, or which candidate to support in an election. Directional decisions are crucial to the outcome of any election, once the most important issues, candidates, and images have been established.

Undoubtedly, though, there are linkages between the perceived importance of issues and images, and voters' *preferences* for certain parties and candidates. The distinction between *cognitive* effects of the media (such as agenda-setting and knowledge acquisition) and *affective* influences (opinion formation and attitude change) must not be overdrawn. There surely is a link between what we know and are concerned about, and what opinions and attitudes we hold. Feelings are not constructed out of thin air, but rather on the basis of beliefs and knowledge. Likewise, cognitions may be formed in response to certain attitudes and opinions. As O'Keefe and Atwood (1981, p. 335) point out in their major review of the research on communication and election campaigns, "the evidence is overwhelming that audiences attend selectively to political information in the mass media." And this selective attention, often motivated by particular atttitudes and ideologies, almost certainly contributes to the formation of beliefs and patterns of knowledge. The relationships between cognitions and attitudes are tenuous and complex, however, and thus are likely to confound evidence of direct media effects on feelings, whereas the relationships between media content and cognitions seem to be more straightforward and easier to demonstrate with empirical evidence.

Having said this, what are some of the more direct implications of issue, image, and interest agenda-setting for elections?

Interest. To the extent that mass media can stimulate interest among potential voters in an election, and thus raise the salience of politics on a larger agenda of concerns, we would expect to find higher levels of turnout among such voters. In our 1976 election study (Weaver et al., 1981), there is evidence to indicate that frequent use of television to follow politics during the primary elections in the spring stimulated subsequent voter interest in the campaign. This finding is consistent with evidence from other campaign studies indicating that the media play an important role in shaping the peaks and valleys of interest in elections, as well as helping to determine its onset (Berelson, Lazarsfeld, & McPhee, 1954; Mendelsohn & O'Keefe, 1976; O'Keefe & Atwood, 1981; Patterson, 1980). And there is evidence to suggest that it is the uninterested voters who decide not to vote either before or relatively early in the campaign. Atkin (1981) likewise rates campaign interests as an important predictor of voting turnout, along with citizen duty salience, preference strength, and political efficacy.

In addition to stimulating voter turnout, there is evidence that high interest in a campaign leads to increased learning about issues, images, and candidates prominent in the campaign. In our 1976 election study, we found that prior knowledge, high interest, and high media exposure were all linked positively to learning (Weaver et al., 1981), even though most such learning was confined to *awareness*—the ability to recognize issues, candidates, and images without the ability to recall positions taken by particular candidates on various issues, etc. Sears and Chaffee (1979), in their review of numerous studies of the 1976 presidential and vice presidential debates, found that the main predictors of debate exposure were interest in politics generally and interest in the campaign, and that exposure to the debates—especially the first one—led to increased learning about the candidates' major domestic positions.

In short, then, there is evidence to suggest that media coverage of an election campaign, especially television coverage of it early on, can lead to increased interest in and learning from the campaign, and increased turnout by voters on election day.[1]

Images. In raising the salience of certain candidates, and particular attributes of candidates, the media play a very important role in forming voters' early perceptions of the election campaign and the final choices available on election day. Obviously, the most basic dimension of a candidate's image is name recognition. If the voters have not heard of a candidate or do not recognize his or her name, they are not likely to have a politically useful image of him or her. Therefore the most fundamental image agenda-setting role performed by the media is simply to familiarize voters with candidates' names.

We found in our 1976 election study (Weaver et al., 1981) that there is a direct, positive relationship between how much media coverage is given to the various candidates before and during the primaries and how many vot-

---

[1] My colleague from the University of Munich in West Germany, Klaus Schönbach, has suggested there is a need to distinguish agenda-setting from information processing, or else all the research findings on learning and information processing become subsumed under the agenda-setting label. I agree with this observation and with his suggestion that agenda-setting should refer to the salience (importance, prominence) of certain objects and their attributes, rather than to the specific relationships between them. Learning various relationships between objects (candidates, political parties, etc.) and attributes (personality traits, issue positions, etc.) is not the same thing as learning the salience of such objects and attributes, although there is probably a relationship between salience and amount of learning of relationships. At least some studies on learning under conditions of low and high involvement suggest that, under low involvement (low relevance and presumably low salience), individuals employ a less taxing information processing strategy that is characterized by peripheral processing of nonmessage content cues such as source expertise, trustworthiness, or attractiveness (Perloff, 1982; Petty & Cacioppo, 1981). Under conditions of high involvement (high relevance and presumably high salience), on the other hand, individuals seem to be more motivated diligently and systematically to process messages, focusing on such attributes as the quality, accuracy, and number of message arguments (Chaiken, 1980; Perloff, 1982; Petty, Cacioppo, & Goldman, 1981).

Whatever the case, it seems useful to distinguish agenda-setting from information processing as media effects, even if the two are correlated. Some of the recommendations in this chapter do assume such a correlation.

ers are familiar with these candidates. Patterson (1980), in his study of 1,200 voters in this same election, found the same thing—after subsequent news coverage focused heavily on Jimmy Carter, he was the sole Democrat to become dramatically more familiar to the voters. Becker and McCombs (1978) likewise found that, from February to March, voters went from being unsure of who was leading the crowded Democratic field of candidates to placing Jimmy Carter at the top of the list—or agenda—of candidates. They concluded that the media were at least partially responsible for these shifts in voter perceptions.

In addition to this evidence of the media's role in determining the agenda, or slate, of candidates in an election, the findings from our 1976 study also suggest that the media are important in raising the salience of certain candidates' characteristics, as well as their names. We found that the image attributes stressed in Chicago *Tribune* coverage and in descriptions used by Evanston, Illinois voters to acquaint their friends with the leading candidates ran along parallel lines. We also discovered, through crosslagged correlational analysis, that, for the most part, the *Tribune* descriptions of Carter and Ford influenced the voters, rather than vice versa. And the voters in our study thought it easier to learn about candidate images than about issues, enhancing the chances for image agenda-setting. They consistently referred to images three or four times as often as to issues in their descriptions of Carter and Ford. Image dimensions pertaining to personality traits and styles of the candidates were better remembered than those pertaining to job qualifications and ideology, a finding duplicated in Patterson's (1980) study. O'Keefe and Atwood (1981), in their review of numerous studies of communication and election campaigns, agree that the media appear to play a major role in the formation of voters' images or stylistic impressions of candidates' personal attributes.

Thus, newspapers and television seem to contribute significantly to determining who will be nominated, and ultimately who will be elected, by focusing news coverage on certain candidates and on certain characteristics of those candidates. By making more salient these candidates and their attributes, the media contribute greatly to the construction of a second-hand reality—one that is not confined to conveying what party spokesmen proclaim and what the candidates say, as the Langs point out in their classic book on mass media and voting (Lang & Lang, 1959).

Issues. As mentioned earlier in this article, there seems to be considerable support for the conclusion that the news media are crucial in determining the public importance of issues in an election campaign, at least those issues generally outside the personal experience of most of the public. However, the power of the media to shape the issue agenda for political leaders and for the public is not unlimited. As we have seen, many important issues are matters of personal experience for the audience, or matters in which saliences have already been shaped by past learning from a variety of media and personal information sources. Irrespective of media emphasis, these issues may assume major importance in an election if the public is greatly concerned about them. This is what happened with such issues as unemployment and inflation in the 1976 U.S. Presidential election. Although the media gave them comparatively little coverage, public concern caused them to be major factors in tipping the balance from Ford to Carter (Miller & Miller, 1977).

We also found that those undecided voters highly interested in the campaign (those with the highest need for orientation) had issue agendas in the last third of the campaign that were substantially more similar to the media agendas than did other voters. And after the election, those voters with a high need for orientation were more likely than other voters to cite issues as more important than either candidate images or political party affiliation in deciding for whom to vote (Weaver & McCombs, 1978).

Findings from our study (Weaver et al., 1981) and from Chaffee and Choe's (1980) work suggest that there is a substantial group of less partisan (more independent) voters who pay close attention to the flow of information during a U.S. Presidential election campaign, and vote on the basis of this information rather than on the basis of the traditional predictor of political party identification. If these patterns hold for other elections, it is tempting to conclude that, even though mass media may indeed reinforce or have little impact on the candidate choices of partisan voters, the media most likely teach those independents who are interested in the campaign (those with a high need for orientation) which issues and candidate characteristics to consider important during the campaign, as well as how the various candidates stand on the issues. And this information can be very important in determining the *outcome* of an election as well as its structure.

When one considers that the outcome of the 1976 U.S. Presidential election hinged on fewer than 15,000 persons (United Press International, 1976) in Ohio and Hawaii (which would have given Ford 270 electoral votes to Carter's 268), the importance of a relatively small group of highly interested undecided voters is apparent. Perhaps, then, in light of the increasing importance of issues in U.S. Presidential elections (Miller, 1977, Miller & Levitin, 1978), the decreasing importance of political party identification (Cantor, 1975), and the increased reliance on campaign information (including issue stands and image attributes) by undecided and interested voters (Chaffee & Choe, 1980; Weaver et al., 1981), the agenda-setting function of newspapers and television will become an even more important factor in determining not only the structure, but also the outcome, of future U.S. Presidential elections.

The Role of the Media. The foregoing conclusions regarding media agenda-setting imply a highly important role for mass media in elections, such as the 1976 U.S. Presidential contest where many voters were unsure of their choices. But if the media can indeed stimulate interest in an election and subsequent voting turnout, the decreasing levels of turnout for U.S. Presidential elections suggest that newspapers and television need to do a more stimulating job of covering such elections—or *not* covering them to such an extent that the voters are weary of them weeks before election day! To maximize interest and turnout in the campaign, the major news media should also stress the citizen duty involved in voting, the distinctions between the parties and candidates, and the fact that even a small number of votes may make a difference in the outcome.

Likewise, with regard to candidates, images, and issues, the media, especially newspapers from which television news seems to take many cues, should make a concerted effort at the beginning of an election year, and even before that time, to cover as many issues as possible and to make the positions of the various political parties and candidates on these issues as clear as possible. This coverage should go beyond clear-cut issues to the more diffuse policy proposals as well. Newspapers and television should also try to cover as many candidates as equally as possible throughout the campaign. By focusing on only one or two winners of early primaries, the choices of voters are unnecessarily restricted long before election day. And there should be more coverage of candidates' job qualifications and ideologies, as well as of their personalities, styles, and campaign activities.

In our study of the 1976 election (Weaver et al., 1981), I and my colleagues agree with Patterson (1980) that the burden on the media is particularly severe during the early nomination phase of a U.S. Presidential election campaign, a period in which our data suggest the media have the most influence on voters. But we do not agree with Patterson's contention that the media cannot be an adequate guide for informed political choice. The media do not have to narrow the field of candidates so early in the campaign; they do not have to concentrate on the clear-cut, conflict-laden issues and gloss over the positions of the candidates on a wide range of more diffuse policy issues; they do not have to focus on the personalities and styles of campaign activities of candidates rather than on their job qualifications and political stances; and they do not have to present information on issues and job qualifications in an uninteresting and dull fashion. Even though we agree with Patterson (1980) that the major themes of the news are dictated more by journalistic values than by political ones, such journalistic values do include a commitment to accuracy, impartiality, and empirical evidence (at least among the high quality media)—values compatible with producing an informed electorate.

Patterson and other scholars contend that the real weakness of the Presidential election system in the United States is the dismantling of the political party. Party leaders, they argue, are more adept than voters at selecting nominees who will meet the public's desire for leadership. Parties are also credited with being ultimately more responsive than the media to the needs of the voters, because parties must win voter support in elections. This leads to the conclusion that the time has come to find ways to increase the party's influence in a nomination system that blends popular participation and party influence.

I personally doubt, however, whether political party elites are much more responsive to voter needs than are the journalists who work for the major news media. In fact, I think it can be argued that the journalists may be more responsive to a wider variety of public needs precisely because many journalists do not have particular "pet causes" or issues to promote. In other words, many journalists in the United States have fewer political axes to grind than do many political party elites who, after all, seek to maintain and increase their own power and positions while at the same time appearing to serve the voters.

In addition, many of those most concerned about new communication technology and the proliferation of channels view the present agenda-setting function of the media as a unifying force in society rather than a divisive one. Blumler and others fear that electronic information delivery systems might lead to less public exposure to serious information on social and political questions, not only because of the ability of each person to be more selective in his or her choice of information, but also because the multiplication of cannels will probably mean a decreased share of the audience for any given news organization, and that this will mean, in turn, decreased revenue to support serious news-gathering efforts.

If media agenda-setting thus serves as an integrative, or unifying, force in society, the question of who sets the agenda becomes of primary importance. In our 1976 election study, we argue that it is the responsibility of the media to use their agenda-setting influence to alert voters to as broad a range of issues and images as possible. This, of course, assumes that journalists should determine what the important issues are, what image qualities need to be stressed, and whose names should be made familiar to the electorate. But, as we note, there is reason to question this assumption. The fact that the public perceptions of the importance of economic issues, with which the public is most familiar, differ from the relative emphasis on them by the media raises doubts about the merits of media choices. So does the fact that the issue agendas of candidates, many of them publicly elected, are not similar to the media agendas.

But are media agendas determined mainly by journalists independently of news sources? The available studies of newsmaking suggest caution in such a conclusion. Some, like those of the Langs (1981) and Cobb and Elder (1972), cited earlier as agenda-building research, suggest that the media are highly important in the origination of public issues, but function in concert with other institutions and groups in creating issues of public concern. In an essay drawing on their study of the 1979 campaign for elections to the European Parliament, Blumler and Gurevitch (1981, p. 469) argue that, in the process of responding to each other, political advocates and media professionals interact in subtle and complex ways, "in the course of which the two sides may virtually be said to constitute a subtly composite unity." They go on to assert that these two sides do not form a new unified whole, but that "it would be extremely difficult to detect, within any given political message, the specific contribution to its shaping that was uniquely made by either side. They are inextricably intertwined.

Future Research. These observations point to the need for future research on media agenda-setting not to be confined to media–audience relationships. We need to continue to examine the interaction of media institutions with news sources *in an agenda-setting framework* to specify more precisely how issues and images originate, and how issue agendas are maintained over time. We need to understand better when media are likely to act as passive transmission belts and when they are more likely to take an active role in filtering and shaping issues and images. Under what conditions are media most likely to pass along the priorities of their news sources? To change those priorities?

But at the same time that we need to know more about the relationships between source agendas and media agendas, we also need to continue the work on how media agendas of issues and images are related to public agendas. And we need to *relate* the findings from both kinds of research to get a fuller and more complete understanding of the agenda-building and agenda-setting processes.

In conducting such studies, it seems worth reemphasizing that we should not draw too sharp a line between cognitive and attitudinal effects of the media. Carter (1965) pointed out some years ago that, although information gain is not always correlated with attitude change, such a correlation is more likely to exist if the information makes salient certain discriminating attributes that enable a person to assign a favorable or unfavorable value to an object (candidate, political party, etc.). To the extent that certain issues and image characteristics stressed by the media help a potential voter to discriminate between candidates or parties, we would expect increased salience of such issues or image qualities to lead to a more favorable evaluation of one candidate over others, or of one political party over others.

McCombs (1972) agrees that research on the affective and cognitive components of attitude indicates that the two are often inextricably bound together, and Chaffee (1975) argues that, from the point of view of a member of a political system, a distinction between opinions and knowledge is likely to be irrelevant. What counts, Chaffee argues, is whether political information relates to the member's action role within the political system —whether that role be a decision to support or not support the system, or to make certain demands upon it.

Extending the agenda-setting concept beyond issues to candidate image characteristics helps link cognitions with attitudes and opinions, but it does not solve the problem of which characteristics are likely to be evaluated in a positive or negative manner by which people. There are some characteristics of candidates that are likely to be perceived by most people as good (e.g., kindness, compassion, generosity) and there are some issues that are likely to be perceived by most people as favoring one candidate or another (unemployment, armed conflict, etc.), but there are many image attributes and issues that are likely to be perceived in differing ways by different people, depending on a whole host of background and personality variables.

Moving beyond elections, it is also necessary to consider the implications of media agenda-setting for subsequent political action. There is some evidence (Janesch, 1982) that problems emphasized by the news media often are addressed by government legislation. We need to know more about the effects of media agenda-setting, not only on public concerns and voting preferences, but also on subsequent behavior of politicians themselves.

Studying the relationships between news sources, media professionals, the public and government actions within an agenda-setting framework is a demanding task, of course, but one worth pursuing if we are to gain a more complete and holistic understanding of the role of mass communication in democratic political systems.

REFERENCES

Atkin, C.K. (1981). "Mass Media Effects on Voting: Recent Advances and Future Priorities." *Political Communication Review 6*, 13–26.

Auh, Taik Sup. (1977). "Issue Conflict and Mass Media Agenda-Setting During the 1974 Indiana Senatorial Campaign." Unpublished doctoral dissertation in mass communication, Indiana University.

Barber, J.D. (1978). "Characters in the Campaign: The Scientific Question." In J.D. Barber (Ed.), *Race for the Presidency: The Media and the Nominating Process* (pp. 147–172). Englewood Cliffs, NJ: Prentice-Hall.

Becker, L.B. (1982). "The Mass Media and Citizen Assessment of Issue Importance: A Reflection on Agenda-Setting Research." *Mass Communication Review Yearbook 3*, 521–536.

Becker, L.B., and McCombs, M.E. (1978). "The Role of the Press in Determining Voter Reactions to Presidential Primaries." *Human Communication Research 4*, 301–307.

Berelson, B.R., Lazarsfeld, P.F., and McPhee, W. (1954). *Voting.* Chicago, IL: University of Chicago Press.

Blumler, J.G. (1980). "Information Overload: Is There a Problem?" In E. Witte (Ed.), *Human Aspects of Telecommunication.* New York: Springer-Verlag.

Blumler, J.G., and Gurevitch, M. (1981). "Politicians and the Press: An Essay on Role Relationships." In D.D. Nimmo and K.R. Sanders (Eds.), *Handbook of Political Communication* (pp. 467–493). Beverly Hills, CA: Sage.

Cantor, R.D. (1975). *Voting Behavior and Presidential Elections.* Itasca, IL: F.E. Peacock.

Carter, R.F. (1965). "Communication and Affective Relations." *Journalism Quarterly 42*, 203–212.

Chaffee, S.H. (1975). "The Diffusion of Political Information." In S.H. Chaffee (Ed.), *Political Communication: Issues and Strategies for Research* (pp. 85-128). Beverly Hills, CA: Sage.

Chaffee, S.H., and Choe, S.Y. (1980). "Time of Decision and Media Use During the Ford-Carter Campaign." *Public Opinion Quarterly 44*, 53-69. (Reprinted in *Mass Communication Review Yearbook 3*, 565-581).

Chaiken, S. (1980). "Heruristic Versus Systematic Information Processing and the Use of Source Versus Message Cues in Persuasion." *Journal of Personality and Social Psychology 40*, 752-766.

Cobb, R.W., and Elder, C.D. (1972). *Participation in American Politics: The Dynamics of Agenda-Building.* Boston: Allyn and Bacon.

Erbring, L., Goldenberg, E.N., and Miller, A.H. (1980). "Front-Page News and Real-World Cues: A New Look at Agenda-Setting by the Media." *American Journal of Political Science 24*, 16-49.

Eyal, C.H. (1979). "Time Frame in Agenda-Setting Research." Unpublished doctoral dissertation, Syracuse University.

Gilberg, S., Eyal, C.H., McCombs, M.E., and Nicholas, D. (1980). "The State of the Union Address and the Press Agenda." *Journalism Quarterly 57*, 584-588.

Janesch, P. (1982). "The Legislature Acted on a Variety of Issues Spotlighted by Papers." *(Louisville) Courier-Journal*, April 18, 1982.

Katz, E. (1980). "On Conceptualizing Media Effects." *Studies in Communications 1*, 119-141.

Klapper, J. (1960). *The Effects of Mass Communication.* Glencoe, IL: Free Press.

Lang, G., and Lang, K. (1981). "Watergate: An Exploration of the Agenda-Building Process." *Mass Communication Review Yearbook 2*, 447-468.

Lang, K., and Lang, G. (1959). *The Mass Media and Voting.* New York: Free Press.

McCombs, M.E. (1972). "Mass Communication in Political Campaigns: Information, Gratification & Persuasion." In F.G. Kline and P.J. Tichenor (Eds.), *Current Perspectives in Mass Communication Research* (pp. 169-194). Beverly Hills, CA: Sage.

MacKuen, M.B., and Coombs, S.L. (1981). *More Than News: Media Power in Public Affairs.* Beverly Hills, CA: Sage.

McLeod, J.M., Becker, L.B., and Byrnes, J.E. (1974). "Another Look at the Agenda-Setting Function of the Press." *Communication Research 1*, 131-166.

Mendelsohn, H., and O'Keefe, G. (1976). *The People Choose a President: Influences on Voter Decision Making.* New York: Praeger.

Miller, H. (1977). "Election Study Notes New Trends in Voter Behavior, Attributes Close Race to a Well-Run Campaign." *ISR Newsletter 5*, 4-5.

Miller, W.E., and Levitin, T.E. (1978). *Leadership and Change.* Cambridge, MA: Winthrop.

Miller, A.H., and Miller, W.E. (1977). "Partisanship and Performance: 'Rational' Choice in the 1976 Elections." Paper presented at the American Political Science Association Convention, Washington, DC.

Nord, D.P. (1981). "The Politics of Agenda Setting in the Late 19th Century Cities." *Journalism Quarterly 58*, 565-574, 612.

O'Keefe, G. (1975). "Political Campaigns and Mass Communication Research." In S.H. Chaffee (Ed.), *Political Communication: Issues and Strategies for Research* (pp. 129-164). Beverly Hills, CA: Sage.

O'Keefe, G. and Atwood, L.E. (1981). "Communication and Election Campaigns." In D.D. Nimmo and K.R. Sanders (Eds.), *Handbook of Political Communication* (pp. 329-357). Beverly Hills, CA: Sage.

Patterson, T. (1980). *The Media Election: How Americans Choose Their President.* New York: Praeger.

Perloff, R.M. (1982). "Political Involvement Revisited: A Critique and a Process-Oriented Reformulation." (Unpublished paper.)

Petty, R.E., and Cacioppo, J.T. (1981). *Attitudes and Persuasion: Classic and Contemporary Approaches.* Dubuque, IA: William Brown.

Petty, R.E., Cacioppo, J.T., and Goldman, R. (1981). "Personal Involvement as a Determinant of Argument-Based Persuasion." *Journal of Personality and Social Psychology 41,* 847–855.

Sears, D.O., and Chaffee, S.H. (1979). "Uses and Effects of the 1976 Debates: An Overview of Empirical Studies." In S. Kraus (Ed.), *The Great Debates: Carter vs. Ford, 1976* (pp. 223–261). Bloomington, IN: Indiana University Press.

Seymour-Ure, C. (1974). *The Political Impact of Mass Media.* London: Constable.

Shaw, D., and McCombs, M.E. (1977). *The Emergence of American Political Issues: The Agenda-Setting Function of the Press.* St. Paul, MN: West.

Siune, K., and Borre, O. (1975). "Setting the Agenda for a Danish Election." *Journal of Communication 25,* (No. 1), 65–73.

United Press International. (1976). "Outcome of '76 Election Hinged on Votes of 15,000." Washington, DC: UPI.

Weaver, D.H., Graber, D.A., McCombs, M.E., and Eyal, C.H. (1981). *Media Agenda-Setting in a Presidential Election: Issues, Images, and Interest.* New York: Praeger.

Weaver, D.H., and McCombs, M.E. (1978). "Voters' Need for Orientation and Choice of Candidate: Mass Media and Electoral Decision Making," paper presented at the conference of the American Association for Public Opinion Research, Roanoke, VA.

Weaver, D.H., McCombs, M.E., and Spellman, C. (1975). "Watergate and the Media: A Case Study of Agenda-Setting." *American Politics Quarterly 3,* 458–471.

Weaver, D.H., Stehle, T.E., Auh, T.S., and Wilhoit, G.C. (1975). "A Path Analysis of Individual Agenda-Setting During the 1974 Indiana Senatorial Campaign." Paper presented at the Association for Education in Journalism Convention, Ottawa, Canada.

Chapter 12
Uses and Gratifications Research and the Study of Social Change

CARL R. BYBEE

Communication Research Center
Department of Speech
University of Oregon
Eugene, OR 97403

The uses and gratifications approach has been hailed as a dramatic break, not just from the mass media effects tradition of the past, but specifically from the conservative commercial and governmental influences which have constrained much of the thinking about media's role in society (Swanson, 1979). In this view, the uses and gratifications approach conceptually relocates a certain degree of autonomous power—power which, until recently, was seen as resting solely in the domain of the communicator—into the hands (and minds) of the audience. Consequently, the cornerstone of the approach is the optimistic conceptualization of the audience as active, consciously using the media to satisfy personal needs and achieve personal goals. From a political perspective, by crediting people with more control over their own activities, "there is less reason to be concerned about the ownership and control of the media, or with the quality of the output or with any problem of long-term or short-term effect" (Elliot, 1974, p. 254). This paper takes the position that the fundamental assumptions of the uses and gratifications approach, particularly the assumptions regarding the nature and extent of audience activity and the ability of the audience consciously to recognize and act in its own best interest, implicitly bind the approach to a limited conceptualization of the distribution and maintenance of political power.

Although there is substantial confusion and debate about the meaning of key concepts (Swanson, 1977, 1979) and whether or not the approach meets the criteria of an emerging theoretical orientation (Elliot, 1974; Katz, 1979; Weiss, 1976), or needs to (Blumler, 1979; Katz, Blumler, & Gurevitch, 1974), a consensus seems to have evolved regarding the parameters of what might loosely be called a uses and gratifications paradigm (Blumler, 1979; McLeod

---

Based on a paper presented at the International Communication Association Conference, Dallas, Texas, May 1983.

& Becker, 1981; Windahl, 1981). This paper offers a critique of that paradigm from a political communication perspective. Political communication is defined here as a concern for the role of communication exchange in the promotion, maintenance, and distribution of political power. Three related points will be made. The first is that the uses and gratifications paradigm does not represent a dramatic break, at the individual or systems level, with the traditional effects perspective, particularly in terms of its implicit conservative bias regarding the process by which political power is distributed in society. The second point is that this conservative bias can best be understood by examining the conceptual linkages of the uses and gratifications paradigm with the theory of democratic pluralism articulated by Dahl (1969) and Polsby (1963), rather than by reviewing the "peculiar" (Elliot, 1974) functionalist roots (functionalist as represented by the work of Merton, 1968), so often defensively re-sifted by supporters of the paradigm (Katz, 1979; McLeod & Becker, 1981; Mendelsohn, 1974).

The third point is derived from an analysis of political participation and power relationships presented by Lukes (1974). Working from a political communication perspective, the potential meaning of the active audience is greatly expanded, resulting in a different context for the interpretation of audience activity and inactivity. Audience members seeking diversion, escape, and relaxation from the mass media can be read, for instance, as citizens, in part seeking noninvolvement in the social and political process. To the extent that these motivations are widely experienced within the disadvantaged sectors of society, a disturbing paradox emerges. Those citizens to whom the society offers the least, make the fewest demands on the society. Murdock and Golding (1979, p. 12) phrase the issue similarly, stating that the central problem in mass communication studies, particularly of a sociological orientation, should be "explaining how radical inequalities in the distribution of rewards come to be presented as natural and inevitable and are understood as such by those who benefit least from this distribution." Lukes' (1974, p. 12) analysis of power relationships provides a number of key insights into this paradox. The explanation of the implications of these insights for future research and theorizing within the uses and gratifications paradigm constitutes the third objective of this paper.

DRAMATIC BREAK OR EVOLUTION: THE INDIVIDUAL LEVEL

The history of mass communication effects research in the United States is the history of a relentless, empirical search, first for direct, powerful, short-term attitudinal effects, and later for the intervening variables which could be regarded as either facilitative or obstructive of those effects. Laboratory work on the varying effectiveness of source and message characteristics, best represented by Hovland and his associates (Hovland, Janis, & Kelley, 1954), flourished in the 1940s and 1950s as the direct effects model was slowly elaborated to take account of the multi-stage process of mass communication. Early in this elaboration process, important intervening variables mediating message effectiveness, such as personality characteristics and social structural variables, were uncovered. Lazarsfeld's field studies (Berelson, Lazarsfeld, & McPhee, 1954; Lazarsfeld, Berelson, & Gaudet, 1948) of voting behavior, while challenging the inflated projections of media influence being obtained in the laboratory, continued to demonstrate the constraining impact of new intervening variables.

The most notable contributions of these voting studies to the growing list of media influence constraining variables were the social relations variable of group interaction—also known as the twostep flow—and the individual difference variables labeled "selective exposure" and "selective perception." While other earlier work is occasionally pointed to as signalling the beginning of the evolution of the uses and gratifications paradigm (Herzog, 1944; Suchman, 1942), these studies were more concerned with the direct linking of specific media content and specific audiences to understand how individuals were integrated into the existing social structure, and the forms this integration took in terms of the legitimation of power and authority (Elliot, 1974). The concern for selective exposure and selective perception, however, constituted the beginning of researchers' search for more general audience orientations toward the media. While identifying primarily defensive orientations of the audience to the media, they called explicit attention to the active, although narrowly defined, motivational character of the audience.

The question then becomes what conceptual baggage was carried along and what was left behind in the process of this transition from a communicator centered model of mass communication effects to the audience centered model represented by the uses and gratifications paradigm. What was left behind was essentially an untenable stimulus–response conception of the media effects process. What was carried along was essentially a limited conception of the media effects process, a lack of explicit social theoretical referents for the interpretation of individual level results, and a consumerist frame of reference.

The limited conception of the media effects process inherent in both pre- and post-uses and gratifications paradigm work reveals itself in a number of related ways. Perhaps the most significant commonality is the truncated view of the media influence process. Both approaches focus attention on the media/audience relationship, taking media content as a given. Imbedded in this assumption is a lack of concern for the nature of the power relationships within society that determine media output (Murdock & Golding, 1979) and for the possibility that there are multiple realities as opposed to one objective reality within which individuals live and construct meaning for their lives (Carey & Kreiling, 1974).

A related commonality is the nature of the methodology employed. Rooted in empiricism and advanced through the variable analytic method, both approaches have suffered from the inability to conceptualize the complexity of symbolic content contained in media messages, or the complex ways in which the audience incorporates this content into their world views (Gitlin, 1978; Swanson, 1979).

These same methodological biases have also contributed to a shortsightedness in both approaches for the understanding of the larger implications of their findings. Without the methodological ability to conceptualize ideology, an organized set of ideas and values regarding the nature of the social-political world, or the theoretical referents to call attention to this methodological deficiency, the interpretive importance of key media effects, such as reinforcement, or key media gratifications sought, such as diversion, is minimized or lost. There is a strong current of resistance to the introduction of the concept of ideology into the uses and gratifications paradigm. It would seem that this is due, in part, to the threat such an introduction would pose to the assumed meaning of audience activeness. Ideology, once conceptualized, brings one to an immediate confrontation with questions of power. To talk about ideology, it is necessary to consider its pervasiveness, its sources, its correspondence to objective reality, and its potential class bias. In light of the answers to these questions, the reallocation of power to the audience that the paradigm presupposes might assume a somewhat hollow ring.

Resistance to the introduction of the concept of ideology may also derive from the recognition that the level of analysis is necessarily forced upward from individual level analysis, micro-functional or action-motivation, which has characterized most uses and gratifications research, to a systems level perspective. While it is true that numerous, apparent functional analyses have been applied to the mass media at the social system level (DeFleur & Ball-Rokeach, 1982; Wright, 1960, 1974), little has been written about the role of the individual, functional or otherwise, within these systems. Specifically, the degree of individual autonomy within a systems level functional analysis has not been addressed, leaving open the question of the degree of compatibility between these system analyses and existing uses and gratifications work done at the individual level.

One last important and relatively unrecognized commonality between the communicator and audience centered approach is in their consumerist frame of reference. While a number of mass communication scholars have called attention to and documented the commercial roots of the traditional communicator centered model of media effects (Blumler, 1979; Gitlin, 1978; McLeod & Becker, 1981), less notice has been paid to the parallels between the uses and gratifications paradigm and evolving marketing philosophy.

Just as contemporary marketing research is attempting to go beyond demographics to psychographics, the uses and gratifications paradigm marks the transition from demographics to audience motivations in predicting media impact. Just as audience demand is offered in the market place as a legitimation of production, whether it be of larger cars or sexually oriented television programming, so the uses and gratifications paradigm is offered as a diagnostic tool for correcting imbalances in the flow of communication as perceived by the audience. While it is true that the paradigm has been criticized for the conservative nature of its micro-functionalist view point (an argument which will be considered later), the sophistication and degree of this criticism has not approached the same level as that which has been directed toward similar audience demand models postulated, for example, by broadcasting executives in defense of current television programming practices. The broadcast executives' defense that "we give the audience what they want" is seen as a relatively vacuous argument, because it doesn't answer fundamental questions, such as "how does content change? How do creators know what will be popular with the audience when there is so little feedback? Why have some programs which have had a relatively small audience when first broadcast been able to build audience interest?" (Cantor, 1980, p. 101).

In addition, many critics recognize the inappropriateness of suggesting that program selection is the equivalent of voting for a particular programming content. What is on the competing channels, the audience's degree of familiarity with the genre (their conditioned acceptance), etc., all challenge the idea that program selection is an example of free choice. However, these same kinds of challenges, posed by Elliot (1974) nearly 10 years ago regarding the uses and gratifications paradigm, have not resurfaced in the literature. It is also interesting to note the parallels between the rhetoric of the consumer movement and those who see the uses and gratifications approach as a significant step forward in improving media policy. In both cases, attention is focused on the act of consumption rather than the act of production. Consequently, the parameters for debate about policy are implicitly set. Audience needs and expectations must be translated into marketplace language in order to be heard. Arguments based on political or social ideals and system concepts are not relevant.

DRAMATIC BREAK OR EVOLUTION: THE SYSTEM LEVEL

DeFleur and Ball-Rokeach (1982) do an admirable job of tracing the roots of the mass society theory and its subsequent impact on theorizing about mass media effects. They, however, do not continue to trace the conceptual trajectory of this social-political theory to its decline and transition into the pluralistic perspective. An extremely brief sketch of that development and its implications for media effects research is provided here.

At the heart of mass society theory is the claim that

> industrialization brings about numerous major changes in the structure of modern society; among them are: Factory replaces family as the premier economic and productive unit; bureaucracy replaces guild as the organizing principle of work; urban areas replace traditional rural communities as the place of residence and the point of psychological contact; and rule-bound associations within the secondary groups replace the primary social ties of kin and friendship as the paramount experience of the social sphere (Wright, 1976, p. 22).

The result is that mass man is cut loose from social restraints resulting in oscillation, atomization, anomie, and alienation. Individuals consequently develop a sense of powerlessness and cynicism. The danger, politically speaking is that apathy, experienced by such individuals toward the political system, may be unpredictably and irrationally transformed into destabilizing political activity (Kornhauser, 1959; Wright, 1976).

While the roots of mass society theory rest in a historical and deep-seated distrust of the masses and their supposed anti-democratic tendencies (Wright, 1976), recent history has provided enough examples of totalitarian or near-totalitarian movements (the rise of Fascism in Europe, the somewhat tamer but similar anti-democratic McCarthy phenomenon in the United States) to keep its theoretical fire burning.

However, McCarthyism was confronted and discredited by the mid-1950s, initiating, particularly in the United States, a period of relative political calm. Even the political disruptions of the 1960s, concerning civil rights and then the Vietnam war, were assimilated into the political mainstream. Consequently, the predictions of mass society theory, of mass politics and mass disruption, were not borne out.

A central solution advanced by political scientists for this problem was the theory of democratic elitism, a modern variant of the pluralistic conception of power (Wright, 1976). The logic of their position is that

> If, as mass society theory suggests, the modern industrial democracy tends toward unstable mass political movements, and if, in this modern industrial democracy, very little political behavior of the sort is empirically manifest, then there must exist other circumstances, conditions, or social processes whose happy consequence is to make democracy relatively "safe" after all (Wright, 1976, p. 28).

The theory of democratic elitism as the explanation of political stability contains two central features (Wright, 1976). The first is that, if rational elites are left alone, that is, somehow buffered from the potentially irrational demands of the masses, they will make wise decisions. The second is that the buffering mechanism involved must somehow maintain a commitment to the democratic ideal of self-government. Consequently, the notion of representation is substituted for the idea of participation as the defining standard of democratic government and pluralism. The dispersal of political power among competing interest groups is offered as the explanation of the stabilizing buffer.

Of particular note to the argument being developed here is that the central feature of political theorizing since the 1950s has been the explanation of stability, just as the central feature of theorizing about the impact of mass communication revolved around its lack of influence and its propensity to reinforce pre-existing attitudes and norms. At first glance, it appears that the explanations presented in these two areas for stabilizing forces are incompatible. Mass communication theorists accounted for the stability by conceptually investing more power into the audiences' role in the communication exchange process. Political scientists accounted for the stability by postulating the importance of competing, representational elite groups. It will be argued below that, rather than incompatible conceptions, these are mutually reinforcing explanations derived from the fundamental conception of power imbedded in the pluralistic model. In this sense, then, just as the initial conceptions of media effects were derived from and compatible with contemporary notions of social and political theory, the uses and gratifications paradigm can also be viewed as a compatible elaboration of contemporary social and political theory. This point will be developed in the next two sections.

THE CONSERVATIVE BIAS OF THE USES AND GRATIFICATIONS PARADIGM: THE CHALLENGE OF FUNCTIONALISM—A BEGINNING AND A FALSE START

Perhaps the most important and most consistent attack on the uses and gratifications paradigm is its alleged conservatism (Carey & Kreiling, 1975; Elliot, 1974; McLeod & Becker, 1981; Swanson, 1979). The basic argument is that the paradigm derives its terminology and has its historical roots in functionalism. Consequently, the standard attack reviews arguments concerning the conservative implications of functionalism, and consequently, its conservative implications for the uses and gratifications paradigm. The position taken here is that the functionalist challenge, as it has been articulated so far, is largely an empty one which tends to obscure a more important conservative anchor. The functionalist challenge is empty, in part, due to the looseness with which functionalism has been applied to the paradigm, but more to the point, due to the special brand of functionalism which has been held up as the theoretical measure. Since the terminology problem has been considered elsewhere (see Elliot, 1974; Swanson, 1977), it is to the second issue we direct our attention.

In tracing the functionalist roots of the uses and gratifications paradigm, most of its critics, as well as supporters, generally arrive at the same two sources, Merton's (1968) exposition of a paradigm for functionalist analysis and Wright's (1960) application of that paradigm to mass communication. Occasionally, Parsons (1964) is also cited as a representative of the functional approach, but is then quickly discounted. Merton is typically selected as the most appropriate representative of functionalism for mass communication researchers because, as a Columbia sociologist, he exerted a substantial amount of influence over several key students with media interests (McLeod & Becker, 1981). The problem is, Merton (1968) was not articulating a functional theory.

As Goode (1973) points out, Merton (1968, p. 42) distinguished between a sociological orientation which indicates the "types of variables which are somehow to be taken into account" and a theory proper which specifies "determinant relationships between particular variables." Merton's often cited contribution to the development of the functional approach to the study of mass communication was a paradigm for functional *analysis,* not a functional theory. To suggest that functionalist analysis is inherently a conservative approach to the analysis of social problems is partly true, because, as McLeod and Becker (1981) point out, change is negatively characterized as the result of dysfunctions in the social system, and because, as Stinchcombe (1968) demonstrates, the impact of history can only be awkwardly handled. However, as Merton (1968), Stinchcombe (1968) and Gans (1972) demonstrate, functional analysis can be used to reveal the logic and impact of even Marxian postulates regarding power.

Functional theory, which Parsons (1964) elevated to a sophisticated level, *is* extremely conservative in that it is an explanation and rationalization of the need for social, political, and economic inequality. Parsonian functionalism is a justification of the concentration of wealth and power and an attack on the logic of participatory democracy. Curiously, the uses and gratifications literature is relatively free of references to this work—work which may have proved somewhat distasteful to the social reform attitudes of many researchers working within the uses and gratifications paradigm, but at the same time provided an articulate statement of an encompassing functional theory to which the uses and gratifications paradigm could have attached itself. It is a bit of an irony that the social "theoretical" umbrella under which the uses and gratifications paradigm has claimed theoretical legitimacy (Katz, 1979) is regarded only as a "context of inquiry" (Merton, 1968), similar to the view of uses and gratifications as only an approach to data gathering.

It should be noted, however, that incorrectly calling functional analysis a social theory, even a flexible social theory, does not get the uses and gratifications paradigm off the conservative hook. It merely suggests that we look elsewhere for an explanation of the nature of the conservative orientation, because the actual application of the uses and gratifications paradigm *has* tended to result in extremely conservative conclusions about the potential for change. Elliot's (1974, p. 253) criticisms of nearly 10 years ago remain largely unanswered:

> No attempt is made to differentiate between media or people on the basis of the interests they represent or the power they possess; no analysis is made in terms of the functions and dysfunctions for different power groups and their ideologies. Dysfunctions, when they appear at all, tend to be negatively labeled phenomena which might prevent society (as a whole) from reaching its ideals, as for example the narcotizing dysfunction identified by Lazarsfeld and Merton (1957).

A relatively unique and still quoted example of the uses and gratifications paradigm as a useful approach to the study of social change is Mendelsohn's work in developing a series of television programs for low-income Mexican-American audiences. Mendelsohn (1974, p. 314) describes the project:

> Working in concert directly with Mexican-American writers, directors and authors, the research team for this project conducted no fewer than twelve separate studies that were designed (1) to delineate a distinctive target audience (urbanized Mexican-Americans earning less than $5,000 yearly and manifesting above-average levels of anomie); (2) to assess important audience needs (e.g. the need for supportive messages designed to alleviate feelings of personal powerlessness); and (3) to determine patterns of media-related wants, uses and gratifications which might help to attract audiences who were unaccustomed to strictly informational mass media vehicles.

Questions the researchers neglected to ask included: Were the Mexican-Americans' perceptions of their personal powerlessness *accurate* from their point of view? For whom is the amelioration of these feelings of powerlessness functional, and for whom is it dysfunctional? To what extent were the media-related wants, uses, and gratifications of this special audience conditioned by their history of experience with the media? And if they were conditioned, for whom were their particular orientations functional or dysfunctional?

THE CONSERVATIVE BIAS OF THE USES AND GRATIFICATIONS PARADIGM: THE CHALLENGE OF THE PLURALIST THEORY OF DEMOCRACY

In this section, the following argument will be developed: The uses and gratifications paradigm is not atheoretical (even though "functionalism" has been refuted as its conceptual home). It can be usefully viewed as an implicit operationization of media effects study within a pluralistic conception of democracy. And while the pluralistic conception of democratic government is important, it is at the same time only a one-dimensional approach to the study of power in society. Consequently, the uses and gratifications paradigm is heir to this limiting conceptualization. In order to make these points, it will be necessary to review the basic assumptions of pluralistic theory, consider the relationships between the uses and gratifications paradigm and these assumptions, examine the criticisms of the pluralistic approach, and, finally, review the implications of these criticisms for the media paradigm.

Assumptions

Dahl (1969, p. 80) offers an intuitive idea of the meaning of power from a pluralistic perspective: "A has power over B to the extent that he can get B to do something that B would not otherwise do." To this definition, Polsby (1963, p. 55) adds, a study of power may be made by analyzing "who participates, who gains and loses, and who prevails in decision-making." The key to this approach is its focus on political behavior and, consequently, on the belief that the exercise of power is overt and therefore observable. It is assumed that grievances are readily recognizable and acted upon. A second assumption is that participation "occurs within decision-making arenas, which are in turn assumed to be open to virtually any organized group" (Gaventa, 1980, p. 5). Conflict, therefore, will be observable in these open arenas, expressed as policy preferences carried into the decision-making process through political participation (Lukes, 1974).

Uses and Gratifications Paradigm

The paradigm fits neatly under the umbrella of pluralistic theory in two ways: in terms of the several roles to be played by media institutions, and in terms of the conceptualization of the audience/citizen. As an institution, the media are seen both as pluralistic interest groups in their own right, and as tools promoting and maintaining other such groups by aiding in the process of political socialization and the provision of information (Kraus & Davis, 1976). Therefore, the media are assumed, not only to make available the necessary range of viewpoints and information to allow an active audience to fashion world views appropriate to their needs, mobilize, and act, but also to keep before the public eye the significant decision-making agendas necessary to allow for public scrutiny. For instance, the close relationship between the organization of news gathering and the *normatively* defined points of political and social decision-making would appear to facilitate this task (Tuchman, 1978).

The paradigm's conceptualization of the active audience dovetails nicely with the pluralistic theory assumptions that people will act on recognized grievances, in an open system, for themselves (Gaventa, 1980). Pluralistic theory requires a rational, motivated, self-interested citizenry. The fact that nonvoting in local as well as national elections is becoming a predominant fact of political life in the United States does not pose a significant problem, given this perspective. Nonvoting in the political area, and, similarly, acceptance of existing media fare, can be read as satisfaction.

Criticism of Pluralistic Theory

The major criticism of pluralistic theory is not that it is wrong but that its definition of power is too narrow. Power, Bachrach and Baratz (1962, p. 7) argue, has two faces:

> Of course power is exercised when A participates in the making of decisions that affect B. Power is also exercised when A devotes his energies to creating or reinforcing social and political values and institutional practices that limit the scope of the political process to public consideration of only those issues which are comparatively innocuous to A. To the extent that A succeeds in doing this, B is prevented, for all practical purposes, from bringing to the fore any issues that might in their resolution be seriously detrimental to A's set of preferences.

The first face of power, then, is the "securing of compliance through the threat of sanctions" (Lukes, 1974, p. 14). This is the visible face of power incorporated into the pluralistic perspective that operates through coercion, influence, authority, force, and manipulation within the decision-making arena.

The second face of power is much less visible, and is exercised essentially through a process of nondecisionmaking. Nondecisionmaking, according to Bachrach and Baratz (1963, p. 44), refers to the "means by which demands for change in the existing allocation of benefits and privileges in the community can be suffocated before they are even voiced; or kept covert; or killed before they gain access to the relevant decision-making arena; or failing all these things, maimed or destroyed in the decision-implementing stage of the policy process."

Westergaard (1979, p. 101), in restating the criticism with particular reference to the media, suggests that the

> liberal democratic theory of a pluralistic form suffers from the same fundamental weakness in its ascription of critical responsibility to the media as it does in its larger denial of any durable concentration of power in western societies. It focuses on diversity of debate, critique and contest within set parameters, but it is indifferent to the existence and social shape of those parameters.

RELEVANCE OF CRITICISMS TO THE USES AND GRATIFICATIONS PARADIGM

Expanding our conceptualization of power to include its second face has important implications for the uses and gratifications paradigm. The disinterested role of media institutions in providing the symbolic raw material for an active audience to construct meaningful self-interested interpretations of reality must be severely redefined. The origins, nature, and shape of the media's symbolic offerings become critical questions which must be addressed in order fully to understand the meaning of the audience/media interaction. The emerging prominence of organizational studies of media production and distribution (Cantor, 1980; Ettema & Whitney, 1982; Gitlin, 1980; Guback, 1974; Tuchman, 1978) must be viewed as relevant to interpretation of audience uses of the mass media, qualifying the meaning of audience activity as operating within these commercially imposed boundaries on media content. In addition, there must be a complementary redirection of attention to the symbolic analysis of media content (Blumler, 1979; Carey & Kreiling, 1974; Elliot, 1974; Swanson, 1977, 1979; Windahl, 1981). It is clear however, that the models for content analysis available from traditional media effects research will not be adequate to this task. Shrinking the unit of analysis to a single action or character type, counting manifest demographic characteristics, will not make visible the implicit ideological boundaries imposed by the existing structure of production and distribution. To uncover the ideological boundaries surrounding themes of power distribution and maintenance will require more subtlety. Work by Williams (1977), the Glasgow University Media Group (1980), and Hall (1979) may help lead the way.

THE USES AND GRATIFICATIONS PARADIGM AND THE THIRD DIMENSION OF POWER

Lukes (1974) has labeled the pluralistic conception of power a one-dimensional view because it focuses on behavior and observable conflict. The second face of power, presented by Bachrach and Baratz (1962, 1963, 1970), and Schattschneider (1960), Lukes (1974, p. 21) labels a two-dimensional view because "it incorporates into the analysis of power relations the question of control over the agenda of politics and the ways in which potential issues are kept out of the political process." However, Lukes still finds several conceptual deficiencies even in the extended position of the second view.

First, he criticizes the two-dimensional view as still too behaviorally oriented. The search for specific cases of nondecisions or exclusions presents a misleading view of the exercise of power. Decisions, whether to include or exclude, are "choices consciously and intentionally made by individuals between alternatives, whereas the bias of the system can be mobilized, recreated, and reinforced in ways that are neither consciously chosen nor the intended result of particular individuals' choices" (Lukes, 1974, p. 21). Furthermore, Lukes argues, the bias of a system is not maintained simply through the accumulation of individual acts, but also through the incorporation of a bias into the "socially structured and culturally patterned behavior of groups, and practices of institutions, which may indeed be manifested by individuals' inaction" (Lukes, 1974, p. 22). In addition, as discussed above, the strict behavioral orientation significantly limits the ability of the critical system observer to *read* the nature of that bias embedded in the cultural artifacts of the system.

The second criticism Lukes (1974) advances concerning the two-dimensional view is the continued emphasis of the pluralists on observable conflict. While the two-dimensional view of power represents an advance in sophistication by calling attention to the exercise of covert as opposed to overt conflict, Lukes argues that it still falls short of a complete conceptualization on two counts. The first is that, for at least two types of power, no conflict is directly observable—for instance, manipulation and authority where power is exercised as agreement based on reason (Bachrach and Baratz, 1970). The second is, as Lukes (1974, p. 23) puts it,

> A may exercise power over B by getting him to do what he does not want to do, but he also exercises power over him by influencing, shaping or determining his very wants. Indeed, is it not the supreme exercise of power to get another to have the desires you want them to have—that is, to secure their compliance by controlling their thoughts and desires?

Even Dahl (1961) recognizes the importance of this phenomena, but fails explicitly to incorporate it into his conception of power, largely due to his focus on actual conflict.

Lukes' (1974) third criticism of the two-dimensional view of power is related to the issue of observable conflict. Nondecisionmaking power is exercised only when a grievance is denied access as an issue into the political process. Lukes argues this implies that individuals who are unable to express their grievances in appropriate ways, directed at appropriate targets, are consequently unharmed by the exercise of power. Furthermore, he asks, since a central tenet in the exercise of power is to minimize the perception of grievances, that is, promote an acceptance of the existing situation, should it be so surprising that individuals may have difficulty recognizing the source of their grievances much less the nature of the grievance itself?

IMPLICATIONS FOR THE USES AND GRATIFICATIONS PARADIGM

While the two-dimensional view of power implied a redefinition of the role of media institutions, the third dimension of power calls for a corresponding redefinition of the meaning of active in conceptualizing the audience. Just as the strictly behavioral orientation of the pluralist theory leads us to an overly narrow conception of the exercise of power, the behavioral orientation of the uses and gratifications paradigm, placing so much faith in the audience's ability to self-report the immediate as well as larger implications of their media orientations, over-emphasizes the degree of autonomy possessed by the audience. If, as the second view of power suggests, the audience cannot see the subtle contours of their social and political environment, it is extremely likely that their world views are correspondingly constrained, in terms of expectations, desires, and behavior. Needs may not be translated into gratifications sought from the mass media because of a conditioning process (conditioning through experience with the media and conditioning explicitly by the media) as to what is probable and possible to expect from the mass media.

Within the three-dimensional view of power, the uses and gratifications paradigm suggests the possibility that we are confronting a situation where certain members of the audience are actively constructing a view of the world and of the media's role in the world which is ideologically loaded. That is, a view which takes into account the reality of their personal experience of political powerlessness and their perception of the lack of entry points, as presented by the media, into the political process. Expressed media demands and expectations do not necessarily equal possible media demands and expectations. While this may seem a new proposition within the standard uses and gratifications' paradigm, it represents a significant advance in the conceptualization of power relationships first articulated by Gramsci (1971) and currently being integrated into thinking about mass communication/power relationships by Williams (1977), Hall (1978, 1979, 1982), Kellner (1979), and others.

In many respects, Swanson's (1977, 1979) recent work, arguing for a reconceptualization of audience activity to include the active construction of meaning, has laid the groundwork for the introduction of the third dimension of power perspective into the uses and gratifications paradigm. What remained missing was a linkage of the process of meaning construction to a social and political inventory of the symbolic raw material available for interpretation. Blumler's (1979) concern regarding the contribution of social structural conditions to the development of specific audience needs and expectations represents a beginning in this direction. It must be recognized, however, that this concern for the manner in which specific material conditions contribute to the construction of meaning, the development of consciousness, has a rich intellectual history in Marxist thought. What appears to hold the uses and gratifications paradigm from borrowing from this history has been its implicit adherence to the pluralistic conception of power and to a strictly quantifiable empirical methodology. It is to be hoped that this paper, in making that implicit connection explicit, will lead media scholars to reexamine the validity of that conceptual home for the study of audience uses of the mass media. It would seem the frustration of researchers continuing to employ strictly empirical methods to the concept of audience activity, which is evolving theoretically to mean more than can be conventionally measured, will also stimulate a re-examination of the uses and gratifications position.

THE THREE VIEWS OF POWER AND IMPLICATIONS FOR RESEARCH IN THE USES AND GRATIFICATIONS PARADIGM

First Dimension. Since it has been argued that most research within the uses and gratifications paradigm has proceeded implicitly from the one-dimensional view, further research from this perspective would only be considered business as usual.

Second Dimension. The primary mechanism by which the second dimension of power is exercised is through the "mobilization of bias:"

> a set of predominant values, beliefs, rituals, and institutional procedures ("rules of the game") that operate systematically and consistently to the benefit of certain persons and groups at the expense of others. Those who benefit are placed in a preferred position to defend and promote their vested interests. (Bachrach & Baratz, 1970, p. 43).

According to Bachrach and Baratz, the mobilization of bias may be found operating through nondecisions in at least four ways: force, the threat of sanctions, directing attention to an existing bias within the political system technically to invalidate a threatening demand or incipient issue, and the strengthening of the existing mobilization of bias through the creation of new obstacles, symbolic or procedural, to hinder the efforts of challengers by delimiting the scope of the issue.

In terms of the uses and gratifications paradigm, then, research is required which will examine the institutional and elite actions which establish the public parameters of conflict and which will examine the symbolic content of those parameters. Recent attempts at the construction of transactional models of the mass communication process are steps in the right direction but they do not go far enough. Typically, such models, while recognizing the importance of media content in determining media impact on even "active" audiences, do not call specific attention to the existence of realities alternative to the one presented, or to the forces responsible for its creation and form. Conceptual bridges are required between the political science concept of agenda building and the mass communication concept of agenda setting and between agenda setting and the uses and gratifications paradigm. Conceptual modification is also required. Agenda setting research must move away from the limiting notions of issue salience to issue framing. The Glasgow University Media Group's (1980) and Gitlin's (1980) work are suggestive of the conceptual types of content analysis and institutional/content interaction required to begin developing a fuller understanding of the nature and origin of the symbolic reality from which an "active" audience can construct their own reality.

Third Dimension. In many respects, the research challenges of the two-dimensional view of power are largely concerned with the recasting of the micro-process orientation of the uses and gratifications paradigm into a richer theoretical context. The challenge of the third dimension is more fundamental. If the audience is to be viewed as potentially not capable of speaking in their own best interest, in what way can an audience-oriented research approach help to uncover this hypothesized dynamic of power? Two research fronts are suggested.

The first has already been incorporated into the research paradigm, but requires refining in terms of the power perspective discussed here. More attention must be paid to the social-structural determinants of the audience's media needs and expectations, paying particular attention to the role the media themselves have in shaping and conditioning those needs and expectations. The existence of explicit connections between the range of media content available and the media demands expressed by the audience must be explored. The concept of accommodation must somehow be incorporated into this study to account for specific media expectations, based not on the media as a functional equivalent of other opportunities for satisfaction—which implies that other solutions actually exist—but as resignation to situations where other options are not perceived as available.

The second front requires a reversal of the current trend within the paradigm toward the conceptual reduction of media expectations to a few universal categories, a reversal which is consistent with the critiques of Carey and Kreiling (1974) and Swanson (1977, 1979). Attention must be devoted to the interpretation of the media expectations that audience members provide in order to understand the origin, meaning, and relationship of those expectations to their lives and to the dominant power structure within which those expectations are constructed.

If the uses and gratifications paradigm is truly to come to grips with the nature of the audience's media experience, it will have to give up the optimistic and simplistic notion that an active audience implies a powerful audience. It must be recognized that the concept of an active audience, as traditionally explicated in the literature, may in fact obscure the powerlessness of the audience. Certain audience media expectations are never voiced because they are perceived as inappropriate or as so unlikely as to make their articulation sound foolish or naive (see Bachrach & Baratz's 1970, rule of anticipated reaction). Other expectations, for some individuals, when expressed, may be significantly modified or tempered due to the sense of powerlessness they feel with respect to the political and social system (Gaventa, 1980). In-depth probing of individual's media expectations may reveal more about the assumptions these individuals hold regarding their locations in the social and political system than about any true media needs. In-depth analysis of the meaning of a commonly expressed media expectation such as diversion may reveal the use of standard media fare not so much for polite relaxation but for opportunities to ridicule a presentation of reality which does not correspond to one's experiences as opposed to mediated life.

Uses and gratifications research is, as Windahl (1981) suggests, at a crossroads. The danger, however, appears that the paradigm will turn back in on itself rather than moving forward to explore the points of mutual concern with existing theoretical traditions.

REFERENCES

Bachrach, P., and Baratz, M. (1962). "The Faces of Power." *American Political Science Review 56,* 947–952.

Bachrach, P., and Baratz, M. (1963). "Decisions and Non-Decisions: An Analytical Framework." *American Political Science Review 57,* 641–651.

Bachrach, P., and Baratz, M. (1970). *Power and Poverty: Theory and Practice.* New York: Oxford University Press.

Berelson, B., Lazarsfeld, P.F., and McPhee, W. (1954). *Voting: A Study of Public Opinion Formation in a Presidential Campaign.* Chicago, IL: University of Chicago Press.

Blumler, J.G. (1979). "The Role to Theory in Uses and Gratifications Studies." *Communication Research 6,* 9–36.

Cantor, M. (1980). *Prime-Time Television: Content and Control.* Beverly Hills, CA: Sage.

Carey, J.W., and Kreiling, A.L. (1974). "Popular Culture and Uses and Gratifications: Notes toward and Accommodation." *In* J.G. Blumler and E. Katz (Eds.), *The Uses of Mass Communication: Current Perspectives on Gratifications Research* (pp. 225–248). Beverly Hills, CA: Sage.

Dahl, R.A. (1961). *Who Governs? Democracy and Power in an American City.* New Haven, CT: Yale University Press.

Dahl, R.A. (1969). "The Concept of Power." *In* R. Bell, D.M. Edwards, and R.H. Wagner (Eds.), *Political Power: A Reader in Theory and Research* (pp. 201–205). New York: Free Press.

DeFleur, M.L., and Ball-Rokeach, S. (1962). *Theories of Mass Communication.* New York: Longman.

Elliot, P. (1974). "Uses and Gratifications Research: A Critique and a Sociological Alternative." *In* J.G. Blumler and E. Katz (Eds.), *The Uses of Mass Communication: Current Perspectives in Gratifications Research* (pp. 249–268). Beverly Hills, CA: Sage.

Ettema, J.S., and Whitney, D.C. (Eds.). (1982). *Individuals in Mass Media Organizations.* Beverly Hills, CA: Sage.

Gans, H.J. (1972). "The Positive Functions of Poverty." *American Journal of Sociology 78,* 275–289.

Gaventa, J. (1980). *Power and Powerlessness: Quiescence and Rebellion in an Appalachian Valley.* Urbana, IL: University of Illinois Press.

Gitlin, T. (1978). Media Sociology: The Dominant Paradigm." *Theory and Society 6,* 205–233.

Gitlin, T. (1980). *The Whole World is Watching.* Berkeley, CA: University of California Press.

Glasgow University Media Group. (1980). *More Bad News.* London: Routledge and Kegan Paul.

Goode, W. (1973). *Explorations in Social Theory.* New York: Oxford University Press.

Gramsci, A. (1971). *Selections from the Prison Notebooks.* New York: International Publishers.
Guback, T. (1974). "Film as International Business." *Journal of Communication 24* (No. 1), 90-102.
Hall, S. (1979). "Culture, the Media and the Ideological Effect. *In* J. Curran, M. Gurevitch, and J. Woollacott (Eds.), *Mass Communication and Society* (pp. 315-349). Beverly Hills, CA: Sage.
Hall, S. (1982). "The Rediscovery of 'Ideology': Return of the Repressed in Media Studies." *In* M. Gurevitch, T. Bennett, J. Curran, and J. Woollacott (Eds.), *Culture, Society and the Media* (pp. 56-91). London: Methuen.
Hall, S., Critcher, C., Jefferson, T., Clarke, J., and Roberts, B. (1978). *Policing the Crisis: Mugging, the State, and Law and Order.* New York: Holmes and Meier.
Herzog, H. (1944). "What Do We Really Know about Daytime Serial Listeners?" *In* P.F. Lazarsfeld and F.N. Stanton (Eds.), *Radio Research 1942-43* (pp. 3-33). New York: Duell, Sloan and Pearce.
Hovland, C., Janis, J., and Kelley, H. (1954). *Communication and Persuasion.* New Haven: CT: Yale University Press.
Katz, E. (1979). "The Uses of Becker, Blumler and Swanson." *Communication Research 6,* 74-83.
Katz, E., Blumler, J.G., and Gurevitch, M. (1974). "Utilization of Mass Communication by the Individual." *In* J.G. Blumler and E. Katz (Eds.), *The Uses of Mass Communication: Current Perspectives on Gratifications Research* (pp. 19-32). Beverly Hills, CA: Sage.
Kellner, D. (1982). "TV, Ideology, and Emancipatory Popular Culture." *In* H. Newcomb (Ed.), *Television: The Critical View* (pp. 386-422). New York: Oxford University Press.
Kornhauser, W. (1959). *The Politics of Mass Society.* New York: Free Press.
Kraus, S., and Davis, D. (1976). *The Effects of Mass Communication on Political Behavior.* University Park: PA: Pennsylvania State University Press.
Lazarsfeld, P.F., Berelson, B., and Gaudet, H. (1948). *The People's Choice.* New York: Columbia University Press.
Lukes, S. (1974). *Power: A Radical View.* London: Macmillan.
McLeod, J.M., and Becker, L.B. (1981). "The Uses and Gratifications Approach." *In* D.D. Nimmo and K.R. Sanders (Eds.), *Handbook of Political Communication* (pp. 67-101). Beverly Hills, CA: Sage.
Mendelsohn, H. (1974). "Some Policy Implications of the Uses and Gratifications Paradigm." *In* J.G. Blumler and E. Katz (Eds.), *The Uses of Mass Communication: Current Perspectives on Gratifications Research* (pp. 303-318). Beverly Hills, CA: Sage.
Merton, R.K. (1968). *Social Theory and Social Structure.* New York: Free Press.
Murdock, G., and Golding, P. (1979). "Capitalism, Communication and Class Relations." *In* J. Curran, M. Gurevitch, and J. Woollacott (Eds.), *Mass Communication and Society* (pp. 12-44). Beverly Hills, CA: Sage.
Parsons, T. (1964). *Sociological Theory and Modern Society.* New York: Free Press.
Polsby, N. (1963). *Community Power and Political Theory.* New Haven, CT: Yale University Press.
Schattschneider, E.E. (1960). *The Semi-Sovereign People: A Realist's View of Democracy in America.* New York: Holt, Rinehart and Winston.
Stinchcombe, A. (1968). *Constructing Social Theories.* New York: Harcourt, Brace and World.
Suchman, E. (1942). "An Invitation to Music." *In* P.F. Lazarsfeld and F.N. Stanton (Eds.), *Radio Research 1941* (pp. 140-147). New York: Duell, Sloan and Pearce.
Swanson, D.L. (1977). "The Uses and Misuses of Uses and Gratifications. *Human Communication Research 3,* 214-221.

Swanson, D.L. (1979). "Political Communication Research and the Uses Gratifications Model: A Critique." *Communication Research 6*, 37-53.

Tuchman, G. (1978). *Making News: A Study in the Construction of Social Reality*. New York: Free Press.

Weiss, W. (1976). "Review of the Uses of Mass Communication: Current Perspectives on Gratifications Research. *Public Opinion Quarterly 40*, 132-142.

Westergaard, J. (1979). "Power, Class and the Media." *In* J. Curran, M. Gurevitch, and J. Woollacott (Eds.), *Mass Communication and Society* (pp. 95-116). Beverly Hills, CA: Sage.

Williams, R. (1977). *Marxism and Literature*. London: Oxford University Press.

Windahl, S. (1981). "Uses and Gratifications at the Crossroads." *Mass Communication Review Yearbook 2*, 174-186.

Wright, C.R. (1960). "Functional Analysis and Mass Communications." *Public Opinion Quarterly 24*, 605-620.

Wright, J.D. (1976). *The Dissent of the Governed: Alienation and Democracy in America*. New York: Academic Press.

Chapter 13
Towards the Democratization of Mass Communication: A Social Search for Equality

JERZY OLEDZKI

Institute of Journalism
University of Warsaw
Warsaw, Poland

This paper focuses on the following issues:

1. The appearance of periodicity in the social need for the expansion in the number of alternative sources of information. It can be said that, in spite of the need to overcome many obstacles, the existing recipients or objects of communication want to communicate for themselves—insuring that they have equal rights to communicate, as do the traditional sources of information;

2. The certain kind of similarity in the problems of development of a communication system in Poland and in other countries developing their own communication systems, i.e., countries which have made changes in their political and socio-economic systems in a relatively short time. The common feature is the constant search for the optimal solution to the question of the social role and responsibility of the media in the configuration of government–society. These countries do not have as long a tradition as the highly industrialized countries of the West have had with their communication systems, where dominance of the commercial, private media still exists.

SOCIAL DEMANDS FOR DIVERSITY IN MEDIA

There are numerous theories on the mutual relations between development and communication, the classical illustrations being Lerner's (1958) hypothesis on the modernization process, and Schramm's (1964) study of the functions performed by mass communication in the process of development. Both authors focus their primary interests on the stages by which particular societies attain the level of an economically and socially developed country

---

Based on a paper presented at the International Association for Mass Communication Research Conference, Prague, Czechoslovakia, 1984.

—described as "modern." In my opinion, what is still lacking are works and studies interpreting on a broader basis the interdependencies taking place today among the stages of development of communication in "modern societies" in non-highly industrialized (or "post-industrial") countries. Among numerous synthetic works, some (see, for example, Merrill & Lowenstein, 1971) on natural evolution of the media (the theory of an "Elite-Popular-Specialized Curve") can be related to the sphere of most industrialized Western countries, rather than to other developed countries. These works do not take into consideration the importance of values formed in the process of social development, such as sense of justice, human dignity, security, aspirations, and values of life, or the right to equal participation in international life. In these works, greater consideration needs to be given to the role performed by the "motive power" of egalitarian tendencies occurring in politically educated and socially mature ("with high political participation and mobile personality," as Lerner would say) societies in states where socialized ownership of the media is constitutionally assured. It seems that the curve of media development in countries dominated by private and commercial media is different from that in countries where the media are subordinated to the state and socio-political organizations.

The society which has accepted the socialist slogans of "liberty, equality, and justice" naturally wants to possess the right to influence the directions of the socially owned media (i.e., owned theoretically by society). Also, since media are seen as tools of government in socialist countries, the nation concerned that the objectives of the workers' state should be realized wants to participate in the media. This results in the existence of a permanent movement towards a change in the status quo; and this means attempts to pluralize the content of the media and extend the number of equal communicators. Such a tendency can be retarded by the political authorities or ruling parties, who interpret such social aspirations as dangerous to their own positions, which they defend by arguing that they are protecting all social interests, i.e., the public good. As a result, the propaganda promoting slogans of "equality, liberty, and justice" turns into an important crisis-causing factor, bringing about a revolution of rising anticipations and frustrations (as Pye, 1963, would say). The disposers of the media in this crisis appear as victims of the egalitarian ideas they promoted, the ideas society demands be realized.

Thus the major power in media development in the new societies—which do not yet have the excessive intensity of information, and the, so-called, "information pollution"[1]—is permanent social demand for news content corresponding to the interests, aspirations, and values of the society. Simple numerical increase in press titles and radio and TV programs does not seem

---

[1] On "information pollution" problems in Japan, see, e.g., Institute for Public Opinion (1972).

to be the proper model of development, unless it is accompanied by a diversity of opinions recognizing various interest of social strata and groups present in every state.[2]

Such development is then a natural, evolutionary tendency towards the democratization of communication.[3] Thus, it is a valid opinion that such development of communication is not self-contained but is an affirmation of the parallel economic and cultural development of the nation and all of its leading social and political institutions. It also is a result of the development of the consciousness of the nation and of real possibilities for the realization of its aspirations and designs.

These generalizations are based on observation of the development of the media in Poland, and Polish experience in this respect allows me to formulate the following hypotheses: (a) In an industrialized country with a high level of general education throughout the society, and a high level of social and political activity, social requirements are increasingly placed on the mass media of communication; (b) a quantitative increase in the media and the resulting universal access to press, radio, and television, but with the same variety of subjects of communication and diversity of views as before, reduces the credibility of these media among recipients; (c) the decrease in credibility of the media influences the growth of criticism in the society, this being motivated by the inadequacy of media content compared to the expectations and knowledge of the society; (d) the intensified distrust in the media and, thereby, in their political disposition, is an important crisis-causing factor; and (e) crisis of trust in authorities and their media demonstrates, among other things, the need for the establishment of a more just (from the viewpoint of the more active social groups), new information order in the country.

CYCLES OF DEMOCRATIZATION IN MASS COMMUNICATION

From recent experience and observation of the development of the Polish press system, one can conclude that there exists a cycle of transfer development of communication aimed at a permanent improvement of the methods and forms of public communication.

In every society, there are various class, strata, and group interests which should be manifested, coordinated, and realized in the sphere of political and economic relations, as well as through public communication media. In

---

[2] By "diversity of opinion," I mean, not only taking account of various groups' ideals, but also the involvement of those groups in the process of actively forming information policy.

[3] The meaning of this idea was defined in the report of the International Commission for the Study of Communication Problems (the MacBride Commission) (1980), as the process whereby: "(a) the individual becomes an active partner and not a mere object of communication; (b) the variety of messages exchanged increases; and (c) the extent and quality of special representation of participation in communication are augmented."

the state where the sphere of ownership relations has undergone revolutionary transformation, public consciousness also undergoes change. The change consists, first, in a high sensitivity to questions of social justice, egalitarianism, equality of all citizens with respect to rights and duties, and also of the chance for expressing their own interests in the public institutions—including the public media of communication. Neglecting these human aspirations, as Polish experience shows, leads to crisis situations favorable to a dynamic start of the cycle of transfer development of communication.

Before generalizing, let me point out the following stimulators of social aspirations for enlarging the number of subjects of communication:

1. Together with intensive economic, social, and cultural development, groups appear with memberships characterized by the "mobile personality" (Lerner, 1958), a search for change, and "cognitive flexibility" (Frey, 1973).[4] Thanks to this activated attitude, they are convinced they can change their own situation into a more favorable one.
2. With highly advanced education, the awareness of one's own importance in a large social group (or nation) increases, and what is important here is the interdependence between the material conditions and people's subjective activity.
3. Becoming conscious of the need to realize their own interests, and the necessity to communicate with the members of their own group, as well as among the other social groups, leads to turning more attention to the role performed by the media (especially in a horizontal sense). As a result, media become an object of particular public evaluation and criticism.
4. People become increasingly convinced of the essential divergence between their social rights and the possibility of exercising them within the frames of the existing formal structures of communication characterized by elitism and monopolization of opinions (in vertical communication).[5]
5. A radical change in past arrangements of relations in society takes place, e.g., even relations based on apparent cooperation and trust break down and turn into conflict.
6. Changes in the technology of communication occur—technological development of the media makes them available to a larger number of people, and gives rise to aspirations to use them.

---

[4] F.W. Frey (1973) synthesizes Lerner's hypotheses into two factors decisive in development: (a) exposure to change for the individual—the result of urbanization, literacy, mass media exposure, physical mobility, and education; all of which tend to constitute the exposure; and (b) cognitive flexibility—the result of empathy, innovativeness, tolerance of deviant behavior, open mindedness, attitudinal modernity, knowledge, etc.

[5] This was mentioned by R.F. Nixon (1974).

In a situation where at least the first five stimulators become active at the same time, a dynamic process of democratization of communication occurs at the level of a large social group/nation. A less dynamic process occurs when the first four stimulators are activated, e.g., without the occurrence of a political crisis. The following states in the development of the process seem to be the rule:

1. emergence of a contradiction between the interests of the already existing subjects of communication, and/or a mounting conflict between the subjects and recipients of communication;
2. the climax stage of criticism and resistance, attack and defense;
3. the stage of diffusing the conflict through establishment of a new subject of communication on an equal footing with the ones already in existence. By the "new subject of communication," I mean a new, active, participating partner in communication, who decides about the program and the content;
4. a symbiosis of all or nearly all subjects of communication, which, after a time, spurs a return to the situation characteristic of Stage I.

The cycle will start anew when some conducive circumstance occurs, i.e., when the above mentioned stimulators, which, acting like enzymes, bring about the evolutionary phenomenon of the self-correcting process of communication and the latter's democratization, following the pattern of a spiral, start to act.

The development of particular stages is shown in Figure 1. It should be pointed out that the start of the process (Stage I) does not mean an automatic step to the next stage. Due to a counter-action of political and economic, as well as social factors (e.g., of strong ethnic or religious groups), the mobility of social groups being activated can be neutralized and will retreat to the preceding stage (from Stage II to I; from III to II). This does not apply to Stage IV, which is a symbiosis and collaboration among all the existing subjects of communication.

POLISH CYCLES OF DEMOCRATIZATION

Taking as an example, the development of the Polish press, we can see two completed cycles of communication development in Poland: 1953 to 1968, and 1968 to 1980. A third cycle was started in 1980/1981 and was restrained somehow. This does not exclude the possibility of its continuation in the future.

As in every other country, all of the activities of the Polish press could be subjects for pride as well as regret. After all, this paper's purpose is to support the more-or-less universal hypotheses presented. In no sense does the paper aim to be a comprehensive overview of the contemporary Polish

III. Expansion of the new subjects of communication

IV. Symbiosis of the existing subjects of communication

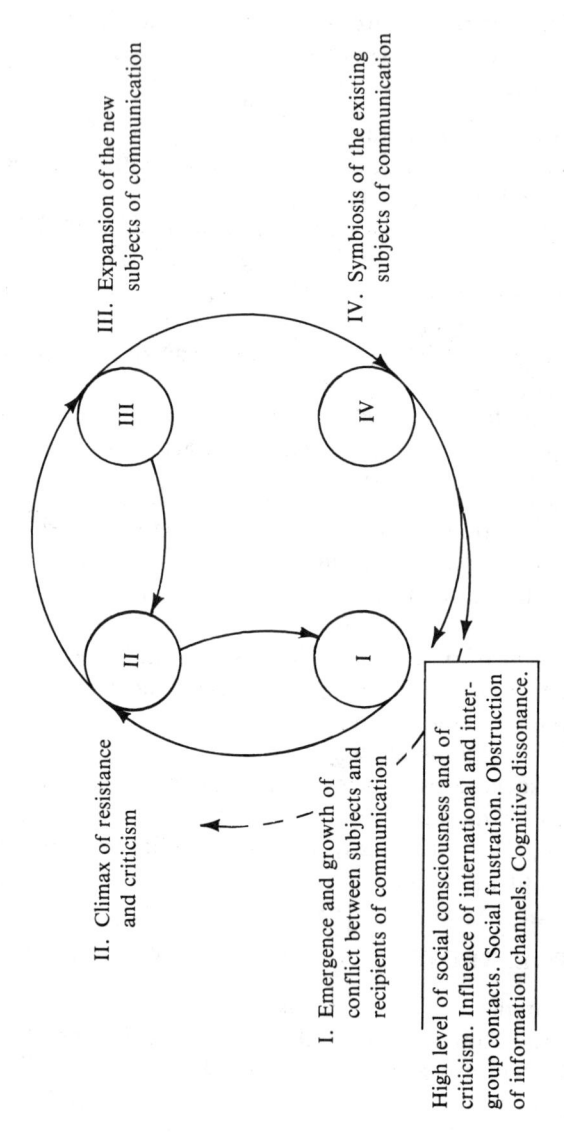

II. Climax of resistance and criticism

I. Emergence and growth of conflict between subjects and recipients of communication

High level of social consciousness and of criticism. Influence of international and inter-group contacts. Social frustration. Obstruction of information channels. Cognitive dissonance.

Figure 1. Stages in the Dynamic Process of Democratization of Communication.

press. Instead, it presents selective general phenomena of social communication; it does not begin to consider the ideological and political background or purposes of various groups.

Poland is among the industrial and developed countries, when one takes all of the parameters of economic and social development (see Table 1). The percentage of illiterates declined from 14.6 in 1946 to 2.7 in 1960. In 1960, 55% of the total population of Poland aged 15 or over had at least a seventh-grade education (by 1980, 89.2%). Beyond this, Poland is one of the few countries in the world whose people are scattered among many nations—the number of persons with Polish origin living abroad is equal to one-third of the total of Poland's population.

This seems to be an important factor in stimulating the interest of Poles in the lives of other nations. Simultaneously, it contributes to tourist exchange and is favorable to the diffusion of cultures, particularly with countries with the largest number of Poles (especially the United States, Canada, the United Kingdom, France, the Federal Republic of Germany, and the U.S.S.R.).

Polish society also values highly the principle of egalitarianism; unequal distribution of wealth and a system with privileges for the political elite are seen as contradictory to the basic principles of socialism.

After the ending of war operations on Polish territories, the process of reestablishment of newspapers began. Some of them reverted to traditions from before 1939. A large majority presented the viewpoints of the various political parties active in that period (i.e., before 1948), although the new system of information—under a changed socio-political system, nationalization of industry, and land reform—began to be decided mainly by the journalists and activists of left-wing parties.

In December 1945, an all-Polish congress of the Trade Union of Journalists of the Polish Republic put forth, among other postulates, one involving the attitude of the journalists in constructing a new Poland as one criteria of value and professional qualifications.[6] This viewpoint became a cornerstone of the Polish press system in future years. The victory of left-wing parties in Sejm (Parliamentary) elections in January 1947 opened a period of political and economic stabilization and of press centralization. In May 1947, the Polish Workers' Party established the Workers' Publishing Cooperative "Prasa" (RSW "Prasa"), with the task of publishing all of the party press. In 1948, the two worker parties (Polish Socialist Party and Polish Workers' Party) merged into the Polish United Workers' Party (PUWP). The youth organizations also merged, and, in November 1949, the peasant parties united. All of this also meant unification of their press and publishing organizations. The process of press centralization was prompt: the 880 titles in 1948 decreased to 576 in 1953, with a substantial increase in circulation.

---

[6] Information on the stages and characteristics of development of the Polish Press are taken from A. Slomkowska (1980).

Table 1. Basic Indicators on Trends of Development in Poland (1946–1982)

Indicators	1946	1950	1955	1960	1965	1970	1975	1980	1982
1. Population (in millions)	23.9	25.0	27.6	29.8	31.6	32.7	34.2	35.7	36.4
2. Percent of urban population	31.8	39.0	43.5	48.3	49.5	52.3	55.3	58.4	59.3
3. Agriculture employment per 1000 population	NA	220.0	193.0	181.6	167.9	160.2	142.9	142.8	138.4
4. Cinema seats per 1000 population	9.2	13.6	16.8	22.1	23.2	19.2	16.2	14.0	13.3
5. Annual attendance to cinema per inhabitant	2.8	5.0	6.7	6.8	5.5	4.2	4.1	2.7	2.5
6. Number of borrowed books from public libraries per inhabitant	NA	1.2	2.0	2.2	3.1	3.9	4.1	4.1	4.0
7. Radio receivers 1) per 1000 population	20.1	58.5	111.0	176.2	178.9	173.5	237.7	242.5	243.8
8. Television receivers 1) per 1000 population	—	—	0.2	14.2	65.9	129.3	189.3	222.6	229.3
9. Telephones per 1000 population	5.0	7.7	12.4	17.9	24.8	32.8	42.9	54.4	57.9
10. Total number of newspapers and periodicals (newspapers only)	702 (63)	626 (42)	638 (45)	988 (53)	1304 (53)	2750 (55)	2702 (56)	2570 (56)	2045 (55)
11. Numbers of newspapers and periodicals published by RSW (newspapers only)	—	40 (18)	113 (42)	125 (42)	165 (43)	202 (45)	236 (46)	274 (45)	255 (44)
12. Average newspapers circulation per 1000 population	NA	249	196	184	206	261	305	299	255
13. Average periodicals circulation per 1000 population	NA	468	463	540	576	817	913	840	596
14. Annual sale of copies per inhabitant									
a/newspapers	a/	2/	50	46	56	70	75	75	59
b/periodicals	b/	2/	13	15	17	19	23	22	15

Sources: Polish Statistical Yearbooks, Warsaw, and data from RSW "Prasa-Ksiazka-Ruch."

NA—Data not available; (1)—Figures relate to the number of licenses issued for radio and television receivers. The Registration of the first bought radio and TV set is obligatory in Poland. This is related to a compulsory monthly subscription. (2)—Data not applicable because of a collective subscription to the factories.

The press actively participated in promoting the plan of reconstruction of the country and the socio-economic education of the nation. Competition of labor, together with an ideological offensive to popularize Marxist philosophy, were promoted. This was accompanied by optimistic visions of accelerated industrialization of the country. Heroism of labor was preached, enthusiasm and feelings of national pride in realizing plans of reconstruction of the Polish economy were promoted, and migration from village to town was supported. An important role was played by the press in support of stamping out illiteracy and in disseminating education and culture among the masses.

In official pronouncements by the leaders of the Polish state, the press was defined as an ideological weapon of the party and the journalists as officers in the ideological front.[7] The necessary performance of organizational tasks by the press was accentuated, and its measure of appraisal was contained, in social support for the concrete services and obligations of the state. As a result, as one witness to those times wrote, many press publications reminded one of military orders. Together with this growth of organized enthusiasm, material on critical phenomena seen by the average citizens began disappearing from the columns of the press (in the interest "of state secret protection"). The major part of circulation (up to 80%) of newspapers and periodicals was sold by a collective subscription organized by the institutions.

The first critical remarks on these methods of press functioning appeared in 1953, during sessions of the CC of PUWP and of the Polish Journalist Association. It was said that propaganda and press were much too enthusiastic, lacking discussion and conflict. However, serious discussion of these problems occurred later, in 1956, in connection with the political crisis in Poland, and with worker strikes, when demands to widen civic liberties and to improve the economic situation of the country were advocated. In those days, for the first time in post-war Poland, demands appeared for freedom of speech and of the press. Within that "creative ferment" it was demanded of the media that they inform honestly about the public's feelings and opinions, and not only the aspirations of the government and political parties. The necessity was also seen to enrich information services on international issues. The basic press organs of PUWP were writing positively about the need for a liquidation of "spheres of slience in the press and in everyday life" (Kupis, 1967, p. 20).[8] As a result, there was also a remarkable increase

---

[7] Based on a book by T. Kupis (1967).

[8] For example, "Trybuna Luda"—the Party daily organ, on July 4, 1956, wrote: "We have to change our relation to the recipient. To manifest more esteem towards him, more faith. From the disbelief in masses resulted distortions in social and political life—from the disbelief in the possibility of proper understanding of the facts by the people (even if they appear to be unfavorable for us)—distortions resulted in propaganda manifested in underestimation of information and intrusive comment."

in press titles (especially sociopolitical, cultural, and children's periodicals), in newspaper circulations, and in a widening of the scope of press information. The press opened to change (parallel to the changes in the political system's method of ruling the country), although on many editorial staffs the journalists themselves did not know what place the press should take in the relation between government and the citizens.

Limitations in typographical equipment, and paper shortages in the 1960s, caused limits in press circulation and reductions in its volume. As a result, there was a tendency by the press to eliminate material on the basis, not of the interests and cognitive abilities of the readers, but on an anticipation of the likes and dislikes of politicans and what they wanted published. More and more, information was published as if it was diplomatic protocol, while the worsening living standards of the people became "a sphere of silence."

The social explosion of December 1970, and the unequivocal self-declaration of the press as standing by the government, caused the same reaction as in 1956. The slogan "The press tells lies" appeared in nearly all of the demonstrations. Apart from appeals for improvement in the nation's economic situation, demands were made for a further democratization of life, as well as for curtailment of state censorship of the press.

When the change in the ruling cabinet took place, the new leadership decided on further development of the press, on modernization of printing facilities, on facilitation of journalists' access to information sources, and on broadening the scope of information on foreign developments. The number of foreign correspondents was increased; cooperation with international information agencies was intensified. A decision was made as well to increase cultural and tourist exchange with Western countries. New social and cultural periodicals were established, and week-end issues of daily newspapers became more varied. Also, various forms of ties between the press and readers were developed (e.g., press days, meetings with readers). These times in the 1970s, were when old time promotion of modest ways of life, and the necessity of austerity, were changed into a "propaganda of success" (in a realization of the effectiveness of the state's general policy), of material abundance and comfort, and of other consumer values. The slogans "construction of the second Poland" and "coming up to the top of highly industrialized countries" were welcomed by the society. After all, they had to mobilize the people to work more effectively.

After several years, however, the growing social aspirations were not accompanied by tangible improvements in the economic standing of the nation. The media, especially television, were not reporting arising anxieties and doubts. Profits had made possible large sums for new investments and modernization of typographical equipment, conditions under which many editors worked had improved, the design of numerous periodicals had been enriched and made more interesting. However, the menaces and unification of contents and surrender of the editorial staffs to decisions and political directives from superior authorities had not disappeared.[9] The contents of all of the media were not well received by the public, most of whom were already involved in the new socialist system. The society was well educated, with aroused intellectual and cognitive aspirations. Its members demanded a realization of the slogans of social justice, honesty, and humanized interpersonal relations, rejecting "newspeak" and any style of "doublethink." The mass media and their political directors had failed to notice these changes, and had not been meeting the public's social aspirations. All the more, the media were not able to perform the role of "stimulator" or "narcotic" (using Schramm's 1964, or more exactly, Lazarsfeld and Merton's 1948, terms). On the contrary, the media irritated recipients who, as a result, began to attach greater importance to face-to-face communication.

The worsening of the economic standing of the country was accompanied by a crisis of trust in state authorities. It was subserved by the picture of reality in the media, resulting from superior authorities' information policy and the censorship records. Particularly in the second half of the 1970s, the media's participation in formation of a program of social and economic development of the country ceased. The centralization of the mass media was progressing, together with dissemination among the masses of the central daily newspapers and TV newscasts, and this made the problem of controlling contents much easier.[10] The use of newspapers and radio and TV programs by Polish citizens was immense. For example, in 1980, TV programs were viewed by 97.8% of Poles aged over 14, radio by 95.6%, and the daily press by 83.6%. (For comparison, in 1974 the corresponding figures were: TV—92.5%, radio—92.6%, newspapers—92.9%.) But the massive character of public contact with the media had not increased public support of the policies of the authorities. On the contrary, the effects of media were the opposite of those desired by the political authorities.

The authors of the report on the state of social communication in Poland during these years had noticed "the growing discrepancy between the picture of reality outlined in the columns of the press and experience; the many

---

[9] A Polish communication specialist offers the following explanation of the phenomenon: "Formalization and, what follows, institutionalization of communication processes in the vertical circulation aggravates the phenomenon of unequal opportunities of both directions of communication. While information addressed from 'above downwards' may have organizational support of the authorities (political or economic), access to advanced technical facilities and, more or less, endorsement of its veracity and even of its official character, it is the other way around with information from 'down upwards.' It is not only difficult to have material published, but it is also frequently treated with disrespect and even, at times, with suspicion" (Szulczewski, 1979, p. 8). The lack of information given by the Polish mass media about the population's life and opinions was described, among others, in the special reports of Press Research Center in Cracow (1980, 1982) and by the Association of Polish Journalists (Brodzki & Surdykowski, 1981).

[10] These remarks are based on work edited by W. Pisarek (1980).

years of lasting contacts with the resulting mechanisms of primitive, uniformed steering, and far-reaching selection of information had formed—at least among part of the recipients—on one hand, the reluctant attitude towards the press as the tool of propaganda, on the other, the skill of reading between the lines, of deciphering the allusions, sometimes even unintended ones...then of inferring information from the lack of information....The paradoxical phenomenon could be observed that a growth in careful reading of the press text resulted in diminishing acceptance of its content" (Pisarek, 1980, p. 23).

The political crisis in the second half of 1980 was caused by the economic crisis and a loss of trust in the ruling group. Among the postulates on how to improve Poland, once again demands appeared to improve the work of the media—it would do this by increasing the scope of influence exerted by the various social groups on the content of information policy. Generally speaking, the opinion that the conflict in 1980–1981 in Poland was one between the public and the structure of power appears to be acceptable (Polish Academy of Sciences, 1982). In its essense, it was rooted in the frustration of "disappointed expectations" (especially of the young, well-skilled generation of workers and technicians who were limited in their possibilities for advancement and their realization of material needs), and in the conflict between values shared by the public and those shared by the authorities (Polish Academy of Sciences, 1982, pp. 305–306). The conflict was aggravated by a blockade (obstruction) of the channels of expressing various views and opinions by the mass media. This precluded an authentic play of interests and negotiations between contradictory attitudes.

There is a strong sense of democratic values in Polish society, which follows in a search for the institutionalization of a system for the articulation of the public pluralistic interests. That is why Solidarity became so popular among Poles. Many of them saw Solidarity as a very convenient vehicle for a broadening of the base for participation in economic and political decision making; that Solidarity would provide a bridge between the people and state institutions.

Agreements that had been reached made possible the initiation of new means of mass communication in 1981 Poland—new trade unions, and social and religious organizations. New periodicals were established (as other titles were eliminated), and air time was given to radio broadcasts of Sunday masses from the churches.

After the introduction of martial law in December 1981, an additional difficulty was created by economic restrictions imposed by the Western countries. There was a lack of spare parts for printing machines and radio and television equipment, and a shortage of newsprint. This caused a further reduction in editorial possibilities and a temporary limitation of radio and TV broadcasts. With reconstruction of the national economy, the reestablishment, by the state, of many publishers is continuing. There is more room for political participation by other groups, including religious associations and trade unions. Censorship law was changed, and its rules are now more liberal. The new (since the Second World War) Press Law came into force in Poland in July 1984, which, in addition to establishing the National Press Council, has also made it possible for individuals to publish periodicals (as semi-private enterprises).

The process of democratization is particularly difficult in the contemporary international political climate, saturated with difficult or even open hostility and intolerance towards opinions other than one's own. Intensified confrontation between two basic political systems, and the ideologies of international relations, are unfavorable for the extension of liberties of speech and opinions in all countries, including Poland.

From a certain perspective, one can say that attaching so great an importance to the events which derogate the principles of equality and social justice testifies to a deep internalization among Poles of the socialist model of social relations, and to a rejection of all authoritarian tendencies. For citizens, this model remains an essential criterion of public estimates of complex socio-political phenomena in the country.

It should be mentioned that, in Poland, a great unifying impact on all society resulted from the guaranteed system of uniform edication for all citizens that was not limited by any status. Similar impact was obtained by accessibility to the mass media, as well as public access to the educational and cultural institutions. The socialist system did create a chance for people to leave behind the many centuries of economic and social humiliation, and it formed a sense of peculiar dignity based on equal citizen rights (Kwaśniewicz, 1983). That sense of dignity, when injured, seems to establish a background for the signs of social dissatisfaction.

Public dissatisfaction with the press always has appeared in Poland during social and economic crises. It does not mean that mass media were playing a decisive role in spreading such unrest, but, I presume, the media contributed to a deepening of the crisis situation. It is comprehensible that different groups in society would prefer to have a pluralistic media with diversity of opinion. And it is known that such mass media can work positively, not only on trust to the state institutions and social organizations, but also that they can affect and create intergroup understanding. They also work as safety valves, or as national stimulants or tranquilizers. A lack of communication between the power elite and the masses is a contributing factor to socio-political unrest. In such circumstances, even if mass media are presenting an accurate picture of public affairs, people usually do not trust them and look for something fictitious, reading "between the lines." They are continually looking for different opinions, which they obtain frequently from abroad. I do not see the importance of the foreign media's impact on raising revolutionary feelings or irritable attitudes toward domestic institutions. I see the contribution of such foreign activity toward the enrichment of an "information environment" (as Read, 1976, called it), since foreign media cannot force persons to act against their wills.

WORLD CYCLES

Confirmation of some of these aspects of democratiziation of communication can be found in the studies of White (1982) and of Matta and Somavia in articles in "Development Dialogue" (No. 2) (1981). A convergence of opinion can also be found in other works (coming, however, from different spheres of theoretical inspiration): the concepts of McClelland (1961) and Hagen (1962); the anthropological theories of cultural diffusion of Rogers (1962) and Katz and Lazarsfeld (1955); the model of the expansion of experience by Moles (1971); the previously mentioned theories of Lerner (1958), Schramm (1964), and, last but not least, Merrill and Lowenstein (1971). It is also worth remembering that the curve of media development (Merrill & Lowenstein, 1971) along stages of "Elite-Popular-Specialized" means, in my opinion, the existence of objective tendencies towards expansion of a diversity of communication subjects according to the "spiral" model. In reality, the subsequent stages differ as well in number of these subjects as in pluralization of the published opinions.

In the history of mankind, the spiral has been drawing ever wider circles, encompassing an increasing number of subjects of communicaiton. The symptoms of this phenomenon are present at the level of individual states and on a global scale. The idea of a new information order may be an example of this. Thanks to this, one can assume that a constant process of decentralization of distribution of information, and of fragmentation of subjects of communication, is taking place. The enzymes in this evolution are always the lack of satisfaction with the existing state of affairs and the desire to change it. There are always the privileged people, in this case the subjects of communication or owners of the media, who resist changes, and there are those who desire such changes, believing that they are in a less advantageous position. What we have is the constant dialectic of the conservative and the progressive factors.

The process of evolution in communication may be characterized in a way similar to that of French social anthropologist C. Levi-Strauss (1952) in his study of progress. It goes on by jerks, and not always in the same direction, as a result of the influence of various political, economic, and technological factors. In sum, however, it does accumulate over long periods of time, giving rise to new subjects of communication. The causative force in this evolution is not nature, but people representing a concrete social and economic force. Yet, they have to be more intellectually active than those who are defending the status quo—after all, they are usually the authors of new programs, ideas, or visions. When, in the course of time, having achieved their goals, they too start defending the situation they created, they become the objects of an attack launched by successive groups, more active intellectually and more mobile. As Otto von Bismarck once put it, "Only he who had been an ardent revolutionary in his youth can become a decent conservative."

We can find global examples of the cycle of transfer development of communication in the 20th century; one cycle having completed all stages of development and the next one having been started recently.

The first example is the struggle of the U.S. news agencies for equal-rights relations with the European agencies operating at the beginning of the 20th century.[11] In sum, a first four-stage cycle of development of international subjects of communication was completed in the span of some 50 years. The French and British agencies were joined by two American agencies and the Soviet TASS. In the 1960s, in step with the emergence of a large group of post-colonial countries on the international arena, voices criticizing the activities of world news agencies became increasingly frequent.[12] The criticism referred particularly to the two U.S. agencies and the slogan of the free flow of information they were promoting.

The culminating second stage of this cycle took place in the 1970s when, at UN sessions and UNESCO conferences, the developing countries demanded recognition of their right to inform others about themselves and their problems. The efforts were crowned with the decisions relating to the necessity of establishing "a new, more just and more effective world information and communication order," adopted by UNESCO in 1978.

In my opinion, we are going through the third stage of this crisis at present: local agencies were launched in the developing countries; special funds for helping to build structures of communication and upgrading the professional skills of journalists are being established. This stage of development is most difficult and will last much longer than the two preceding ones. The experience gained to date shows that in order for a subject of international communication to have equal-rights relations with other subjects, it has to manifest the same journalistic efficiency and have the support of a political and economic potential recognized worldwide.

---

[11] See Cooper's *Barriers Down* (1942) and works by H.I. Schiller, e.g., *Communication and Cultural Domination* (1976). We can find a similar history of development and motives of activity in the history of the United Press International (formerly the United Press Association); see Tremaine (1978).

[12] UNESCO reports (1947–1951) pointed out that some parts of the world are not covered by international news agencies.

CONCLUSIONS

Undoubtedly, the phenomenon of democratization of communication is at the same time an outcome and a cause of the development of human civilization. One should seek its sources in man himself, who is striving to learn new things and usually does so through contacts with other people. Largely conducive to this development is the progress made in mutual communication, which is transforming the world into a global community of people; we are inhabitants of mutually dependent countries, where all are neighbors who are more or less well informed about the life of others. One can also say that the process of democratization is convergent with the processes of oligarchization of all sorts of contesting groups.

This oligarchization happens at the level of occupational, political, and national groups, as well as in all countries which want a new, more just, and more effective world information and communication order established. Such an order must not entail liquidation of the existing international news agencies, or replace them with bureaucratized governmental agencies minding only their own interests. The present state of world communication problems verifies the existence of a tendency to expand the freedom to express opinions, enhance their variety, and improve the flow of information among nations. Thus, efforts for further democratization of communication, and for meeting the need to inform and to be well informed, which is one of the fundamental human rights, are worthy of support. At the same time, any attempts to introduce governmental censorship or to terminate media pluralism are deserving of punishment.

There is no difference of opinion on the subject of imbalance in the flow of information in the world, especially in the developed countries–developing countries relation. The asymmetry in the international information flow is almost identical with the world asymmetry in the possession of economic and military power. However, it is difficult to reach agreement on the steps that should be taken to do away with this inequality. I do not think that lack of funds is the only reason. It is rather the lack of a general consensus in understanding the role and functions of the media in society, and the absence of an unequivocal answer to the question of what the aims and uses of communication are.

REFERENCES

Brodzki, S., and Surdykowski, J. (1981). *Raport o stanie komunikacji spolecznej w Polsce* (Report about the State of Social Communication in Poland). Warszawa: Association of Polish Journalists.

Cooper, K. (1942). *Barriers Down.* New York: Farrar & Rinehart.

Frey, F.W. (1973). "Communication and Development." *In* I. de S. Pool, F.W. Frey, W. Schramm, N. Maccoby, and E.B. Parker (Eds.), *Handbook of Communication* (pp. 337–461). Chicago, IL: Rand McNally.

Hagen, E.E. (1962). *On the Theory of Social Change: How Economic Growth Begins.* Homewood, IL: Dorsey.

Institute for Public Opinion (Japan) (1972). *Survey on Information Desired by Audience.* Tokyo: Japanese Broadcasting Corporation.
International Commission for the Study of Communication Problems. (1980). *Many Voices, One World.* (MacBride Report). Paris: UNESCO.
Katz, E., and Lazarsfeld, P.F. (1955). *Personal Influence; the Part Played by People in the Flow of Mass Communications.* Glencoe, IL: Free Press.
Kupis, T. (1967). *Wspolczesna prasa polska* (Contemporary Polish Press). Warsaw.
Kwaśniewicz, W. (1983). "Makrostrukturalne aspekty kryzysu lat osiemdzieseatych" (Macrostructural aspects of crisis of the Eighties). *Studia Sosjologiczne* (No. 4).
Lazarsfeld, P.F., and Merton, R.K. (1948). "Mass Communication, Popular Taste, and Organized Social Action." *In* L. Bryson (Ed.), *The Communication of Ideas.* New York: Harper.
Lerner, D. (1958). *The Passing of Traditional Society: Modernizing the Middle East.* New York: Free Press.
Levi-Strauss, C. (1952). *Race and History.* Paris: UNESCO.
McClelland, D.C. (1961). *The Achieving Society.* Princeton, NJ: Van Nostrand.
Merrill, J.C., and Lowenstein, R.L. (1971). *Media, Messages, and Men: New Perspectives in Communication.* New York: D.McKay.
Moles, A. (1971). *La Communication.*
Nixon, R.F. (1974). "Access to the Media: By Whom, How, For What Purpose, With What Consequence." Paper presented at the International Association for Mass Communication Research Conference, Leipzig.
Pisarek, W. (Ed.). (1980). *Komunikowanie nasowe w Polsce. Próba bilansu lat siedemdziesiatych* (Mass Communication in Poland: An Attempt to Balance the Seventies). Krakow.
Polish Academy of Sciences. (1982). *Polacy 81, Postrzeganie Kryzysu i konfliktu* (Poles '81, Perception of Crisis and Conflict). Warszawa: Polish Academy of Sciences.
Press Research Center (Cracow). (1980). *Komunikowanie masowe w Polsce. Próba bilansu lat siedemdzieseatych* (Mass Communication in Poland. An Attempt to Evaluate the Seventies). Krakow: Press Research Center.
Press Research Center (Cracow). (1982). *Raport o stanie komunikacje spolecznej w Polsce (sierpien 1980-13 grudnia 1981)* (Report about the State of Social Communication in Poland. August 1980 - 13 December 1981). Krakow: Press Research Center.
Pye, L. (Ed.). (1963). *Communications and Political Development.* Princeton, NJ: Princeton University.
Read, W.H. (1976). *America's Mass Media Merchants.* Baltimore, MD: John Hopkins University Press.
Rogers, E.M. (1962). *Diffusion of Innovations.* New York: Free Press.
Schiller, H.I. (1976). *Communication and Cultural Domination.* White Plains, NY: International Arts and Sciences Press.
Schramm, W. (1964). *Mass Media and National Development: The Role of Information in the Developing Countries.* Stanford, CA: Stanford University Press.
Slomkowska, A. (1980). *Prasa w PRL, Szkice historyczne* (The Press in Polish People's Republic. Historical Essays). Warsaw.
Szulczewski, M. (1979). *Informacja spoleczna* (Social Information). Warsaw.
Tremaine, F. (1978). "United Press International: Origin, Organization, and Operations." New York.
UNESCO. (1947-1951). *Reports on the Facilities of Mass Communication: Press Film, Radio* (5 vol.). Paris: UNESCO.
White, R.A. (1982). "Contradictions in Contemporary Policies for Democratic Communication." Paper presented at the International Association for Mass Communication Research Conference, Paris.

Chapter 14
Information Technology and National Development in Latin America

JOSEP ROTA
School of Telecommunications
Ohio University
Athens, OH 45701

TATIANA GALVAN
Department of Communication
National University of Mexico
Mexico City, Mexico

INTRODUCTION

In order to understand a modern society thoroughly, it is also necessary to understand the way by which and the extent to which that society is permeated with information, as well as the level of its technological development and the degree to which both technology and information are integrated into its socio-economic and cultural structures.

That process of understanding, however, becomes more difficult when there is little pertinent research in a society, particularly in a less developed one. In such a case, the historical articulation of information and technology with socio-economic and cultural structures will usually be reconstructed from alien economic, political, and cultural perspectives. Worse yet, those extraneous perspectives typically will be the ones of developed societies. Since the paucity of research in Latin American countries is a common characteristic, the reconstruction of their history can only be done in relatively general terms, sometimes precluding the possibility of more comprehensive explanations.

In the industrialized countries, the modern information technologies have become a kind of bridge to establish relations with new concepts and, therefore, with new possibilities for development. In Latin America, however, where the various countries are confronted with serious economic and social shortcomings, those potential bridges have actually become immense fractures in the system. The fractures are so wide and deep-rooted that they

---

Based on a paper presented at the International Communication Association Conference, San Francisco, 1984.

make it very difficult to build the bridges that would shorten the distance between the present state and the eventual solution of the economic and socio-cultural shortcomings of the region through a process of gradual development.

From this perspective, one can understand that a "functional" economy requires certain equilibriums in order to maintain the stability of the system. In a developed society, the widespread presence of large quantities of information and of a "living" technology (living in the sense that it is integrated with the social system as a whole) would seem to be, and most likely is, indispensable. Conversely, in underdeveloped societies, the information structure is poor, and technology, especially educational technology, does not reach those who need it most.

In this paper, we explain some of the reasons why this is happening, as well as some of the effects of technology, particularly information technology, on the local culture of Mexico and, by extension, on other Latin American countries.

HISTORICAL DEVELOPMENT: THE MEXICAN ECONOMY AFTER 1940, A LATIN AMERICAN EXAMPLE

By the 1940s, Mexico already had an economic infrastructure which was rich enough for the development of new industrial enterprises. It had an important network of roads, railroads, and other means of communication and transportation (to a large extent, especially for the railroads, the legacy of Porfirio Diaz, the last President before the Revolution of 1910). Its agricultural infrastructure was reasonably solid, since it allowed for the subsistence of the masses, the earning of foreign currencies through exports, and the production of goods needed by the industrial sector. Also, there existed a disproportionate concentration of the national income, which facilitated the importation of certain technologies instead of others and helped to explain the subsequent patterns of importation of technology, the uses that new technologies were put to, and their socioeconomic consequences (Unger, 1977).

At the same time, there were three main trends that characterized the industrial sector of the developed countries: increasing automation, the development of products and technologies of ever-increasing complexity, and the growth of direct foreign investment by private investors and multinational corporations of industrialized countries in the manufacturing sector of the less developed ones (Unger, 1977).

According to Wionczek (1971), a Mexican authority on technology, foreign investment, and development, foreign investment was concentrated mostly in the manufacturing sector of Mexico during and after the 1940s. This is explained by the fact that other areas of the Mexican economy, such as mining, transportation and communications, oil, and the light and power companies, were subjected to a process of Mexicanization or outright nationalization. Sooner or later, all those economic activities became a part of the State-owned and State-run companies.

The growth of the manufacturing sector of Mexico is closely related to the official industrialization policies of the government during the so-called period of "stabilizing development" that took place between 1958 and 1969. It brought with it a large influx of private foreign investment.

According to data presented by Wionczek (1971), Mexico was third, after Canada and Great Britain, in the amount of direct foreign investment by the largest U.S.-based multinational corporations, as early as 1967. Of the 187 largest corporations accounting for more than 70% of all direct investment in the manufacturing sector of foreign countries by U.S. companies in 1967, 179 had invested in Mexico, usually through subsidiaries. The corresponding figures for Canada and Great Britain were 183 and 180, respectively. The total number of Mexican companies that were subsidiaries of, or were affiliated with, U.S.-based corporations, regardless of size, was 625; the largest number of any Latin American country and the fifth largest in the world, after Canada (1967 subsidiaries), Great Britain (1189), France (670) and West Germany (632). Since the Mexican economy is far less developed than that of the other four countries, the figure represents a relatively greater concentration of national companies in the hands of U.S.-based multinational corporations.

In the absence of alternative plans and strategies for national development, the government of Mexico decided to confront the challenge of multinational manufacturing companies in three indirect ways. One consisted of increasing the pressure to force the Mexicanization of new segments of the industrial sector. Another was to force those plants controlled by foreign companies, to increase their consumption of goods and other supplies produced in Mexico. The third, more recent, was to make the granting of import permits dependent upon meeting certain export goals that woud offset the foreign currencies spent in the imports (Wionczek, 1971). These three alternatives, however, were not always very successful.

Thus in the field of industrial technology, foreign influence has been quite definitive in Mexico, while in other sectors of the national economy, where the government participates more directly, the possibilities for foreign investment have been reduced and, therefore, the attendant technological influence has been more limited.

Nevertheless, even in certain crucial areas where the Mexican government has direct participation, there is a huge technological gap that neither the government nor private sector investors have been able to bridge. Those areas include some of the most dynamic fields of technology, such as electronics, and the information and education technologies. In those critical fields, Mexico and other Latin American countries are almost totally dependent upon foreign developers and suppliers. This can be explained, at least in part, by the nature of dependency as a dominant characteristic of Latin American societies. But another important factor that contributed to the existence and growth of the technological gap is that, until very recent years, Latin American countries, including the larger ones, failed to prepare adequate human and technical resources. In the absence of those resources, both the technological gap and the degree of their dependency increased. The government has been urged to train experts in many fields of technology, something that had practically been ignored since the 1940s, with all its detrimental consequences for national development.

Technological dependency is not limited just to investments, patents, trademarks, designs, and equipment. Rather, it also includes a high degree of dependency in management and human resources, as well as in the planning and development of new technologies which were produced according to the needs of the exporting companies and not as a function of the national needs of Latin American countries. Likewise, Latin Americans failed to construct a national, or at least a Latin American or regional, theory of technology and its relation to national development as a function of local needs and local definitions of what development ought to be like. Consequently, they applied a theory (whether explicit or implicit) and a conceptualization of technology and its socio-economic and cultural role that was borrowed from a different setting. Such a theory turned out to be utterly dysfunctional once it was applied in Latin American countries without the benefit of a previous process of critical analysis and structural adaptation.

ORGANIZATIONAL DIFFERENCES: A DEVELOPED AND AN UNDERDEVELOPED MODEL OF ORGANIZATIONAL GROWTH

From the budding origins of American capitalism, more than a century and a half ago, until recent times, American companies have grown in a way that cannot be compared with those of Mexico and Latin America. Mexican capitalism, conceived as a modern form of economic organization, began its consolidation much later than its North American counterpart, despite some nineteenth-century early nuclei of industrial development in Mexico. And Mexican capitalism began its consolidation (still a far from finished process) at a time when large foreign corporations, particularly in the United States and in Great Britain, had reached their transnational phase and had penetrated and even controlled many foreign markets, notably in Mexico and many other Latin American countries.

In the United States, according to authors, like Fombrun and Astley (1982), the growth of organizations took place through a sequential process involving (a) *horizontal integration,* as a firm spans geographical markets; (b) *vertical integration,* as a firm moves to guarantee its sources of supply and outlets for its products; and (c) *diversification* across related and unrelated domains in the process of developing a portfolio of complementary business. More specifically, horizontal interdependence exists between firms with common markets or products. Vertical interdependence links organizations at different stages of production. Symbiotic interdependence links organizations that complement each other in the rendering of services to individual clients. Following Pennings (1981), the authors state that these stages of growth can be described in terms of a strategic absorption of environmental elements with which the focal organization is, in sequence, horizontally, vertically, and then symbiotically interdependent.

Related processes of integration and diversification took place among Mexican companies differently, more consonant with the general characteristics of underdevelopment. Accordingly, the consolidation of Mexican corporations (we refer here to the larger ones) has usually implied the absolute supremacy of only one company (or a group of individuals, frequently interrelated by family ties) that has managed to establish a monopoly in some sector of the economy which is then used as a base to expand into other sectors. A relevant example here would be Televisa. Televisa, at present the national private monopoly of commercial television in Mexico, began, several decades ago as a radio station and then expanded into a national radio network. Several years later, in 1950, the owners of the radio network, by then already related with important newspaper and magazine chains, were among the originators of commercial television. Twenty or thirty years after that, Televisa had already become, not only the national monopoly of commercial television, but also the base upon which a large private empire had been built, directly owning more than 70 companies in fields that included, besides television, radio, the film industry, magazines, night clubs, theaters, hotels, museums, and record companies. Other Mexican companies that exist in most of those fields do not represent any real competition for the implacable monopoloy.

Consequently, the processes of horizontal and vertical integration and diversification that have increasingly characterized North American corporations have not occurred in Mexico and other Latin American countries, at least not in instances where the consolidated corporations *compete* for the same market in approximately even terms with other, similar corporations.

There are other differences that distinguish North American from Latin American organizational growth. In the United States, such growth usually ends up in a transformation of the organization from a local, or national company into a multinational or transnational one. Contrastingly, even the largest Mexican and other Latin American corporations usually do not extend beyond national boundaries. (Televisa is a notable exception; in recent years it has expanded into the U.S. market, becoming one of the largest TV networks there.)

An additional but important difference is that, while in the United States the increasing concentration of economic power occurs in the hands of private *corporations,* the government holds the largest concentration and control of economic power in Mexico. (This became more overwhelming after the government took over the national banking system in September 1982. In that way, the Mexican government now directly controls more than half of the national economy, as measured by its direct participation in the Gross National Product.

In the Mexican *private* sector, we find the domination of certain areas by monopolistic and oligopolic groups and, in other areas, a dispersion of economic power. A similar pattern exists in most other Latin American countries, except that, in most of them, the government tends to control less in the economic sector.

Furthermore, the concentration of economic power in the United States is mostly in the hands of organizations or corporations, while in Mexico and other Latin American countries such a concentration is usually controlled by individuals (either by themselves or organized in closely knit groups, generally comprising members of a reduced elite only).

Another difference has to do with the concentration or dispersion of political power. In the face of increasing concentration of economic power in relatively fewer private corporations, what we find in the United States is a comparatively greater dispersion of political power (at least as compared to Latin American countries). The opposite happens in Mexico, where political power is highly concentrated.

The consequences of those differences are very important. Since power is so markedly concentrated in the hands of a small elite in Mexico and in other Latin American societies, whatever modern technology is introduced into these countries actually serves, on the one hand, to strengthen the power of that elite. On the other hand, it widens the already large gap that separates the elite, as well as the middle and upper classes, from the rest of the population; that is, from a majority of the inhabitants that constitute the lower middle class, the working class, and *"los marginados,"* the dispossessed ones or the rural and urban poor. Hence, and in marked contrast to what happens in the United States and in other industrialized societies, the introduction of new technologies in Latin America has so far not carried the real possibility, perhaps not even the hope, of a process of democratization. Namely, the democratization of information, knowledge, and, ultimately, power.

THE HISTORICAL CONTEXT OF THE DEVELOPMENT OF INFORMATION TECHNOLOGY IN MEXICO AND LATIN AMERICA

On the basis of what we have already stated, we can now point out the principal elements and characteristics that, in our opinion, give shape to the historical context within which information technology has evolved in Mexico and, by extension, in other Latin American countries.

There are three main characteristics: (a) dependency, (b) the lack of national policies of technological development, and (c) discontinuities between culture and technology.

Dependency
It is well known that new information technologies are not created in Latin America. Quite the contrary, this is a region of importers of the technological products developed in the industrialized countries of the North. Moreover, Latin Americans not only import those products, but also the premises, theories (whether implicit or explicit), models, the underlying values and cultural foundations, and the strategic priorities that support those new technologies in their countries of origin. And they use them all, whether they are actually applicable to their own (and different) contexts or not. Conceptual dependency is even worse than the material one, even though such a form of dependency is probably a distinctive characteristic of the global state of dependency and of the Latin American condition as satellites or peripheral countries in relation to the structure of world power and domination.

By "dependency" we understand, at the very least, (a) the inability of a country to produce for itself the products that it needs in an area of strategic importance, which necessarily leads it to import those products from foreign countries. (It can import those products from any number of countries, but, in fact, the number of suppliers is usually very reduced and politically homogeneous). Such an inability is, by and large, the result of a lack of a locally originated and advanced technology, the nonexistence of a self-sufficient and autonomous manufacturing sector, the lack of capital, and the scarcity of trained technicians and other personnel. And (b), as a consequence of the preceding characteristics, dependency also means the loss of autonomy in decision making. That is, dependence on others not only for products, but also on their definitions of priorities, interests, and approaches, on their logic as exporters and dominators.

In the field of information, dependency also implies at least four additional characteristics; namely, cost, functionality, structural imposition, and strategic risk.

(a) *Cost*. Even though in the past, even the recent past, the argument that importing information technology was cheaper than producing it for a less developed country was well established, the recent economic history of Latin America, which is synonymous with inflation-devaluation-recession, has totally invalidated that argument (if it were indeed ever valid). Let us consider a simple example. A small electronic component, that costs US$10 in the United States, in mid 1982 cost only 270 pesos in Mexico (cheaper than its equivalent in U.S. currency, since the Mexican peso was overvalued).

Two years later, however, and after several devaluations, the same component would cost more than 1,700 pesos—an increase of more than 600%, without taking into consideration that, until August 1982, there was a free and open currency market and now it is more difficult to buy foreign currencies. We leave it to the imagination of the reader to figure out what it means for a country to take that small example and raise it to the level of the massive importations that the entire economy of a dependent country needs if it hopes to function properly.

Another aspect of "cost" refers to the attendant difficulties of implementing any new information technology. The absence of an adequate technical infra-structure and of trained personnel in an organization means that many of its members, at all hierarchical levels, will have to be trained, and also that it will be necessary to introduce many other changes into the organization. This usually consumes more time and resources than the organization has available. Consequently, the new information technology will frequently end up by being forced upon or superimposed on top of the organization, neither whose structure nor employees have been prepared to absorb it. The economic and human, as well as other costs, tend to be high.

(b) *Functionality.* By the term "functionality" we refer to the way in which new technological products, especially those in the field of information, will integrate or not with the cultural structure of a given country. Some would argue that it is irrelevant to postulate a relation between technology and culture. They would say that technology is, in itself, "neutral;" that its use is limited to performing specific tasks, such as transmitting messages or operating a machine; and that activities such as these have no relation with culture. However, any new technology, particularly if it has to do with information, cannot be regarded as neutral. Those technologies are used for certain purposes and by certain individuals who live in a given culture.

In an industrialized society, the number of people who have access to new information technologies is constantly and dramatically growing. The tendency appears to be eventually to give everybody access to those technologies. In a dependent society, access to the new information technologies is substantially more restricted. Some of the reasons have to do with costs, functional illiteracy, and lack of cultural adaptation. But we also have to consider that the members of the local elite will probably be more concerned with the possibility of using those technologies as another tool for the preservation of their privileges and domination than with democratization. From this perspective, new information technologies have tended to have rather dysfunctional effects in Latin America both for cultural integration and for the possibility of reducing the economic, information, and, ultimately, power imbalances that exist.

(c) *Structural imposition.* We have stated that, when one imports new information technologies, one also tends to import, along with them, their underlying cultural, socio-economic, and conceptual premises. Those premises have been developed in, and correspond to, a socio-cultural tradition which is different from the Latin American. They are derived from a different reality, which demands from its members certain styles of social participation that do not fit within the outline of a dependent society. Thus, when a new technology is forced into a peripheral society ("directly adopt" instead of "critically and functionally adapt"), we can be sure that certain problems will ensue. First, it may threaten or weaken some structural elements of the receiving culture. (It may "unstructure" it.) Second, it may inhibit the growth of adaptive mechanisms from within the receiving culture, since there generally exists a contradiction, or at least an incompatibility, between some of the underlying elements of the cultural structure of the receiving system and the implicit cultural frames of reference of the industrialized society that exports the technology. Third, such a contradiction or incompatibility will be a likely source of value confusion, with its inherent cultural and socio-psychological consequences.

(d) *Strategic risks.* Information technologies do not operate alone. They are not self-sufficient pieces of hardware. Rather, they require, among other things, software, definitions about their applications, and maintenance. These three elements are frequently imported too, at least in part. This implies the same problems we have previously discussed. In addition, there is what we call "strategic risk," since a piece of hardware is useless without software, applications, and maintenance. Inasmuch as these elements are wholly or partially imported, there is always the risk that the user will not be able to get them and will only have an expensive but useless piece of hardware. The thread that binds together a foreign supplier and a local user can be very weak, either because the supplier may decide to cut ties with the foreign user, for whatever reasons (no matter how valid), or because of uncontrollable independent events (such as massive devaluations and sudden foreign currency controls) that can unexpectedly appear. If the weak thread does indeed break, the modern and complex piece of hardware will be rendered useless.

On top of those risks, we have to add an additional problem which is very frequent in less developed societies. It has to do with the speed with which it is possible adequately to train the technicians who will satisfy the demand generated by this new activity. The discrepancy between supply and demand is not only quantitative. It has other dimensions; for example, the time it takes to develop a school or college curriculum, to train the instructors, and to prepare the first class of graduates may be too long. Improvisation is thus unavoidable.

Lack of a National Policy of Technological Development

In Mexico and in other Latin American countries, there is no national policy of technological development capable of orienting and giving a minimum degree of rationality, within the socio-economic conditions of its own system, to the introduction and use of new technologies. This is due to three principal factors.

First is the lack of both basic and applied research, since funding is generally too scarce for research activities, both from the public and the private sectors. One consequence is that, to a large extent, there is not sufficient factual data to permit an adequate and reliable diagnosis of the Latin American reality, from which it is then possible to define global economic and other development objectives, and design a policy that will be a dependable map, that will show an efficient way to follow, in order to arrive at the established objectives and other development goals.

Second is the existence of a large, unwieldy, inefficient government bureaucracy that has only recently (in the last four decades, but mostly in the past 12 to 20 years) begun to incorporate into its apparatus a small but growing cadre of professionals who are technically qualified to devise the policies and plans that are needed for a rational and consistent process of national development. Until recently, whatever development projects or activities existed had been decided upon without a general plan that would give congruence to all those projects and activities. Some of them, perhaps many of them, were well conceived and executed, but as isolated entities that did not constitute a part of a well integrated national plan. The leaders of the government bureaucracies did not include (until about 12 or 14 years ago, in the case of Mexico) planning as a necessary part of any government program, even though many of those leaders were very skillful at political operations and decision making. Recent planning activities have tended to be partial, instead of global (at a national level), and have been limited to certain crucial sectors, like education and industrial development. There still is no encompassing or global development policy and plan in Mexico, nor in any other Latin American country.

The third factor has been the generalized tendency in Mexico, and in most other countries of Latin America, to try to articulate the national economy principally around a single and dominant sector. A recent and dramatic example is the articulation of the Mexican economy, after 1976, on the basis of oil, even though the country has other assets, deserving a level of similar importance, that were ignored by the administrations. Mexico, for example, has the twelfth largest industrial plant, among all the non-Socialist countries of the world. (This plant, one might add, has sometimes been built, not with the support of the government, but almost despite its resistance expressed in the form of low-level bureaucratic obstacles, incongruous laws and rules, etc.) Furthermore, the predominance that a single sector has had over the entire economic system, at least in large countries like Mexico, has not been constant throughout recent history. If oil is the articulating factor today, before it was the manufacturing industry. And before that, agriculture (cash crops). Such changes have also contributed to making it even more difficult to devise a long-range plan of national development.

Because of the absence of a national development policy, there has been (a) a lack of *continuity* among the actions implemented by each government: thus, different, and incompatible, technologies have been adopted; (b) there has been a lack of any real technological *integration,* both from economic and cultural points of view; and (c) there has been a lack of *rationality* or *equilibrium* among the various decisions implemented in the field of technology. So, for example, we frequently witness one sector of the economy, and even the various branches of the same organization, struggling to use incompatible instruments of different origins.

Discontinuities Between Culture and Technology in Mexico and Other Latin American Countries

There are at least seven instances of such discontinuities.

(a) The first can be found within the technological system Latin American countries have adopted since technology was brought into those countries in a partial and local way, where the various areas, or structural components, are isolated among themselves, rather like a large group of isolated islands. Each island is the object of attention of a group of people, but this group is unrelated to the groups that busy themselves on the other islands. The islands may be spatially close, but, in practical terms, since they are isolated from each other, it is as if they were light years apart. The technologies imported into Latin America, both in each country as a whole and in each economic sector within the country, as well as sometimes in the different units of the same institution, represent nothing more than an atomized and desintegrated collection of technological components. This can be explained by an external and an internal factor. The external factor is represented by the competition, among the various technology exporting companies in the industrialized countries, in order to win buyers for the products they sell. A technology exporting company is not so much interested in helping to develop an adequate level of technological integration and consistency in a foreign country as it is in opening a market for its products. Its goal is to sell, not to construct policies for foreign societies. The internal factor stems from the lack of policy definition and planning previously mentioned. However, this limitation is not only found in the field of technology in general, or information technology in particular. Rather, it is a general characteristic of the way in which Latin American societies have tended to adopt technology and other alien objects throughout most of their history.

(b) The second discontinuity occurs between the technological system and the cultural system of the receiving country. Technology has been imported and adopted in a disarticulated, discontinuous way, generally for the benefit of a few people. At the same time there has been no learning process —in the school, at home, in the world place—among the rest of the population about technology (or specific technologies) and its economic and social function. In addition, the technologies that Latin Americans have utilized have not been developed in their own countries, as part of the natural evolution of their economies and cultures. Instead, they have imported those technologies directly from countries that represent different economic and socio-cultural systems. Logically, this has rendered the integration of the imported technologies into Latin American cultures all the more difficult. Such a difficulty has been worsened even more because, according to some Latin American thinkers like Salas de Gomez Gil (1977), the image of the scientist and the inventor is more an ideal than a real norm in the Latin American tradition. It is, therefore, difficult to integrate into culture and daily lives.

(c) Throughout their recent historical evolution, Latin Americans have skipped whole stages in the process of technological development as compared to the stages traversed in the countries from which they imported the technologies. This results in great voids in the development process, which, in turn, are the cause of incongruencies and lack of connections among the various structural components of the system, especially in comparison with the structures of the systems that exported these technologies.

(d) The rural–urban discontinuity that is a distinguishing characteristic of Latin America has given rise to what the Mexican sociologist Pablo Gonzalez Casanova (1965) has called "internal colonialism." This form of colonialism (conceived as the domination by a *cacique*—a local political boss or tyrant—over the rest of the population), helps to explain the gradual cultural impoverishment of the rural dwellers. This, in turn, makes their potential participation in modern technological activities an even more difficult and alien enterprise compared to their participation if internal colonialism and other forms of oppression were absent.

Internal colonialism worsens the problems and contradictions of the rural–urban discontinuities that so dramatically characterize Latin American societies; but it is not their cause. The urban world of Mexico and most other Latin American countries is a "modern" one, a world that has altered its traditional culture and which frequently imitates the life-style and culture of the United States. In the urban world, modern technologies are seen as relatively natural objects, at least for the middle and upper classes. The rural world, on the other hand, which comprises both country people *and* those who live in the huge and impoverished fringes of the larger cities, is much more traditional in its culture and life-styles. In the rural world, change is introduced much more slowly, and, consequently, new things and modern products and life-styles, including technology, are opposed with greater resistance.

(e) A fifth discontinuity can be found between the modern concepts and practices of management and control, which are so fundamental for all technological systems, and the reality of economic underdevelopment, where the notions of management and control are seen differently. This difference includes alternative perceptions of, among other things: time, human relations, and task performance. These perceptions are, of course, quite functional for the traditional cultural styles of Latin America (they are "alternative" only from the ethnocentric perspective of technological cultures). However, they are no longer functional for the management and control of technological systems.

(f) Sixth, there is also a "psychological discontinuity" which can be conceived as the feeling of *strangeness* that a prototypical Latin American person usually experiences when he or she is faced with new technologies. This feeling is probably due, among other possible causes, to the sensation of being confronted with something which is alien and therefore not integrated into his or her culture, but which, at the same time, is presented as a powerful symbol of modernity, of sophistication, of power, of capacity for achievement, all of which are seen as highly desirable. For an industrialized (or "modern") society, like the United States both the new technologies and what they have come to symbolize stem from its own dynamics and are perceived as a natural element of the socio-cultural environment by a majority of its members. Most of the members of more traditional societies experience the new technologies as something forced upon them, superimposed, and, therefore, artificial.

(g) Finally, the seventh discontinuity, also cultural, is expressed as a *resistance* opposed by many (most) of the members of a given society to the acceptance of new technologies. Indeed, we believe that, for large segments of the Latin American population, the adoption of a new technology is perceived as neither necessary nor a question with which they are concerned. Even though one can think of many exceptions, we cannot deny that a very large proportion of Latin Americans is still traditional enough to reject, or at least resist, the change implicit in many new things. Such a rejection or resistance does not necessarily imply "primitivism," as some critics of Latin American culture might be tempted to declare. Rather, it can be interpreted as logical resistance to what is, after all, alien, perhaps even culturally incompatible; to what is perceived, or at least intuitively felt, as an imposition of an outside element that may threaten certain cherished cultural values. Thus, far from being a primitive reaction, such an attitude can be reinterpreted as a logical mechanism of cultural defense.

A new technology can also be rejected or opposed when it is clearly and objectively useless within the *micro*-economic perspective of an individual or a small group of people, even if the task that they perform could be carried out more efficiently with a new technology in a *different* cultural or economic setting. In other words, many new technologies which probably are very useful in certain environments, are neither factually nor ideally possible in the socio-economic and cultural conditions of a different environment.

A CONCLUDING REMARK

A *mistaken* conclusion that one could derive from an analysis of the relationship between economic development and culture is that economic underdevelopment is a consequence of cultural underdevelopment. This definitely is not our belief. In this paper, we have developed the argument that economic development and cultural development belong to totally different domains, even though each one is affected by the other in numerous ways. There are no "underdeveloped" or "developed" cultures (the terms do not apply to culture); there are just *different* cultures. Modern technology is a product of a given culture; one should not expect that it be perceived and used in an identical way in different cultures. We have also tried to point out that the degree of economic development of a given society, together with the form and structure of its culture, will determine how, and if, technology will be integrated into that society.

Latin America is facing serious problems in the field of technology, as are most Third World countries. For example, technology's management and use (in ideological, political, and economic terms) are oriented to the maintenance of the equilibrium of a social system that greatly benefits a small elite, while there is a huge segment of poverty-stricken, dispossessed people who do not receive any visible benefits. For those practically excluded from the development process, technology is a meaningless concept; alien to them and their everyday lives. Of course, it can be argued that, even though they do not directly use technology, they are affected by it because of what others do with it (in schools, hospitals, transportation systems, mass media, etc.). The point here, however, is that technology has not become a part of their direct experience, their culture, and their patterns of everyday life. Even if they do not "see" it, technology has infiltrated their lives and has begun to have an impact on various structural foundations of their cultural system. Simultaneously, technology is probably increasing the isolation of the rural and urban poor, it may make it even more difficult for them eventually to be able to bridge the knowledge gap (and other gaps as well) that separate them from the rest of the society. Even though it does not directly touch them, technology is helping to create a new culture for the rural and urban poor, a cruel form of oppressive culture that we may call the *"culture of underdevelopment."*

REFERENCES

Fombrun, C., and Astley, W. (1982). "The Telecommunications Community: An Institutional Overview." *Journal of Communication 32* (No. 4), 56–68.
Gonzalez Casanova, P. (1963). *La Democarcia en mexico*. Mexico: Editorial Era.
Pennings, J.M. (1981). "Strategically Interdependent Organizations." *In* P. Nystrom and W. Starbuck (Eds.), *Handbook of Organizational Design* (Vol. 2, pp. 433–455). New York: Oxford University Press.

Salas de Gomez Gil, M.L. (1977). *El Cientifico en Mexico: su imagen entre los estudiantes de ensenanza media.* Mexico: Universidad Nacional Autonoma de Mexico.

Unger, K. (1979). "El Proceso Mexicano de Industrializacion Sustitutiva de Importaciones: Problemas y Politicas." *Comercio Exterior 27* (No. 9), 1083–1091.

Wionczek S. (1971). *Inversion y Technologia Extranjera en America Latina,* Mexico, Cuadernos de Joaquin Moritz.

Chapter 15
International Information: Bullet or Boomerang?

RENÉ JEAN RAVAULT

Départment des Communications
Université du Québec à Montréal
Montréal, Québec H3C 3P8, Canada

During the last 10 years, international communication has more and more captivated the attention of a growing number of social scientists throughout the world. This increased interest in the subject seems to parallel the appearance, growth, and expansion of the demand from Third World countries, especially the non-aligned nations, for a *New World Information Order*. This demand has been progressively shaped and articulated at UNESCO meetings dealing with either transnational cultural problems or international information issues including, more recently, the implantation of new transborder telecommunication technologies (Hamelink, 1983, pp. 56–72).

While this demand for a *New World Information Order* has been the source of tumultuous debates both within UNESCO and in the industrialized Western World, especially by the commercial media which firmly oppose it, most scholars and researchers seem to support it, document it, reinforce it, and do their best to publicize it to a large educated audience.

Among the main promoters of the *New World Information Order* in the Western World, besides the experts who have been involved in the elaboration of the MacBride Commission's report (International Commission for the Study of Communication Problems, *Many Voices, One World, Communication and Society, Today and Tomorrow,* 1980), are researchers like Antonio Pasquali (1963, 1967), Herbert Schiller (1969, 1976, 1980), Kaarle Nordenstreng (Nordenstreng & Schiller, 1979; Nordenstreng & Varis, 1974), Dallas Smythe (1981a), Cees J. Hamelink (1983), Hervé Bourges (1978), Armand Mattelart (1974, 1976; Mattelart & Dorfman, 1979; Mattelart & Schmucler, 1983; Mattelart, Delcourt, & Mattelart, 1983), and Yves Eudes (1982). They are often quoted by the students of contemporary issues in international communications.

In fact, more than just supporting the implementation of the *New World Information Order,* about some parts of which they take exception in divergent fashions, all these critics seem to agree on the necessity to denounce and debunk the reigning international information structure. To them, this structure is grossly imbalanced and benefits only the multinational corporations and transnational banks of the Western World, instead of contributing to the socio-economic and cultural development of the Third World countries.

Their analysis, paralleling, inspiring, and reflecting the analyses made by the spokespersons of the non-aligned countries, suggests that there is a strong relationship between the economic domination of the North over the South and the cultural domination of the First World over the Third World. According to them, as well as many spokespersons of the developing countries, the implementation of the *New World Information Order* should go along with the implementation of the *New World Economic Order*. Often getting more radical than most Third World's spokespersons, these researchers are proposing a *New World Information Order* in which economic and cultural dissociation of the developing countries from the West seems to be the ultimate solution or panacea.

Taking issue against this extremely radical solution (which, amazingly, presents striking similarities with the economic and cultural solutions of the "have not" or fascists countries opposing the "have" just before World War II), this paper contends that the cultural dissociation proposal is based upon a victimizing view of the communication process in which the receiver is considered to be passive and totally receptive to the "messages" broadcast or diffused by powerful producers or senders.

This victimizing view of the communication process has been notoriously referred to by Wilbur Schramm as the "Bullet Theory." According to Schramm, this theory characterizes the paradigm which dominated research in communications before and around World War II. During the last 30 years, the "Bullet Theory" has progressively been considered as ill-founded and abandoned by communication researchers, as Schramm (1971, pp. 6–11; emphasis added) puts it:

> one must recall how frightening World War I propaganda, and later Communist and Nazi propaganda, were to many people. . . . The unsophisticated view point was that if a person could be reached by the insidious forces of propaganda carried by the mighty power of the mass media, he could be changed and converted and controlled. . . . I have . . . called this the Bullet Theory of communication. Communication was seen as a magic bullet that transferred ideas or feelings or knowledge or motivations almost automatically from one mind to another. . . . In the early days of communication study, the audience was considered relatively passive and defenseless, and communication could *shoot something into them*. . . But scholars began very soon to modify the Bullet Theory. It did not square with the facts. The audience, when it was hit by the Bullet, refused to fall over. *Sometimes, the Bullet had an effect that was completely unintended.*

Founding their proposal of cultural dissociation of the Third World from the First upon this antiquated "Bullet Theory" of communication, the researchers noted above make the Third World nations run the risk of no longer having the opportunity to use First World transnational communications structures and contents to their own advantage, as the "Boomerang Theory" suggests.

Contrary to the obsolete "Bullet Theory," the "Boomerang Theory" does not consider the receiver as a passive target, but gives him or her a power to respond to one-way communications in stronger and more efficient ways. According to the "Boomerang Theory," the receivers, even deprived of diffusion means, can use information provided by the "cultural dominator" to their own advantage. They can even use this information in order to make decisions and elaborate military, diplomatic, political, and economic strategies totally unintended by the sender and sometimes quite detrimental to the "dominating sender."

Dissociating Third World countries from transnational communication networks would put them in the situation of their "dominators" who, while talking instead of listening, have not been able to foresee and react properly to decolonization, the uprise of national and ethnic minorities all over the world, the growing economic competition of newly industrialized countries, and almost all of the geopolitical and economic changes which have been taking place lately.

After having demonstrated the methodological weaknesses of the "Bullet Theory" used by the experts and researchers who dominate the field of international communications, this paper points out evidence suggesting that an analysis based upon the "Boomerang Theory" would equally, or even more appropriately, account for the nature of the relationships between communication, culture, politics, and economics at the international level. It will also elaborate policies benefitting the culture and the economy of all the countries involved in transnational communications.

In conclusion, it will be pointed out that there still are ways to cope with international communication issues other than the quasi national-socialist ultimate solution of cultural and economic dissociation surprisingly revamped by Dieter Senghaas (1977) and Cees J. Hamelink (1983).

THE METHODOLOGICAL FLAWS OF THE "BULLET THEORY" OF THE SUPPORTERS OF THE NEW WORLD INFORMATION ORDER

The understanding of the communication process upon which the critics of the reigning information order settle their arguments is similiar to what Schramm has described as the "Bullet Theory." Evidences of that are legion. Here are some of the most blatant.

The most striking aspect of this theory is certainly the passivity or powerlessness of the receiver vis-à-vis the powerful of the senders who, as they wish, impose thoughts, beliefs, ideologies, and ways of looking at the world on their audience. A blatant manifestation of this understanding comes from Hamelink (1983, p. 114):

> Insofar as information processes are a reflection of existing power relations, they will in general follow a synchronic mode. In this mode, there is a great distance between sender and receiver; the receiver is supposed to synchronize with the input from the sender. The sender becomes the specialist who alone can select, process, and distribute the messages. Messages are "prescribed" to the *passive receiver* who is expected to register and store them in his "archives." In the synchronic mode, there is no dialog that can possibly make the receiver an *active participant* in the process or enable him to question the message and search for ways to relate the messages to everyday reality (emphasis added).

From this quotation it is clear that the receivers, whatever the system— synchronic or diachronic—is always "passive." They get some power and become an *active participant* only when they have the opportunity to become a sender.

The flaw in this approach lies in its inability to conceive of the receiver in any other situation than the very communication event in which she or he is involved: as if the possibility to question the sender, to give feedback, to talk or to dialog with him or her was the most important thing to do on earth. Among many others, an instance of such a belief is held by Oswaldo Capriles, who attributes the success of Paulo Freire's popular education strategies to the fact that, contrarily to the monologue of traditional pedagogy, they are settled upon a "real dialog" (Capriles, 1982, p. 122).

But, to question or talk back to the sender may very well turn out to be a waste of time. There are many other ways to deal with him or her. Asian, and more especially the Japanese silence, should be a source of meditation for excessively talkative Westerners.

No matter how naive the confusion of the receiver with a passive victim and the sender with the only active participant is, it seems to be present in almost all the work of the promoters of the *New World Information Order.*

To underline the fact that this confusion is largely shared among UNESCO researchers, the following passage from the MacBride report about "Vertical Flow" is quite revealing:

> Ideally, communication is a continual exchange between equals, or at least between reciprocally responsible partners. In practice, this ideal has never been and probably cannot be entirely realized. The flow is vertical instead of horizontal and is mostly in one direction—from the top downwards. Inevitably, this has an effect on the style of work of communication professionals. They consider their task in terms of effectiveness, "getting the message across", translating information into simple terms, winning and holding attention. These skills are certainly necessary: a professional who fails to interest his audience is no professional. But this concept of communication tends to eclipse the equally important objective of encouraging access and participation

for the public. The ordinary man or woman becomes excluded, accepting the idea that professional skill and equipment are prerequisites of communication. Meanwhile, improvements in techniques are designed solely to place added resources at the disposal of the producer or sender of messages (International Commission for the Study of Communication Problems, 1980, p. 149).

This typical confusion of communication with diffusion which is both deplored and accepted, since the only way out proposed by these researchers is to allow the receiver to become a modest producer, is, of course, complemented by the belief in the total power of those who control the means of diffusion. Indeed, according to the "Bullet Theory," the one who controls the gun and triggers the bullet has a power of life and death over his or her target. Conversely, in communication, the one who controls the means of diffusion and fashions the content is able to control what the audience believes, thinks or wants...

On this point, which was noted in the quotation from Hamelink, Armand Mattelart (1974, p. 69) is quite explicit: "through their media, the ruling class (la bourgeoisie) not only imposes but also foreshadows the attitudes and the tastes the public will adopt and later reflect through interviews from marketing surveys."

Mattelart seems to have borrowed this belief from the work of Antonio Pasquali and other Latin American communication scholars who, according to Capriles, launched analytical studies of the sender (the "who" in the Lasswellian formula) as well as analyses of radio and television programming. These studies were published between 1966 and 1969 and significantly contributed to a strong opinion movement among intellectuals aimed at debunking demagogical communication systems responsible for the inculcation of the dominant market ideology, as well as the spreading of news controlled by private local mass media industries connected to multinational press agencies (Capriles, 1982, p. 132). According to Capriles, who synthesises the ideas of this new school of Latin American communication researchers, "private mass media industries consciously hold and use an inculcation power which contributes significantly to the establishment of a consumers' society and to the global expansion of the market economy" (Capriles, 1982, p. 108).

Since these researchers from or close to UNESCO promote the idea that the presently reigning international information structure supports the reigning transnational economic system, it is not surprising that they attempt to adapt in the field of international communication the "Bullet Theory" argument that advertising is creating and promoting false needs. Hamelink is a case in point. As he puts it: "in many Third World countries, information processes, such as advertising, carry messages that induce people to acquire goods and services which bear no relation to real needs" (Hamelink, 1983, p. 102).

Consistently with the "Bullet Theory," the methodology used by these experts does not deal with the public, the receivers and, a fortiori, their "true" or "false" needs (see Bogart, 1967).

On this occultation of the role played by the receiver and his or her attitudes and present and past perceptions, the distinction between information and communication Hamelink attempts to make is quite revealing:

> In general, this study prefers the phrase national *information* policy to that used by the MacBride Commission, national *communication* policy. Although no fundamental differences are implied, the concept of information is used for the following reasons. First it corresponds better with the formula of a new international information order. Second, and more important, communication tends to be associated with mass commmunication only. In this study, the proposed policy making has to be *comprehensive, encompassing* also point-to-point forms of information transfer, as, for example, in informatics. Moreover, such policy making should address not only *problems of infrastructure* but also those relating to the *information contents* that these infrastructures carry (Hamelink, 1983, p. 101) (emphasis added).

Indeed, it is quite fascinating that a researcher who seems willing to propose an approach as "comprehensive" and as "encompassing" as possible did not pick on the classical distinction between "information" and "communication" in which the first, more limited concept can be equated with the process of broadcasting or diffusion, while the second should involve both sender and receiver, specific attention being given to the two communication agents, each within its own social and cultural context, as well as through their psycho-sociological history.

Instead of doing these separate studies of the communicating agents, Hamelink and his colleagues stick to the study of production and dissemination infrastructure problems to which they generously add the study of information content.

Some researchers do take into account the "socio-historical environment" which forces them to pay attention to the roles played by culture and ideology within the traffic of signs and symbols, within the processes of production of meaning. In other words, they study the cultural forms imposed by, or inculcated through, mass communication as a part of the analysis of the entire cultural formation process (with its relationship to economy). However, as Capriles (1982, p. 143) acknowledges, so far, the essential point has been left aside, since: "the analysis, now, has to go back towards the receivers who shall be the subject of a research aiming at making sense out of the 'black box' of communication, i.e., the ingestion or digestion process of this mass culture."

As Hamelink himself admits at the beginning of his book, no research is done on *how* the receiver is affected, how she or he perceives these contents and uses these infrastructures: "Admittedly, we need more research on precisely *how* the process of cultural 'imports' affects the receivers in the long term, especially with respect to cultural norms and behavior" (Hamelink, 1983, p. 3).

But this blatant and admitted lack of knowledge which could decisively confirm or refute the validity of the "Bullet Theory," upon which their understanding of the synchronic mode of communication rests, does not prevent these researchers from using a pseudo-scientific and pseudo-empiric phraseology to contend that what happens at the diffusion level also happens at the reception.

Again, Hamelink is a case in point, since, just after admitting this methodological crucial flaw, he goes on pretending: *"One conclusion still seems unanimously shared:* the impressive variety of the world's cultural systems is waning due to a process of 'cultural synchronization' that is without historic precedent" (Hamelink, 1983, p. 3) (emphasis added). And, on the next pages: *"all the evidence* indicates that centrally controlled technology has become the instrument through which diversity is being destroyed and replaced by a single global culture" (Hamelink, 1983, pp. 4-5) (emphasis added). Or, again: "The international flow of communications has, *in fact,* become the main carrier of transnational cultural synchronization" (Hamelink, 1983, p. 7) (emphasis added).

But the use of pseudo-empirical and scientific concepts such as "fact," "evidence," or "conclusion unanimously shared" does not veil the point that when these researchers are talking about the "global culture synchronization" they are only referring to the standardization or synchronization of production and dissemination infrastructures and information contents. It is not through the study of a gun and its bullets that a detective can learn if someone has been aimed at, if this person has been hit or not, wounded or not, killed or not. If the ridiculous aspect of such an investigation would not escape the critical mind of any detective novel reader, it seems that similar practices in international communication studies performed among the world's brightest experts can "get away with murder."

Indeed, for Hamelink as for most of these researchers, what is wrong with the traditional criticisms of the reigning practice of international communication is not the fact that those critics did not study what foreign audiences do with imported mass communication products, but rather that: "The crucial question of control over economic, technological, and marketing structures in international communciation are left untouched" (Hamelink, 1983, p. 71).

Again, in this "Bullet Theory" approach, the control (be it economic, technological, or whatever) over the entire international communication process, is reduced to the control of international diffusion structures.

The "Bullet Theory" occults the fact the receivers also could exercise a certain control; for instance, in exposing themselves to the "information content" or not, in interpreting it in the way intended by the sender or not, and in using it in a way benefitting the sender or not.

Of course, it is methodologically easier to study production and diffusion structures from either a political or an economic point of view, as well as information contents through categories of classification used by the producers themselves or by a specific school of content analysis, and, from there, assume what the media do to people rather than studying what receivers do to media structures and information contents!

It is at the easiest level that these researchers address their tough questions.

> With the transfer of technology, the following questions must always be posed: Which social group receives the economic, political, and cultural benefits? In the case of communication technology, it is especially important to ask, "Who benefits economically; that is who gets more income from the application of new communication techniques?" Moreover, who benefits culturally. Who is going to use the new technology? Who can exploit their prestige value? Which groups can communicate more effectively by adopting this technology? (Hamelink, 1983, p. 17).

And Hamelink provides his readers with the easy answer:

> In most Third World countries, past experience indicates that these benefits will accrue principally to three groups: the transnational corporations which deliver the products; the transnational banks which finance the purchase of the products; and a "new class" of officials—managers and military personnel connected with the ruling government who will be among the few able to use the products (Hamelink, p. 17).

This analysis, essentially shared by such authors as Armand Mattelart and Hector Schmucler (1983), is dangerously limited in time ("past experience indicates") and space.

In time, it does not take into account the smartness of some receivers belonging or not to the "new class of officials" who may eventually decide in their "passive wisdom" to let their country go bankrupt, as the "new Soviet ruling class" did with Russia's foreign debt in a notorious "past experience." What would happen then to the supposedly "accrued benefits" of the multinational corporations and transnational banks of the industrialized countries of the West? And proletarian revolutions are not always necessary to allow smart receivers belonging to the "old class of officials" in the South to behave in an economic fashion which may turn out to be quite detrimental to their alleged allies, the "transnational banks" of the North. Indeed, in an amazing article entitled, "Where the Latin American Loans Went?" Larry A. Sjaastad shows how "Wealthy individuals recycled about one-third of the money into investments in the U.S. and Europe." And, for this economist:

Herein lies the potential for the great ripoff. The foreign liabilities of the debtor countries are largely sovereign debt, subject to default or repudiation if the governments cannot or choose not to pay. The foreign assets, on the other hand, are quite private. If, say, Argentina defaults, U.S. banks cannot seize the deposits of Argentine citizens (Sjaastad, 1984, pp. 195, 198).

In space, the UNESCO experts' analysis remains at a micro-economic level, dealing only with communication industries and not taking into account what the receiving countries might do in other economic areas or other industrial sectors with these new technologies' hardware and software as well as with the information they give access to.

The last flaw of this application of the "Bullet Theory" to international communications comes from the naive classification of information contents according to the sender's own categories. Since they do not seem to be willing to know what the receivers do with the information, these researchers have a tendency to consider that communication contents always fulfill, for the audience, the functions that the producer intended them to fulfill.

The articulation of the victimizing approach suggested by the "Bullet Theory" with the content analysis of mass media programming, in a way consistent with programming categories used by broadcasters or producers, has been launched by the Venezuelan researcher Antonio Pasquali. As Capriles, also a Venezuelan communication researcher, points out, Pasquali first demonstrated that existing transnational communication structures did not offer any opportunity for the reversal of their active/passive, sender/receiver polarization. He then studied programming structures through comparison analyses of the different "styles" and "categories" of content: foreign vs. domestic content, information vs. entertainment, fiction, and advertisements. He referred to the results of these quantitative and qualitative content analyses to demonstrate the "alienating nature" of television programming in several countries of Latin America (Capriles, 1982, p. 127).

Using this approach, Kaarle Nordenstreng and Tapio Varis, in their UNESCO-subsidized work, point out:

> The majority of U.S. exports are entertainment programmes. Many of the major exporters do not distribute newsfilm or documentaries at all. Even when newsfilms and sports programmes are included, they do not compose a significant part of the total export when measured in hours. The ratio between entertainment and information programmes is usually 90 per cent and 10 per cent respectively (Nordenstreng & Varis, 1984, p. 32).

From these kinds of statistics based upon definitions of content given by the producers, Hamelink, among others, infers the impact of these imported cultural products upon the receivers who, supposedly, took them into account. As (Hamelink, 1983, p. 9) puts it: "Creation of social myths and false heroes and overemphasis on entertainment and violence are all instruments of alienation and cultural disorientation."

Furthermore, after having inferred these consequences of U.S.-made entertainment upon its foreign receivers, he goes into the advertisers' classification categories of advertising content and accordingly states: "The messages produced and distributed by the transnational advertising agencies can be divided into two categories: informative and persuasive" (Hamelink, 1983, p. 13). And, again, he infers the function fulfilled by these ads upon the receivers of Third World countries in the following fashion: "Transnational advertising aimed at Third World countries, however, floods them with messages for consumer goods which *inform* very little but *persuade* very strongly" (Hamelink, 1983, p. 13) (emphasis added).

The success of these advertising persuasion strategies, which seems to be tremendous, since, as Hamelink (1983, p. 14) puts it: "Products are not adapted to suit local needs, local needs, through advertising, are adapted to the products." This is not demonstrated by the analysis of the receivers' buying behavior, or even the survey of stock turnovers or the merchants' profits and losses, but instead by the very remote indicator of "the number of trademarks registered in Third World countries [which] indicates the rate of their introduction and the source of foreign consumer goods" (Hamelink, 1983, p. 13).

The methodological problem with an approach which uses such remote indicators as trademarks registrations, or worse, the media content classification categories used by producers in order to infer the behavior of receivers, is that, again, it does not take into account the possibility that a receiver can use the content of mass communication in ways that were not at all intended by the producer. Manifestations of this difference between the function of a "message" as intended by the sender and the function actually fulfilled have been brought foreward by Elihu Katz and David Foulkes in their article "On the Use of the Mass Media as 'Escape': a Clarification of a Concept" (1962). This, also, has been found in many other studies. Synthesizing their results, Schramm (1973, pp. 255-256), notes:

> Man is an extraordinary efficient learning machine. He can learn from nearly any source and any experience. When he exposes himself six hours a day to such an enormous flow of information and entertainment as the mass media carry, there is bound to be a great deal taken in and retained....One of the most interesting findings...has been the amount of *incidental* learning—incidental meaning facts, ideas, and attitudes that were not intended to be part of the learning from the message. This means that *such information can be acquired—is acquired—from programs intended to entertain rather than inform* (emphasis added).

After such a statement, it becomes obvious that inferring the audience's "alienation and cultural disorientation" from contents intended to "entertain," and customer's "persuasion" from a flood of advertising messages intended to "persuade," is a methodological aberration. Some of the students of communication who are part of this trend go even further; sharing the pessimistic popular culture approach criticized by Katz and Foulkes (1962), they suggest, as René Prédal does in a (1984) article that, because of the way they are produced, financed, and distributed, French documentaries often fulfill an advertising function for their subsidizers. If news and documentaries can fulfill persuasive, entertaining, and even alienating functions, it never occurred to them that media receivers can be as smart or even smarter than they are and obtain information out of fictions and advertisments.

Nevertheless, this does not seem to bother either these experts and researchers or their learned audiences. One reason is that most of the experts belonging to social sciences, such as literature, linguistics, sociology, cultural anthropology, political sciences, economy of development, and so on, have a tendency to discard theories and discoveries coming from the field of communication, organizational communication, and especially human communication, which they consider as "administrative research" and as a mere appendage of the very "bourgeois" American social-psychology, or micro-sociology.

But, the credibility of their methodologically weak argumentation, more likely, comes from the fact that, to a large extent, it supports the claim of effectiveness made by the producers, be they advertisers or mass communication industries' owners or employees.

Attacking the reigning world information structures on the ground that they are unethical or unfair because, through them, the rich get richer, the poor get poorer, and the Third World countries are losing their cultural identity, does not seriously harm mass communication industries of the West. Rather, it confirms their undocumented pretense of "effectiveness" and helps them get more clients to come to advertising agencies and buy more advertising time and space in the media.

However, it would be unfair to conclude this first part without mentioning that at least one of these researchers, Yves Eudes (1982) has made a very serious attempt to consider studies of receivers in order to account for the effects of American cultural exports. And, as a matter of fact, his analysis of the methodological and epistemological value of these studies is quite revealing.

Indeed, Eudes' book, *"La Conquête des Esprits"* (the Conquest of Minds), aptly subtitled *"L'appareil d'exportation culturelle américain"* (American cultural export machinery), is quite puzzling. On the one hand, as the title and subtitle suggest, Eudes, through a thorough analysis of the American government's cultural export machinery, shared, with the critical researchers referred to, the tendency to infer what an audience does with what it is exposed to from the in-depth study of the machinery behind the production and dissemination of specific messages. And, like his colleagues, Eudes has a tendency to suggest that the impact of the American federal government's cultural export machinery upon overseas' and especially Third World's audiences is tremendous. In most chapters of his book, allusions to the effectiveness of this machinery abound. However, the last two chapters cast some doubts and, even sometimes at the very conclusion, invalidate this omnipresent affirmation.

The next to last chapter, entitled "L'évaluation de l'impact" (measuring the impact), is even more puzzling. While the results from available studies on foreign audiences generally confirm Eudes' and other critical experts' guesses or inferences about the effectiveness of industrialized countries' cultural export machinery, he has the intellectual scrupulousness to question the epistemological and methodological validity of these studies. Pointing out the complexity of international communication and transcultural phenomena, as well as the nature and the almost infinite number of variables involved, he seriously questions the relevance of quantitative research in these areas. Eudes cast more doubts when, to these epistemological and methodological difficulties, he adds the political and institutional motivations of the researchers and their employers. As he puts it: "not only is it impossible to deduce an increase in mutual understanding from the consumption of cultural products but, further, mutual understanding, if established, does not necessarily generate an approval of the United States' international policies. Expected causal relationship cannot be empirically demonstrated and their validity, at best, remains at the level of deduction" (Eudes, 1982, p. 230).

If this observation considerably weakens the posture of the espousers of the "Bullet Theory" in transnational communications, it also forces us to admit that, if there is no methodologically satisfactory way to check out the validity of the "Bullet Theory," there are no means either to demonstrate the adequacy of the "Boomerang Theory."

However, if there are "events," "facts," "past experience," and so on, which apparently may be considered as manifestations of the "Bullet Theory," there are at least as many events, facts, past experience, and so on, which can equally illustrate the fitness of the "Boomerang Theory."

A SAMPLE OF SOME TRANSNATIONAL COMMUNICATION SITUATIONS AND EVENTS BEST ACCOUNTED FOR BY THE "BOOMERANG THEORY"

Amazingly enough, excellent illustrations of the "Boomerang Theory" are provided by several of the experts and critical researchers whose postures were questioned in the preceding part of this article.

As the previously reported progression of Eudes' argumentation in the last two chapters of his book suggested, he concludes in a way which strongly contradicts the general impression of effectiveness of the U.S. cultural export machinery:

> In most situations, poverty and oppression, tend to generate a systematic rejection of the ruling elites who, then, are considered as "denationalized" through their consumption of foreign cultural products. In such situations the practice of the American culture is mainly perceived as a sign of treason. Conversely, the national culture becomes a strategic agent in the resistance to the implantation of "interdependence" (Eudes, 1982, p. 252).

The contribution of the media and advertising to this "Boomerang" process is further emphasized by Hamelink who suggests that: "As a result of this bombardment by advertising, the elite sectors, with higher incomes, tend to be integrated increasingly into the international economy, while the poor, spending scarce resources on unneeded things, lag farther behind in essentials such as health and education. This creates a widening gap between the rich and poor and contributes to an explosive social disintegration" (Hamelink, 1983, p. 16).

In such situations, one could wonder what happens to the cultural "integration," "homogenization," and "synchronization" that the present international information structure is supposed to generate? In fact, instances of this kind of situation can be found in many places during this century of decolonization and national as well as ethnic revival. The most striking and recent case is certainly Iran. "There, an indigeneous information system, Shi'ite Islam, discovered itself intact at the end of a decade or more of vigorous importation of Western culture and on the crest of a wave of oil prosperity. The whole quest for modernization was rejected along with the Shah and the electronic culture, technically advanced though it was, was suddenly seen to have been an excrescence, an imposition, a conflict-bearing overseas culture which appealed to a particular Western-leaning elite, but which had not and could not penetrate the entire culture" (Smith, 1980, p. 59).

Similar backlash or "Boomerang" situations seem to be present in many countries of Latin America and more especially, Central America. While Cuba and Nicaragua have expelled their Americanized or "Gringoized" urban elites and middle classes, conflicts between these classes seem to rage in other countries where American culture is omnipresent within the local media.

Despite the fact that they are not yet at the same stage of progression, the cases of Iran and Latin America present striking similarities, the most blatant of which is certainly the simultaneous growth of two opposed modes of communication. On the one hand, there are the new mass media, such as television channels like N.I.R.T. in Iran or those denounced by Pasquali, Beltran, Mattelart, Schiller, etc., in Latin America. On the other hand, there are person-to-person, group-to-group, traditional, religious, pedagogical, and ideological or political communication modes which rest upon people's responsibility, values, motivations, and beliefs. In Iran, this was the case of the Ayatollah's communication networks; in Latin America, this is the way used by religious, cultural, pedagogical, and political animators or "agitators" trained through a kind of Paulo Freire's educational system or, even sometimes, directly under the Cubans. While this second kind of communication mode, based upon people's immediate needs and responsibilities, enjoys a high level of respect and credibility, the first one, despised by the Ayatollahs in Iran and the animators-agitators in Latin American for its dominant, vertical (top-to-bottom, elite-to-masses), distant, and foreign nature, suffers from an obvious lack of credibility. According to Majid Tehranian (1982, p. 28), in Iran, this lack of credibility of the dominant mass media has been acknowledged by the Shah's last Prime Minister, Sharif-Emani, who once said, "If we say it is daytime when it is daytime, people will deduce it is nighttime." And, illustrating the previously mentioned opposition between traditional media effectiveness and official or imported mass media weaknesses, Tehranian (1982, p. 29) goes on:

> The technological feat of covering this vast and mountainous country by a large network of microwave communication systems within a decade or so was thus largely counter-communicative. Meanwhile, in direct contrast, the traditional religious communication system was thriving. Its success depended on several factors. It used informal channels and small as opposed to big media. Its message was familiar and designed in terms of the archetypical legends of Persian historical memory. And it was credible, because it corresponded to the living reality of its audience and delivered by legitimate opinion leaders.

Besides this recent and continuing evidence of the boomerang effect, in the past and especially during periods of decolonization, as Hamelink himself recognizes, the media have contributed to this "Boomerang" or resistance phenomena, as in Algeria where radio was considered as part of the colonial oppression through which "Frenchmen were talking to Frenchmen" (Hamelink, 1983, p. 108).

In many instances, mass media have provided colonized audiences with a clear understanding of their dominator's views of the world. This knowledge of their enemy's expectations and values helped them to elaborate shrewd strategies of resistance which successfully led them to independence.

On this point Hamelink (1983, p. 30) relates the example of Algeria where, "in order to support the resistance movement, the women of their own accord decided to take off the veil. By conforming to French expectations, Algerian women were above suspicion and were allowed to pass the patrol posts with loads of grenades in their handbags." And, giving other examples of boomerang effect related to foreign cultural invasion of dependent countries, Hamelink continues:

At the same time, devices introduced by the French, such as the radio, were adapted as a means of internal communication in the movement of independence from France. A similar phenomenon occurred [in Chile] during the rule of Allende. In the working class district of Santiago, North American television series were viewed with close attention; the symbols, however, were interpreted in accord with the prevalent resistance to North American influences (Hamelink, 1983, p. 31).

This awareness of the possibility for exported cultural products to generate a backlash against the exporting country rather than supporting it is not so new:

In the early days of Hollywood exporting there was some anxiety in Washington as to its possible unfortunate consequences for the American reputation abroad. From time to time such anxieties have again surfaced; some surveys have shown that familiarity with Hollywood products does not necessarily induce love of the United States. Occasionally foreign regimes—including those of Hitler and Stalin—have used careful selections of especially unsavoury Hollywood films, deliberately to reflect discredit on the USA (Tunstall, 1977, pp. 271-272).

Furthermore, if transnational communications can be politically, diplomatically, and militarily exploited in a boomerang fashion by the receiving countries, there are also many instances of such behavior on the scene of international economy. On this point, the shrewd strategies of the "old class of Latin-American officials" on the scene of international finance have been previously mentioned. Regarding the scene of international trade, I have elsewhere (Ravault, 1980a, b, 1981) pointed out that the post-war American mass communications flooding of Japan and Germany contributed significantly to the economic "miracle" of these two countries, providing them with crucial information about the domestic American market which they, later, flooded back with industrial exports.

Many other examples could be mentioned to point out that, indeed, the "Bullet Theory" is "full of holes." In many instances, the receiver using his or her own cultural and experimental background can, to a large extent, control the meaning that a foreign message has for him or her. Through the "Boomerang Theory" the function of communication can no longer be limited to the function intended by the producer or sender, it can have an adverse or perverse effect. As in the case of Iran, foreign cultural imports can contribute to the revival of a cultural and ethnocentric background, according to which, eventually, international communications are interpreted and evaluated.

This rather new phenomenon is accounted for by Jean Cazamajou and Jean-Pierre Martin (1983, p. 158), who point out: "it is precisely in a period when a set of international networks of trade, communications, and intellectual relations progressively puts together national elites that a reverse movement is taking place. On the contrary, this movement involves members of vertical strata belonging to the social fabrics of specific countries." And, to these authors, this phenomenon is connected with the alleged homogenizing functions of the mass media: "These ethnic revivals the vitality of which is obvious but the future doubtful, first appear as a common revolt against what John Updike calls 'cultural cannibalism' of the dominant society" (Cazamajou & Martin, 1983, p. 142).

Even if Cazamajou and Martin have doubts, there is enough evidence that the *Ethnic Revival in the Modern World* (Smith, 1981) is here to stay:

> "Varied phenomena such as independence movements among French Canadians, Scots and the like; the 'nationalistic' and assimilationist issues of the Ukranians, Jews and Belorussians, the language conflicts between the Flemings and the Waloons in Belgium and the religious conflict in Northern Ireland; the deportation of Indians, Chinese, and Arabs from Burma, Africa, Zanzibar; the social psychological differences between Irish and Italian Americans; struggles for political and economic primacy in Black Africa, the terrorist activities of the Palestinians, the South Moluccans, or the Armenians against current Turkish officials; and the status tensions of Indians, Mestizos, Creoles, and others in parts of Latin America" (Burgess, 1978, p. 271) demonstrate we still are very far from the situation of global synchronization or total homogenization of the whole world, as alarmingly alluded to by the experts of the "Bullet Theory" paradigm.

This trend, which is rooted far back into history, instead of decreasing in intensity has significantly grown during the last 15 or 20 years, as Marshall Murphrey (1973, pp. 6-7) insists:

> It has been an assumption in race relationship research...that regardless of peripheral countercurrents, the mainstream of human events has been moving towards the disestablishment of race as a central determinant in human society ...increased acceptance of common values and increased participation in a common set of groups, associations and institutions. Unfortunately, this is an assumption not borne out by the events of the last decade. The tide of ethnic, regional, and racial aspiration runs high...encouraging the retention of distinctive tradition.

If we closely compare the quotations from the "Bullet Theory" contenders with the ones reported in the second part to support the "Boomerang" contention, we have the strong feeling that their authors are not living on the same planet and/or do not belong to the same generation. And this, probably, is another evidence of the weaknesses of the synchronization or homogenization view.

More and more, the "Bullet Theory" experts become aware of this "rising resistance" against homogenizing and synchronization modes of international communication. For instance, Schiller himself, recently pointed out in a somewhat contradictory fashion:

> it must be admitted that to date the transnationals have been quite successful in promoting their integrationist program, one that they enjoy calling "interdependence." Simultaneously, their armed forces are everywhere gearing up to intervene should the "dissociation option" be taken up. One fact is clear. The world business system has not contained the movements toward national independence that have grown up during the past four decades. Battles will become more intense. The most recent struggles in Nicaragua and El Salvador are not exceptional develoments (Schiller, 1983, p. xi).

This quote from Schiller deserves two comments. First, it underlines the acknowledgement that the success of the transnationals in promoting their "interdependence" program is significantly limited by their inability to contain "the movements towards national independence that have grown up during the past four decades." Second, the quote reveals that, in order to progress, "interdependence," "homogenization," or "synchronization" have to be supported and promoted not only by the private and public cultural export machinery of the industrialized countries but also by "their armed forces."

This last point is crucial, since it underlines the fact that, in probably every situation where the "Bullet Theory" seems to make sense, the *persuasion* of the media have been paralleling the *action* of the armed forces.

The best instance of that is certainly provided by the leading piece of work in the "Bullet Theory" literature: Serge Tchakhotine's *The Rape of the Masses: The Psychology of Totalitarian Propaganda* (1940), which analyses and denounces Goebbels' propaganda machinery. In this tragic period of German history as well as during the events Mattelart (1974) analyzes in Chile, the military, the police, the paramilitary, and other militia forces played a rather significant role.

In other words, the "Bullet Theory" of communication only stands when bad guys' propaganda is supported by bad guys' real bullets and real guns. Otherwise, propaganda wars, as between France and Germany just before World War II, remain "funny wars" ("La drôle de guerre"). Since they already are utopianly asking for a *New Economic International Order,* in addition to a *New World Information Order,* Third World countries and their supporting experts should as well ask for a *New World Military Order.*

As pointed out earlier, the reigning international information structure has provided Third World people with "entertainments" (Nordenstreng & Varis, 1974) contributing to their awareness of their "true" economic, political, and military situation of dependence. Hamelink, himself, acknowledges this change: "In many dependent countries, the importation of an inadequate cultural system is actively stimulated by a small leading elite and is passively accepted by the majority. A change in this process has been evident in recent years, with an increasing awareness that the imported culture is usually accompanied by such a high degree of dependence that the recipients are completely blown off their feet" (Hamelink, 1983, p. 26).

But, even if Hamelink considers the widening debate on the "New International Information Order" as one of the most important manifestations of the Third World resistance movement against the synchronization of communication and culture, the very existence of Hamelink's, Schiller's, Mattelart's and UNESCO's Western experts' thinking is blatant evidence of receivers' ability to resist the culturally homogenizing forces disseminated by global corporations' media.

Of course, this last, crucial evidence, could be rejected by snobbish leftist intellectuals, pointing out that it is not the illiterate populace of the developing world which is able to unveil, analyze, and criticize the pro-global corporations propaganda content of Walt Disney's cartoons, as did Mattelart and Dorfman (1979).

However, as Pierre Bourdieu and Jean-Claude Passeron humbly put it: "Intellectuals scarcely believe in peoples' defenses, that is: in others' freedom. They are fond of keeping for themselves the professional monopoly of freedom of thought" (Bourdieu & Passeron, 1963).

Consequently, and in spite of their acknowledgement of the weaknesses of the "Bullet Theory" upon which their analyses and recommendations are based, the large majority of these researchers and UNESCO experts still believe and strive for the implementation of a *New World Information Order* in which Third World resistance against economic "interdependence" should be achieved through cultural "dissociation."

CONCLUSION

The "Bullet Theory" is full of methodological holes, and the "Boomerang Theory" could as well if not better, account for what is happening on the scene of international communications. Thus, there are better solutions based upon more serious studies of the recipient as a "communication agent" than this revamping of a pre-World War II proposal for economic and cultural dissociation.

Indeed, instead of desperately trying to avoid considering the many ever-increasing manifestations of the "Boomerang Theory" in the developing and newly industrialized countries, serious attention should be paid to the more and more numerous demonstrations of the failure of the "Bullet Theory" as applied to transnational communication practices of countries belonging to the industrialized Western World.

If such an analysis is done, it seems obvious that the most successful countries are not at the disseminating end of the transnational communication networks, be they "strategic or entertaining," but rather at the receiving end (Ravault, 1980a, b, 1981, 1984, 1985).

What, then, seems to be most needed for all countries involved in a world in which "escaping interdependence" seems to be a genuine utopia is not a return to pre-World War II economic and cultural dissociation of the have-not countries, which may very well lead us back precisely to what the United Nations Organization and UNESCO have been established to stand against; but rather a genuine opening of Western countries that, so far, have been legally and, worse, psychosociologically closed to most foreign (and more especially Third World) culture and communication products.

Indeed, because of the fact, briefly noted by Hamelink (1983, p. 81) that "the Federal Communications Commission in the United States has placed severe restrictions on the entry of foreign broadcasting into its territory," as well as the self censoring behavior of American audiences who seem to believe that America is the "top Banana" country in the industrialized and technologized world and consequently believe that they do not have anything to learn from foreign cultures which they seem to consider as "ethnocentric errors" (Carey, 1975, p. 7) and the spreading belief among American finance and business top decision-makers that "Global companies must... operate as if the world were one large market—ignoring superficial, regional, and national differences" (Levitt, 1983, p. 92), America is suffering from "linguistic and cultural myopia," which "is losing" her "friends, business and respect in the world" (Fulbright, 1979, p. 15).

The core countries of capitalism are seriously disadvantaged by their inability to comprehend adequately, not only what is going on in the world, but, most important, how foreign decision-makers perceive and make sense out of what is going on in the world and, consequently, will act or react to it. Then, being almost always "taken by surprise," the core countries of capitalism seem to demonstrate an increasingly dangerous tendency to overreact in a rather brutal fashion. These reactions having often taken the form of direct or disguised military interventions, they, sometimes, manifest themselves through unilaterally decided financial reforms or monetary measures which may very well end up jeopardizing the whole, so painfully elaborated, international monetary order, as we are witnessing nowadays.

If the *New World Information Order* based upon a balanced communication traffic (instead of cultural dissociation), as originally proposed and supported by a good number of Third World countries, were implemented, it would be able to make the core countries of the industrialized and technologized world better informed about how different social and ethnic strata of different nations in the world do perceive and make sense out of what is going on. Then, tremendous progress in the wisdom and welfare of all the people involved in this new and balanced communication process could be accomplished.

In order to improve its ability and susceptibility to be communicated to by the rest of the world, the First World will have to appreciate the value of other cultures and, to a certain extent, adapt itself to them.

Through such a mutual adaptation, diversity will be protected and even stimulated by senders as well as receivers of international communication. The cultural sovereignty of each and every nation will be respected, honored, learned, and even subsidized (as the Japanese recently did with some movies to be produced in Québec by Québekers).

REFERENCES

Bogart, L. (1967). *Strategy in Advertising*. New Yrk: Harcourt, Brace and World.
Bourdieu, P., and Passeron, J.-C. "Sociologues des Mythologies et Mythologies des Sociologues." *Les Temps Modernes* (No. 206), 998–1021.
Bourges, H. (1978). *Décoloniser l'Information*. Paris: Cana.
Burgess, E. (1978). "The Resurgence of Ethnicity: Myth or Reality?" *Ethnic and Racial Studies 1*, 265–285.
Capriles, O. (1982). "La Nouvelle Recherche Latino Américaine en Communication." *Communication & Information 5* (No. 1), 97–146.
Carey, J.W. (1975). "A Cultural Approach to Communication," *Communication 2*, 1–22.
Cazamajou, J., and Martin, J.-P. (1983). *La Crise du Melting-Pot, Ethnicité et Identité aux Etats-Unis de Kennedy à Reagan*. Paris: Aubier-Montaigne
Eudes, Y. (1982). *La Conquête des Espirits, l'appareil d'exportation culturelle américain*. Paris: Maspéro.
Fulbright, J.W. (1979). "We're Tongue-Tied." *Newsweek* (July 30, 15).
Hamelink, C.J. (1983). *Cultural Autonomy in Global Communications*. New York: Longman.
International Commission for the Study of Communication Problems. (1980). "Many Voices, One World, Communication and Society, Today and Tomorrow. (McBride Report.) Paris: UNESCO.
Katz, E., and Foulkes, D. (1962). "On the Use of the Mass Media as 'Escape': A Clarification of a Concept." *Public Opinion Quarterly 26*, 381–395.
Levitt, T. (1983). "The Globalization of Markets." *Harvard Business Review*, (No. 3), 92–102.
Mattelart, A. (1974). *Mass Media, Idéologies et Mouvements Révolutionnaires, Chili, 1970–1973*. Paris: Anthropos.
Mattelart, A. (1976). *Multinationales et Systèmes de Communication, les Appareils Idéologiques de l'Impérialisme*. Paris: Anthropos.
Mattelart, A., and Dorfman, A. (1979). *Donald l'Imposteur*. Paris: Alain Moreau.
Mattelart, A., and Schmucler, H. (1983). *L'Ordinateur et le Tiers Monde*. Paris: Maspero.
Mattelart, A., Delcourt, X., and Mattelart, M. (1983). *La Culture contre la Démocratie? L'audiovisuel à l'heure transnationale*. Paris: La Découverte.
Murphrey, M. (1973). "The Study of Race and Ethnic Relations in Southern Africa, Salisbury." Inaugural lecture, University of Rhodesia.
Nordenstreng, K., and Schiller, H.I. (Eds.) (1979). *National Sovereignty and International Communication*. Norwood, NJ: Ablex.
Nordenstreng, K., and Varis, T. (1974). *Television Traffic—A One-Way Street? A Survey and Analysis of the International Flow of Television Programme Material*. Paris: UNESCO.
Pasquali, A. (1963). *Communicación y Cultura de Masas*. Caracas: Universitad Centrale del Venezuela.
Pasquali, A. (1967). *Al Aparato Singular*. Caracas: Universitad Centrale del Venezuela.

Prédal, R. (1984). "Les Films Documentaires Francais: Mode de Financement et Production de Sens." In B. Miège (Ed.), *Les Actes du Congrès: Information, Economie et Société* (pp. 383-394). Grenoble: Les Presses Universitaires de Grenoble.
Ravault, R.J. (1980a). "Some Possible Economic Dysfunctions of the Anglo-American Practice of International Communications. Unpublished dissertation, University of Iowa.
Ravault, R.J. (1980b). "De l'Exploitation des 'Despotes Culturels' par les Téléspectateurs." In A. Méar (Ed.), *Recherches Québécoise sur la Télévision* (pp. 169-188). Montréal: Albert Saint Martin.
Ravault, R.J. (1981). "Information Flow: Which Way is the Wrong Way?" *Journal of Communication 31* (No. 4), 129-134.
Ravault, R.J. (1984). "Irresponsible Information and Stagflation: An Overlooked Relationship Between Communication and Economics." In S. Thomas (Ed.), *Studies in Mass Communication, Vol. 1: Studies in Mass Communication and Technology* (pp. 15-33). Norwood, NJ: Ablex.
Ravault, R.J. (1985). "The Ideology of the Information Age in a Senseless World." In F. Fejes and J.D. Slack (Eds.), *The Ideology of the Information Age.* Norwood, NJ: Ablex (in press).
Schiller, H.I. (1969). *Mass Communications and American Empire.* Boston, MA: Beacon Press.
Schiller, H.I. (1976). Communication and Cultural Domination. White Plains, NY: International Arts and Sciences Press.
Schiller, H.I. (1980). *Who Knows: Information in the Age of the Fortune 500.* Norwood, NJ: Ablex.
Schiller, H.I. (1983). "Foreword." In C.J. Hamelink, *Cultural Autonomy in Global Communications* (pp. ix-xii). New York: Longman.
Schramm, W. (1971). "The Nature of Communication Between Humans." In W. Schramm and D. Roberts (Eds.), *The Process and Effects of Mass Communication* (Revised ed.). Urbana, IL: University of Illinois Press.
Schramm. W. (1973). *Men, Messages, and Media, a Look at Human Communication.* New York: Harper & Row.
Senghaas, D. (1977). *Weltwirtschaftsordnung und Entwicklungspolitik.* Frankfurt: Surhkamp.
Sjaastad, L.A. (1984). "Where the Latin American Loans Went." *Fortune III* (Nov. 26), 195, 198, 202.
Smith, A.D. (1980). *The Geopolitics of Information.* New York: Oxford University Press.
Smith, A.D. (1981). *The Ethnic Revival in the Modern World.* New York: Cambridge University Press.
Smythe, D.W. (1981a). *Dependency Road: Communications, Capitalism, Consciousness, and Canada.* Norwood, NJ: Ablex.
Smythe, D.W. (1981b). "Communications: Blindspot of Economics." In W.H. Melody, L. Salter, and P. Heyer (Eds.), *Culture, Communication, and Dependency* (pp. 111-126). Norwood, NJ: Ablex.
Tohakhotine, S. (1940). *The Rape of the Masses; the Psychology of Totalitarian Propaganda.* London: Labour Books Service.
Tehranian, M. (1982). "Development Theories and Messionic Ideologies: Dependency, Communication and Democracy in the Third World." Paper presented at the International Association for Mass Communication Research Conference, Paris.
Tunstall, J. (1977). *The Media Are American, Anglo-American Media in the World.* London: Constable.

Author Index

A
Abreu, H., 161, *162*
Alexander, J.C., 170, 171*n, 174*
Altheide, D.L., 23, *23,* 28, 42, *48,* 55, *60*
Althusser, L., 17, *23*
Anderson, P., 4, *24*
Arana, A., 3, *24*
Astley, W., 233, *243*
Atkin, C.K., 184, *191*
Atwood, L.E., 184, 186, *192*
Auh, T.S., 182, *191, 193*

B
Bachrach, P., 204, 205, 206, 208, 209, *210*
Baerns, B., 90, 91*n,* 93*n,* 94, 96*n, 103, 104*
Ball-Rokeach, S., 27, *46,* 170, *174,* 197, 198, *210*
Baratz, M., 204, 205, 206, 208, 209, *210*
Barber, J.D., 183, *191*
Baudrillard, J., 58*n, 60*
Bauer, R.A., 173, *174*
Becker, H., 42, *46*
Becker, L.B., 174, *174,* 180, 182, 186, *191, 192,* 195, 197, 200, 201, *211*
Belloni, M.L., 153*n, 163*
Bendix, R., 50, *60*
Beniger, J.R., *128*
Bent, D.H., *104,* 107*n*
Berelson, B., 168, *174,* 184, *191,* 196, *210, 211*
Bernstein, C., 41*n,* 42, 43, 44, *46*
Blumler, J.G., 168, 169, 171, 172, *174, 175,* 191, *194,* 195, 197, 207, *210, 211*
Bogart, L., 250, *264*
Boneschi, M., 76, *87*
Boorstin, D.J., 35, *46*
Borre, O., 180, 182, *193*
Bourdieu, P., 262, *264*
Bourges, H., 245, *264*
Bowman, W.W., 27, *47*
Boyland, J., 35, *46*
Bregues, S.G., 153*n, 162*
Broder, D.S., 38, *46*
Brodzki, S., 223*n, 228*
Brooks, S.C., 33, *47*
Burstein, P., *128*

Butler, D., 168, *175*
Byrnes, J.E., 180, 182, *192*

C
Cacioppo, J.T., 185*n, 193*
Cantor, M., 198, 205, *210*
Cantor, R.D., 187, *191*
Capriles, O., 248, 249, 250, 253, *264*
Carey, J.W., 197, 200, 205, 209, *210,* 263, *264*
Carter, R.F., 190, *191*
Cater, D., 11, *24*
Catledge, T., 31, *46*
Cazamajou, J., 259, 260, *264*
Chaffee, S.H., 26, 27, *46,* 185, 187, 190, *192, 193*
Chagas, C., 153*n, 163*
Chaiken, S., 185*n, 192*
Chilberg, J., 63, 66*n,* 72
Choe, S.Y., 187, *192*
Chu, G.C., 130, *147*
Clarke, J., *211*
Clausse, R., 93, *104*
Cobb, R.W., 181, 189, *192*
Cohen, B.M., 6, *24*
Comstock, G.A., 26, 27, *46*
Cook, F.L., 26, 28*n,* 33, *46*
Coombs, S.L., 178, 179, 192, *192*
Cooper, K., 227*n, 228*
Costella, A.F., 153*n, 163*
Critcher, C., *211*
Crotty, W.J., 38, *62*
Curtis, B., 52, *60*

D
Dahl, R.A., 91, *104,* 195, 203, 206, *210*
Dahlgren, P.H., 21, *24*
Davis, D., 27, 47, 203, *211*
Davison, W.P., 35, *46*
DeFleur, M.L., 27, *46,* 170, *174,* 197, 198, *210*
Delcourt, X., *264*
Deutsch, K.W., 92, 93, *104*
Divorski, S.W., 28, *47*
Donsbach, W., 63, 66*n,* 67*n,* 71

267

AUTHOR INDEX

Dorfman, A., 245, 262, *264*
Dreier, P., 45, *46*
Dreifus, R.A., 159, *163*

E

Edelman, M., 33, *46*
Edelstein, A.S., 130, *147*
Ehrenreich, B., 54, *60*
Ehrenreich, J., 54, *60*
Elder, C.D., 181, 189, *192*
Elliot, P., 54, *60*, 194, 195, 198, 200, 202, 205, *210*
Entman, R.M., 23, *24*, 40, *47*
Erbring, L., 180, 181, 182, *192*
Ettema, J.S., 205, *210*
Eudes, Y., 245, 255, 256, 257, *264*
Ewen, S., 45, *46*
Eyal, C.H., 177, 180, 182, 184, 185, 187, 188, *192, 193*

F

Fishman, M., 27, 28, 30, 41, *46*, 55, *60*
Fombrun, C., 233, *243*
Foucault, M., 52, *60*
Foulkes, D., 254, 255, *264*
Frey, F.W., 216, 216n, *228*
Friendly, F.W., 27, *46*
Fulbright, J.W., 263, *264*

G

Gallup, G.H., 32, *47*
Gans, H.J., 19, *24*, 27, 28, *47*, 54, 55, *60*, 201, *210*
Garbayo, C., 153n, *163*
Gaudet, H., 192, *211*
Gaventa, J., 203, 209, *210*
Gerbner, G., 26, *47*
Gilberg, S., 177, *192*
Gitlin, T., 4, 19, *24*, 27, 45, *47*, 197, 205, 208, *210*
Goes, W. de, 161, 162, *163*
Goetz, S.G., 26, 28n, 33, *46*
Gold, D.A., 11, *24*
Goldenberg, E.N., 180, 181, 182, *192*
Golding, P., 195, 196, *211*
Goldman, R., 185n, *193*
Gonzalez Casanova, P., 241, *243*
Goode, W., 201, *210*
Gordon, A.C., 28, *47*
Gordon, M., 26, 28, 33, *46, 47*

Graber, D.A., 27, *47*, 177, 182, 184, 185, 187, 188, *193*
Gramsci, A., 4, *24*, 207, *211*
Greenfield, J., 27, *47*
Gross, L., 26, *47*
Guback, T., 205, *211*
Gurevitch, M., 168, 171, 173, *174, 175*, 190, *191*, 194, *211*

H

Hagen, E.E., 226, *228*
Halberstam, D., 5, 7n, *24*
Hall, S., 4, *24*, 55, *60*, 205, 207, *211*
Hallin, D.C., 3, 3n, 10, 11, 17, 21, *24*
Hamelink, C.J., 245, 247, 248, 249, 250, 251, 252, 253, 254, 257, 258, 259, 262, 263, *264*
Harrison, M., 168, *175*
Heath, L., 28, *47*
Heinz, J.P., 28, *47*
Hellweg, S.A., 62, *71*
Herzog, H., 196, *211*
Hinker, P.J., 133, *147*
Hobsbawm, E.J., 54, *60*
Hoskin, K., 52, *60*
Hoveland, C., 26, *47*, 196, *211*
Hull, C.H., *104*, 107n
Hummell, H.J., 99, *104*
Huntington, S.J., 14, *24*

I

Irle, M., 70, *71*
Isaacson, W., 17, *24*
Ives, J., 168, 173, *174*

J

Janesch, P., 191, *192*
Janis, I.L., 26, *47*
Janis, J., 196, *211*
Jefferson, T., *211*
Jenkins, J.G., *104*, 107n
Johnstone, J.W.C., 27, *47*

K

Katz, E., 30, *47*, *192*, 194, 195, 201, *211*, 226, *229*, 254, 255, *264*
Katzman, N.I., 26, 27, *46*
Kavanagh, D., 168, *175*
Kay, G.B., 50, 51, 53, 56, *60*
Kelley, H., 26, *47*, 196, *211*
Kellner, D., 207, *211*

AUTHOR INDEX

Kepplinger, H.M., 62, 63, 63n, 65n, 66n, 67n, 71
Klapper, J., 26, 47, 192
Knight, G., 54, 55, 57, 59, 60
Knoche, M., 96, 104
Kohler, I., 66, 71
Köhler, W., 66, 72
Kornhauser, W., 199, 211
Kraus, S., 27, 47, 203, 211
Kreiling, A.L., 197, 200, 205, 209, 210
Kriz, J., 104, 106n
Krolls, A., 120, 128
Kupferberg, S., 35, 47
Kupis, T., 221n, 221, 229
Kwasniewicz, W., 225, 229

L

Lafer, C., 148, 163
Lamounier, B., 148, 163
Lang, G., 41n, 44n, 47, 181, 186, 189, 192
Lang, K., 41n, 44n, 47, 181, 186, 189, 192
Lazarsfeld, P.F., 30, 47, 168, 174, 184, 191, 196, 202, 210, 211, 223, 226, 229
Lee, C.-C., 130, 145, 147
Lee, Y.-L., 131, 131n, 145, 147
Leff, D.R., 26, 28n, 33, 46, 47
Lerg, W.B., 93, 104
Lerner, D., 213, 216, 226, 229
Lester, M., 35, 41, 47
Levi-Strauss, C., 226, 229
Levitin, T.G., 187, 192
Levitt, T., 263, 264
Linz, J., 151, 163
Lippman, W., 89, 104, 170, 175
Lisch, R., 104, 106n
Liu, A.P.L., 131, 133, 147
Lo, C.Y.H., 11, 24
Loderhose, W., 72
Loffler, M., 102, 104
Long, N.E., 45, 47
Lowenstein, R.L., 214, 226, 229
Lu, K., 147
Luhmann, N., 89, 104
Lukes, S., 195, 203, 204, 205, 206, 211

M

MacKeun, M.B., 178, 179, 182, 192
MacLean, M.S., Jr., 92, 105
Mandell, L., 63, 72
Marconi, P., 153n, 157, 163

Marcuse, H., 10, 24
Markham, J.W., 130, 133, 147
Martin, J.-P., 259, 260, 264
Marx, K., 52, 60
Maslow, J.E., 3, 24
Massing, M., 10, 24
Mattelart, A., 153n, 163, 245, 249, 261, 262, 264
Mattelart, M., 245, 264
Mazzoleni, G., 76, 87
McCain, T.A., 63, 66n, 72
McClelland, D.C., 226, 229
McClure, R.D., 77, 87
McCombs, M.E., 26, 27, 43n, 46, 48, 174, 174, 177, 180, 182, 184, 185, 186, 187, 188, 190, 191, 192, 193
McConnell, G., 29, 47
McGinniss, J., 77, 87
McGrath, J.E., 63, 65n, 72
McGrath, M.F., 63, 65n, 72
McLeod, J.M., 174, 174, 180, 182, 192, 194, 195, 197, 200, 201, 211
McPhee, W., 168, 174, 184, 191, 196, 210
Mecklin, J., 5, 24
Mendelsohn, H., 184, 192, 195, 211
Menningen, W., 100, 104
Merrill, J.C., 214, 226, 229
Merton, R.K., 195, 201, 202, 211, 223, 229
Michelson, S., 26, 27, 47
Miliband, R., 4, 24
Miller, A.H., 180, 181, 182, 187, 192
Miller, H., 187, 192
Miller, W.E., 187, 192
Moles, A., 226, 229
Molotch, H.L., 26, 27, 28n, 33, 41, 45, 46, 47
Morales, Q., 21, 24
Morentz, J.W., 43n, 47
Mott, J., 50, 51, 53, 56, 60
Mueller, C., 45, 47
Muller, U., 90n, 105
Murdock, G., 195, 196, 211
Murphrey, M., 260, 264

N

Nahr, G., 103, 104
Nicholas, D., 177, 192
Nie, N.H., 85, 87, 104, 107n
Nimmo, D., 77, 87
Nissen, P., 100, 104
Nixon, R.F., 216n, 229

Noble, D.F., 54, *61*
Noelle-Neumann, E., 170, *175*
Nord, D.P., 183, *192*
Nordenstreng, K., 245, 253, 261, *264*

O

O'Keefe, G., 184, 186, *192*
Oliphant, C.A., 130, *147*
Onis, J. de, 13, *24*

P

Paletz, D.L., 23, *24*, 40, *47*
Parsons, T., 201, *211*
Pasquali, A., 245, *264*
Passeron, J.-C., 262, *264*
Pateman, C., 169, *175*
Patterson, T., 38, *47*, 77, 85, *87*, 168, 170, *175*, 177, 186, 188, *192*
Pennings, J.M., 234, *243*
Pereira Filho, M., 161, *163*
Perloff, R.M., 185n, *192*
Peterson, S., 21, *24*
Petrocik, J.R., 85, *87*
Petty, R.E., 185n, *193*
Phillips, S.L., 62, *71*
Pinheiro Machado, J.A., 158, *163*
Pisarek, W., 223n, 224, *229*
Pitkin, H.F., 6n, *24*
Plamenatz, J., *175*
Polsby, N., 168, *175*, 203, *211*
Predal, R., *265*
Protess, D.L., 26, 28n, 33, *46*, *47*
Pye, L.W., 130, *147*, 214, *229*

R

Ravault, R.J., 259, 263, *265*
Read, W.H., 226, *229*
Reiger, C.C., 29, *47*
Reindl, H., 110, *128*
Riemann, H., 92, *104*
Ritsert, J., *104*, 106n
Rivers, W.L., 27, *48*
Roberts, B., *211*
Roberts, C.M., 11n, *24*
Roberts, D.F., 26, 27, *46*
Robinson, M.J., 4, *24*, *175*
Rogers, E.M., 117, *128*, *229*
Ronnenberger, F., 90, 91, 92, *104*, *105*
Rosengren, K.E., 89, *105*
Ruhl, M., 90n, 93, *105*
Rutherford, P., 54, *61*

S

Salas de Gomez Gil, M.L., 241, *244*
Salisbury, H.E., 35, 36, *48*
Santoro Libri, M.A., 77, *87*
Saxer, U., 93, *105*
Scavone, L., 153n, *163*
Schattschneider, E.E., 205, *211*
Schenk, M., 92n, *105*
Schiller, H.I., 45, *48*, 227n, 229, 245, 261, *264*, *265*
Schmidt, H., 103, 105n, *105*
Schmucler, H., 252, *264*
Schramm, W., 27, *48*, 213, 223, 226, *229*, 246, 254, *265*
Schudson, M.S., 54, *61*
Schulz, W., 88, *105*
Schwartzenberg, R.-G., 77, *87*
Sears, D.O., 185, *193*
Seidler, F.W., 110, *128*
Senghaas, D., 247, *265*
Seymour-Ure, C., 168, 173, *175*, 177, *193*
Shaw, D., 63, *72*, 180, *193*
Shoemaker, F.F., 117, *128*
Shribman, D., 22, *25*
Sigal, L.V., 11n, *25*
Sigel, R.S., 63, *72*
Sills, D.L., 31, *48*
Siune, K., 168, *175*, 180, 182, *193*
Sjaastad, L.A., *265*
Slawski, E.J., 27, *47*
Slomkowska, A., 219n, *229*
Smith, A., 54, *61*, 168, *175*
Smith, A.D., 257, 260, *265*
Smith, Z.N., 32, 32n, *48*
Smythe, D.W., 245, *265*
Souza, A. de, 148, *163*
Spellman, C., 43n, *48*, 180, *193*
Starck, K., 131, 132, *147*
Steffens, L., 17, *25*, 35, *48*, 92, *105*
Stehle, T.E., 182, *193*
Steinbrenner, K., 107n, *104*
Stinchcombe, A., 201, *211*
Stumpf. A.G., 161, *163*
Suchman, E., 196, *211*
Surdykowski, J., 223n, *228*
Swanson, D.L., 194, 197, 200, 205, 207, 209, *211*, *212*
Szulczewski, m., *229*

T

Taylor, I., 57, 59, *60*

AUTHOR INDEX

Tehranian, M., 258, *265*
Tiemens, R.K., 62, 63, 66*n*, 72
Tohakhotine, S., 261, *265*
Tremaine, F., *229*
Tretiak, D., 131, *147*
Trumbull, R., 7, *25*
Tuchman, G., 27, *48*, 54, 55, *61*, 89, *105*, 203, 205, *212*
Tunstall, J., 259, *265*
Tyler, T.R., 26, 28*n*, 33, *46*

U
Unger, K., 231, *244*

V
Valentine, D., 27, *48*
Varis, T., 245, 253, 261, *264*
Verba, S., 85, *87*
Volosinov, V.N., 6*n*, *25*

W
Wagner, H., 90, *105*
Wakshlag, J., 63, 66*n*, 72
Walden, B., 173, *175*
Wang, K., 131, 132, *147*
Weaver, D.H., 43*n*, *48*, 177, 180, 182, 184, 185, 187, 188, *193*
Weber, M., 51, 54, *61*
Weiss, W., 194, *212*
Westergaard, J., 204, *212*
Westin, A., 17, *25*
Westley, B.H., 92, *105*
White, R.A., 226, *229*
Whitney, D.C., 205, 210
Wilhoit, G.C., 182, *193*
Wilke, J., 90*n*, *105*
Williams, R., 4, *25*, 205, 207, *212*
Wills, G., 27, *48*
Windahl, S., 195, 205, 210, *212*
Wionczek, S., 231, 232, *244*
Woodward, R., 41, 41*n*, 42, 43, 44, *46*
Wren-Lewis, J., 56, *61*
Wright, C.R., 197, 201, *212*
Wright, E.O., 11, *24*
Wright, J.D., 199, *212*
Wyckoff, G., 77, *87*

Y
Yao, I.P., 133, *147*
Yu, F.T.C., 35, *46*, 130, 133, *147*

Z
Zekman, P., 32, 32*n*, *48*
Zucker, H.G., 126, *128*

Subject Index

A
Abstraction, 53 (*see also* Forms, formality)
Administration, administrative labor, 49–60
Adversary culture, 4
Advertising, 253–256
Agenda building, 182–183
Agenda setting, 15–16, 176–191
  assumptions, 176–178
  media roles in, 176–191
  research on, 190–191
  stability of, 189–190
  timing of, 179
Alton Telegraph, 14
American Broadcasting System, 8, 17, 34

B
Better Government Association (BGA), 28–29, 32, 34, 39–40
Boomerang effect (Communication), 247–249, 256–262
Brazil
  armed forces, 149, 159–162
  human rights, 149, 159–160
  politics, decompression process, 148–151
  press, 148–162
    legislation, 152–153
    liberalization, 148–157, 162
    as mechanism of political action, 148–151
  redemocratization, 148–162
Bullet theory (Communication view), 246–253, 256, 259–263

C
Camera perspectives, influence on perception of politicians, 62–71
Campaign broadcasts
  candidates and, 81–82, 85–86
  intensity of, 82–84
  low interests of viewers in, 77, 84
  personalization of, 77, 85
Candidates (*see also* Politicians)
  attitudes toward, 184–185
  evaluations of, 183–184

Candidates (cont.)
  images, 179, 185–187
  name recognition of, 186–187
Capitalism, 51–56
Carter administration
  Central American policy, 13–15, 22
  and human rights, 12–15
Catholic Church, 18–19
Censorship, self, 154–155
Central America
  media coverage, 3–23
  public opinion, 22
Central America in Revolt (CBS documentary), 7–10, 18–19, 22
Chicago Sun-Times, 32, 37–38
Chicago Tribune, 37
China, Central Committee, 133
China Daily, 146
Chinese press, U.S. coverage, 129–146
Chinese-U.S. relations, normalization, 131–133
Choice, indetermination of, 7
Christian Democratic Party (Italy), 76, 81
Class, 51–56
Coalition journalism, 36–41
  ad hoc coalitions, 37–38
  mobilized coalitions, 38–41
Cold war
  ideology, 6–9, 12–15, 17–20
  and news media, 5–23
  politicization, 8
Columbia Broadcasting System, 7–10, 18–19, 20, 22
Committee to Re-Elect the President (CREEP), 41–43
Commodities
  commodity form, 50–53
  equivalence of, 54–55 (*see also,* Positivism)
Communication
  control, 245–247
  democratization, 213–228
  development, 213–227
  in elections, 167–174
  international, 245–264

SUBJECT INDEX

Communication (cont.)
  political, 167-174
  transnational, 245-264
Communism (China), 129-133
Communist party (Brazil), 159
Communist party (China), 129-132
Compulsory military service, Germany, 109-111, 117
Conscientious objection
  consequences, 110-112
  criticism, 110-112, 118-121
  Germany, 108-128
    history, 109-110
    press coverage, 123-125
  goals, 110-113, 117
  legitimization, 109, 112, 116-117, 126-128
  motives, 110-113, 117, 119
  public opinion, 118-121
Consensualism, 55-59
Conservatism, 200-204
Conservatives, criticism of media by, 4-5, 10
Content analysis, 88-89
Contradictions, social, 50-53
Credibility gap, 9-10
Cultural revolution (China), 129
Culture, international, 245-264
Cycles, of democratization, 215-227

D
Debates, political, 62
Decisionmaking, 203-210
Democratic Alliance (China), 133
Democratic pluralism, 195, 202-204
Democratic political systems, 167-174
Democratic Revolutionary Front (El Salvador), 16
Democratization
  in Brazil, 148-162
  cycles, 215-227
  of mass communication, 213-228
Development, relation to communication, 214-215
Diffusion research, 92
Discourse, discursive forms, 49-50, 57-59
Dissemination, of information, 92-93, 97
Dissociation, economic and cultural, 246-247

E
El Salvador, media coverage, 3-23
El Salvador White Paper, 3-4, 13-15
Elections
  campaigns, media performance, 167-168

Elections (cont.)
  communication in, 167-174
  in El Salvador, news coverage, 15-16
  media agenda setting, 176-191
  outcomes of, 187
  role of television, 75-87
Electoral process
  administrative elections, 76-76, 80
  effects of television, 75-76, 84-87
  in Italy, 75-87
Enlightenment Daily (China), 129, 132-133, 136-146
Equality, formal, 53
O Estado de S. Paulo, 150, 152-153, 155

F
Farabundo Marti Front for National Liberation (El Salvador), 16
Folha de S. Paulo, 151, 155, 157-158, 160, 162
Foreign policy, China, 129-146
Forms, formality, 50-56, 59-60
"Fortress America," as new world image, 21-23
"Four Modernizations" (China), 132, 145
Freedom of the press (Brazil), 157-162
Functional analysis, 200-202
Functionalism, 23, 195, 200-204

G
Gatekeeping, 89-90, 92, 153
Gazeta Mercantil (Brazil), 150
Geisel administration (Brazil), 148-149, 151-152, 157-162
German Press Council, 91
German Public Relations Association, 91
Germany
  conscientious objection, 108-128
  journalism, 88-107
  public relations, 88-107
Gesetz der guten Gestalt, 66
O Globo (Brazil), 155-156, 162
Government
  credibility, 9-10
  media relation to, 11-15, 21
Gratification research (*see,* Uses and gratification research)
Growth, organizational in Latin America, 233-235
Guatemala, News coverage of, 9

H
Hegemony, 3-23
Human rights, 13-15, 22
Humanism, 57-59
Hypodermic model of media influence, 27, 29

I
Ideological change, 16-21
Ideology, 6, 16-21, 53 (*see also* Humanism)
Imperialism, American, 130, 139
Indo-China War, 139-140
Influence, patterns of, 88-107
Information
  bureaucratization, 153-154
  international, 245-264
  systems, 90-91
  technology in Latin America, 230-243
  transnational, 245-264
"Instrumentalism," 10-11
Interaction, 88-107
International information, 245-264
Iran hostage crisis, 21
Issues, salience of, 176, 186-187
Italy, elections, role of television, 75-87

J
Jornal da Tarde (Brazil), 155
Jornal de Brasilia, 155, 161
Jornal do Brasil, 155-156, 162
Journalism, 88-107
  coalition (*see* Coalition journalism)
  persistence of routines, 11-16
  political, 167-174

K
Kennedy administration, and Vietnam news coverage, 5-7

L
Land reform, in El Salvador, news coverage, 16
Language, 6
Latin America
  discontinuities between culture and technology, 240-242
  information technology, 230-243
    history, 235-242
  national development, 230-243
Leaping impacts models of media influence, 34-36
Legitimacy, 16

M
Manchete (Brazil), 161
Mass communication
  democratization, 213-228
  effects research, 194-210
Media
  American, 3-23
  audience relationship, 195-198, 202-211
  development, world cycles, 226-227
  effects, 26-27
    cognitive, 184, 190
  functionalism, 195, 200-204
  Germany, 108-128
  influence, 26-46
  penetration, 258-260
  performance, 91-92, 94, 187-188
  pluralism, 202-210
  policy, 26-46
    partnerships, 39-40
  production, control, 246-247
  role in agenda setting, 176-191
  systems, 96-100
  and voting behavior, 196
Mexico
  economy, 231-233
  information technology in, 231-242
  national development, 231-242
Mirror model of media influence, 27
Muckraking (*see* Truncated muckraking model)
Muckraking model of media influence, 29-33

N
National Broadcasting Company, 20
National development, Latin America, 230-243
National Liberation Front (South Vietnam), news coverage of, 9
New China News Agency (NCNA), 132-133, 141-142
New world economic order, 246, 261
New world information order, 215, 217, 245-248, 261-263
New world military order, 261
New York Times, 5, 13, 31, 35, 41
News, 49-50, 53-59
News coverage, of U.S. in China, 129-146
News media, 88-107
  American, 3-23
  conflict with government, 5-11
  ideological change, 3-23

SUBJECT INDEX

News, sources, 12-13, 96-100
Newspapers, 94-95
  Brazil, 148-162
  effect on public policy making, 26-46
Nicaragua, news coverage of, 12, 15, 17

O

Objective journalism, 6
Objects, 50-53 (see also Subjects)
Opinião (Brazil), 158
Organizational growth, 233-235

P

Particularity, 55-59
Partisanship, distrust of, 18-21
Peking Review, 130-131
Pentagon papers, 29, 35, 41
People's Daily (China), 129-133, 136-146
Perception
  conformity of, 66-70
  homogeneity of, 65-70
  leveling of, 66-71
  tendency of, 65-70
Ping-pong diplomacy, 131
Pluralism, 202-210
Poland, democratization of mass communication, 231-228
Policy, public, 34-36
Polish journalists, 219-221
Polish press system, 214, 217-226
  censorship, 222-225
  sphere of silence, 221-222
Polish United Workers Party, 219-221
Political advertising
  candidates and, 81-83
  costs and expenditures, 79, 83-84, 87
Political advocacy, 173
Political campaigns, 62-63
Political communication
  "election tribunes," 76-77, 85
  image campaign, 77, 85
  Italy, 75-87
  and private television, 75-87
Political parties
  of the left, 76, 81, 86
  and television, 75-77, 85
Political systems, democratic, journalism in, 167-174
Politicians
  effect of camera perspectives on perception of, 62-71
  effect of distance on perception of, 63-67

Politicians (cont.)
  perception of, 62-71
Population, as an administrative category, 53-54, 56-57
Positivism
  of commodities, 54
  as mythology, 59
  of subjects, 54, 57
Power, 49-60
  and decision making, 203-210
  and ideology, 204-210
  media effect on, 202-203, 208-211
Press
  Brazil, 148-162
  roles of, 178-180, 187-188
Propaganda, 129
Property, 50-53 (see also Commodities; Humanism)
  absolute and real, 55
Public, as sphere and subjectivity, 49-60
Public opinion, on Central America, 22
Public policy, 34-36
Public relations, 88-107
Publicity, of state subjects, 49-60
Pure Food and Drug Act (1906), 29

R

Radio, influence, 95-100
Reagan administration,
  and Central American news coverage, 3-5, 10, 12-15, 19, 22
  influences on news media, 3-23
Reality, in news media, 88
Reference News (China), 46
Revolution
  American reporting of, 8-9
  news coverage, 8-9, 15-16, 21
Right, 50-56 (see also, Humanism)

S

Selection
  by news media, 88-89
  systems, 92-93
Semantics, 90-91, 93
"Sixty Minutes" (CBS program), 32
Social change, 194-210
Social values, 214-217
Socialist party (Italy), 81-86
Socialization, Mexican American audience, 202
Society, mass media effects, 194-210

State (*see also* Administration)
  as force, 51-53
  as newsworthy, 49-50
  political and juridical, 56
  publicity, 49-60
Subjects, subjectivity, 49-60
Syntax, 90-91
Systems, theory, 91

T

Technological development, Latin America, 235-242
Telecommunications, international, 245-264
Television, 95-100
  access criteria, 81
  electoral, 76-87
  local and private, 75-80, 84-87
  political, 168-169
  in political campaigns, 62-71
  role in Italian elections, 75-87
Third World, 247-249, 261-262
  news coverage, 15, 19
Time, 5-6, 17
Transmission, of information, 92-93
Truncated muckraking model of media influence, 31-33
20/20 (ABC news magazine), 17, 34

U

UNESCO, 245, 248-249, 253, 262-263
United States
  Department of Justice, 35, 41
  news coverage in China, 129-146
Universality, 55-59
Uses and gratification research, 194-210
  conservative bias, 200-203
  and functionalism, 195, 200-204
  methodology, 197-198
  pluralism, 202-210

V

Vietnam war, media coverage, 3-23
Voters, 177-179
  turnout, 184-185

W

Washington Post, 11, 41-44
Watergate, 29, 35, 41-45
"White Paper" (Communist Interference in El Salvador), 3-4, 13-15
Wire editors, views on Central American coverage, 14